高橋　和希

BEFORE I WROTE THIS SERIES, I WENT TO EGYPT FOR BACKGROUND RESEARCH. I WAS PARTICULARLY STRUCK BY HOW OPEN-HEARTED AND FRIENDLY THE EGYPTIAN PEOPLE WERE. WHEN THEIR SMILING FACES GREETED ME, I ENDED UP BUYING STONES THAT I WASN'T INTERESTED IN BUYING, RIDING DONKEYS THAT I HAD NO INTEREST IN RIDING, AND BUYING PHOTOGRAPHS THAT WERE FORCED ON ME. BUT ONE LOOK AT THOSE FACES, AND YOU JUST HAD TO FORGIVE THEM!

—KAZUKI TAKAHASHI, 1997

Artist/author Kazuki Takahashi first tried to break into the manga business in 1982, but success eluded him until **Yu-Gi-Oh!** debuted in the Japanese **Weekly Shonen Jump** magazine in 1996. **Yu-Gi-Oh!**'s themes of friendship and fighting, together with Takahashi's weird and wonderful art, soon became enormously successful, spawning a real-world card game, video games, and two anime series. A lifelong gamer, Takahashi enjoys Shogi (Japanese chess), Mahjong, card games, and tabletop RPGs, among other games.

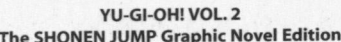

YU-GI-OH! VOL. 2
The SHONEN JUMP Graphic Novel Edition

This graphic novel contains material that was originally published in English in the second two-thirds of **SHONEN JUMP** #4, all of **SHONEN JUMP** #5 and #6, and the first one-third of #7.

STORY AND ART BY
KAZUKI TAKAHASHI

Translation & English Adaptation/Anita Sengupta
Touch-Up Art & Lettering/Kelle Han
Cover & Graphic Design/Sean Lee
Senior Editor/Jason Thompson

Managing Editor/Annette Roman
Associate Managing Editor/Albert Totten
Senior V.P. of Editorial/Hyoe Narita
Production Manager/Nobi Watanabe
Director of Licensing & Acquisitions/Rika Inouye
V.P. of Marketing/Liza Coppola
V.P. of Strategic Development/Yumi Hoashi
Publisher/Seiji Horibuchi

PARENTAL ADVISORY
Yu-Gi-Oh! is rated "T" for teens. It may contain violence, langugage, alcohol or tobacco usage, or suggestive situations. It is recommended for ages 13 and up.

Printed in Canada.

Published by VIZ, LLC
P.O. Box 77010 • San Francisco, CA 94107

SHONEN JUMP Graphic Novel Edition
10 9 8 7 6 5 4 3 2 1
First printing, August 2003

www.viz.com

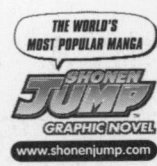

THE WORLD'S MOST POPULAR MANGA
SHONEN JUMP GRAPHIC NOVEL
www.shonenjump.com

SHONEN JUMP GRAPHIC NOVEL

YU-GI-OH!™

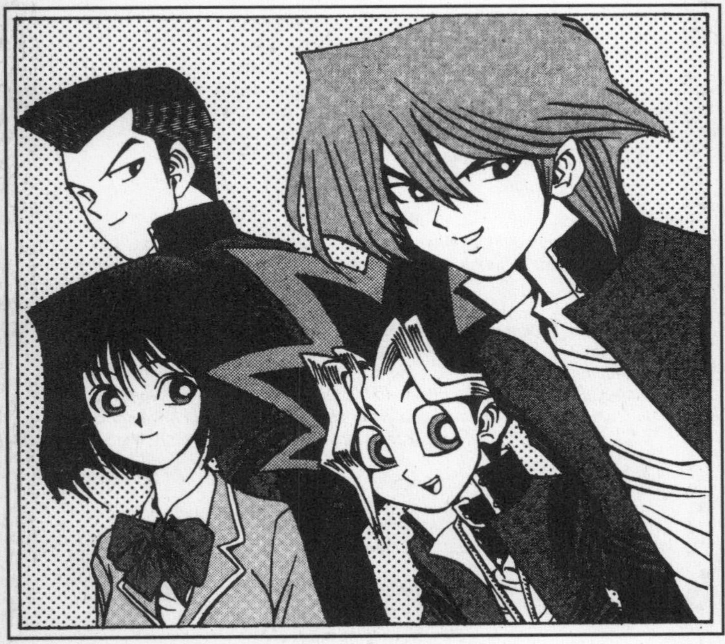

Vol. 2
THE CARDS WITH TEETH

STORY AND ART BY
KAZUKI TAKAHASHI

THE STORY SO FAR...

Shy and easily picked on, 10th-grader Yugi spent most of his time alone playing games...until he solved the Millennium Puzzle, a mysterious Egyptian artifact passed down from his grandfather. Possessed by the puzzle, Yugi became a different person, and challenged bullies and criminals to weird games where the loser *loses their mind!* Now, Yugi has become *Yu-Gi-Oh!*, the King of Games...and the Shadow Games have begun!

DARK YUGI

武藤遊戯

YUGI MUTOU

The main character. Normally he's a nice guy—even a pushover—until his *other* personality takes over. Afterwards, he doesn't remember what happened.

城之内克也
KATSUYA JONOUCHI
Yugi's classmate, a tough guy who gets in lots of fights. He used to think Yugi was a wimp, but now they are good friends. In the English anime he's known as "Joey Wheeler."

真崎杏子
ANZU MAZAKI
Yugi's classmate and childhood friend. She fell in love with the charismatic voice of Yugi's alter ego, but doesn't know that they're the same person. Her first name means "Peach." In the English anime she's known as "Téa Gardner."

本田ヒロト
HIROTO HONDA
Yugi's classmate, a friend of Jonouchi. In the English anime he's known as "Tristan Taylor."

武藤双六
SUGOROKU MUTOU
Yugi's grandfather, the owner of the Kame ("Turtle") game store, which sells rare and interesting games.

Yu-Gi-Oh!

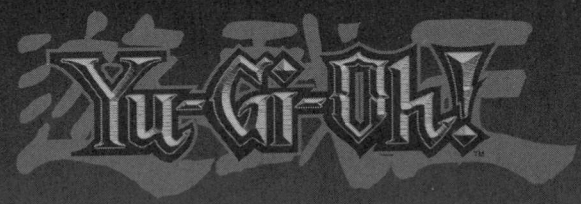

Vol. 2

CONTENTS

Duel 8: The Poison Man

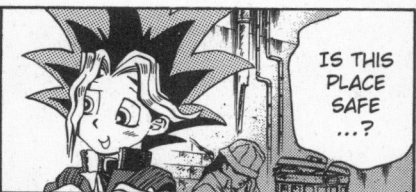

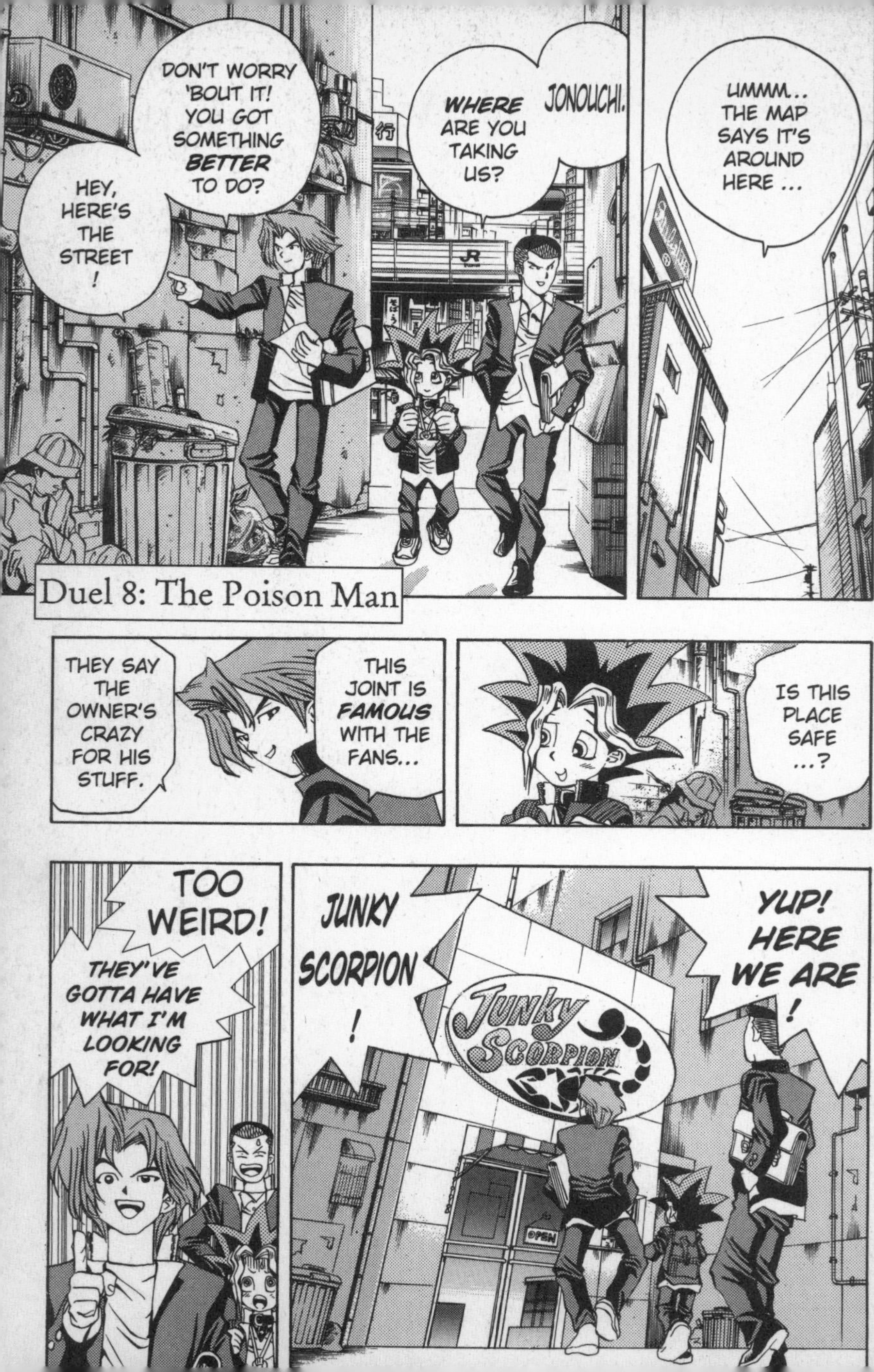
UMMM... THE MAP SAYS IT'S AROUND HERE ...
JONOUCHI.
WHERE ARE YOU TAKING US?
DON'T WORRY 'BOUT IT! YOU GOT SOMETHING BETTER TO DO?
HEY, HERE'S THE STREET!
IS THIS PLACE SAFE ...?
THIS JOINT IS FAMOUS WITH THE FANS...
THEY SAY THE OWNER'S CRAZY FOR HIS STUFF.
YUP! HERE WE ARE!
Junky Scorpion
JUNKY SCORPION!
OPEN
TOO WEIRD!
THEY'VE GOTTA HAVE WHAT I'M LOOKING FOR!

Duel 8: The Poison Man

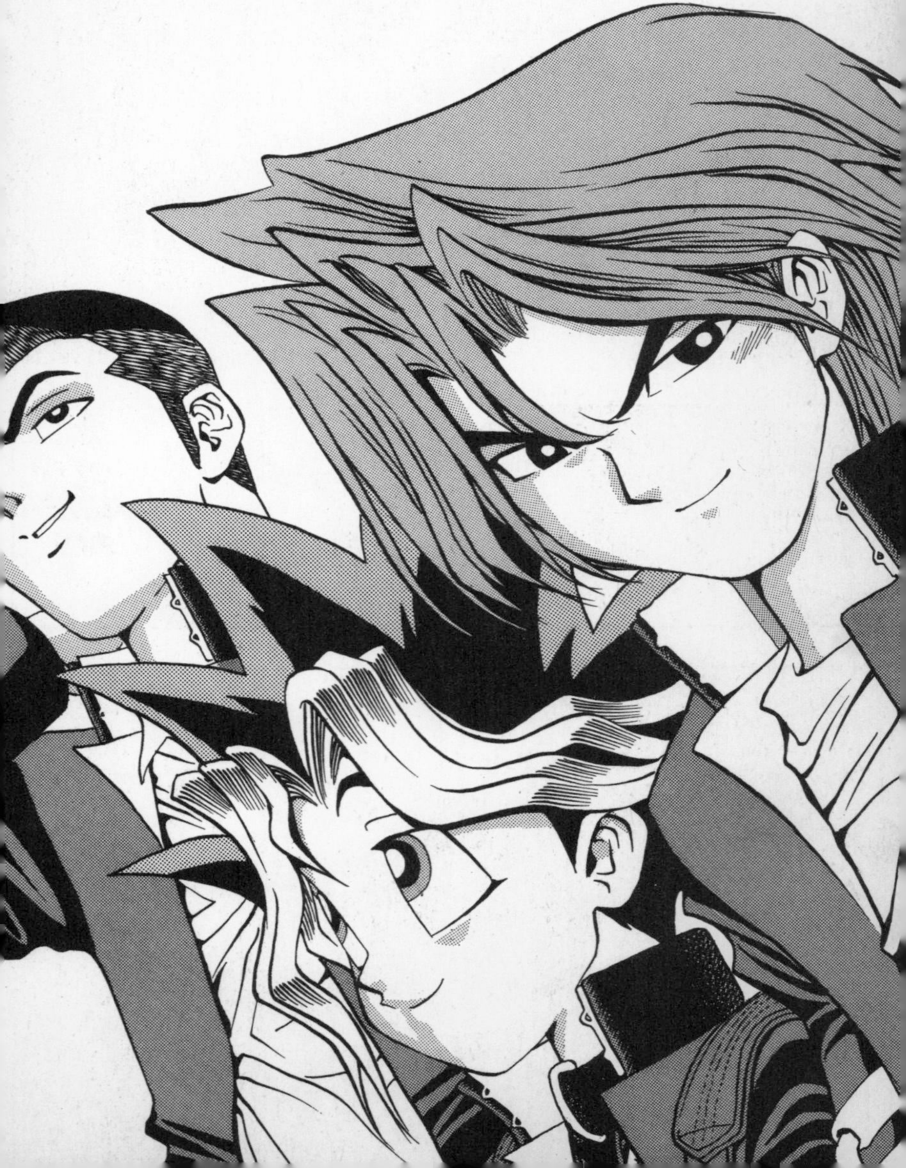

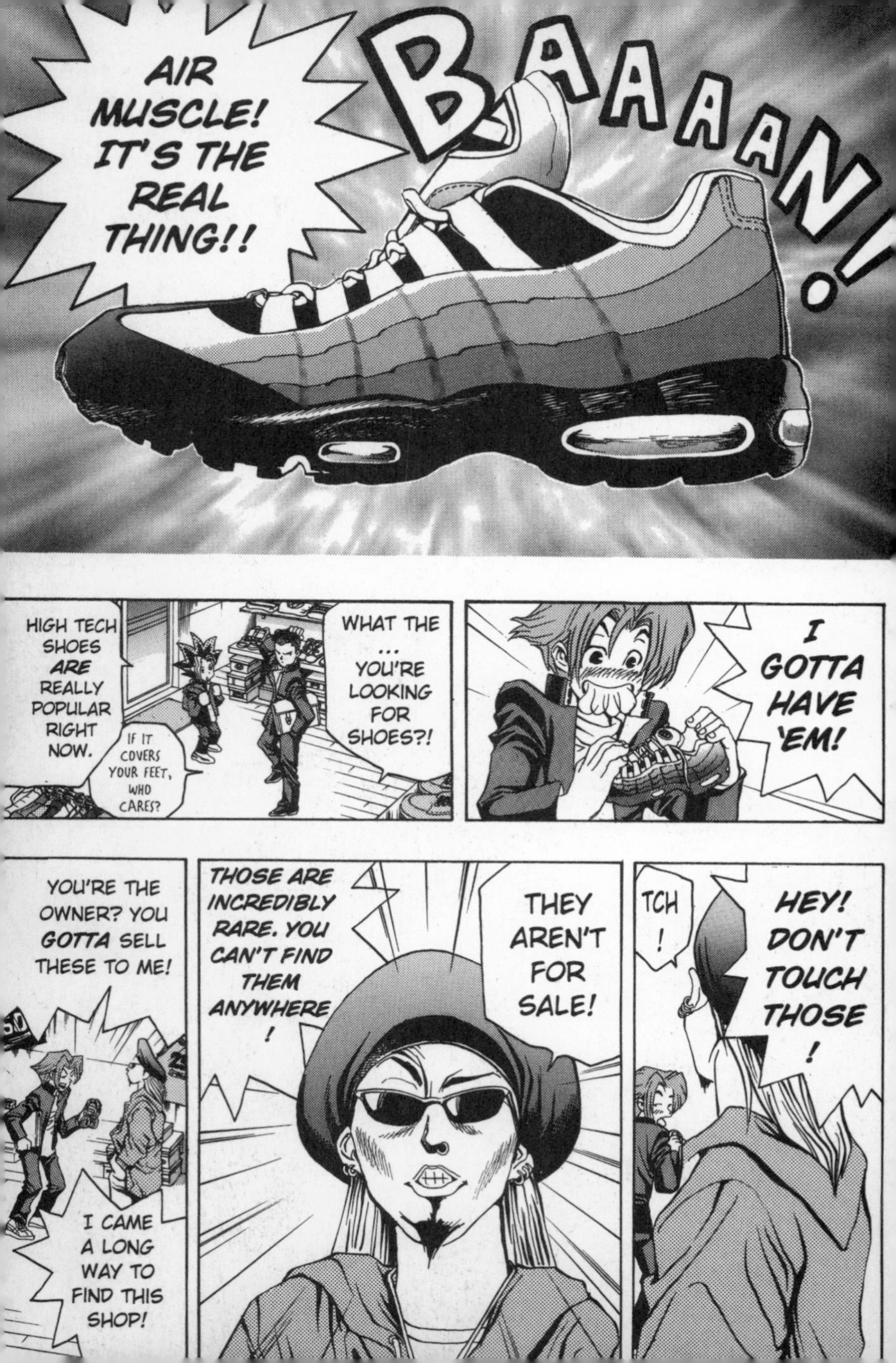
BAAAAN!!
AIR MUSCLE! IT'S THE REAL THING!!
I GOTTA HAVE 'EM!
WHAT THE ... YOU'RE LOOKING FOR SHOES?!
HIGH TECH SHOES ARE REALLY POPULAR RIGHT NOW.
IF IT COVERS YOUR FEET, WHO CARES?
HEY! DON'T TOUCH THOSE!
TCH!
THEY AREN'T FOR SALE!
THOSE ARE INCREDIBLY RARE. YOU CAN'T FIND THEM ANYWHERE!
YOU'RE THE OWNER? YOU GOTTA SELL THESE TO ME!
I CAME A LONG WAY TO FIND THIS SHOP!

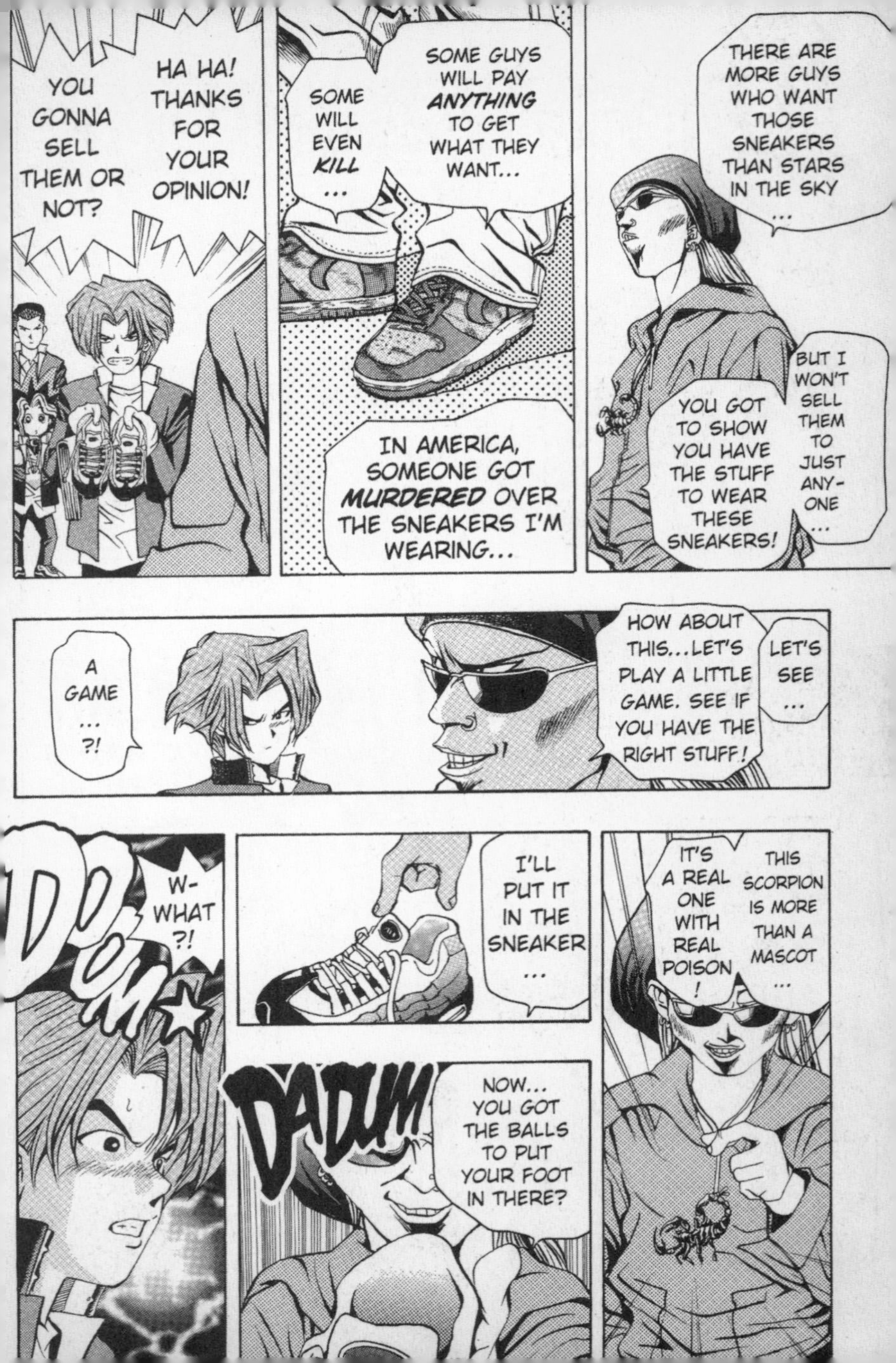
THERE ARE MORE GUYS WHO WANT THOSE SNEAKERS THAN STARS IN THE SKY ...
BUT I WON'T SELL THEM TO JUST ANY-ONE ...
YOU GOT TO SHOW YOU HAVE THE STUFF TO WEAR THESE SNEAKERS!
SOME GUYS WILL PAY ANYTHING TO GET WHAT THEY WANT...
SOME WILL EVEN KILL ...
IN AMERICA, SOMEONE GOT MURDERED OVER THE SNEAKERS I'M WEARING...
HA HA! THANKS FOR YOUR OPINION!
YOU GONNA SELL THEM OR NOT?
LET'S SEE ...
HOW ABOUT THIS...LET'S PLAY A LITTLE GAME. SEE IF YOU HAVE THE RIGHT STUFF!
A GAME ...?!
THIS SCORPION IS MORE THAN A MASCOT ...
IT'S A REAL ONE WITH REAL POISON!
I'LL PUT IT IN THE SNEAKER ...
DADUM
NOW... YOU GOT THE BALLS TO PUT YOUR FOOT IN THERE?
DOOM
W-WHAT ?!

READ THIS WAY

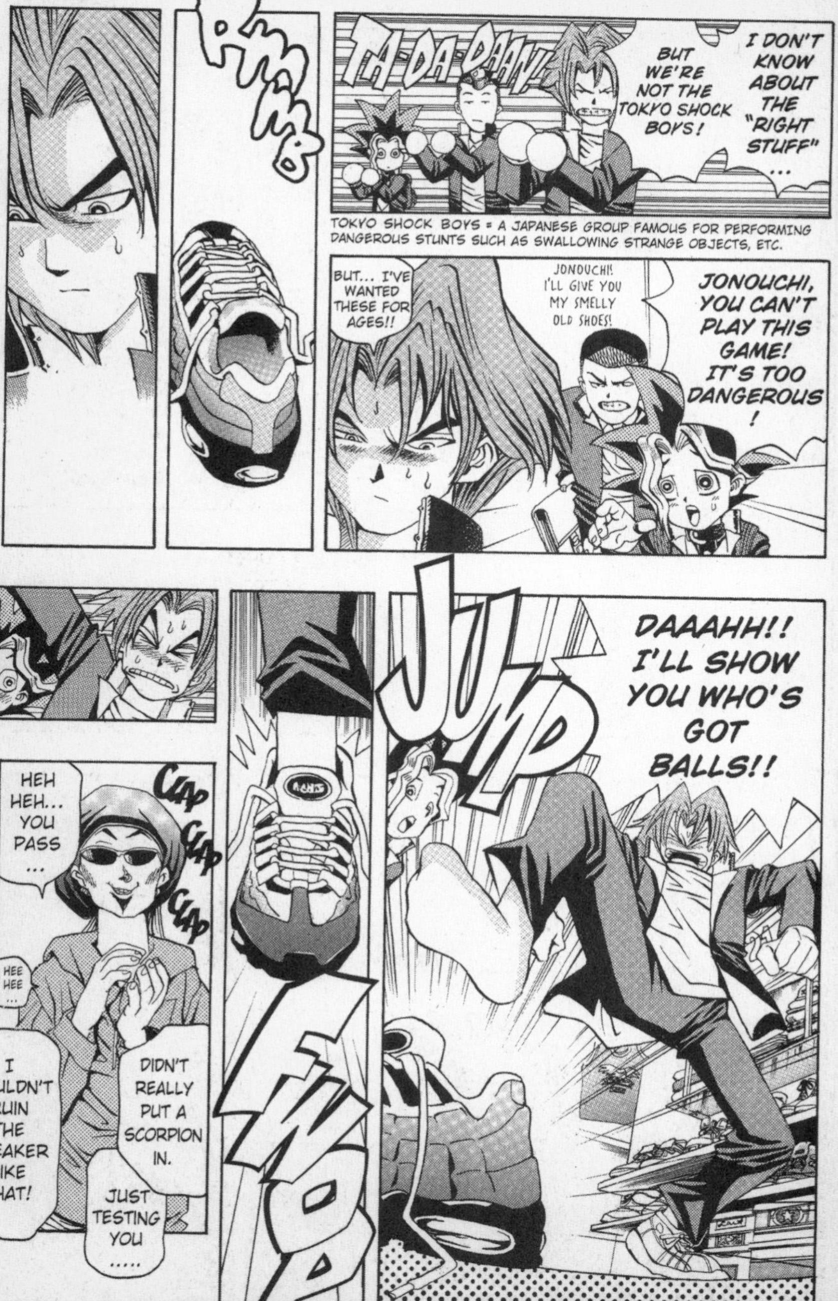
TA-DA-DAAN!
I DON'T KNOW ABOUT THE "RIGHT STUFF"...
BUT WE'RE NOT THE TOKYO SHOCK BOYS!
JONOUCHI, YOU CAN'T PLAY THIS GAME! IT'S TOO DANGEROUS!
JONOUCHI! I'LL GIVE YOU MY SMELLY OLD SHOES!
BUT... I'VE WANTED THESE FOR AGES!!
JUMP
DAAAHH!! I'LL SHOW YOU WHO'S GOT BALLS!!
CLAP CLAP CLAP
HEH HEH... YOU PASS...
HEE HEE...
DIDN'T REALLY PUT A SCORPION IN.
JUST TESTING YOU.....
I WOULDN'T RUIN THE SNEAKER LIKE THAT!

TOKYO SHOCK BOYS = A JAPANESE GROUP FAMOUS FOR PERFORMING DANGEROUS STUNTS SUCH AS SWALLOWING STRANGE OBJECTS, ETC.

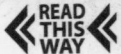

READ THIS WAY

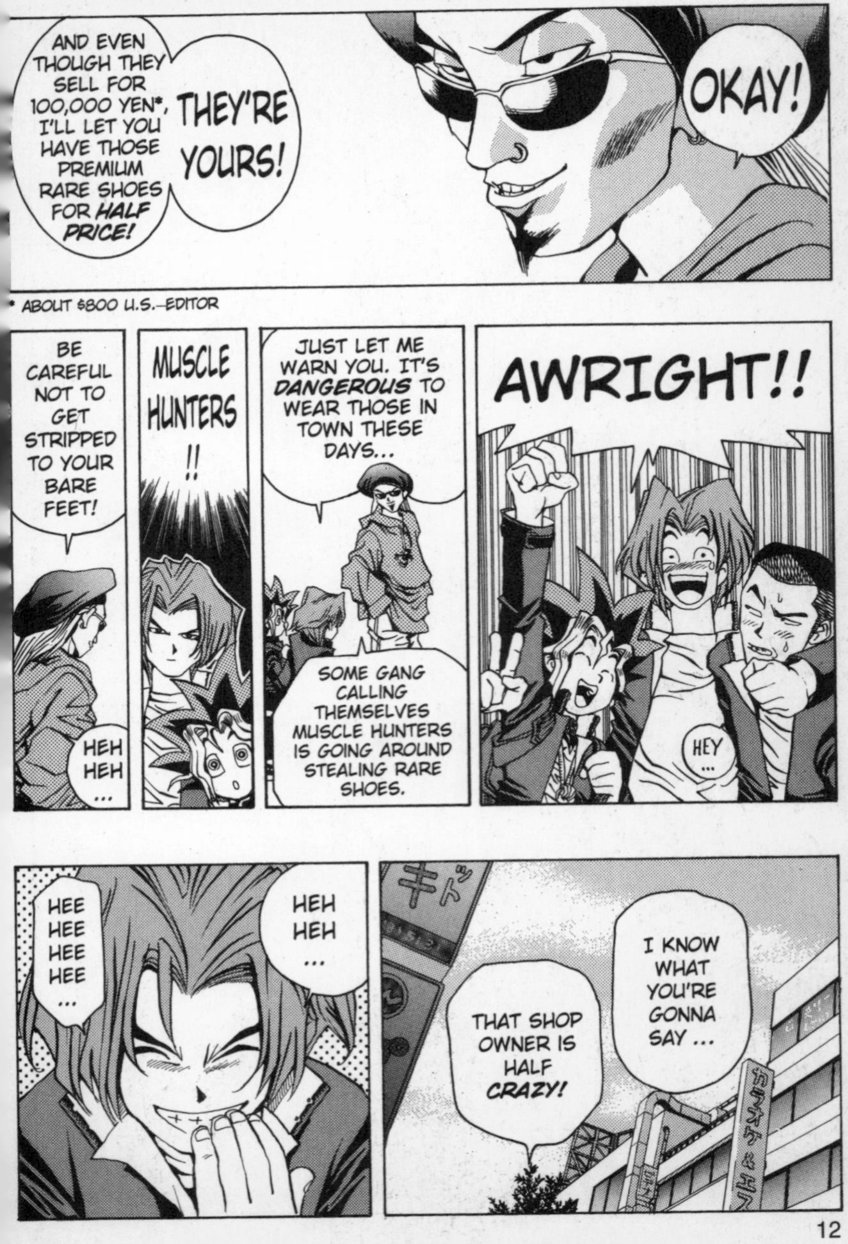
OKAY!
AND EVEN THOUGH THEY SELL FOR 100,000 YEN*, I'LL LET YOU HAVE THOSE PREMIUM RARE SHOES FOR HALF PRICE!
THEY'RE YOURS!
AWRIGHT!!
HEY ...
JUST LET ME WARN YOU. IT'S DANGEROUS TO WEAR THOSE IN TOWN THESE DAYS...
SOME GANG CALLING THEMSELVES MUSCLE HUNTERS IS GOING AROUND STEALING RARE SHOES.
MUSCLE HUNTERS !!
BE CAREFUL NOT TO GET STRIPPED TO YOUR BARE FEET!
HEH HEH ...
I KNOW WHAT YOU'RE GONNA SAY ...
THAT SHOP OWNER IS HALF CRAZY!
HEH HEH ...
HEE HEE HEE HEE ...

* ABOUT $800 U.S.–EDITOR

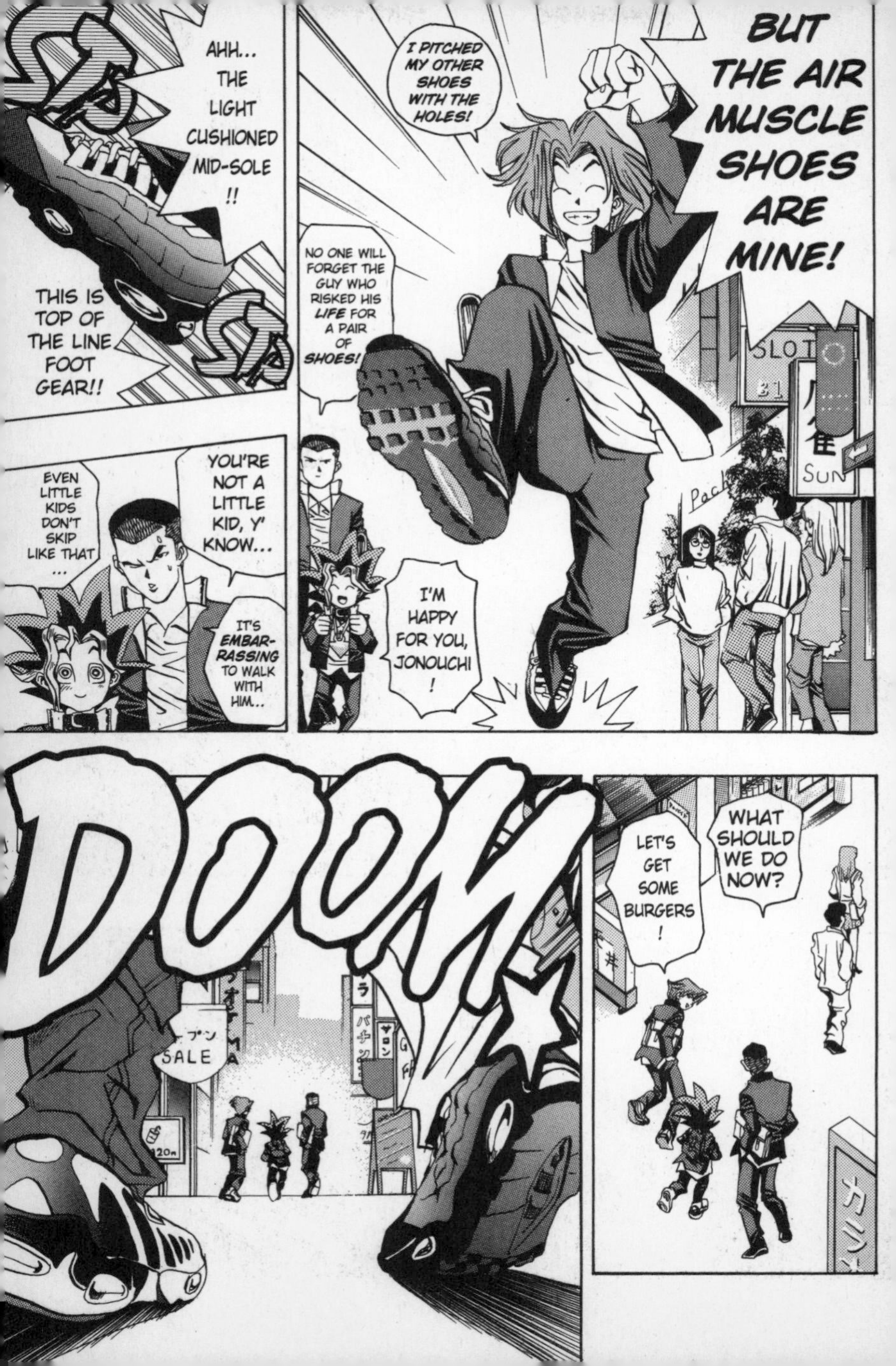
BUT THE AIR MUSCLE SHOES ARE MINE!
I PITCHED MY OTHER SHOES WITH THE HOLES!
NO ONE WILL FORGET THE GUY WHO RISKED HIS LIFE FOR A PAIR OF SHOES!
SLOT
SUN
I'M HAPPY FOR YOU, JONOUCHI!
STP
AHH... THE LIGHT CUSHIONED MID-SOLE!!
THIS IS TOP OF THE LINE FOOT GEAR!!
STP
YOU'RE NOT A LITTLE KID, Y' KNOW...
EVEN LITTLE KIDS DON'T SKIP LIKE THAT...
IT'S EMBARRASSING TO WALK WITH HIM...
WHAT SHOULD WE DO NOW?
LET'S GET SOME BURGERS!
DOOM
SALE

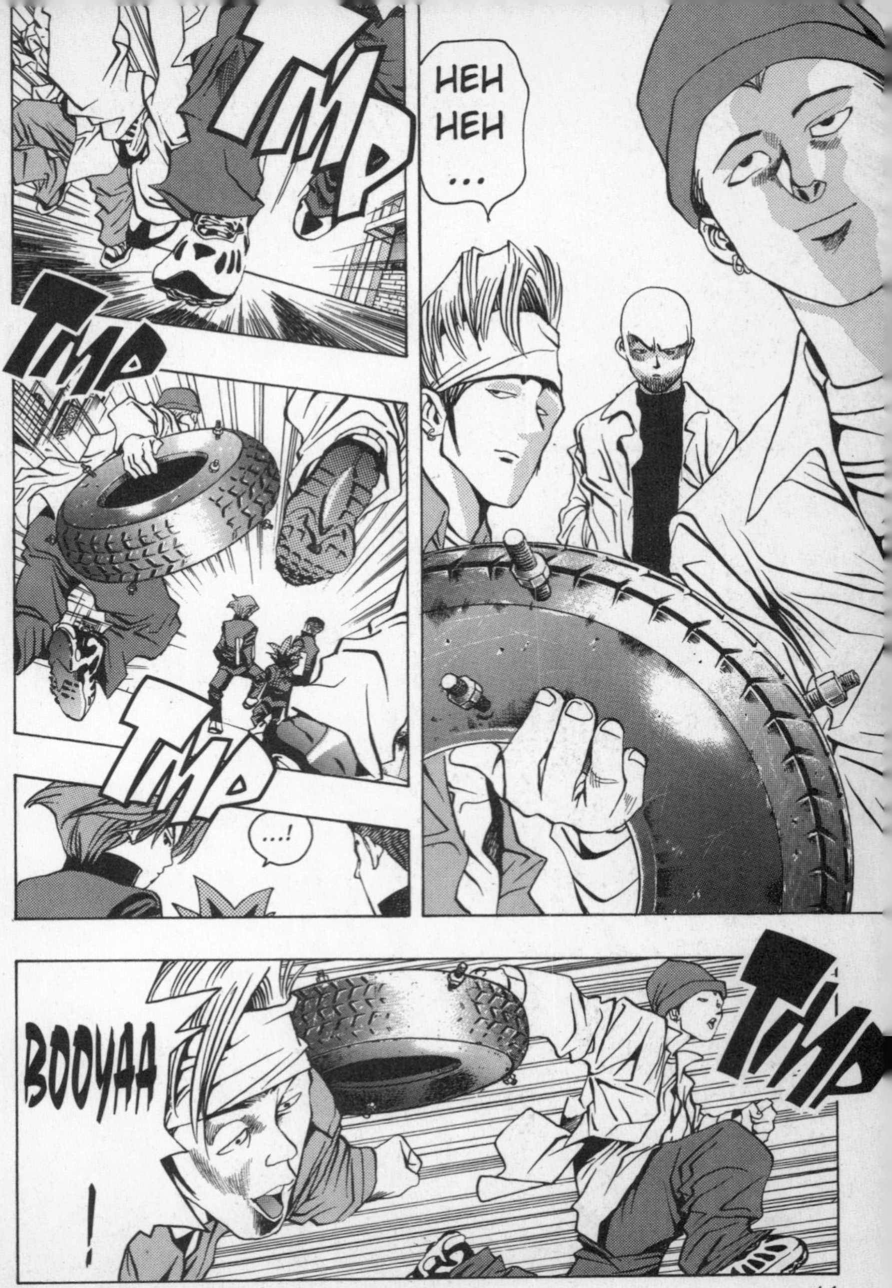
HEH HEH ...
TMP
TMP
TMP
...!
TMP
BOOYAA !

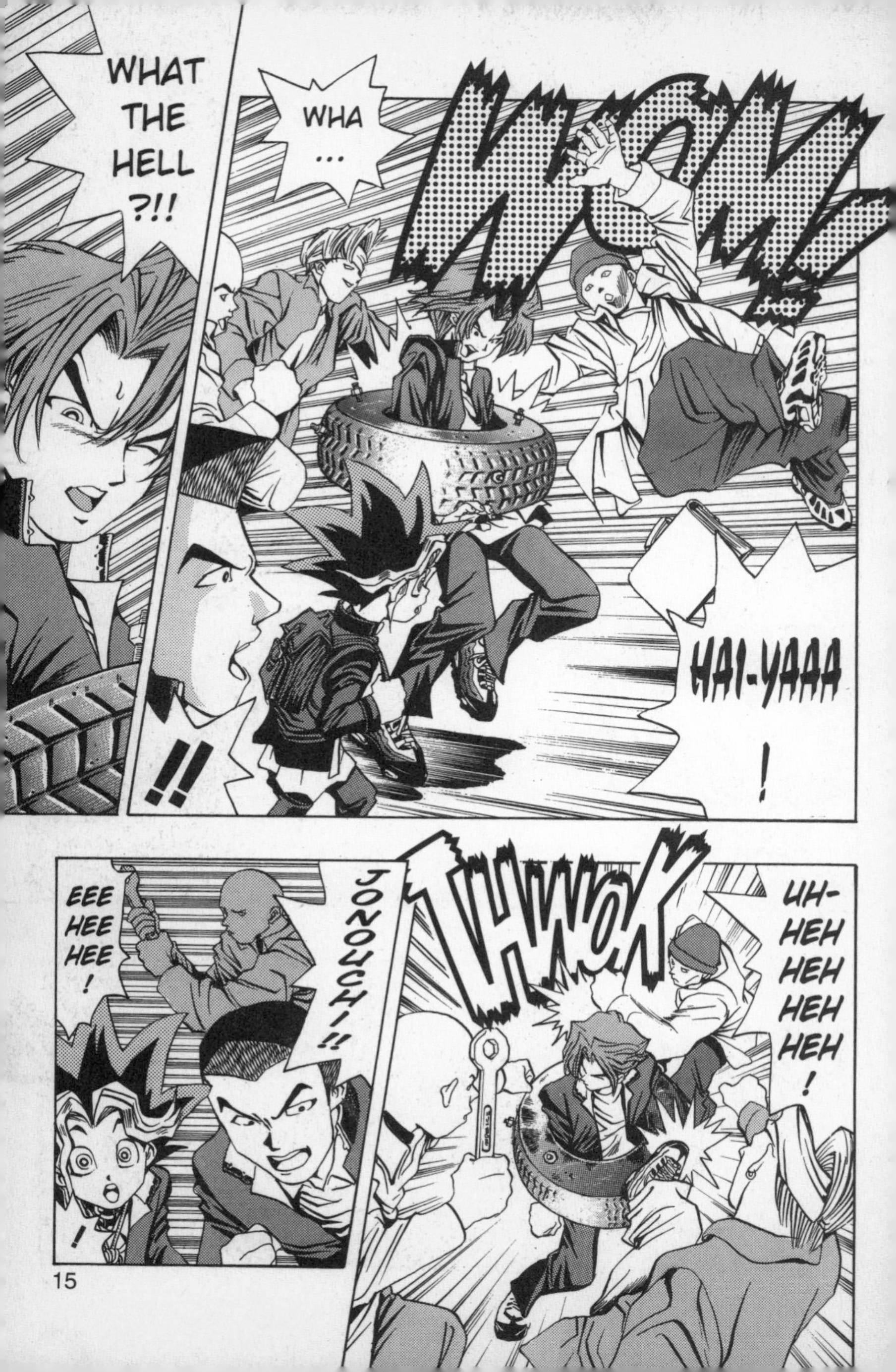
HAI-YAAA
!
WHA
...
WHAT THE HELL ?!!
!!
UH-HEH HEH HEH HEH
!
THWOK
JONOUCHI!!
EEE HEE HEE
!
!

READ THIS WAY

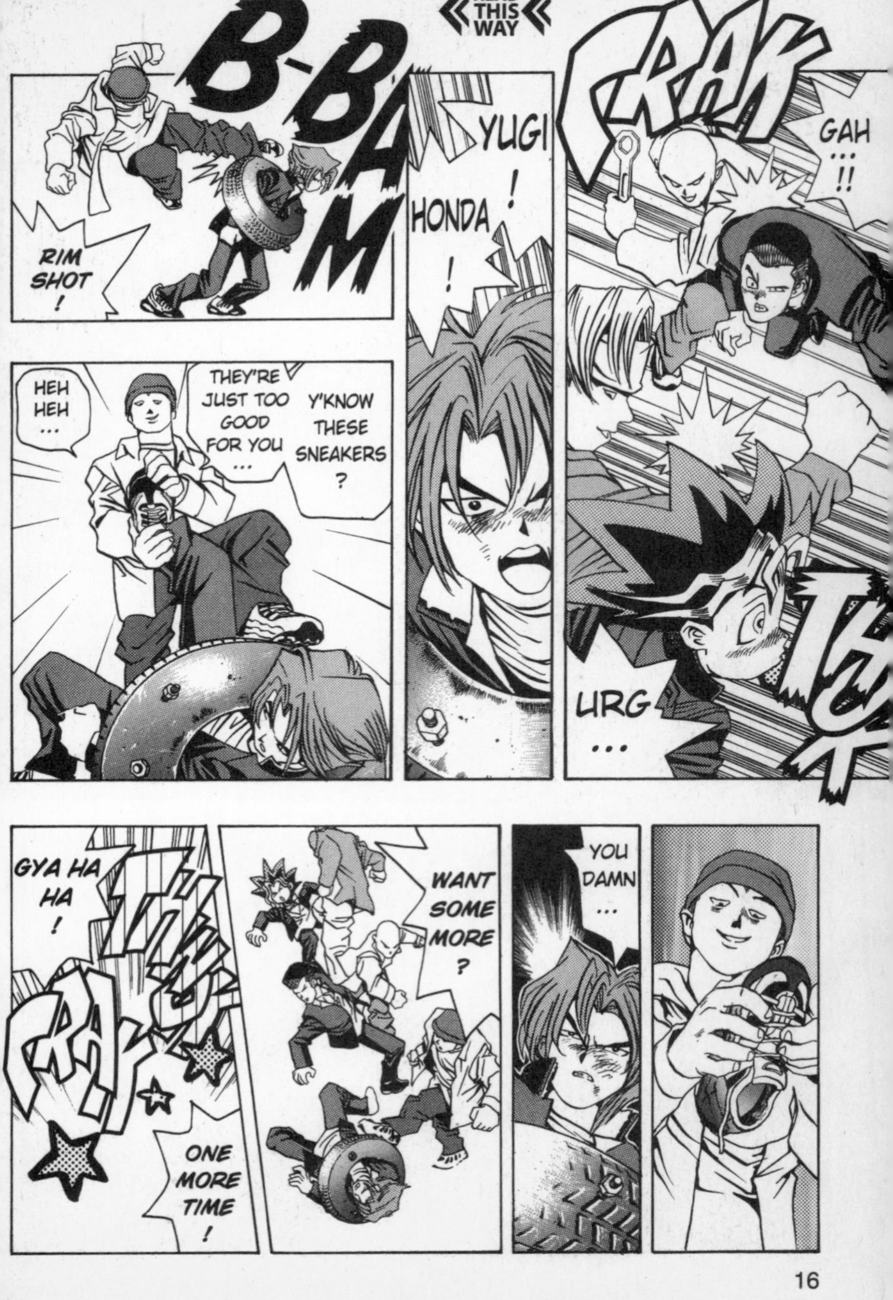
CRAK
GAH …!!
THUK
URG …
YUGI !
HONDA !
B-BAM
RIM SHOT !
Y'KNOW THESE SNEAKERS ?
THEY'RE JUST TOO GOOD FOR YOU …
HEH HEH …
YOU DAMN …
WANT SOME MORE ?
ONE MORE TIME !
GYA HA HA !

READ THIS WAY

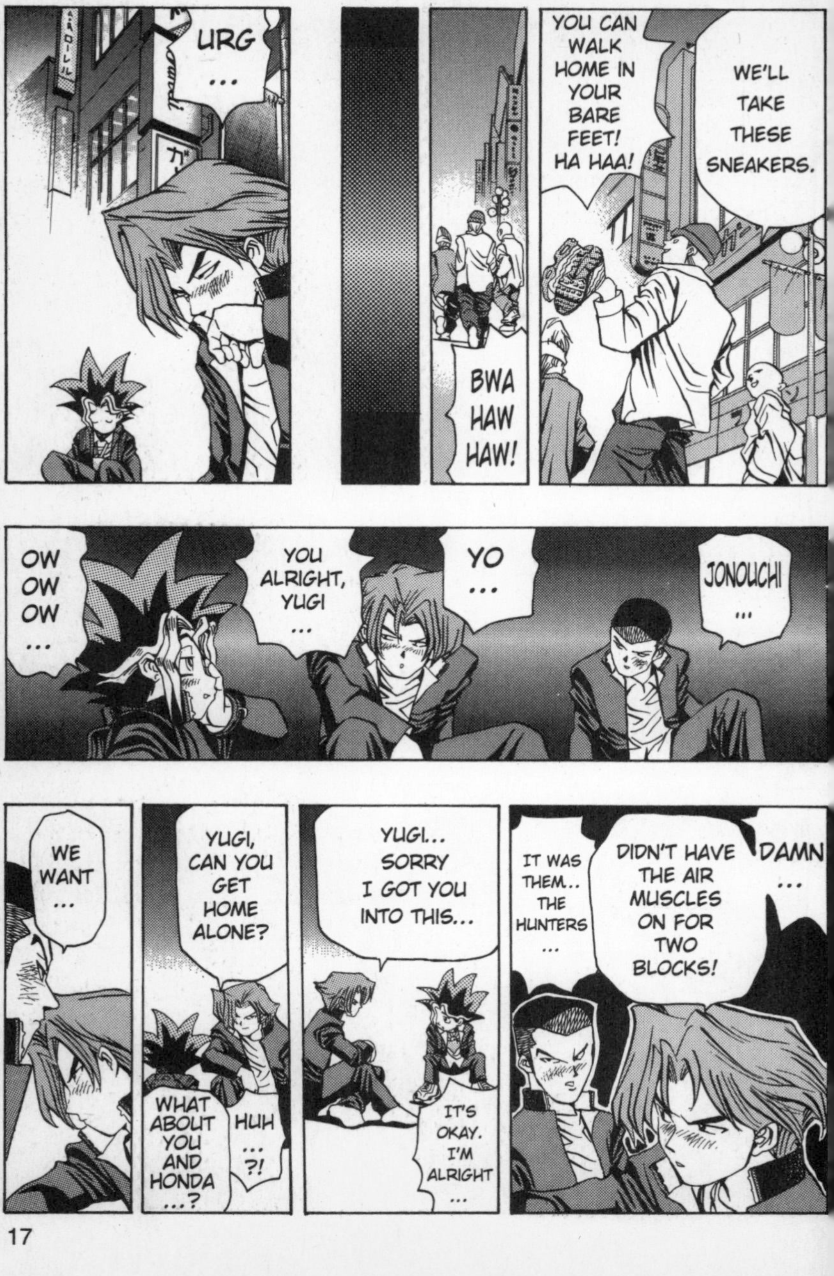
WE'LL TAKE THESE SNEAKERS.
YOU CAN WALK HOME IN YOUR BARE FEET! HA HAA!
BWA HAW HAW!
URG ...
JONOUCHI ...
YO ...
YOU ALRIGHT, YUGI ...
OW OW OW ...
DAMN ...
DIDN'T HAVE THE AIR MUSCLES ON FOR TWO BLOCKS!
IT WAS THEM... THE HUNTERS ...
YUGI... SORRY I GOT YOU INTO THIS...
IT'S OKAY. I'M ALRIGHT ...
YUGI, CAN YOU GET HOME ALONE?
HUH ...?!
WHAT ABOUT YOU AND HONDA ...?
WE WANT ...

READ THIS WAY

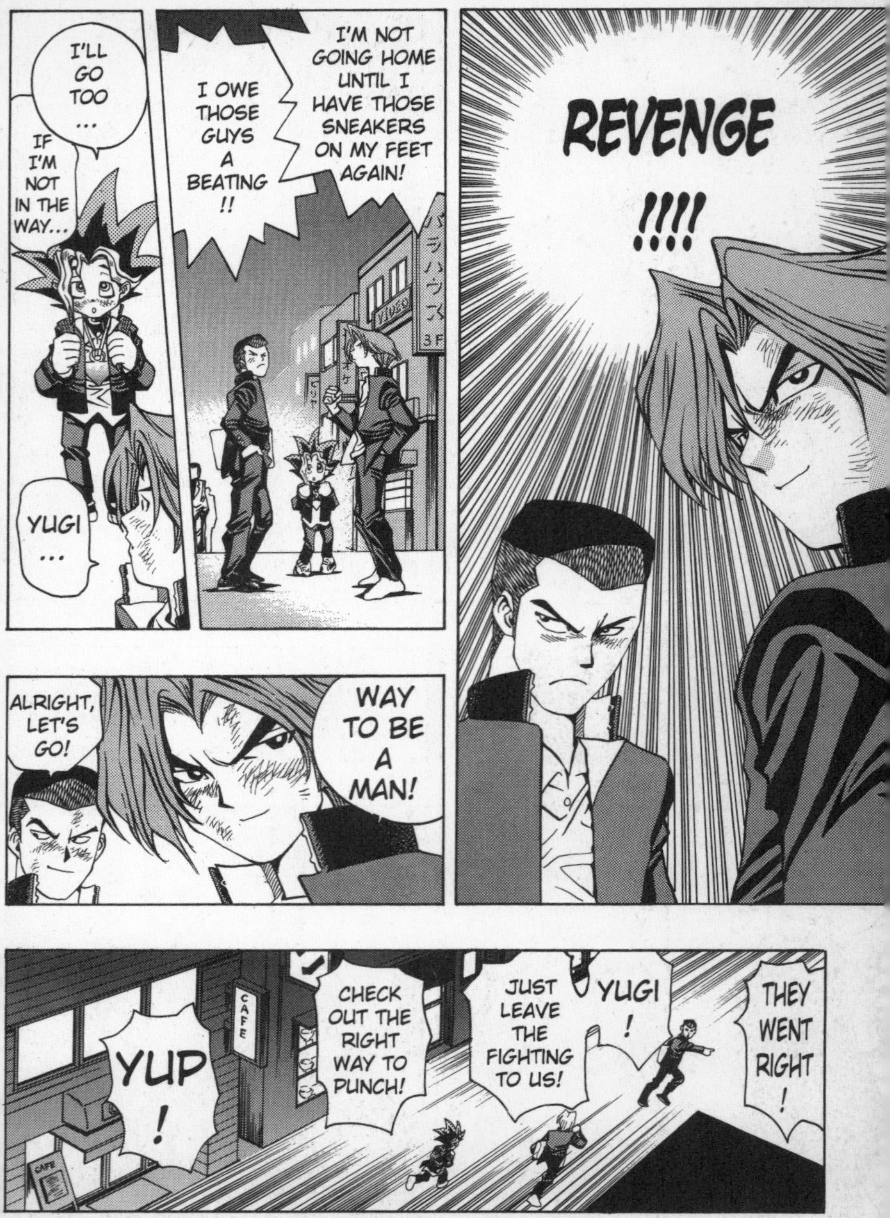
REVENGE !!!!
I'M NOT GOING HOME UNTIL I HAVE THOSE SNEAKERS ON MY FEET AGAIN!
I OWE THOSE GUYS A BEATING !!
I'LL GO TOO ...
IF I'M NOT IN THE WAY...
YUGI ...
WAY TO BE A MAN!
ALRIGHT, LET'S GO!
THEY WENT RIGHT !
YUGI !
JUST LEAVE THE FIGHTING TO US!
CHECK OUT THE RIGHT WAY TO PUNCH!
CAFE
YUP !

READ THIS WAY

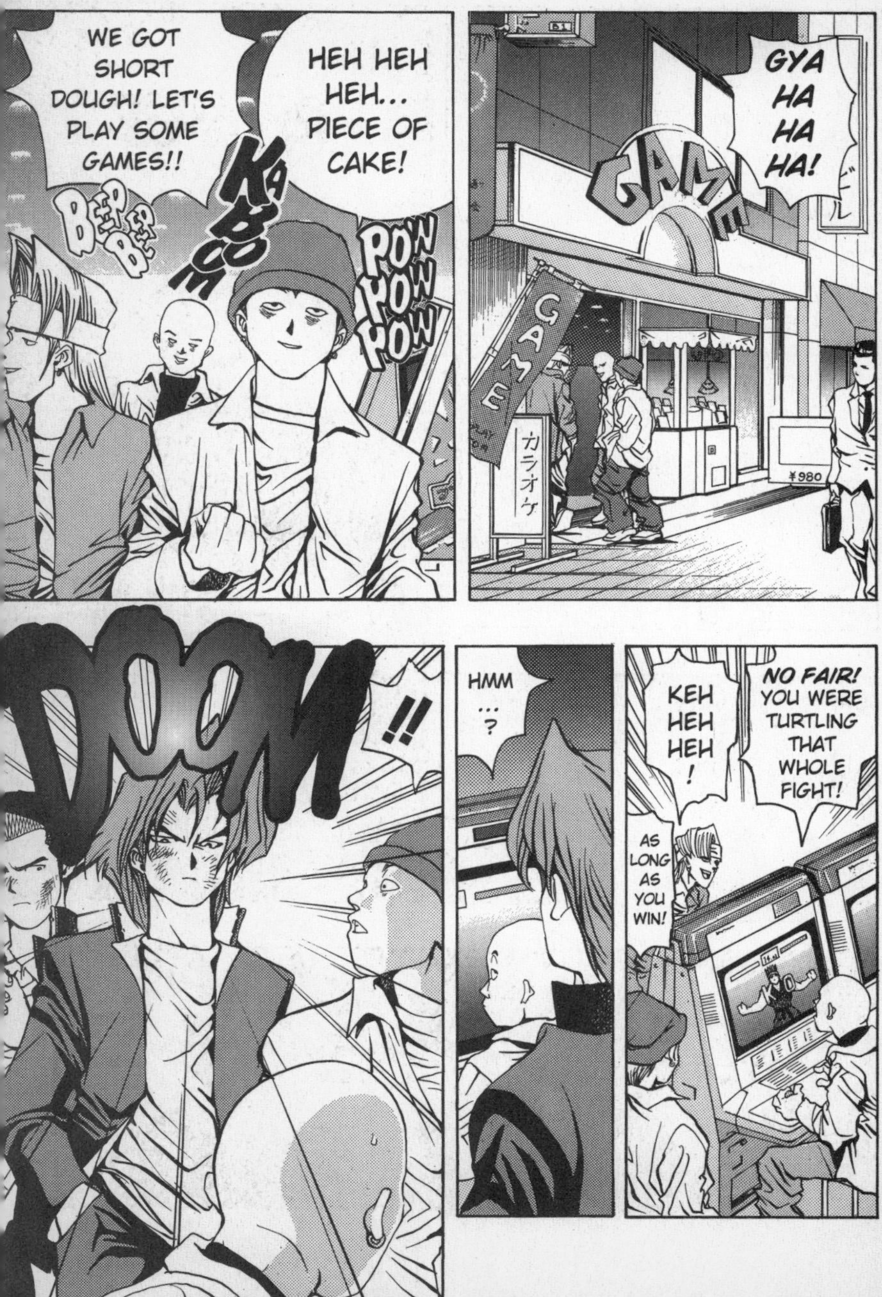
GYA HA HA HA!
GAME
GAME
カラオケ
¥980
HEH HEH HEH... PIECE OF CAKE!
WE GOT SHORT DOUGH! LET'S PLAY SOME GAMES!!
POW POW POW
KABOOM
BEEP BEEP
NO FAIR! YOU WERE TURTLING THAT WHOLE FIGHT!
KEH HEH HEH!
AS LONG AS YOU WIN!
HMM ...?
DOOM!!

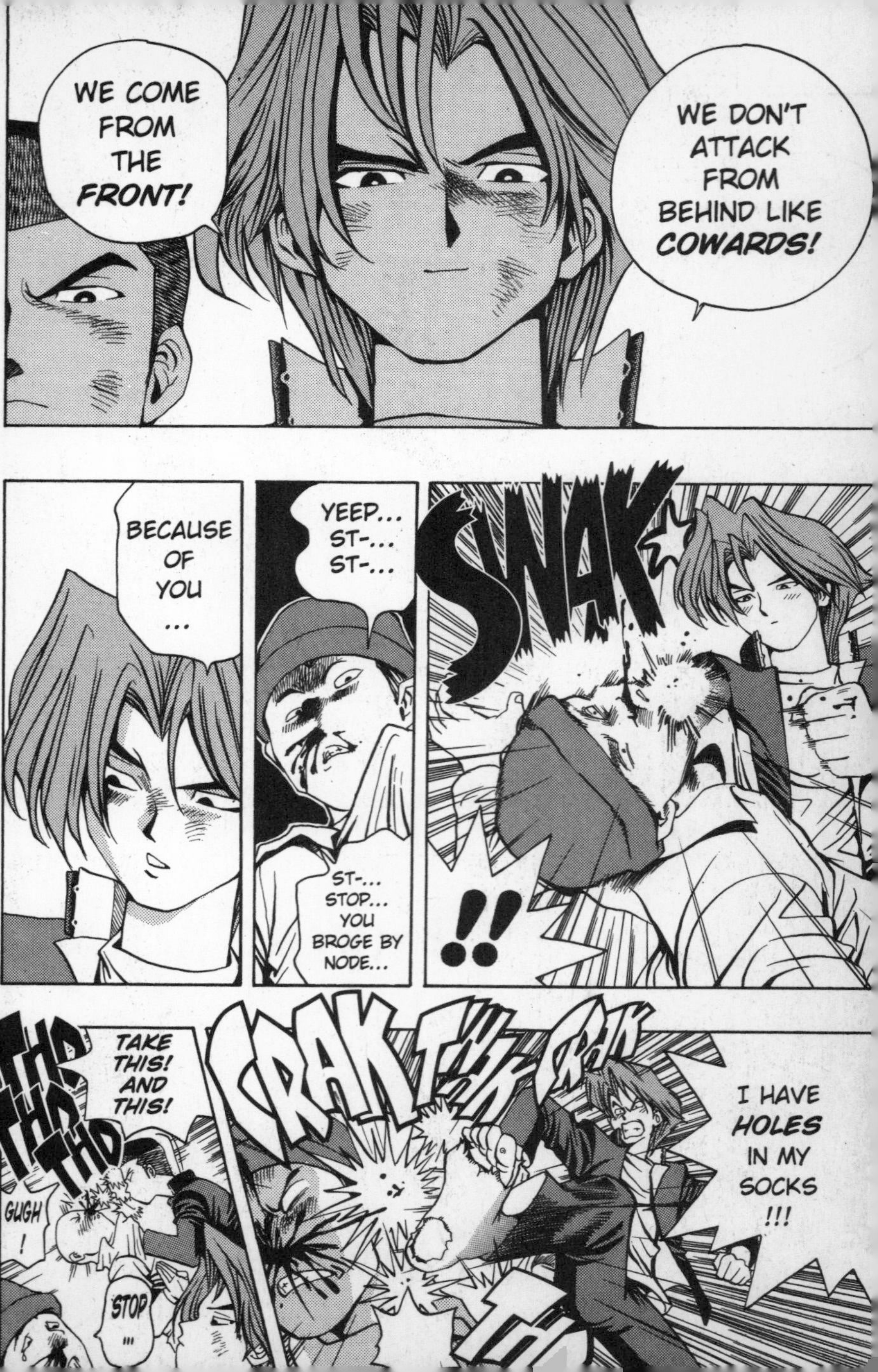
WE COME FROM THE FRONT!
WE DON'T ATTACK FROM BEHIND LIKE COWARDS!
BECAUSE OF YOU ...
YEEP... ST-... ST-...
ST-... STOP... YOU BROGE BY NODE...
SNAK
!!
THD THD THD
TAKE THIS! AND THIS!
GUGH !
STOP !!!
CRAK
I HAVE HOLES IN MY SOCKS !!!

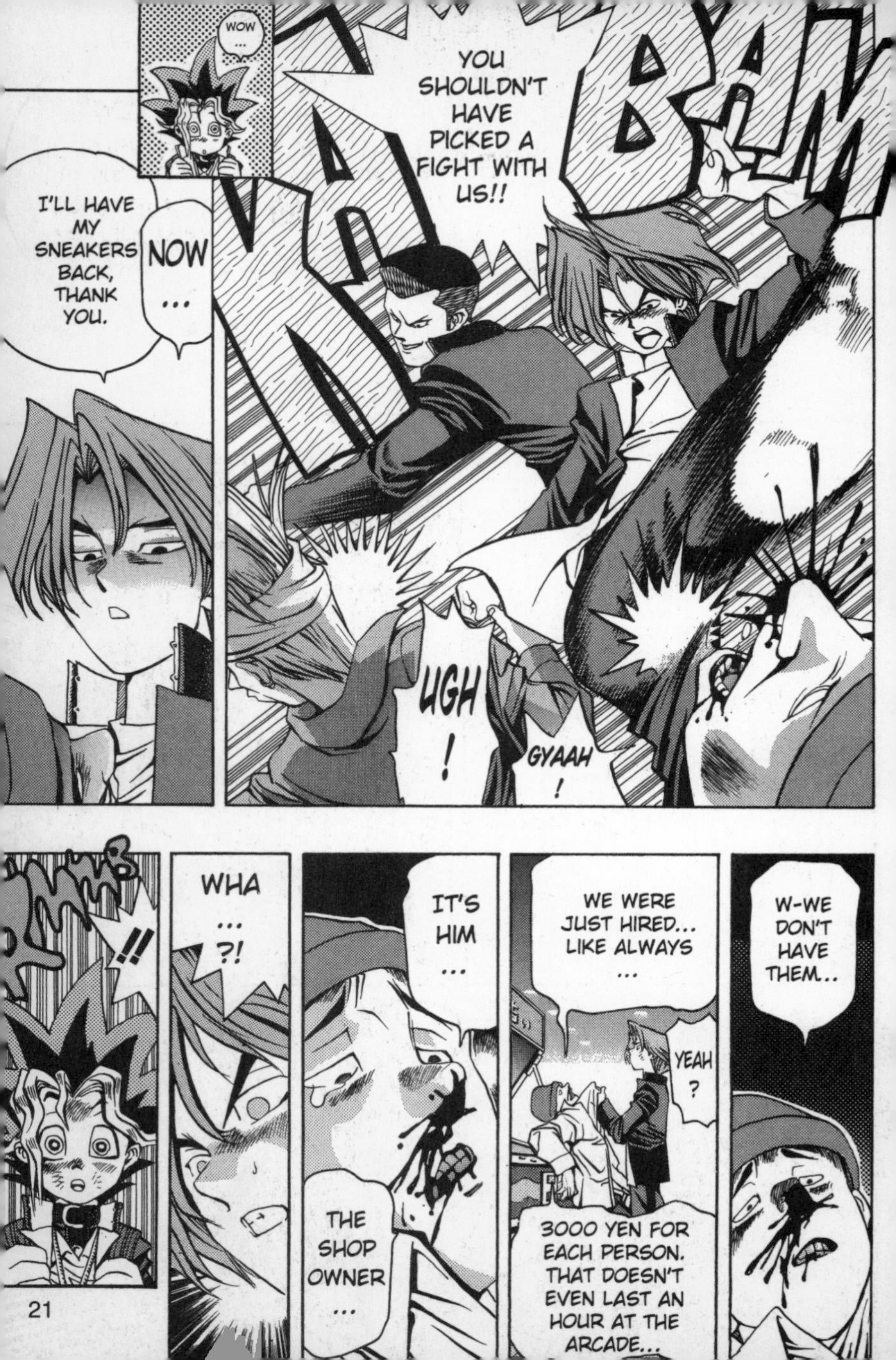
BAM
YOU SHOULDN'T HAVE PICKED A FIGHT WITH US!!
UGH!
GYAAH!
WOW...
NOW...
I'LL HAVE MY SNEAKERS BACK, THANK YOU.
W-WE DON'T HAVE THEM...
WE WERE JUST HIRED... LIKE ALWAYS...
YEAH?
3000 YEN FOR EACH PERSON. THAT DOESN'T EVEN LAST AN HOUR AT THE ARCADE...
IT'S HIM...
THE SHOP OWNER...
WHA...?!
!!

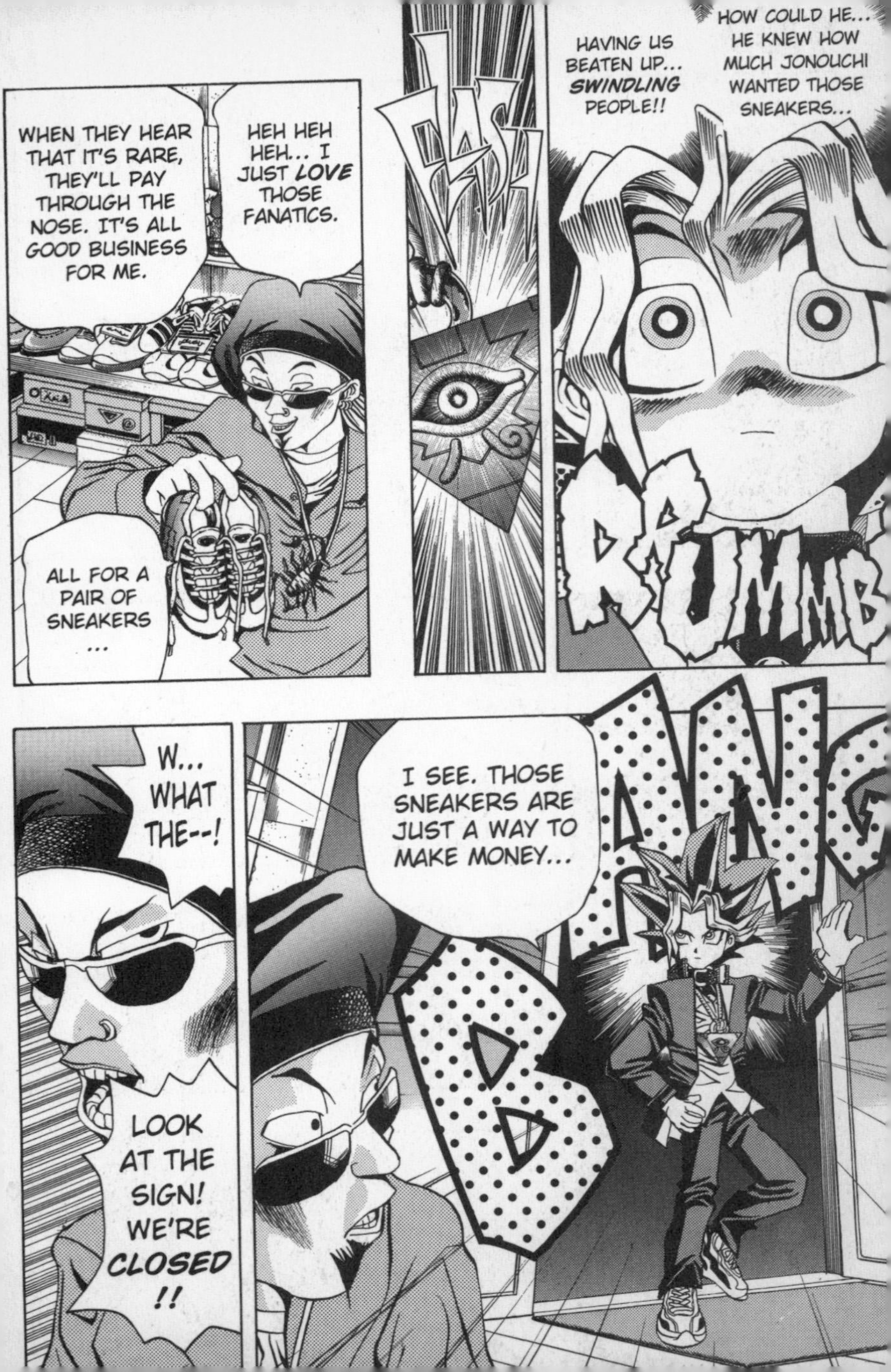
HOW COULD HE... HE KNEW HOW MUCH JONOUCHI WANTED THOSE SNEAKERS...
HAVING US BEATEN UP... *SWINDLING* PEOPLE!!
HEH HEH HEH... I JUST *LOVE* THOSE FANATICS.
WHEN THEY HEAR THAT IT'S RARE, THEY'LL PAY THROUGH THE NOSE. IT'S ALL GOOD BUSINESS FOR ME.
ALL FOR A PAIR OF SNEAKERS ...
I SEE. THOSE SNEAKERS ARE JUST A WAY TO MAKE MONEY...
W... WHAT THE--!
LOOK AT THE SIGN! WE'RE *CLOSED* !!

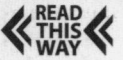

READ THIS WAY

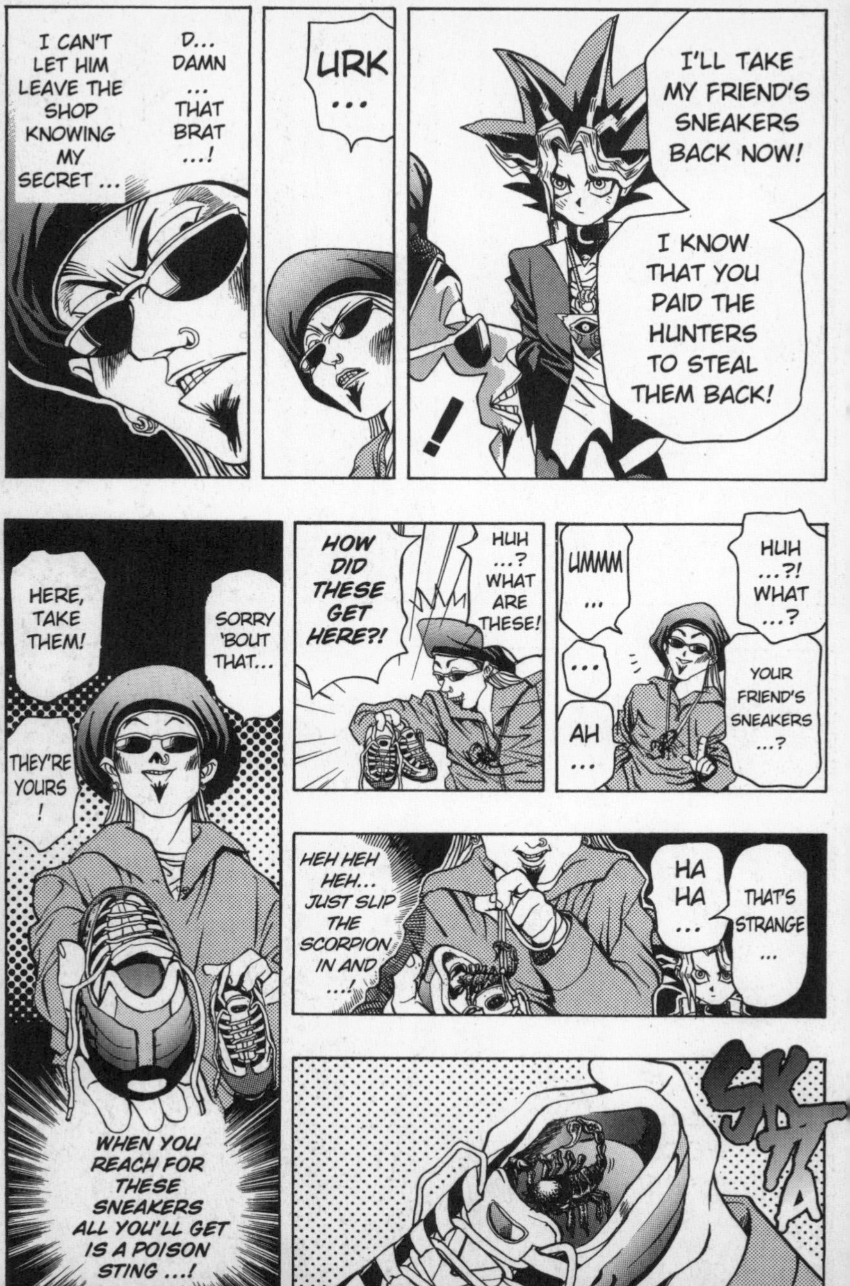
I'LL TAKE MY FRIEND'S SNEAKERS BACK NOW!
I KNOW THAT YOU PAID THE HUNTERS TO STEAL THEM BACK!
!
URK ...
D... DAMN ... THAT BRAT ...!
I CAN'T LET HIM LEAVE THE SHOP KNOWING MY SECRET ...
HUH ...?! WHAT ...?
UMMM ...
YOUR FRIEND'S SNEAKERS ...?
...
AH ...
HUH ...? WHAT ARE THESE!
HOW DID THESE GET HERE?!
THAT'S STRANGE ...
HA HA ...
HEH HEH HEH... JUST SLIP THE SCORPION IN AND ...!
SKA
SORRY 'BOUT THAT...
HERE, TAKE THEM!
THEY'RE YOURS!
WHEN YOU REACH FOR THESE SNEAKERS ALL YOU'LL GET IS A POISON STING ...!

READ THIS WAY

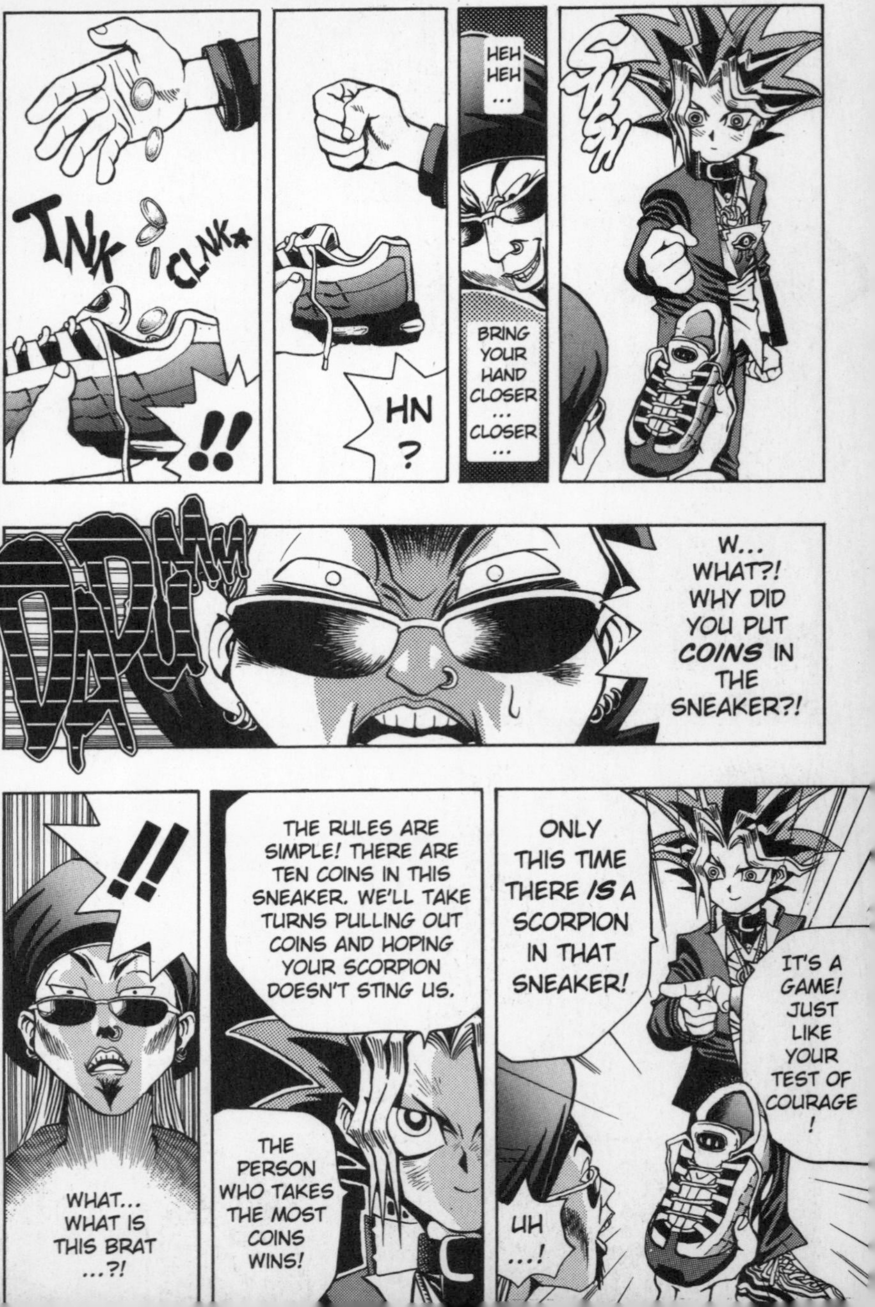
HEH HEH ...
BRING YOUR HAND CLOSER ... CLOSER ...
HN ?
TNK
CLNK★
!!
W... WHAT?! WHY DID YOU PUT *COINS* IN THE SNEAKER?!
ONLY THIS TIME THERE *IS* A SCORPION IN THAT SNEAKER!
IT'S A GAME! JUST LIKE YOUR TEST OF COURAGE!
UH ...!
THE RULES ARE SIMPLE! THERE ARE TEN COINS IN THIS SNEAKER. WE'LL TAKE TURNS PULLING OUT COINS AND HOPING YOUR SCORPION DOESN'T STING US.
THE PERSON WHO TAKES THE MOST COINS WINS!
!!
WHAT... WHAT IS THIS BRAT ...?!

READ THIS WAY

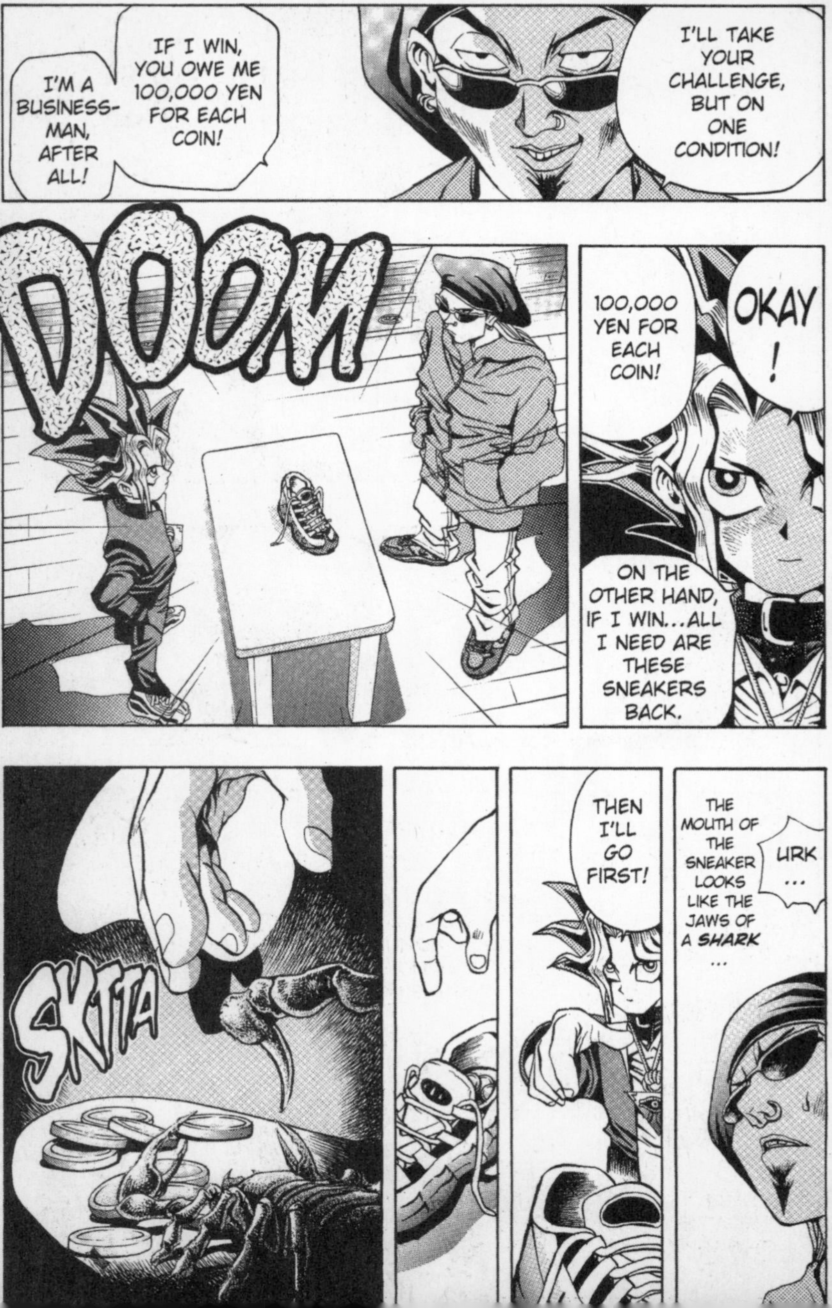
I'LL TAKE YOUR CHALLENGE, BUT ON ONE CONDITION!
IF I WIN, YOU OWE ME 100,000 YEN FOR EACH COIN!
I'M A BUSINESS-MAN, AFTER ALL!
OKAY!
100,000 YEN FOR EACH COIN!
ON THE OTHER HAND, IF I WIN...ALL I NEED ARE THESE SNEAKERS BACK.
DOOM
URK...
THE MOUTH OF THE SNEAKER LOOKS LIKE THE JAWS OF A ***SHARK***...
THEN I'LL GO FIRST!
SKTTA

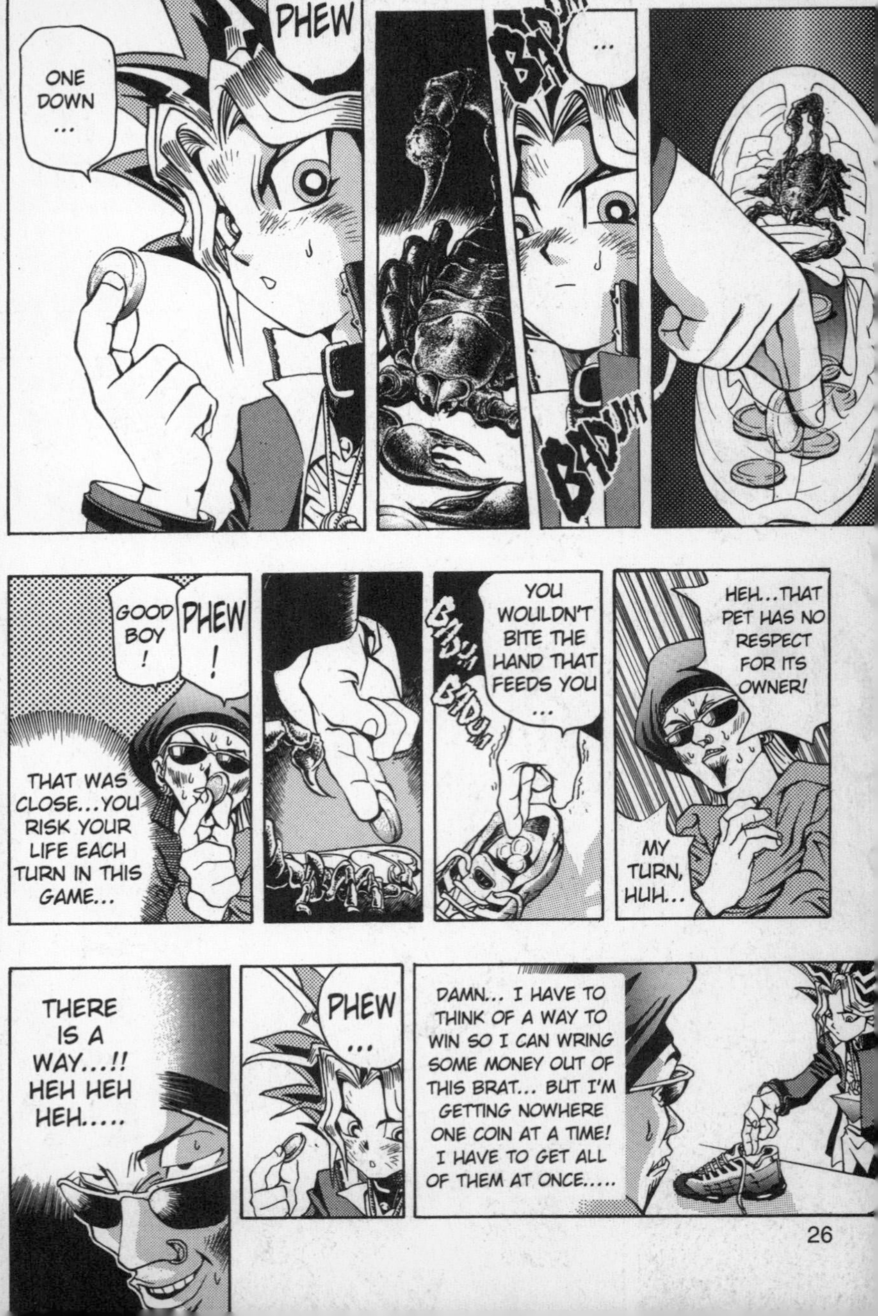
BADUM
...
BADUM
PHEW
ONE DOWN ...
HEH...THAT PET HAS NO RESPECT FOR ITS OWNER!
MY TURN, HUH...
YOU WOULDN'T BITE THE HAND THAT FEEDS YOU ...
BADUM
BADUM
PHEW !
GOOD BOY !
THAT WAS CLOSE...YOU RISK YOUR LIFE EACH TURN IN THIS GAME...
DAMN... I HAVE TO THINK OF A WAY TO WIN SO I CAN WRING SOME MONEY OUT OF THIS BRAT... BUT I'M GETTING NOWHERE ONE COIN AT A TIME! I HAVE TO GET ALL OF THEM AT ONCE.....
PHEW ...
THERE IS A WAY...!! HEH HEH HEH.....

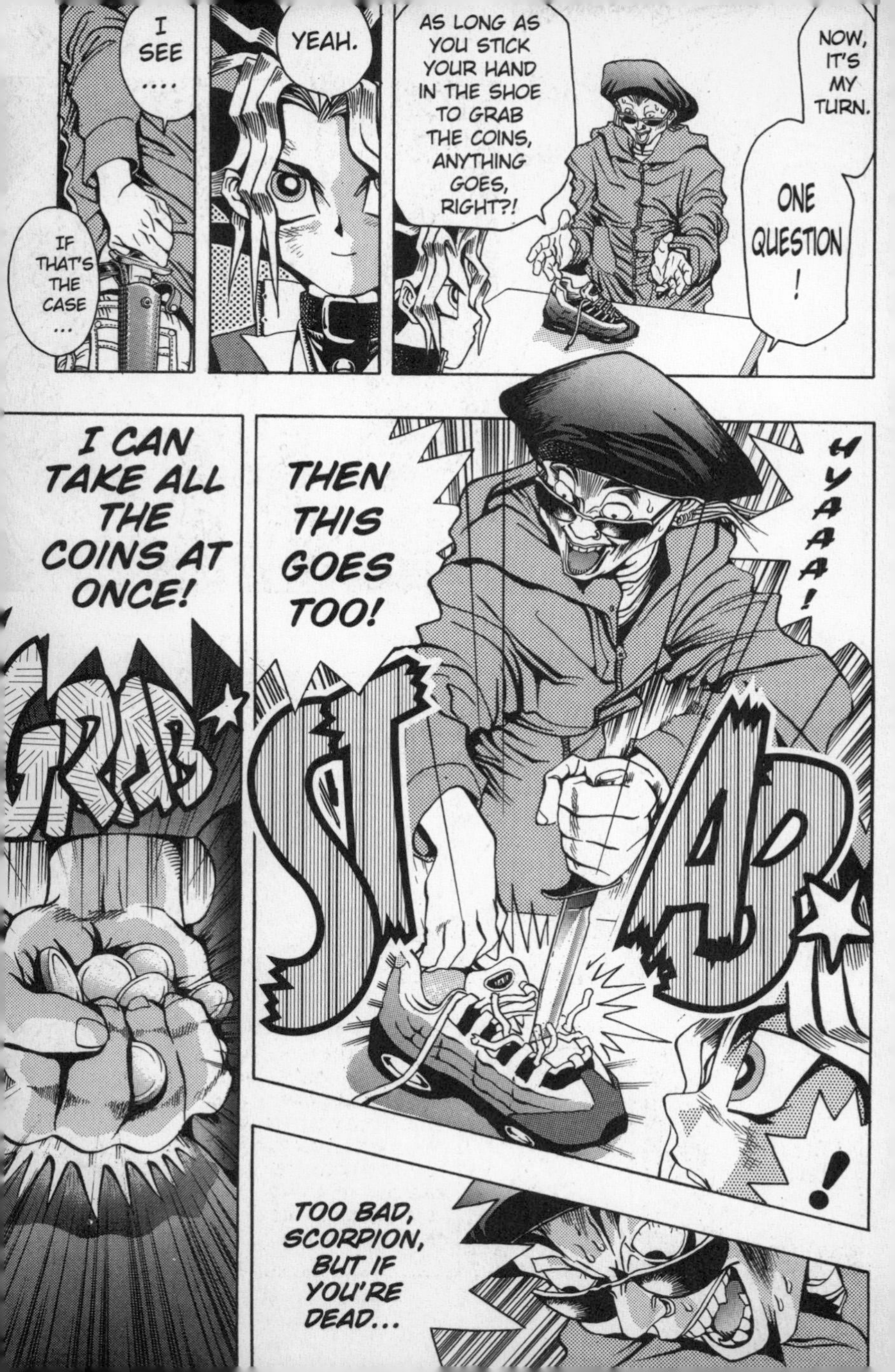
NOW, IT'S MY TURN.
ONE QUESTION!
AS LONG AS YOU STICK YOUR HAND IN THE SHOE TO GRAB THE COINS, ANYTHING GOES, RIGHT?!
YEAH.
I SEE....
IF THAT'S THE CASE...
HYAAAA!
THEN THIS GOES TOO!
STAB
!
TOO BAD, SCORPION, BUT IF YOU'RE DEAD...
I CAN TAKE ALL THE COINS AT ONCE!
GRAB

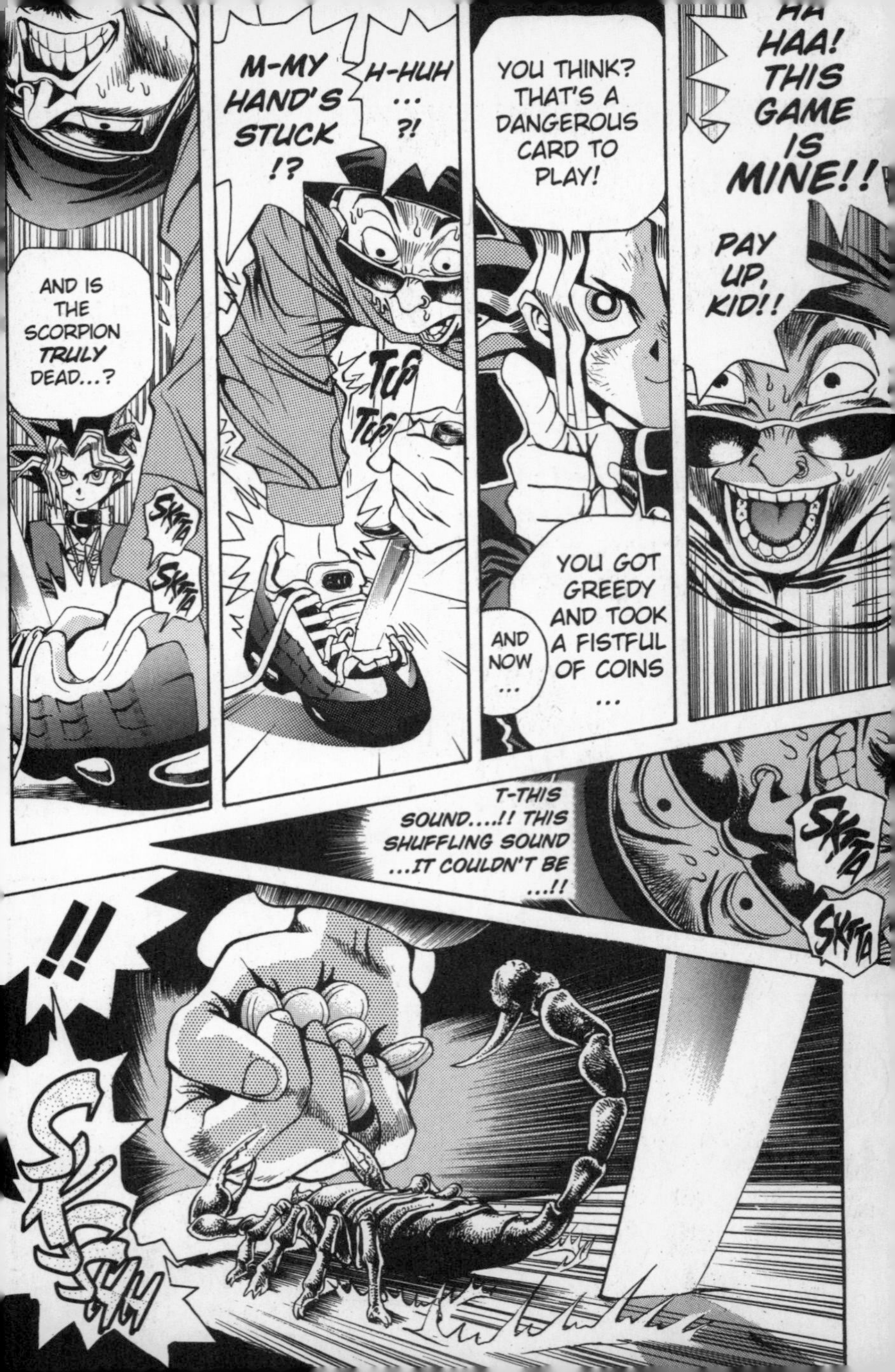
HA HAA! THIS GAME IS MINE!!
PAY UP, KID!!
YOU THINK? THAT'S A DANGEROUS CARD TO PLAY!
YOU GOT GREEDY AND TOOK A FISTFUL OF COINS...
AND NOW...
H-HUH...?!
M-MY HAND'S STUCK!?
TUP
TUP
AND IS THE SCORPION TRULY DEAD...?
SKTTA
SKTTA
SKTTA
SKTTA
T-THIS SOUND....!! THIS SHUFFLING SOUND ...IT COULDN'T BE ...!!
!!

READ THIS WAY

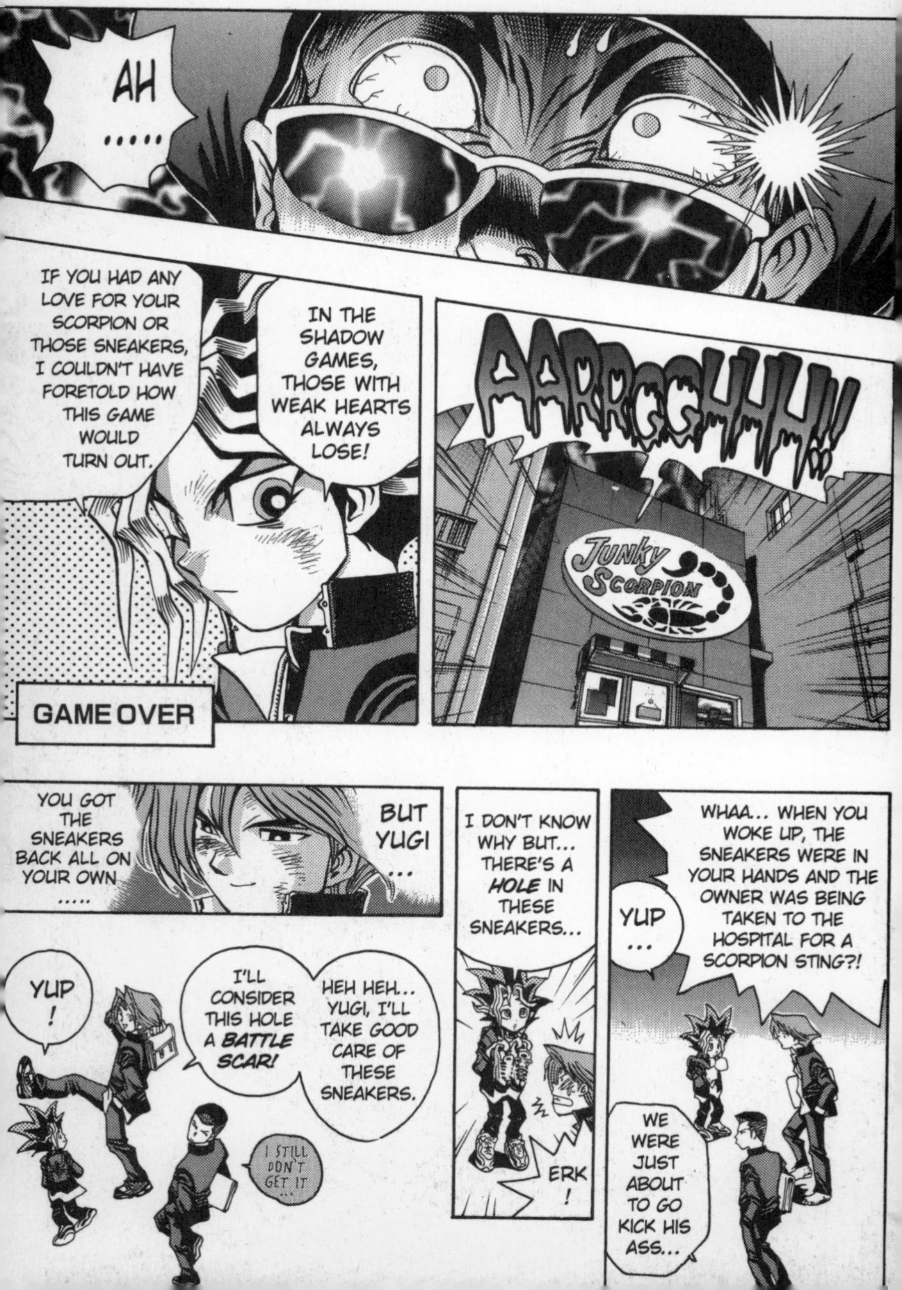
AH .....
AARRGGHHH!!
IF YOU HAD ANY LOVE FOR YOUR SCORPION OR THOSE SNEAKERS, I COULDN'T HAVE FORETOLD HOW THIS GAME WOULD TURN OUT.
IN THE SHADOW GAMES, THOSE WITH WEAK HEARTS ALWAYS LOSE!
GAME OVER
Junky Scorpion
WHAA... WHEN YOU WOKE UP, THE SNEAKERS WERE IN YOUR HANDS AND THE OWNER WAS BEING TAKEN TO THE HOSPITAL FOR A SCORPION STING?!
YUP ...
WE WERE JUST ABOUT TO GO KICK HIS ASS...
I DON'T KNOW WHY BUT... THERE'S A *HOLE* IN THESE SNEAKERS...
ERK !
BUT YUGI ...
YOU GOT THE SNEAKERS BACK ALL ON YOUR OWN .....
HEH HEH... YUGI, I'LL TAKE GOOD CARE OF THESE SNEAKERS.
I'LL CONSIDER THIS HOLE A *BATTLE SCAR!*
YUP !
I STILL DON'T GET IT ...

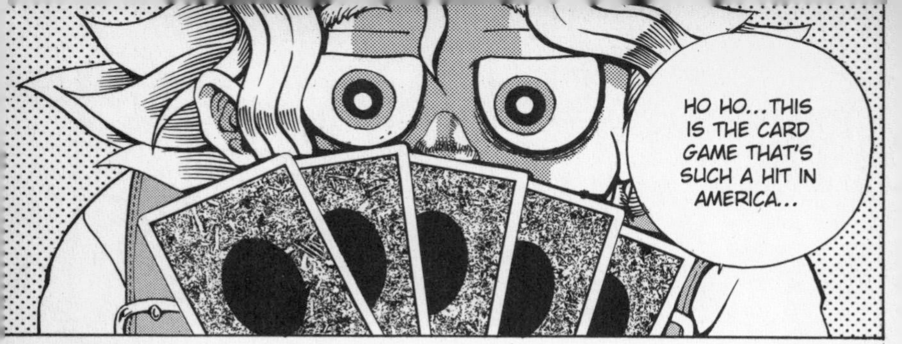
HO HO...THIS IS THE CARD GAME THAT'S SUCH A HIT IN AMERICA...

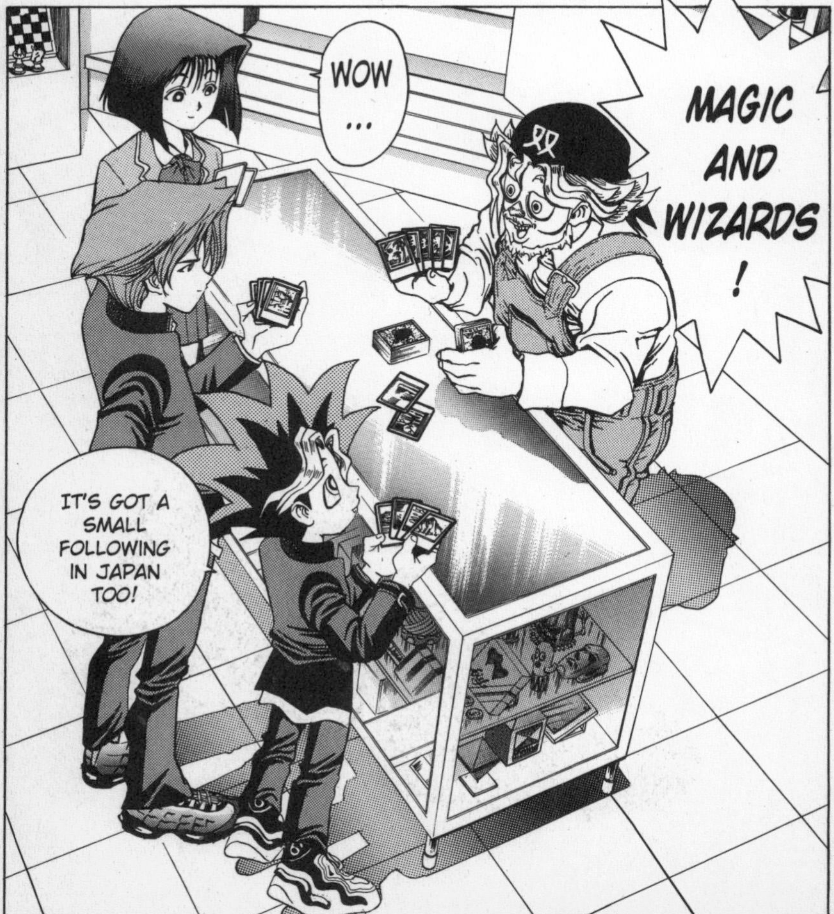
MAGIC AND WIZARDS!
WOW...
IT'S GOT A SMALL FOLLOWING IN JAPAN TOO!

Duel 9: The Cards with Teeth (Part 1)

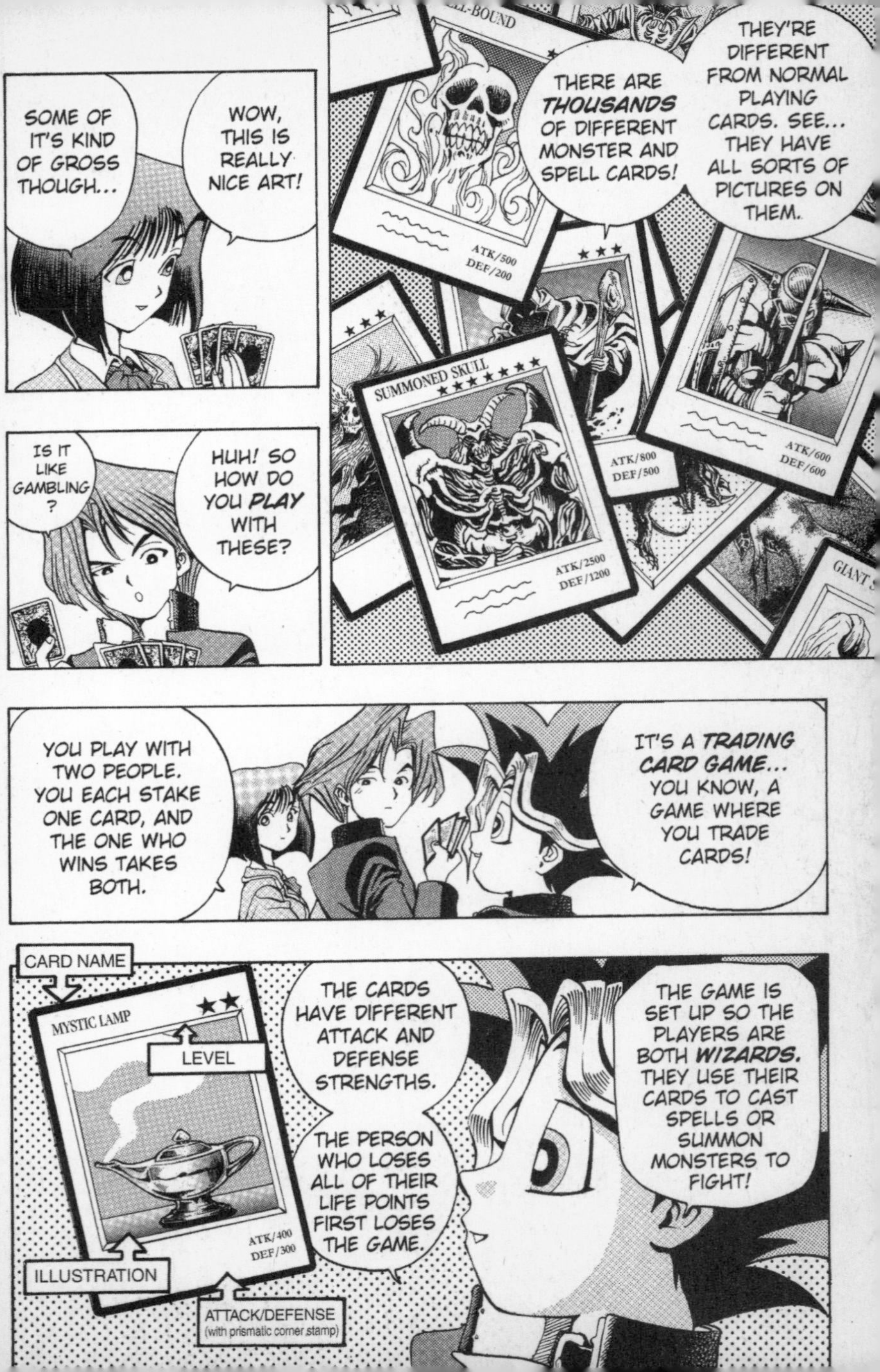
THEY'RE DIFFERENT FROM NORMAL PLAYING CARDS. SEE... THEY HAVE ALL SORTS OF PICTURES ON THEM.
THERE ARE THOUSANDS OF DIFFERENT MONSTER AND SPELL CARDS!
ATK/500 DEF/200
ATK/800 DEF/500
ATK/600 DEF/600
SUMMONED SKULL
ATK/2500 DEF/1200
WOW, THIS IS REALLY NICE ART!
SOME OF IT'S KIND OF GROSS THOUGH...
HUH! SO HOW DO YOU PLAY WITH THESE?
IS IT LIKE GAMBLING?
IT'S A TRADING CARD GAME... YOU KNOW, A GAME WHERE YOU TRADE CARDS!
YOU PLAY WITH TWO PEOPLE. YOU EACH STAKE ONE CARD, AND THE ONE WHO WINS TAKES BOTH.
THE GAME IS SET UP SO THE PLAYERS ARE BOTH WIZARDS. THEY USE THEIR CARDS TO CAST SPELLS OR SUMMON MONSTERS TO FIGHT!
THE CARDS HAVE DIFFERENT ATTACK AND DEFENSE STRENGTHS.
THE PERSON WHO LOSES ALL OF THEIR LIFE POINTS FIRST LOSES THE GAME.
CARD NAME
MYSTIC LAMP
LEVEL
ILLUSTRATION
ATK/400 DEF/300
ATTACK/DEFENSE
(with prismatic corner stamp)

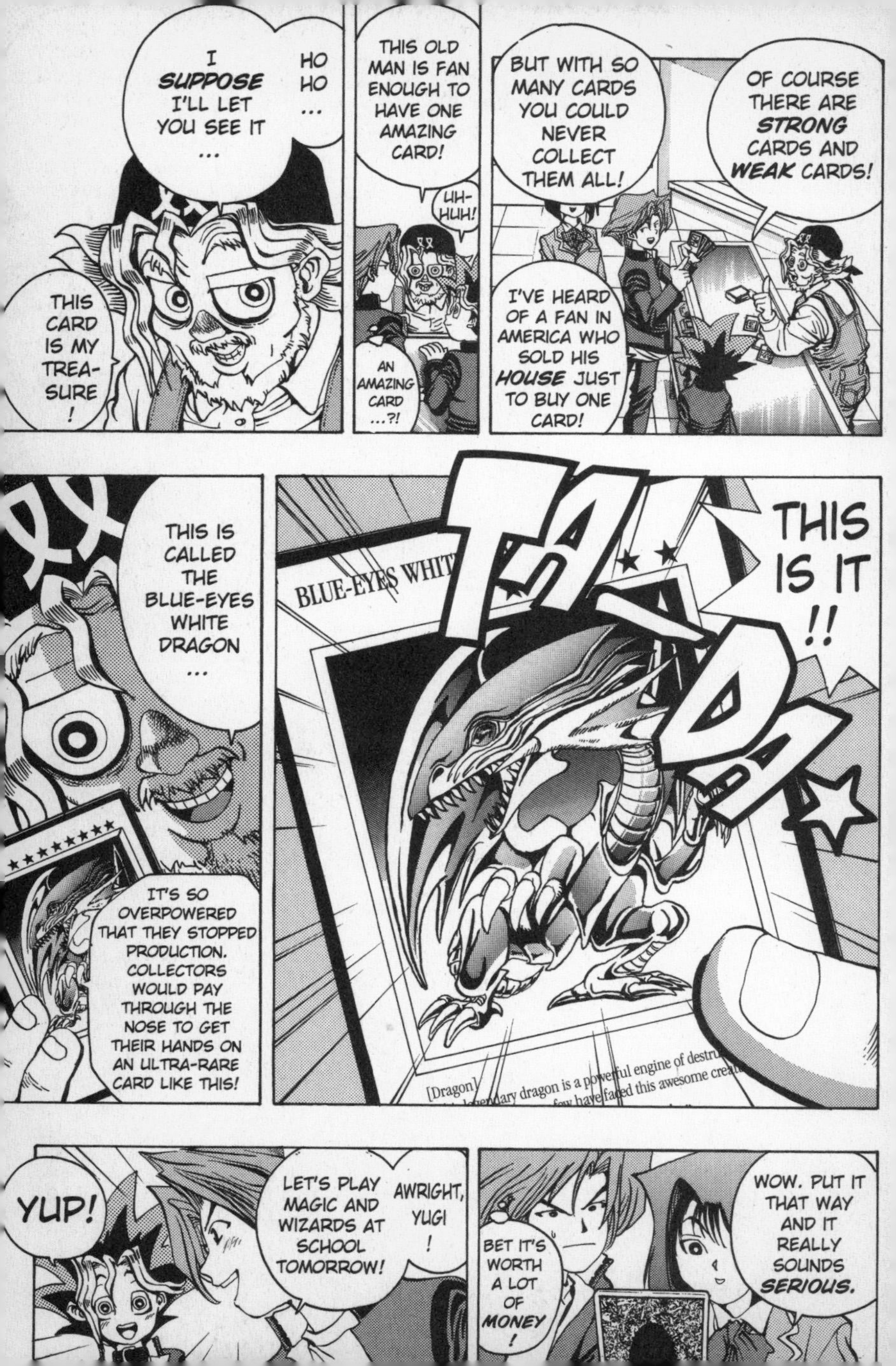

OF COURSE THERE ARE STRONG CARDS AND WEAK CARDS!
BUT WITH SO MANY CARDS YOU COULD NEVER COLLECT THEM ALL!
I'VE HEARD OF A FAN IN AMERICA WHO SOLD HIS HOUSE JUST TO BUY ONE CARD!
THIS OLD MAN IS FAN ENOUGH TO HAVE ONE AMAZING CARD!
UH-HUH!
AN AMAZING CARD ...?!
HO HO ...
I SUPPOSE I'LL LET YOU SEE IT ...
THIS CARD IS MY TREA-SURE!
THIS IS IT!!
TA-DA
BLUE-EYES WHIT
[Dragon]
THIS IS CALLED THE BLUE-EYES WHITE DRAGON ...
IT'S SO OVERPOWERED THAT THEY STOPPED PRODUCTION. COLLECTORS WOULD PAY THROUGH THE NOSE TO GET THEIR HANDS ON AN ULTRA-RARE CARD LIKE THIS!
WOW. PUT IT THAT WAY AND IT REALLY SOUNDS SERIOUS.
BET IT'S WORTH A LOT OF MONEY!
AWRIGHT, YUGI!
LET'S PLAY MAGIC AND WIZARDS AT SCHOOL TOMORROW!
YUP!

READ THIS WAY

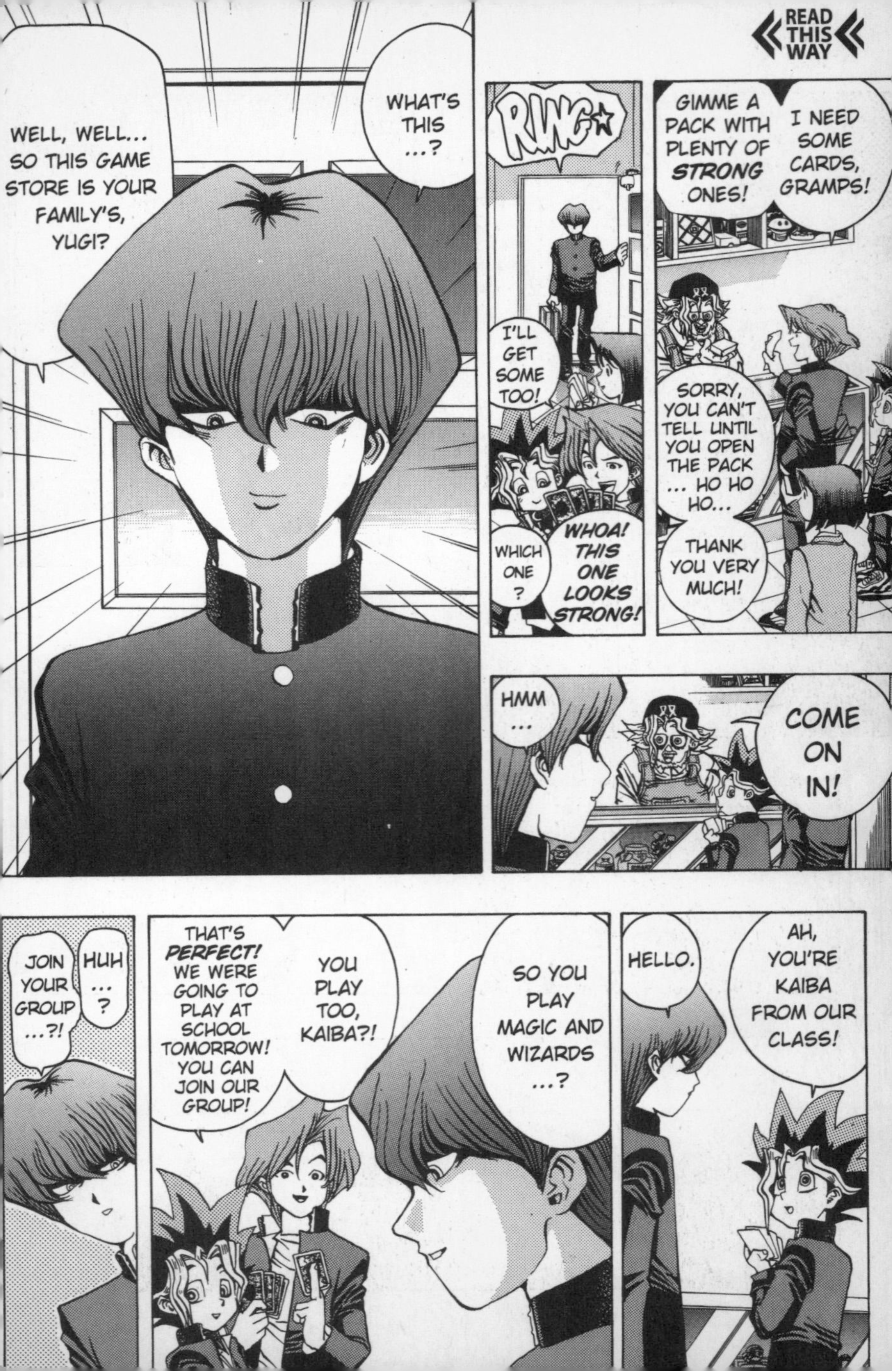
I NEED SOME CARDS, GRAMPS!
GIMME A PACK WITH PLENTY OF *STRONG* ONES!
SORRY, YOU CAN'T TELL UNTIL YOU OPEN THE PACK ... HO HO HO...
THANK YOU VERY MUCH!
RING☆
I'LL GET SOME TOO!
WHOA! THIS ONE LOOKS STRONG!
WHICH ONE ?
COME ON IN!
HMM ...
WHAT'S THIS ...?
WELL, WELL... SO THIS GAME STORE IS YOUR FAMILY'S, YUGI?
AH, YOU'RE KAIBA FROM OUR CLASS!
HELLO.
SO YOU PLAY MAGIC AND WIZARDS ...?
YOU PLAY TOO, KAIBA?!
THAT'S *PERFECT!* WE WERE GOING TO PLAY AT SCHOOL TOMORROW! YOU CAN JOIN OUR GROUP!
HUH ... ?
JOIN YOUR GROUP ...?!

READ THIS WAY

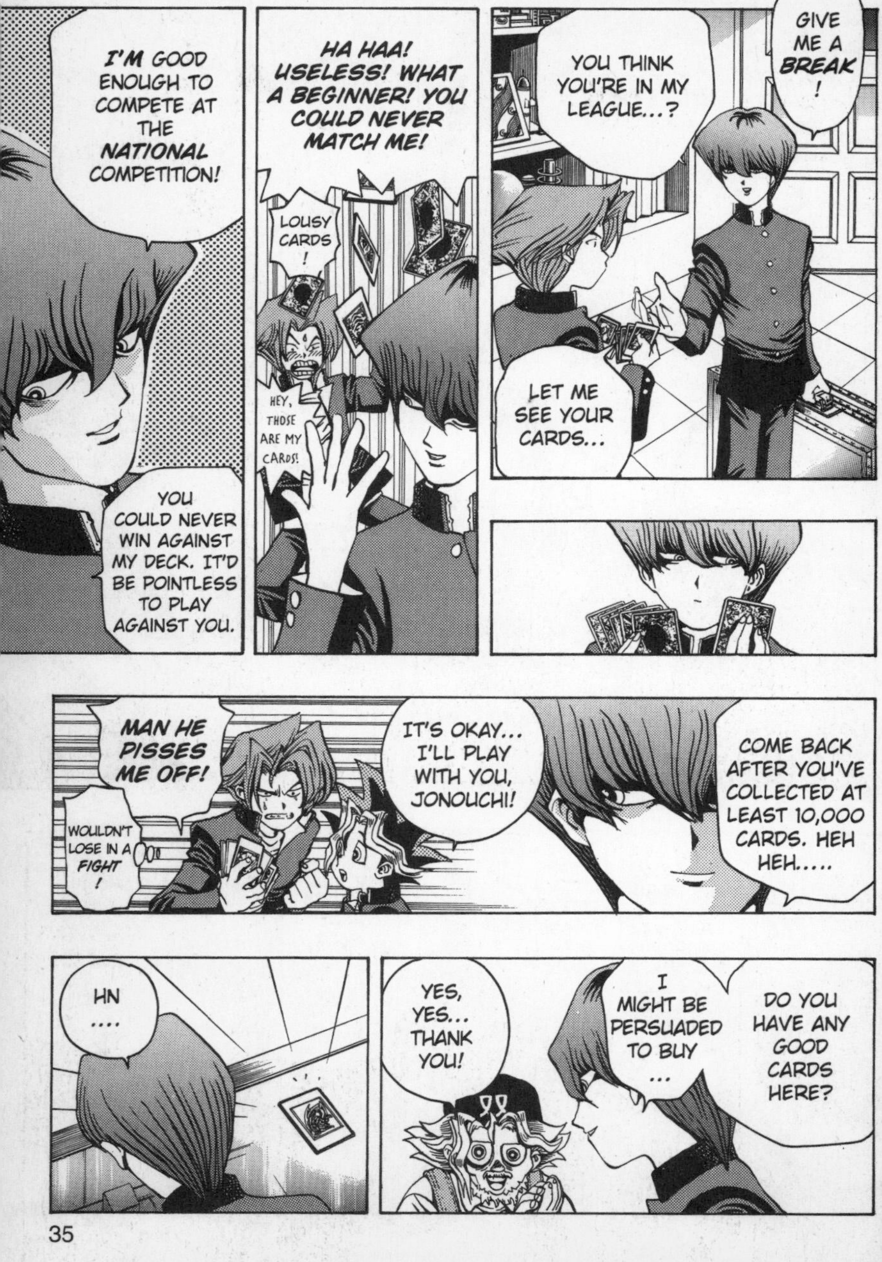
GIVE ME A BREAK!
YOU THINK YOU'RE IN MY LEAGUE...?
LET ME SEE YOUR CARDS...
HA HAA! USELESS! WHAT A BEGINNER! YOU COULD NEVER MATCH ME!
LOUSY CARDS!
HEY, THOSE ARE MY CARDS!
I'M GOOD ENOUGH TO COMPETE AT THE NATIONAL COMPETITION!
YOU COULD NEVER WIN AGAINST MY DECK. IT'D BE POINTLESS TO PLAY AGAINST YOU.
COME BACK AFTER YOU'VE COLLECTED AT LEAST 10,000 CARDS. HEH HEH.....
IT'S OKAY... I'LL PLAY WITH YOU, JONOUCHI!
MAN HE PISSES ME OFF!
WOULDN'T LOSE IN A FIGHT!
DO YOU HAVE ANY GOOD CARDS HERE?
I MIGHT BE PERSUADED TO BUY...
YES, YES... THANK YOU!
HN ....

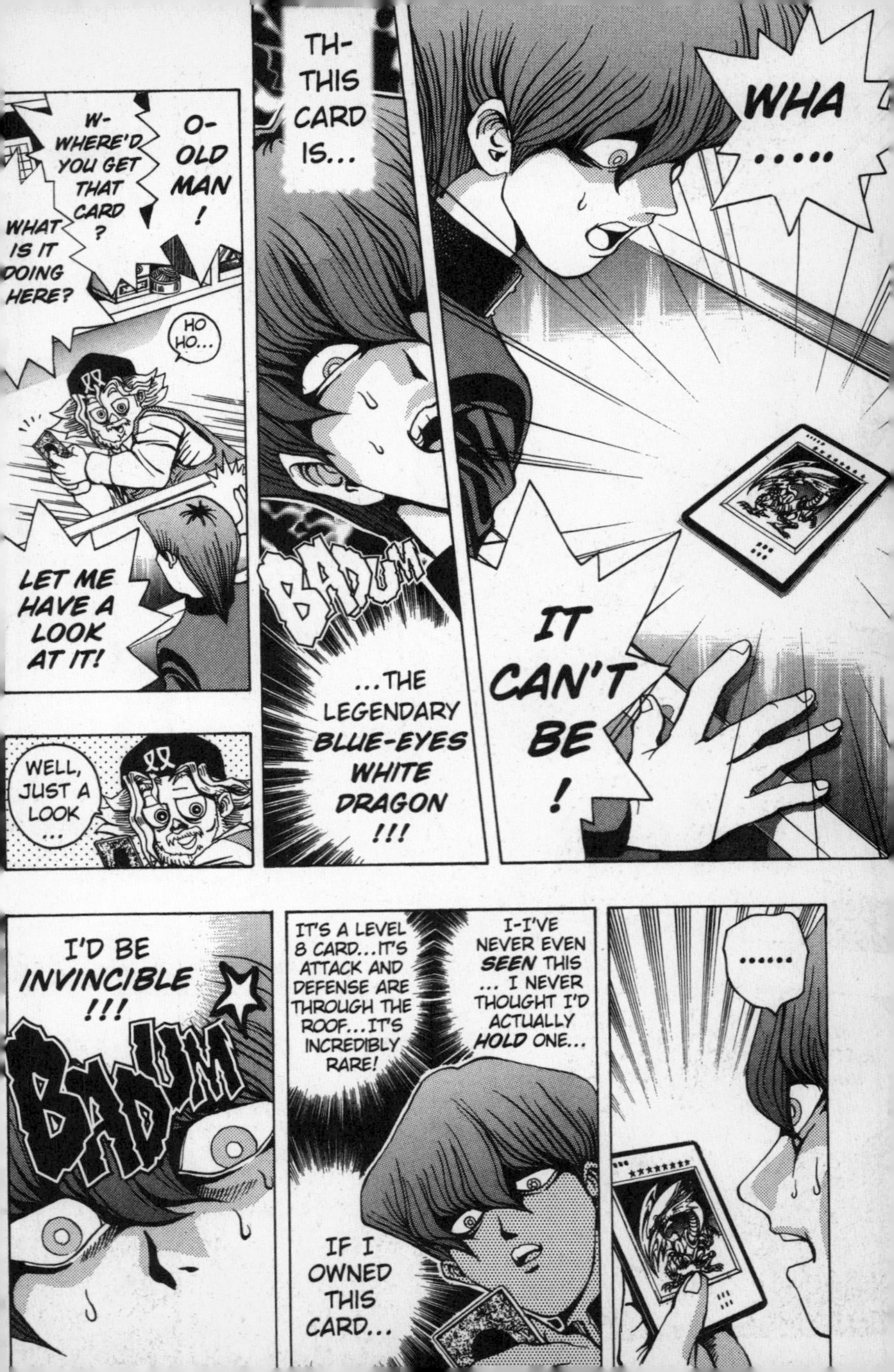
WHA .....
IT CAN'T BE !
TH- THIS CARD IS...
BADUM
...THE LEGENDARY BLUE-EYES WHITE DRAGON !!!
O- OLD MAN !
W- WHERE'D YOU GET THAT CARD ?
WHAT IS IT DOING HERE?
HO HO...
LET ME HAVE A LOOK AT IT!
WELL, JUST A LOOK ...
......
I-I'VE NEVER EVEN SEEN THIS ... I NEVER THOUGHT I'D ACTUALLY HOLD ONE...
IT'S A LEVEL 8 CARD...IT'S ATTACK AND DEFENSE ARE THROUGH THE ROOF...IT'S INCREDIBLY RARE!
IF I OWNED THIS CARD...
I'D BE INVINCIBLE !!!
BADUM

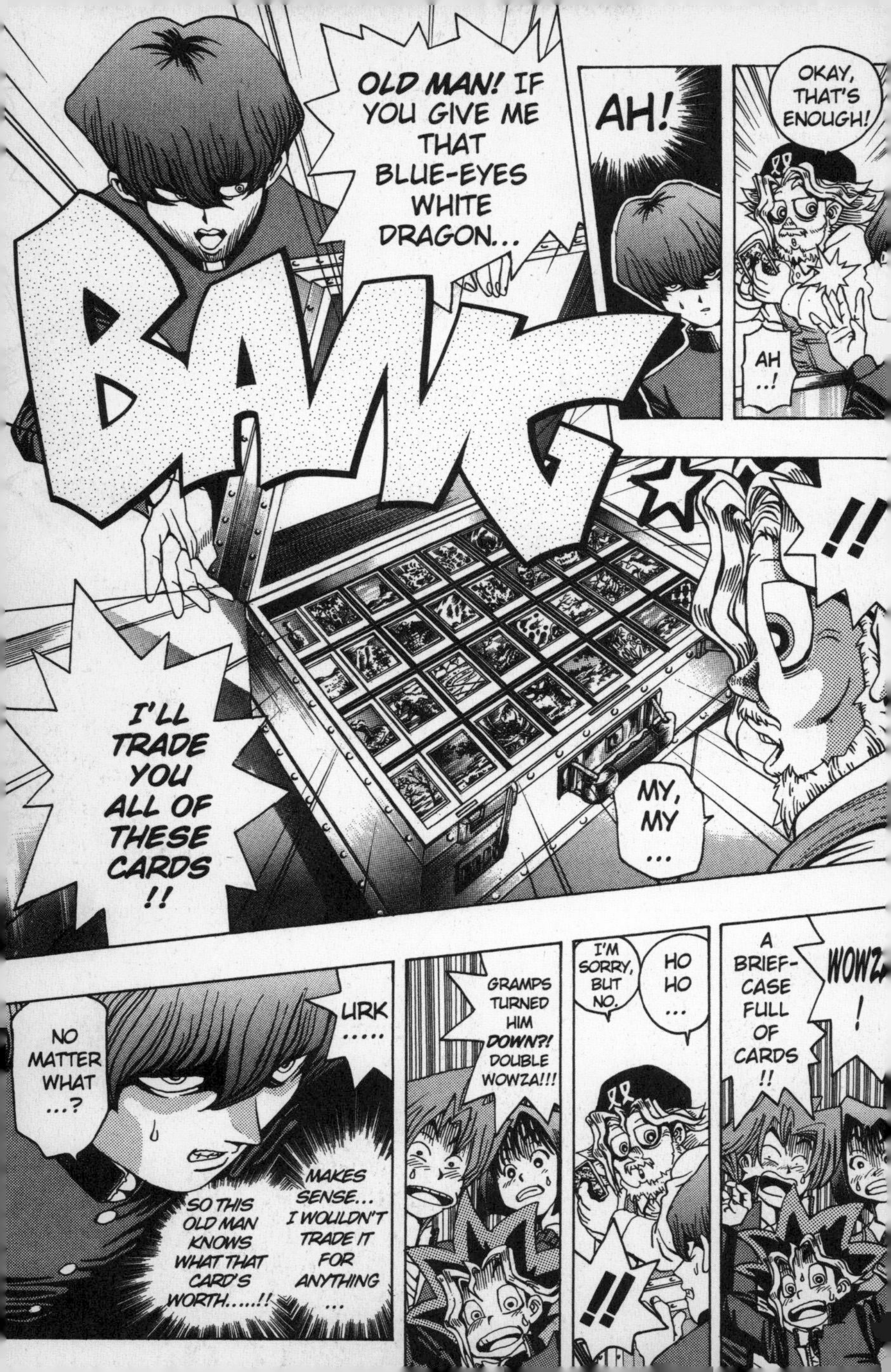

OKAY, THAT'S ENOUGH!
AH ..!
AH!
OLD MAN! IF YOU GIVE ME THAT BLUE-EYES WHITE DRAGON...
BANG
I'LL TRADE YOU ALL OF THESE CARDS !!
MY, MY ...
!!
WOWZA!
A BRIEF-CASE FULL OF CARDS !!
HO HO ...
I'M SORRY, BUT NO.
GRAMPS TURNED HIM DOWN?! DOUBLE WOWZA!!!
!!
URK .....
NO MATTER WHAT ...?
MAKES SENSE... I WOULDN'T TRADE IT FOR ANYTHING ...
SO THIS OLD MAN KNOWS WHAT THAT CARD'S WORTH.....!!

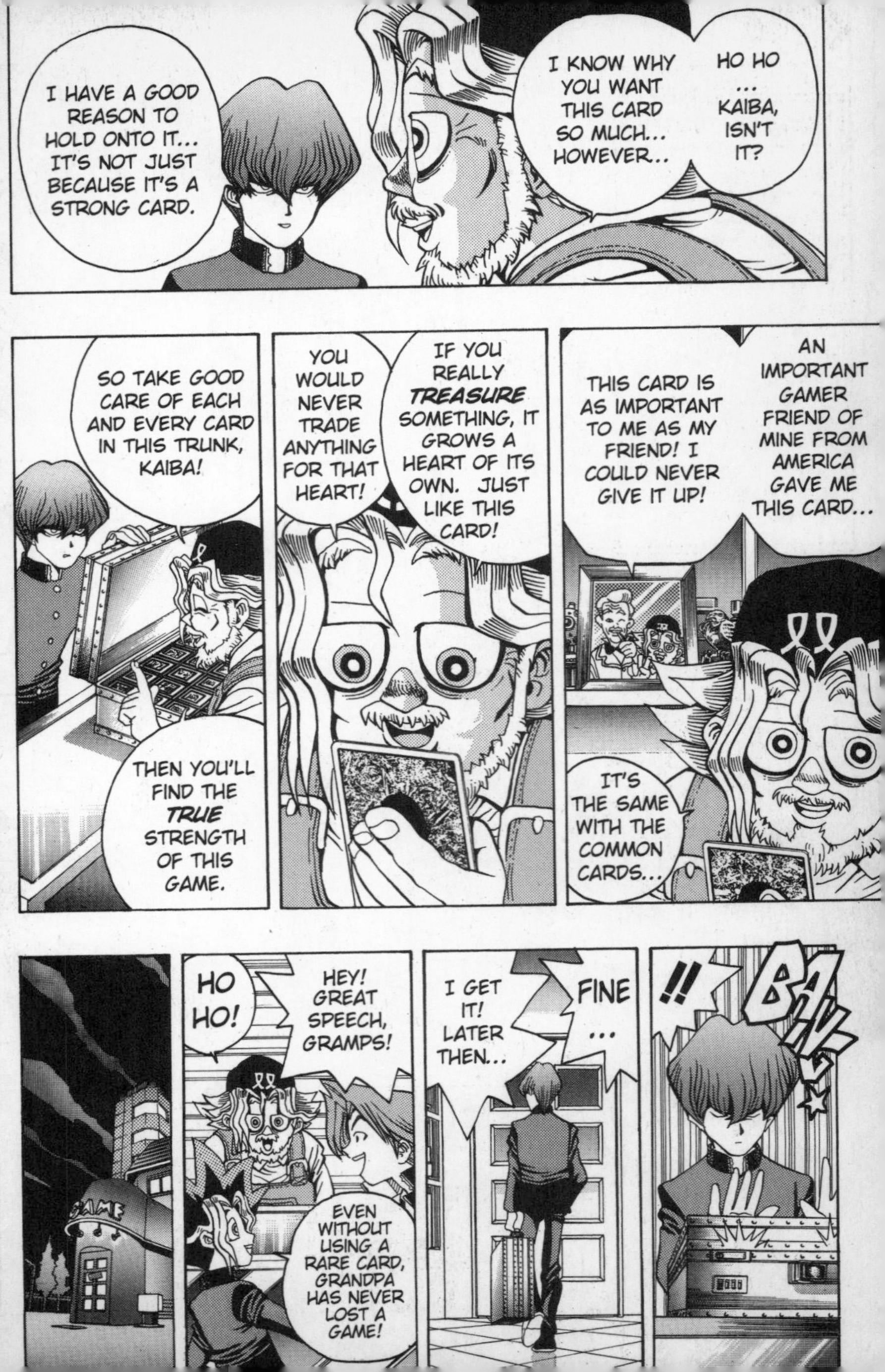
HO HO ... KAIBA, ISN'T IT?
I KNOW WHY YOU WANT THIS CARD SO MUCH... HOWEVER...
I HAVE A GOOD REASON TO HOLD ONTO IT... IT'S NOT JUST BECAUSE IT'S A STRONG CARD.
AN IMPORTANT GAMER FRIEND OF MINE FROM AMERICA GAVE ME THIS CARD...
THIS CARD IS AS IMPORTANT TO ME AS MY FRIEND! I COULD NEVER GIVE IT UP!
IT'S THE SAME WITH THE COMMON CARDS...
IF YOU REALLY *TREASURE* SOMETHING, IT GROWS A HEART OF ITS OWN. JUST LIKE THIS CARD!
YOU WOULD NEVER TRADE ANYTHING FOR THAT HEART!
SO TAKE GOOD CARE OF EACH AND EVERY CARD IN THIS TRUNK, KAIBA!
THEN YOU'LL FIND THE *TRUE* STRENGTH OF THIS GAME.
BANG
!!
FINE ...
I GET IT! LATER THEN...
HEY! GREAT SPEECH, GRAMPS!
HO HO!
EVEN WITHOUT USING A RARE CARD, GRANDPA HAS NEVER LOST A GAME!
GAME

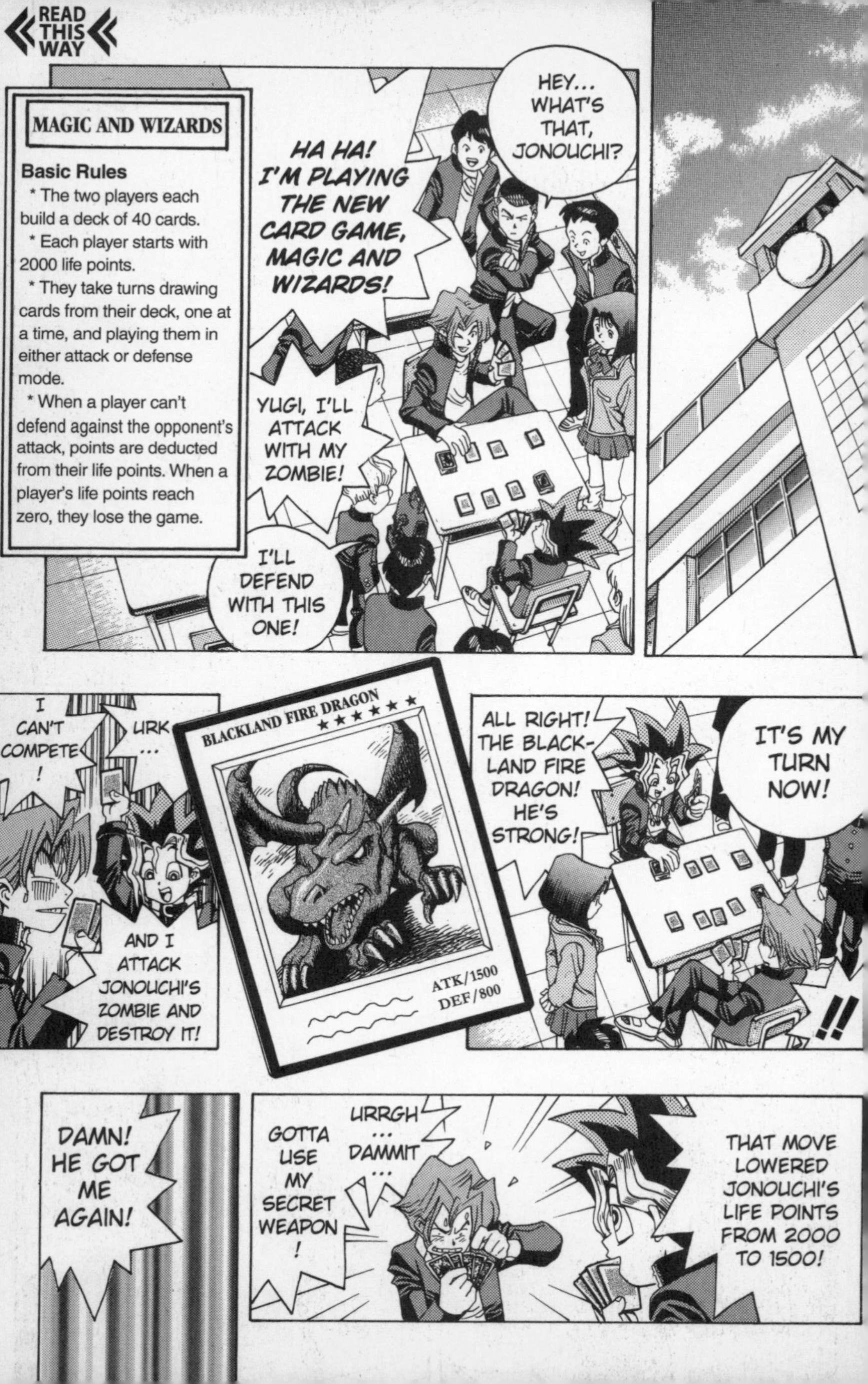
READ THIS WAY
HEY... WHAT'S THAT, JONOUCHI?
HA HA! I'M PLAYING THE NEW CARD GAME, MAGIC AND WIZARDS!
MAGIC AND WIZARDS
Basic Rules
* The two players each build a deck of 40 cards.
* Each player starts with 2000 life points.
* They take turns drawing cards from their deck, one at a time, and playing them in either attack or defense mode.
* When a player can't defend against the opponent's attack, points are deducted from their life points. When a player's life points reach zero, they lose the game.
YUGI, I'LL ATTACK WITH MY ZOMBIE!
I'LL DEFEND WITH THIS ONE!
IT'S MY TURN NOW!
ALL RIGHT! THE BLACK-LAND FIRE DRAGON! HE'S STRONG!
!!
BLACKLAND FIRE DRAGON
ATK/1500
DEF/800
URK...
I CAN'T COMPETE!
AND I ATTACK JONOUCHI'S ZOMBIE AND DESTROY IT!
THAT MOVE LOWERED JONOUCHI'S LIFE POINTS FROM 2000 TO 1500!
URRGH... DAMMIT...
GOTTA USE MY SECRET WEAPON!
DAMN! HE GOT ME AGAIN!

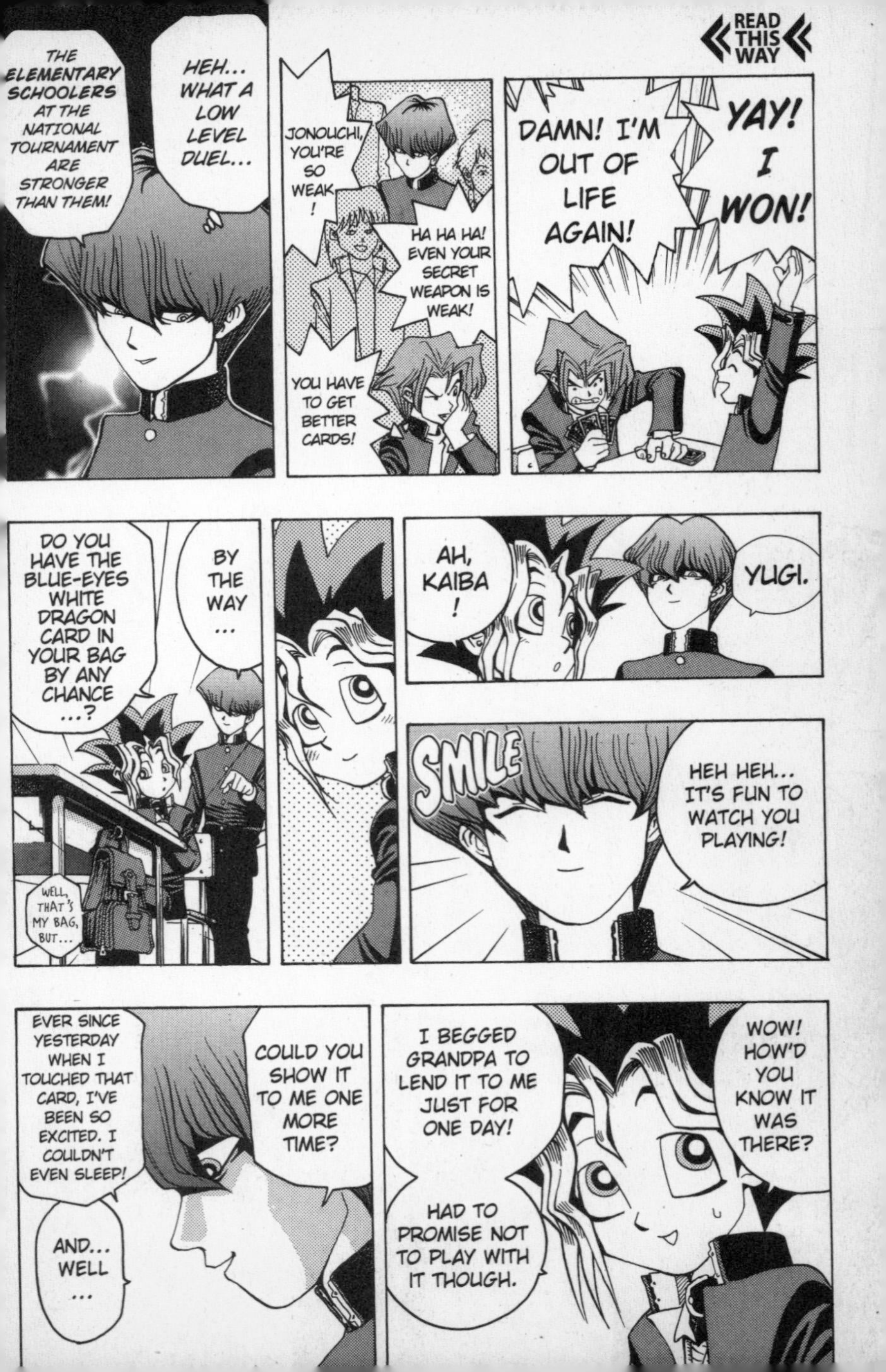
READ THIS WAY
YAY! I WON!
DAMN! I'M OUT OF LIFE AGAIN!
JONOUCHI, YOU'RE SO WEAK!
HA HA HA! EVEN YOUR SECRET WEAPON IS WEAK!
YOU HAVE TO GET BETTER CARDS!
HEH... WHAT A LOW LEVEL DUEL...
THE ELEMENTARY SCHOOLERS AT THE NATIONAL TOURNAMENT ARE STRONGER THAN THEM!
YUGI.
AH, KAIBA!
SMILE
HEH HEH... IT'S FUN TO WATCH YOU PLAYING!
BY THE WAY...
DO YOU HAVE THE BLUE-EYES WHITE DRAGON CARD IN YOUR BAG BY ANY CHANCE...?
WELL, THAT'S MY BAG, BUT...
WOW! HOW'D YOU KNOW IT WAS THERE?
I BEGGED GRANDPA TO LEND IT TO ME JUST FOR ONE DAY!
HAD TO PROMISE NOT TO PLAY WITH IT THOUGH.
COULD YOU SHOW IT TO ME ONE MORE TIME?
EVER SINCE YESTERDAY WHEN I TOUCHED THAT CARD, I'VE BEEN SO EXCITED. I COULDN'T EVEN SLEEP!
AND... WELL...

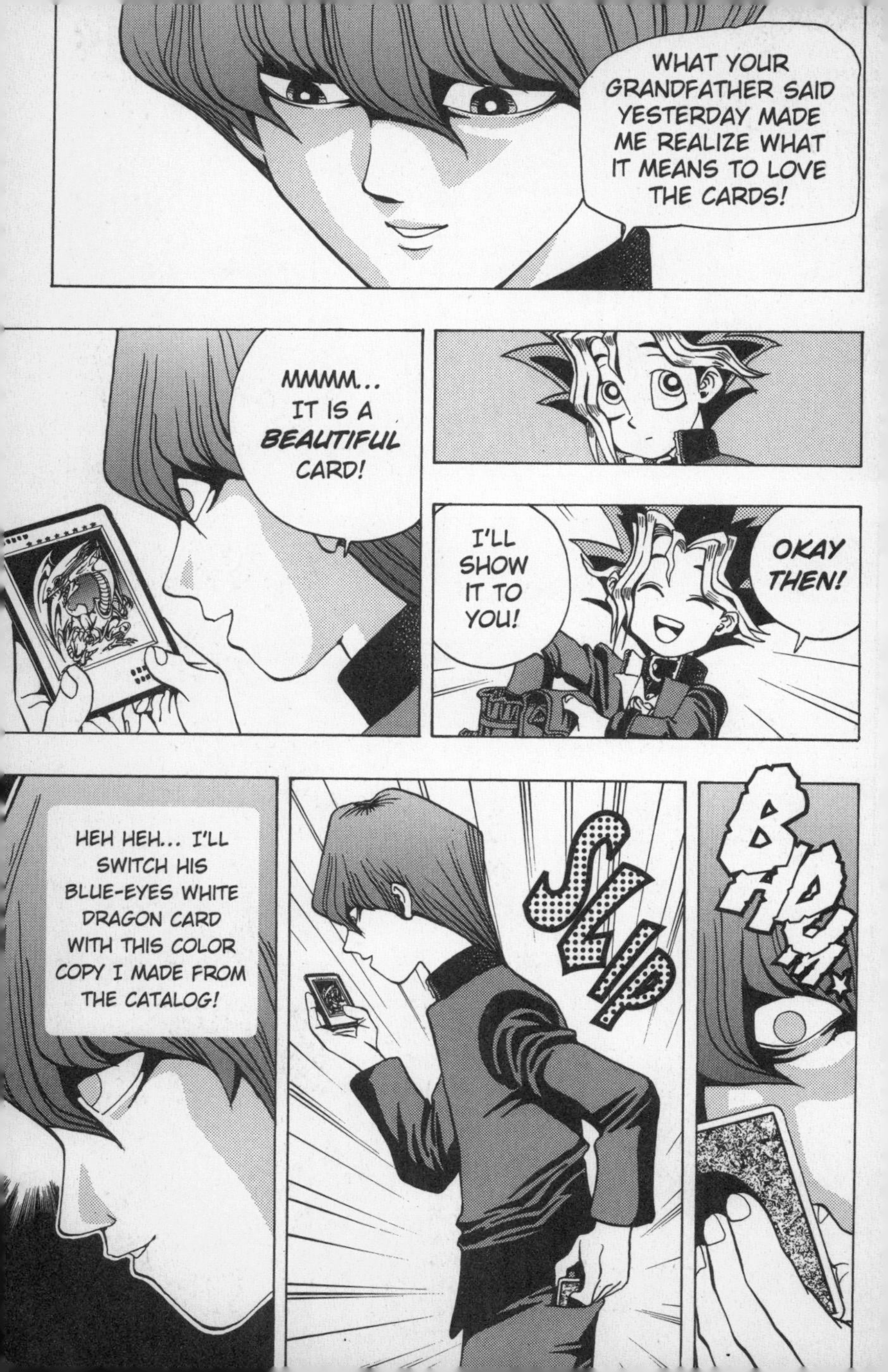
WHAT YOUR GRANDFATHER SAID YESTERDAY MADE ME REALIZE WHAT IT MEANS TO LOVE THE CARDS!
OKAY THEN!
I'LL SHOW IT TO YOU!
MMMM... IT IS A *BEAUTIFUL* CARD!
BADUM★
SLIP
HEH HEH... I'LL SWITCH HIS BLUE-EYES WHITE DRAGON CARD WITH THIS COLOR COPY I MADE FROM THE CATALOG!

READ THIS WAY

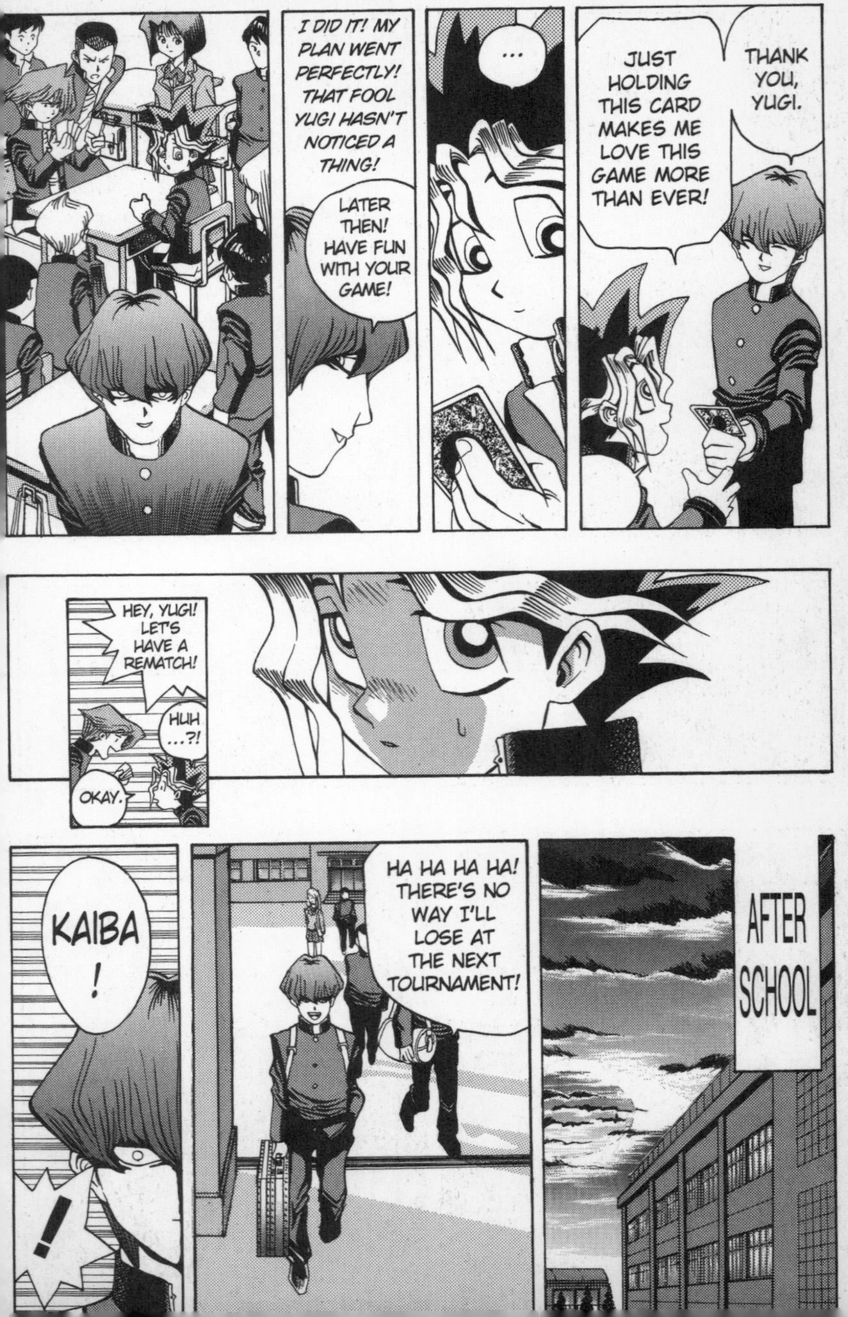
THANK YOU, YUGI.
JUST HOLDING THIS CARD MAKES ME LOVE THIS GAME MORE THAN EVER!
...
I DID IT! MY PLAN WENT PERFECTLY! THAT FOOL YUGI HASN'T NOTICED A THING!
LATER THEN! HAVE FUN WITH YOUR GAME!
HEY, YUGI! LET'S HAVE A REMATCH!
HUH ...?!
OKAY.
AFTER SCHOOL
HA HA HA HA! THERE'S NO WAY I'LL LOSE AT THE NEXT TOURNAMENT!
KAIBA !
!

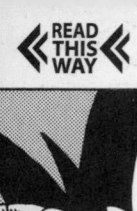

READ THIS WAY

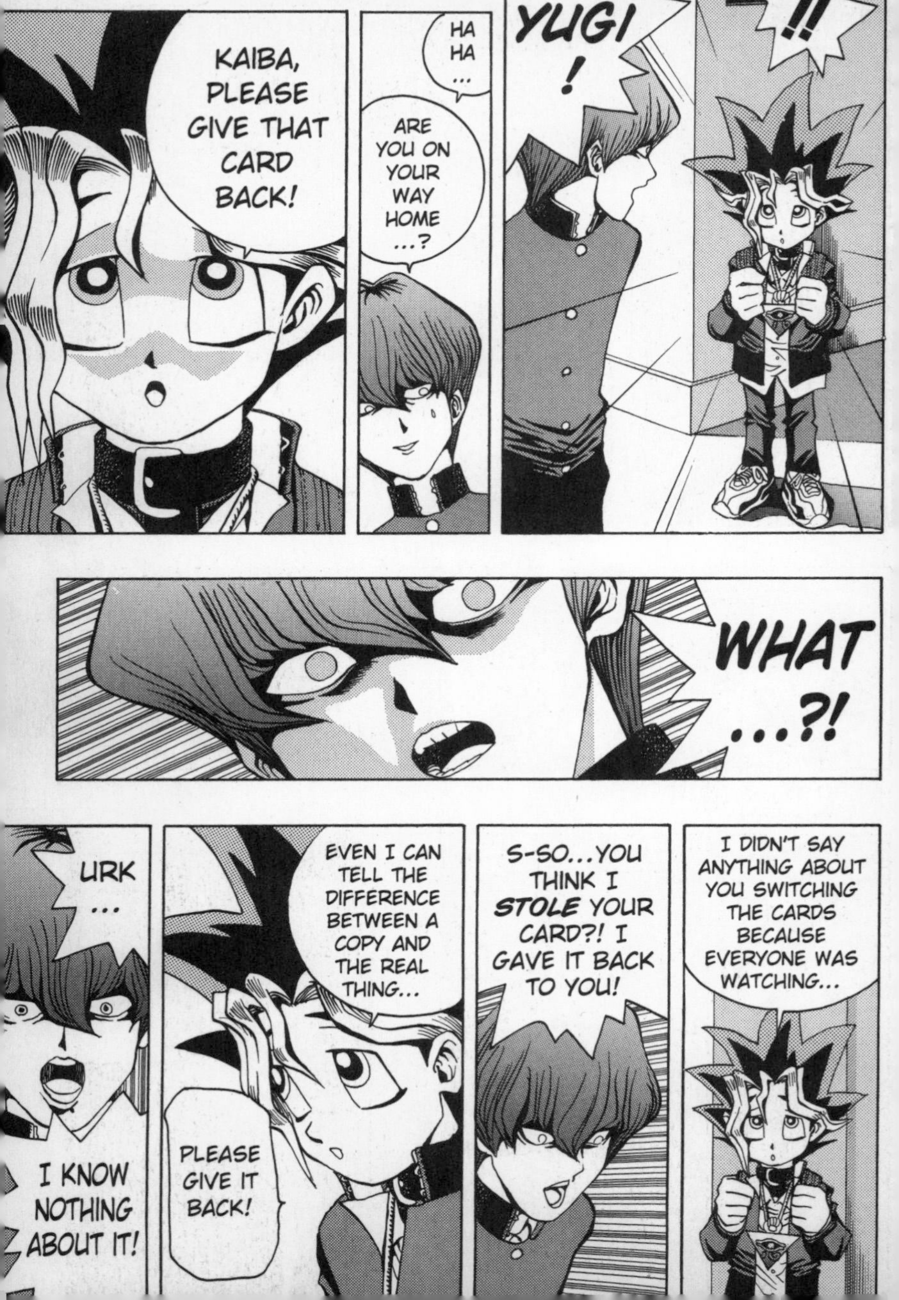
!!
YUGI!
HA HA ...
ARE YOU ON YOUR WAY HOME ...?
KAIBA, PLEASE GIVE THAT CARD BACK!
WHAT ...?!
I DIDN'T SAY ANYTHING ABOUT YOU SWITCHING THE CARDS BECAUSE EVERYONE WAS WATCHING...
S-SO...YOU THINK I *STOLE* YOUR CARD?! I GAVE IT BACK TO YOU!
EVEN I CAN TELL THE DIFFERENCE BETWEEN A COPY AND THE REAL THING...
PLEASE GIVE IT BACK!
URK ...
I KNOW NOTHING ABOUT IT!

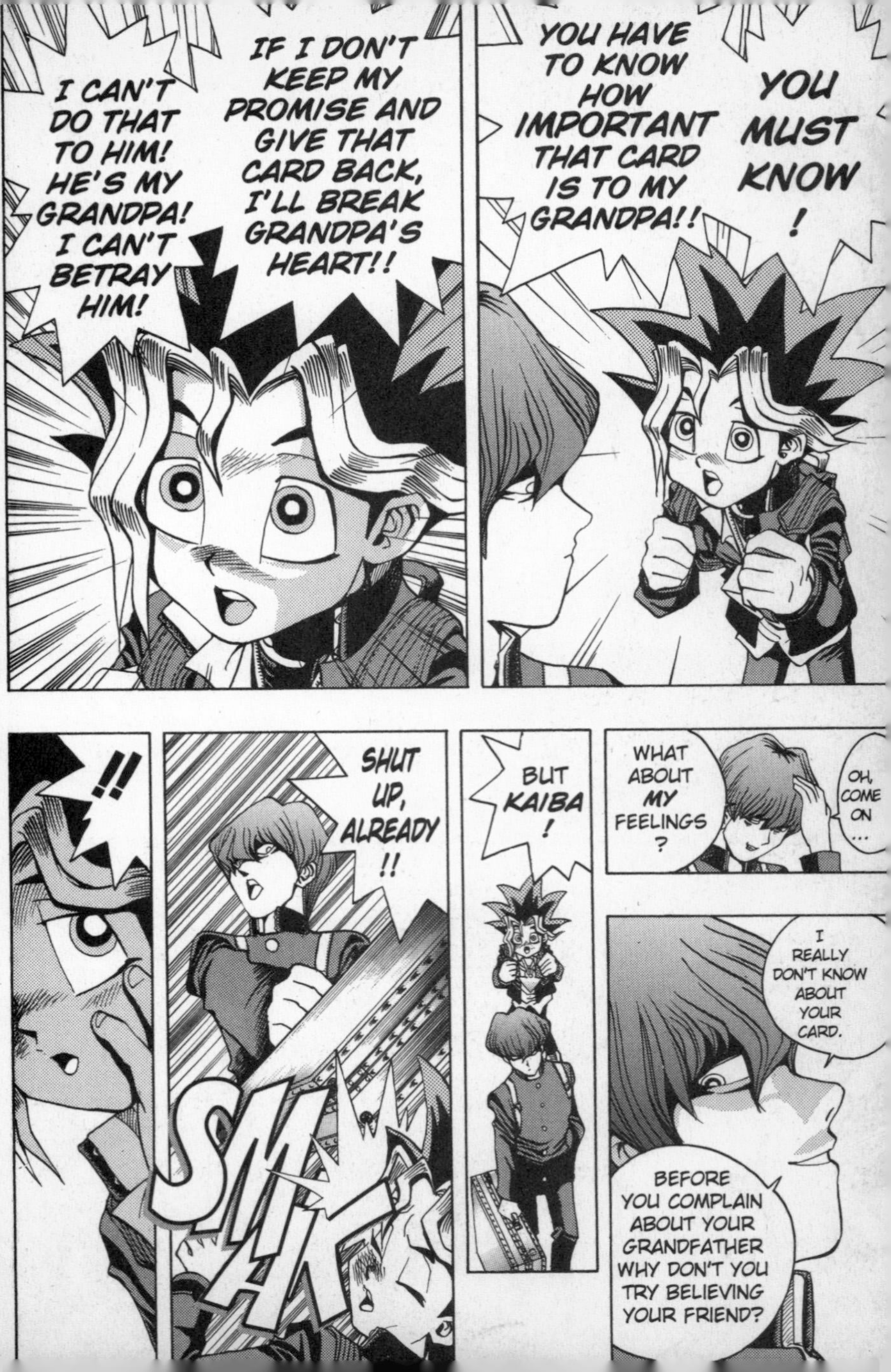
YOU MUST KNOW!
YOU HAVE TO KNOW HOW IMPORTANT THAT CARD IS TO MY GRANDPA!!
IF I DON'T KEEP MY PROMISE AND GIVE THAT CARD BACK, I'LL BREAK GRANDPA'S HEART!!
I CAN'T DO THAT TO HIM! HE'S MY GRANDPA! I CAN'T BETRAY HIM!
OH, COME ON...
WHAT ABOUT MY FEELINGS?
BUT KAIBA!
I REALLY DON'T KNOW ABOUT YOUR CARD.
BEFORE YOU COMPLAIN ABOUT YOUR GRANDFATHER WHY DON'T YOU TRY BELIEVING YOUR FRIEND?
SHUT UP, ALREADY!!
!!

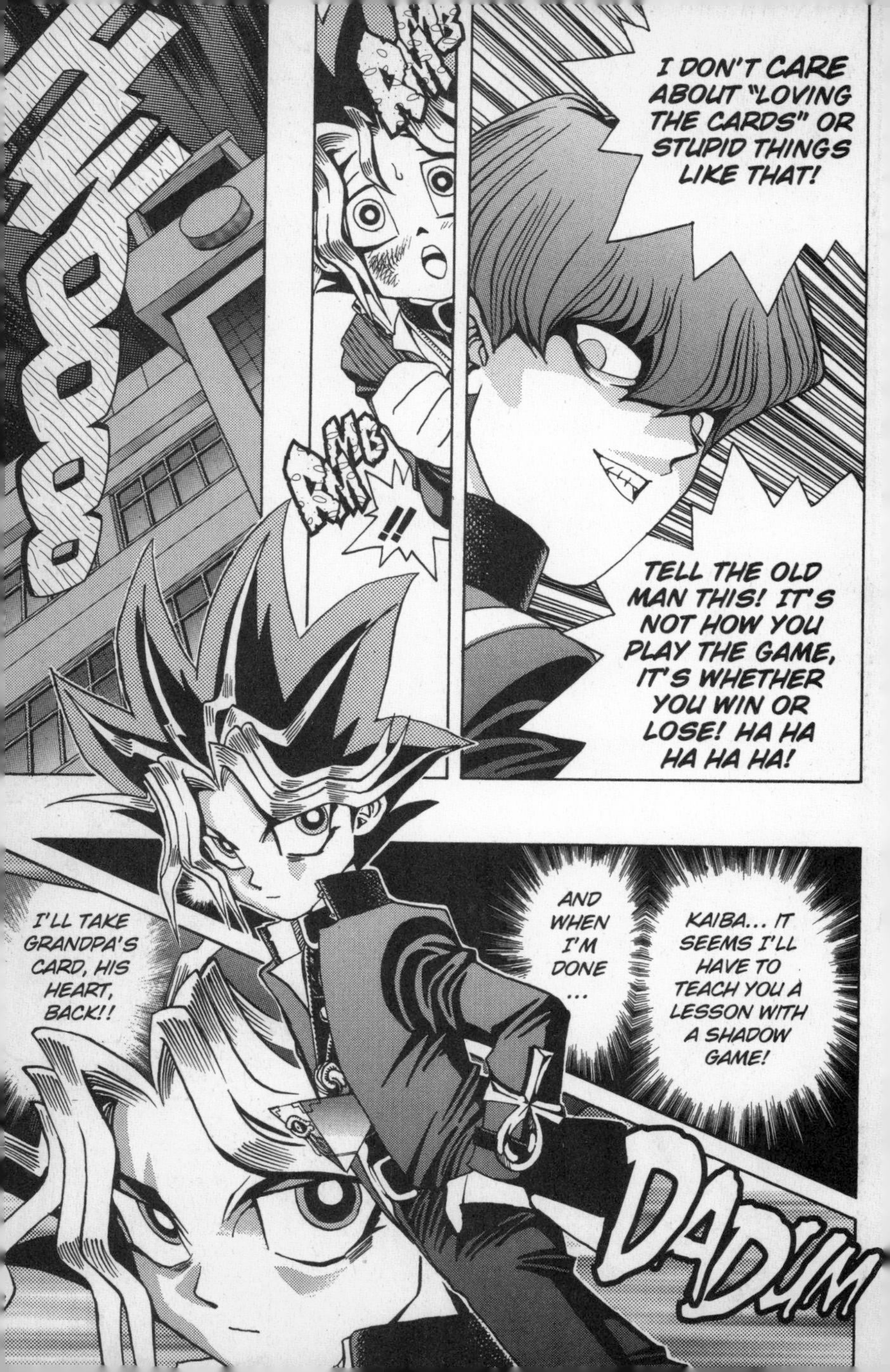
I DON'T CARE ABOUT "LOVING THE CARDS" OR STUPID THINGS LIKE THAT!
TELL THE OLD MAN THIS! IT'S NOT HOW YOU PLAY THE GAME, IT'S WHETHER YOU WIN OR LOSE! HA HA HA HA HA!
DMB
DMB
!!
KAIBA... IT SEEMS I'LL HAVE TO TEACH YOU A LESSON WITH A SHADOW GAME!
AND WHEN I'M DONE ...
I'LL TAKE GRANDPA'S CARD, HIS HEART, BACK!!
DADUM

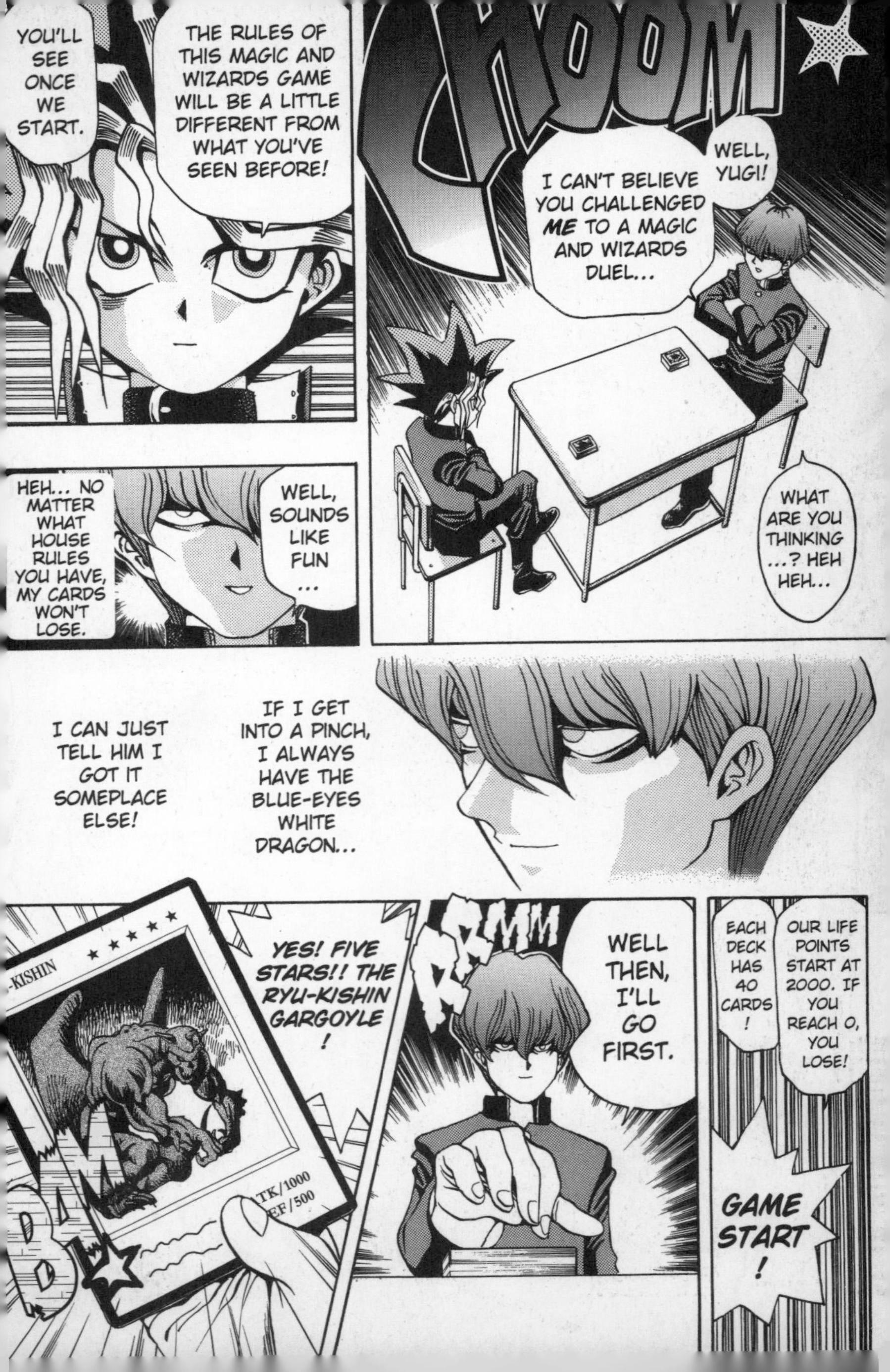
THE RULES OF THIS MAGIC AND WIZARDS GAME WILL BE A LITTLE DIFFERENT FROM WHAT YOU'VE SEEN BEFORE!
YOU'LL SEE ONCE WE START.
VOOM
WELL, YUGI!
I CAN'T BELIEVE YOU CHALLENGED ME TO A MAGIC AND WIZARDS DUEL...
WHAT ARE YOU THINKING ...? HEH HEH...
WELL, SOUNDS LIKE FUN ...
HEH... NO MATTER WHAT HOUSE RULES YOU HAVE, MY CARDS WON'T LOSE.
IF I GET INTO A PINCH, I ALWAYS HAVE THE BLUE-EYES WHITE DRAGON...
I CAN JUST TELL HIM I GOT IT SOMEPLACE ELSE!
OUR LIFE POINTS START AT 2000. IF YOU REACH 0, YOU LOSE!
EACH DECK HAS 40 CARDS!
GAME START!
WELL THEN, I'LL GO FIRST.
YES! FIVE STARS!! THE RYU-KISHIN GARGOYLE!
-KISHIN
TK/1000
EF/500

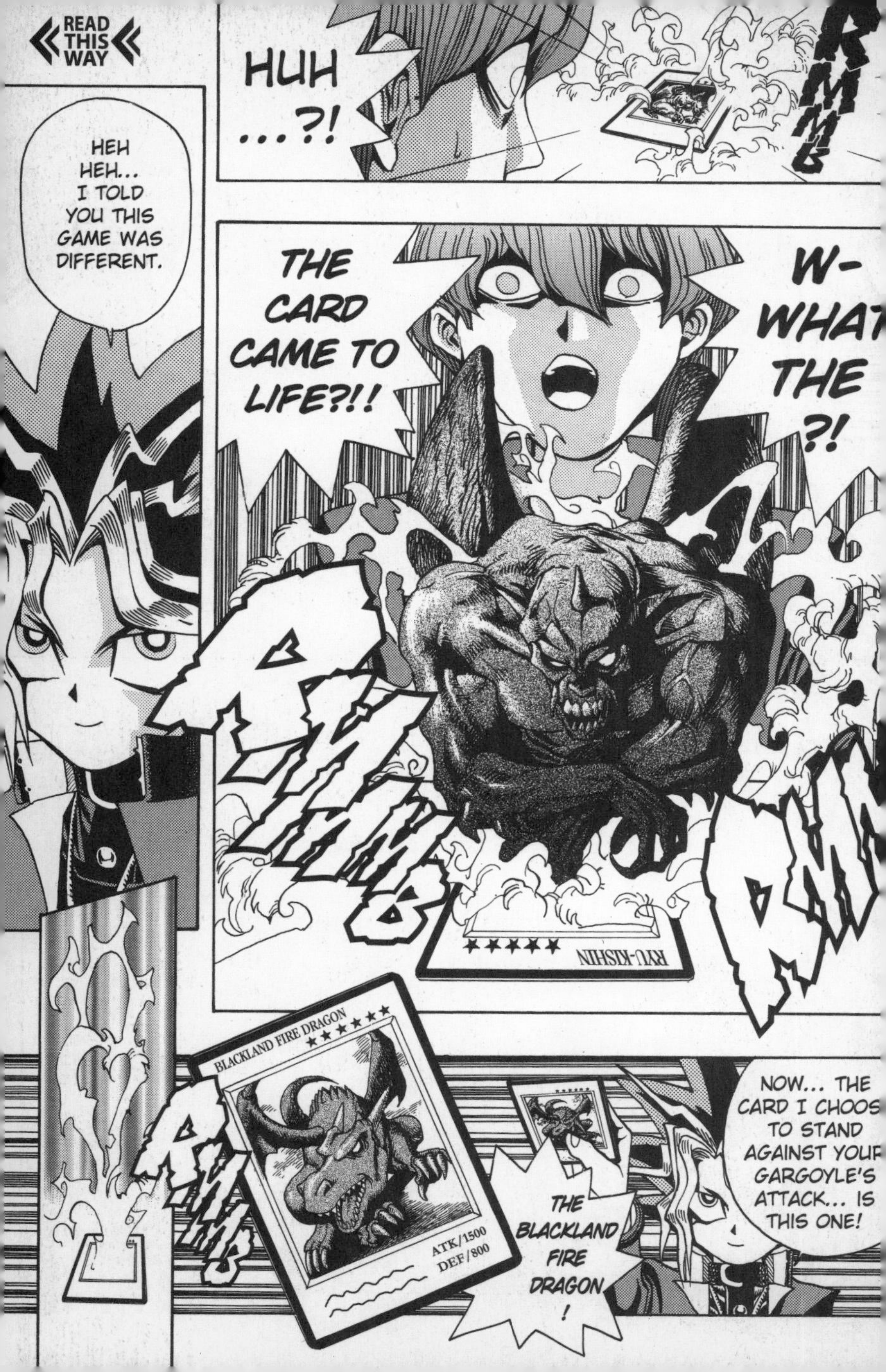
READ THIS WAY
HUH ...?!
RMMMB
W-WHAT THE ?!
THE CARD CAME TO LIFE?!!
RYU-KISHIN
HEH HEH... I TOLD YOU THIS GAME WAS DIFFERENT.
NOW... THE CARD I CHOOS TO STAND AGAINST YOUR GARGOYLE'S ATTACK... IS THIS ONE!
THE BLACKLAND FIRE DRAGON !
BLACKLAND FIRE DRAGON
ATK/1500
DEF/800

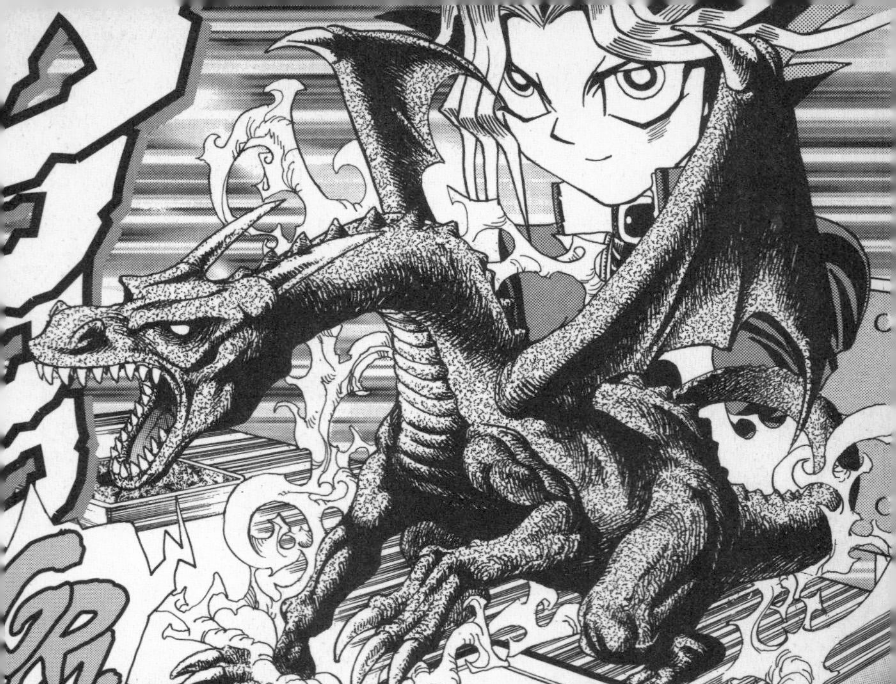

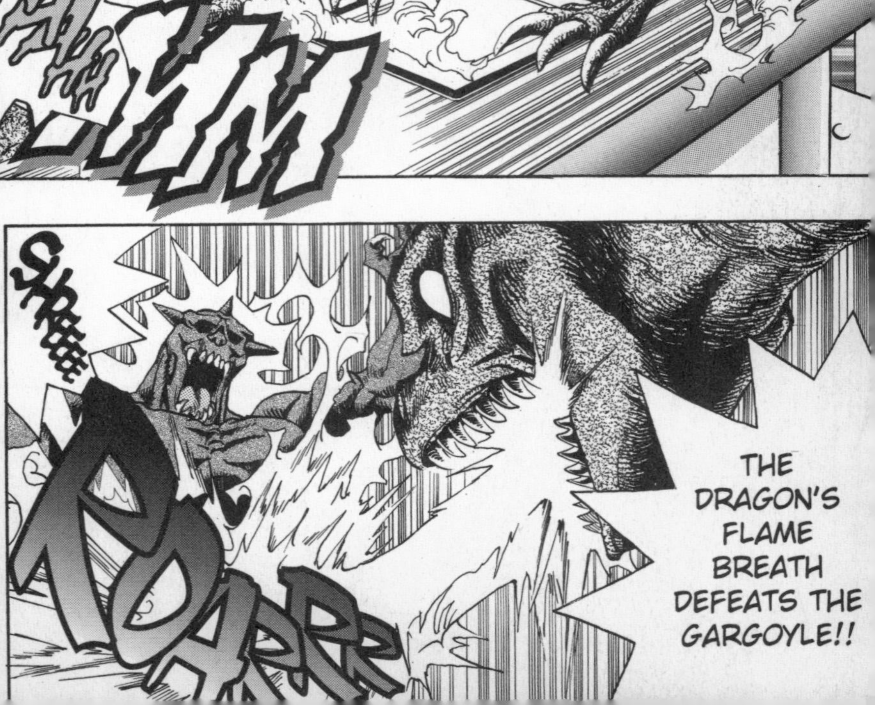
THE DRAGON'S FLAME BREATH DEFEATS THE GARGOYLE!!

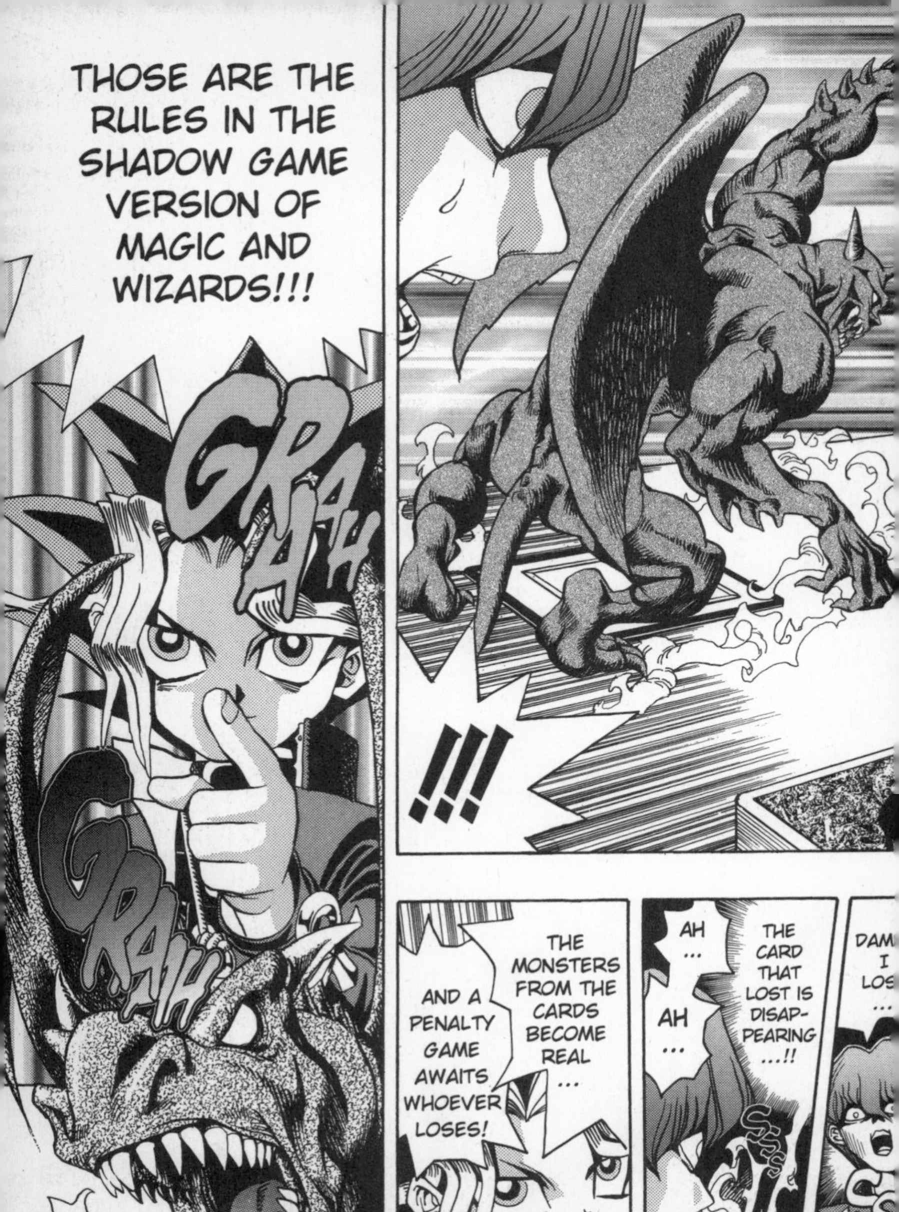
!!!
DAM
I
LOS
...
WHA
...?
THE CARD THAT LOST IS DISAP-PEARING ...!!
AH ...
AH ...
THE MONSTERS FROM THE CARDS BECOME REAL ...
AND A PENALTY GAME AWAITS WHOEVER LOSES!
THOSE ARE THE RULES IN THE SHADOW GAME VERSION OF MAGIC AND WIZARDS!!!
GRAAH
GRAAH

TO BE CONTINUED...

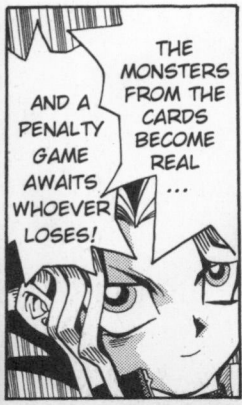

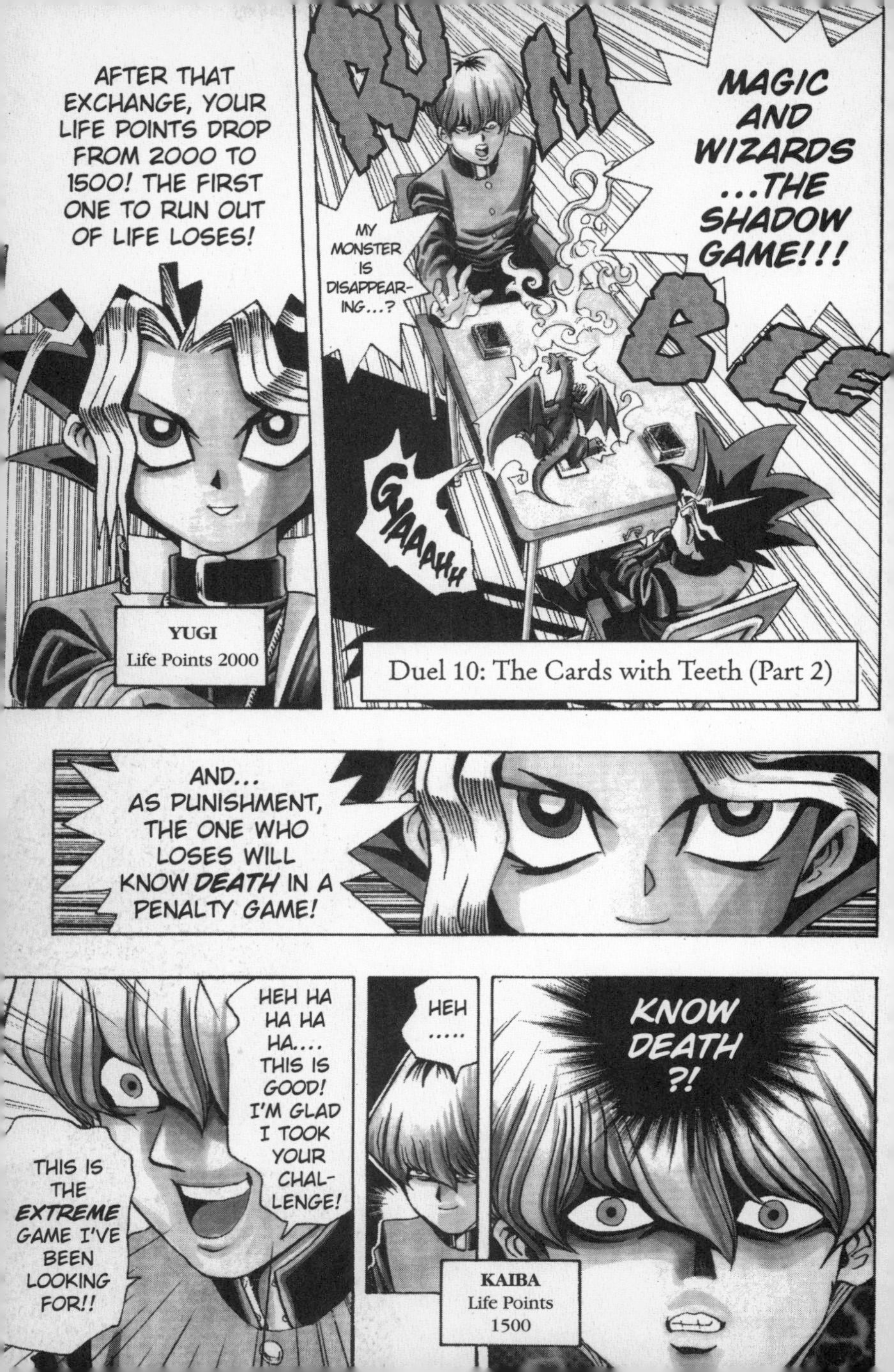
AFTER THAT EXCHANGE, YOUR LIFE POINTS DROP FROM 2000 TO 1500! THE FIRST ONE TO RUN OUT OF LIFE LOSES!
YUGI
Life Points 2000
RUMBLE
MAGIC AND WIZARDS ...THE SHADOW GAME!!!
MY MONSTER IS DISAPPEARING...?
GYAAAAHH
Duel 10: The Cards with Teeth (Part 2)
AND... AS PUNISHMENT, THE ONE WHO LOSES WILL KNOW *DEATH* IN A PENALTY GAME!
HEH HA HA HA HA.... THIS IS GOOD! I'M GLAD I TOOK YOUR CHALLENGE!
THIS IS THE *EXTREME* GAME I'VE BEEN LOOKING FOR!!
HEH .....
KNOW DEATH ?!
KAIBA
Life Points 1500

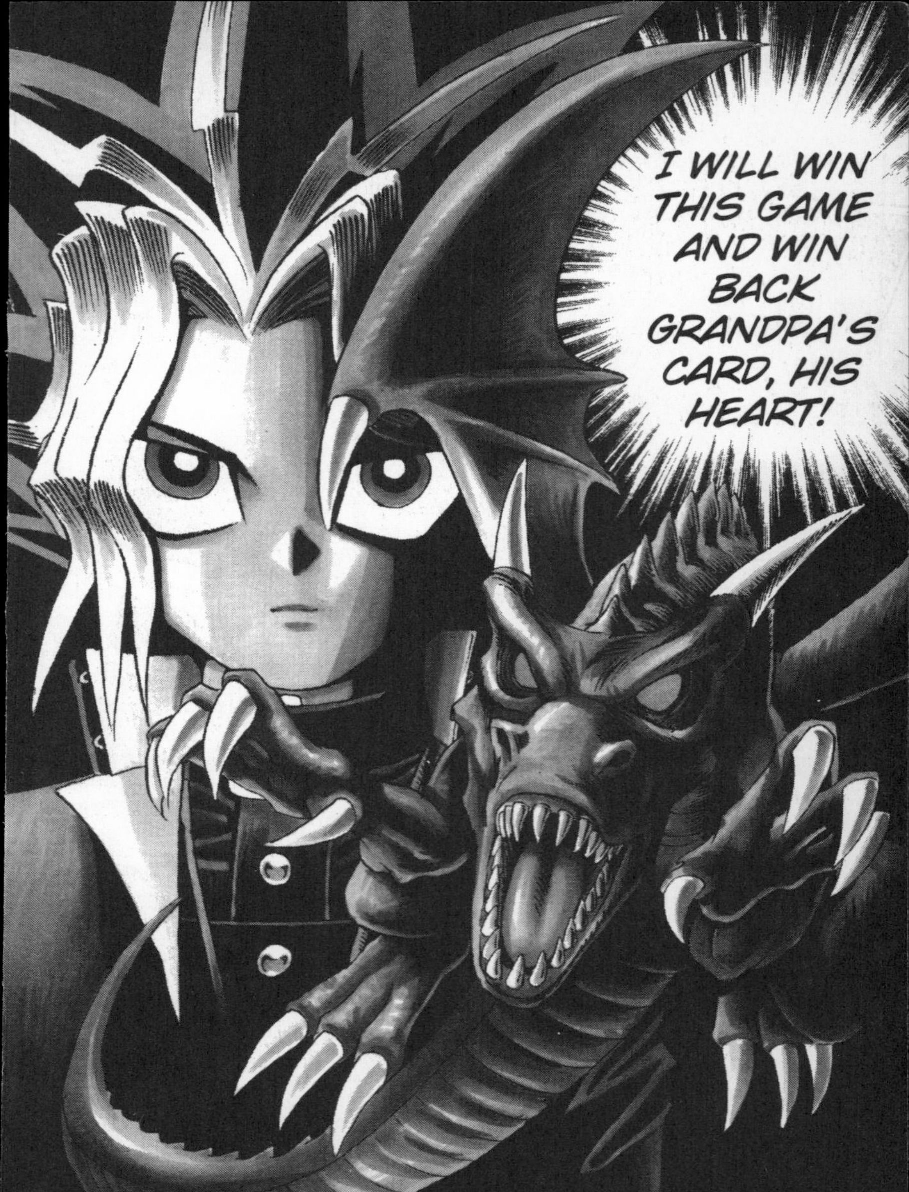
I WILL WIN THIS GAME AND WIN BACK GRANDPA'S CARD, HIS HEART!

Duel 10: The Cards with Teeth (Part 2)

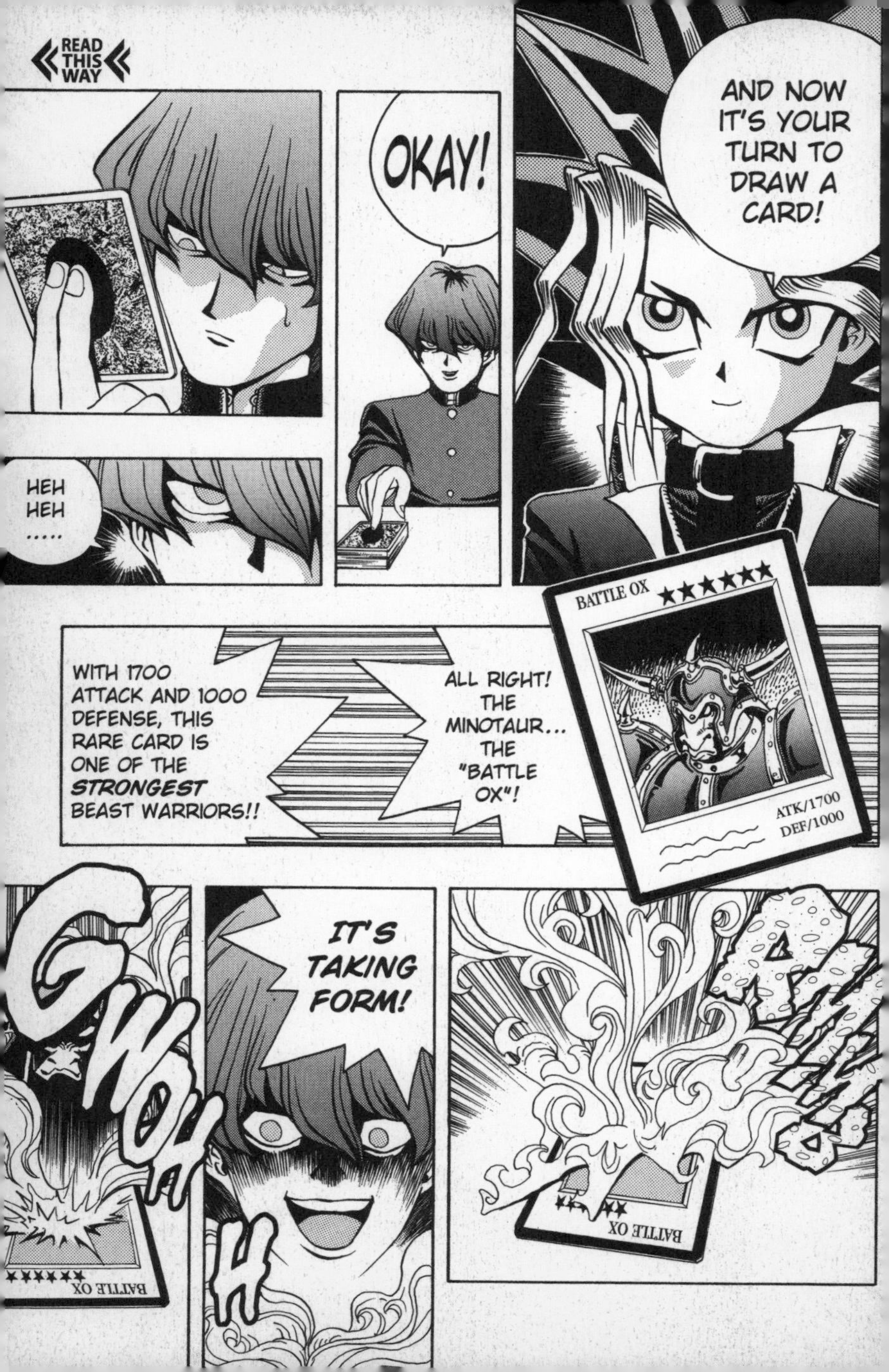
READ THIS WAY
AND NOW IT'S YOUR TURN TO DRAW A CARD!
OKAY!
HEH HEH .....
BATTLE OX
ATK/1700
DEF/1000
ALL RIGHT! THE MINOTAUR... THE "BATTLE OX"!
WITH 1700 ATTACK AND 1000 DEFENSE, THIS RARE CARD IS ONE OF THE STRONGEST BEAST WARRIORS!!
IT'S TAKING FORM!

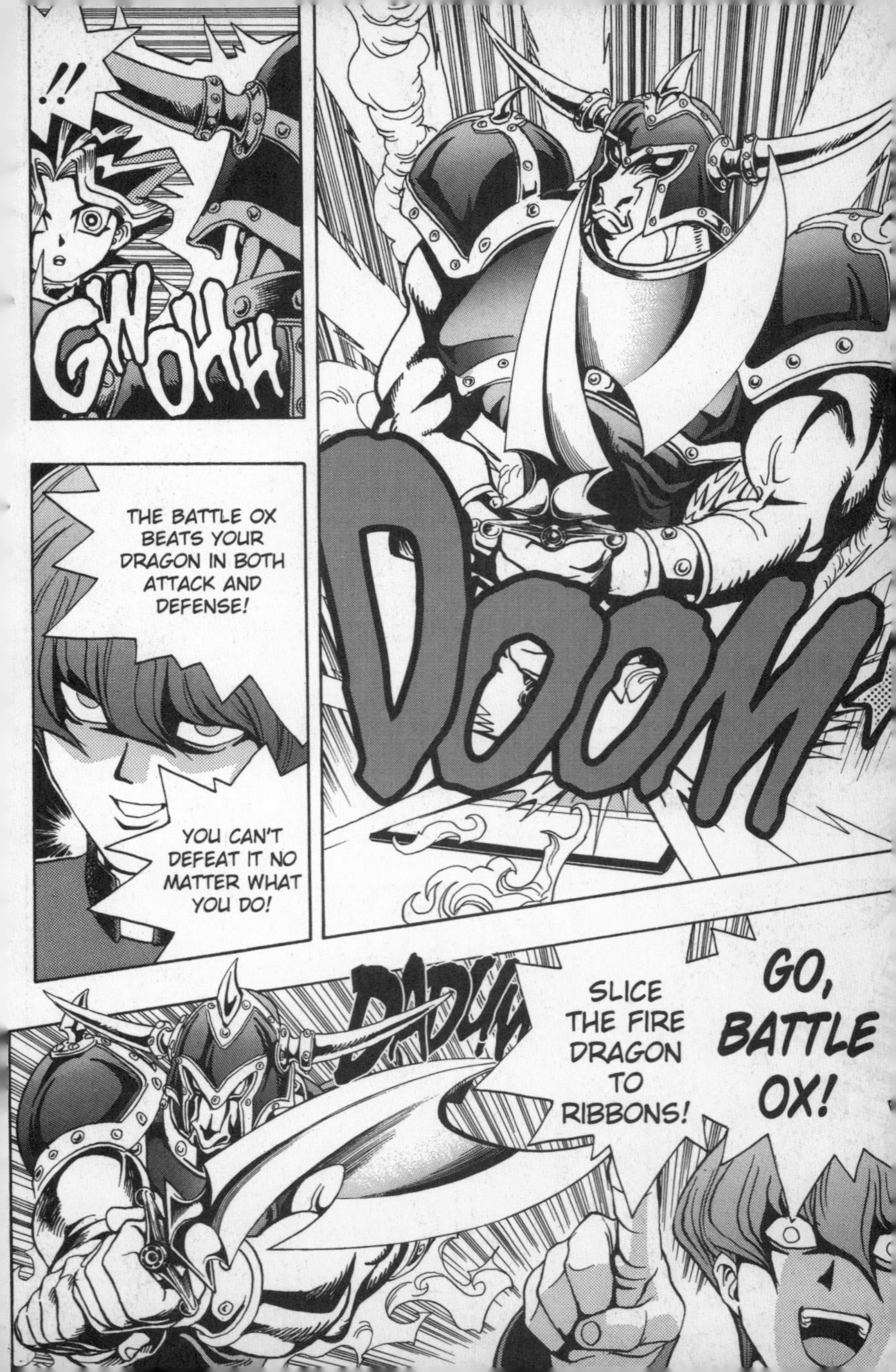
DOOOM
!!
GNOHH
THE BATTLE OX BEATS YOUR DRAGON IN BOTH ATTACK AND DEFENSE!
YOU CAN'T DEFEAT IT NO MATTER WHAT YOU DO!
GO, BATTLE OX!
SLICE THE FIRE DRAGON TO RIBBONS!
DADUN

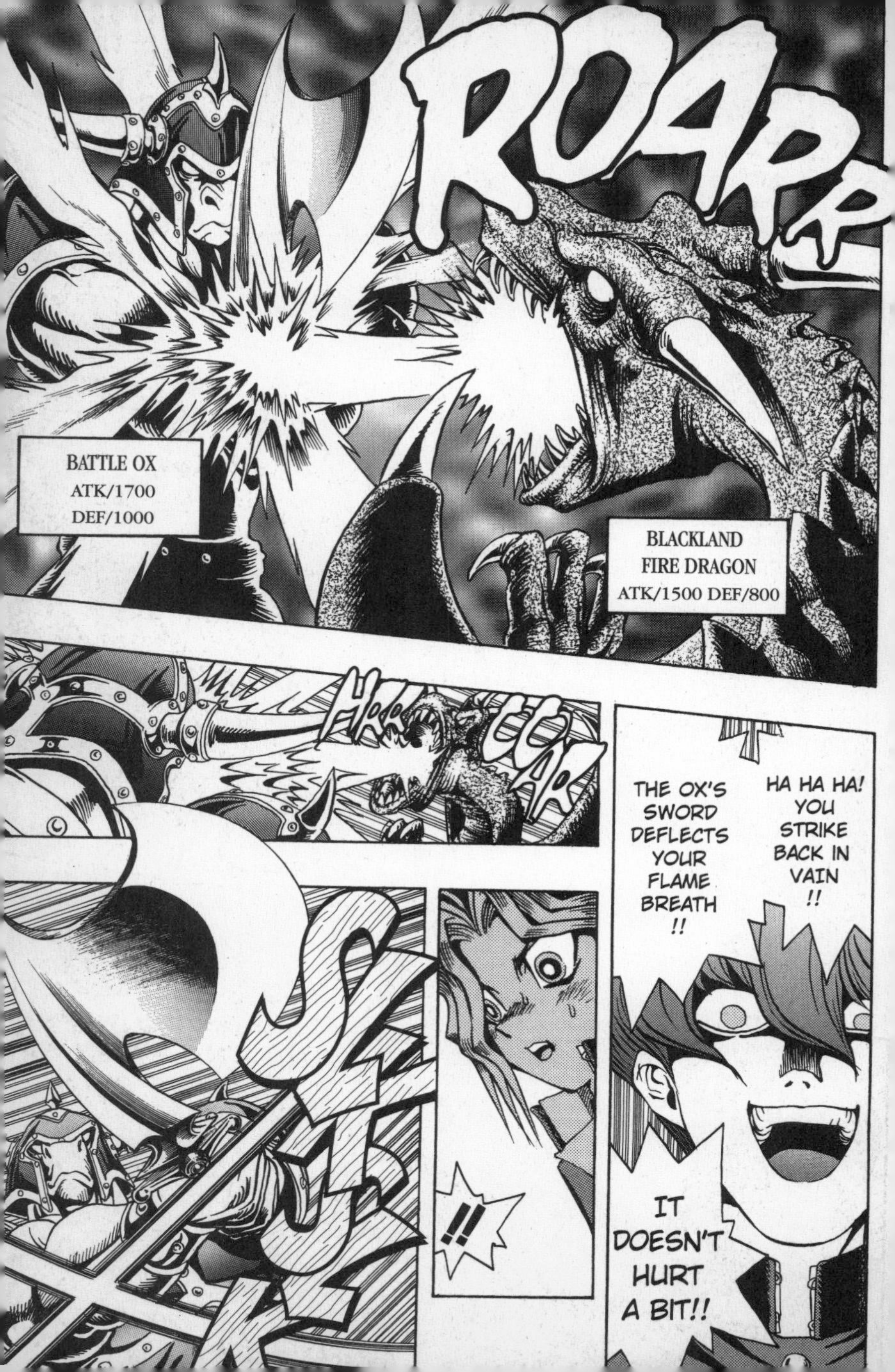
ROARR
BLACKLAND FIRE DRAGON ATK/1500 DEF/800
BATTLE OX ATK/1700 DEF/1000
HA HA HA! YOU STRIKE BACK IN VAIN !!
THE OX'S SWORD DEFLECTS YOUR FLAME BREATH !!
IT DOESN'T HURT A BIT!!
!!

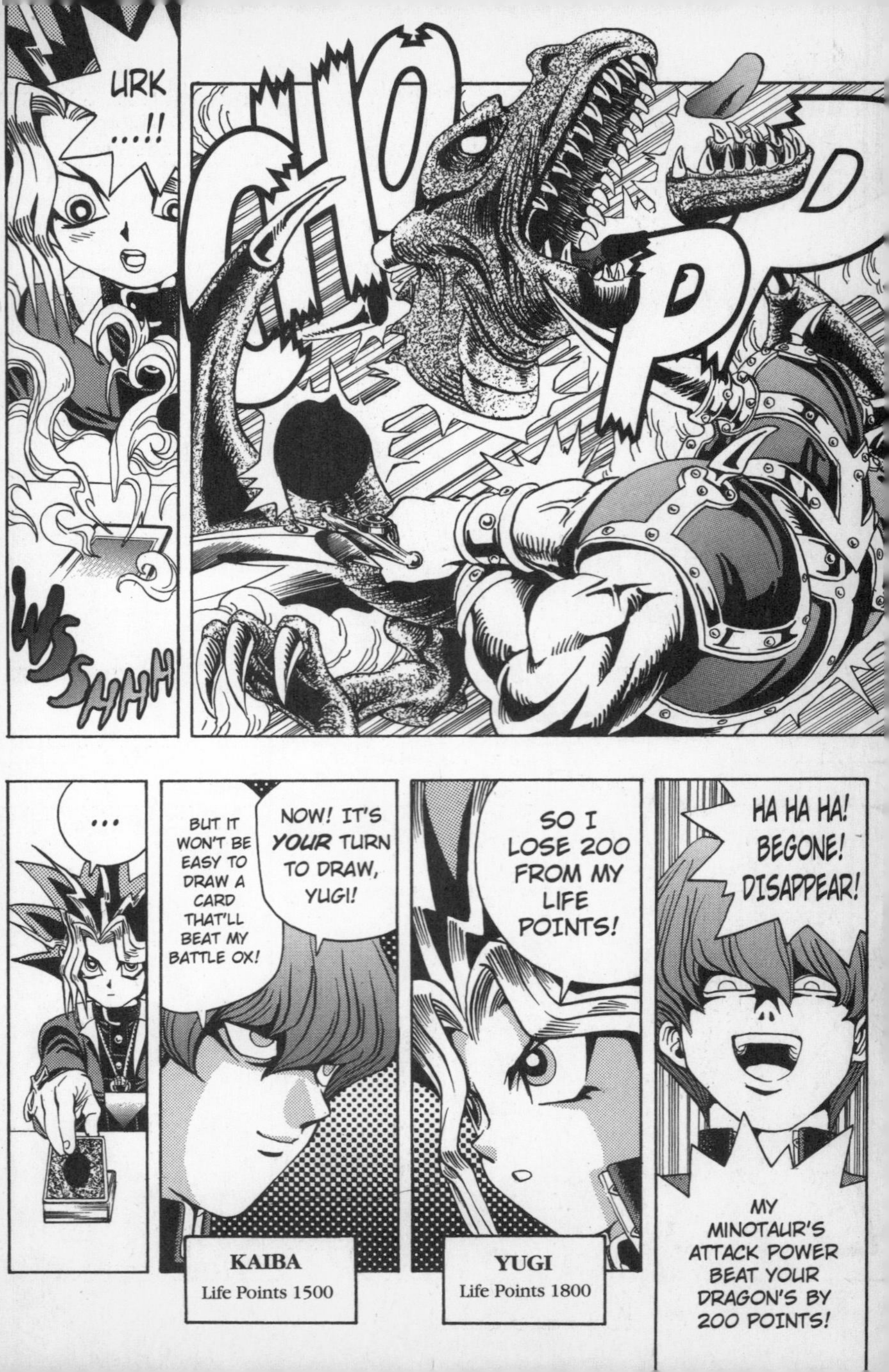
URK ...!!
HA HA HA! BEGONE! DISAPPEAR!
MY MINOTAUR'S ATTACK POWER BEAT YOUR DRAGON'S BY 200 POINTS!
SO I LOSE 200 FROM MY LIFE POINTS!
YUGI
Life Points 1800
NOW! IT'S *YOUR* TURN TO DRAW, YUGI!
BUT IT WON'T BE EASY TO DRAW A CARD THAT'LL BEAT MY BATTLE OX!
KAIBA
Life Points 1500
...

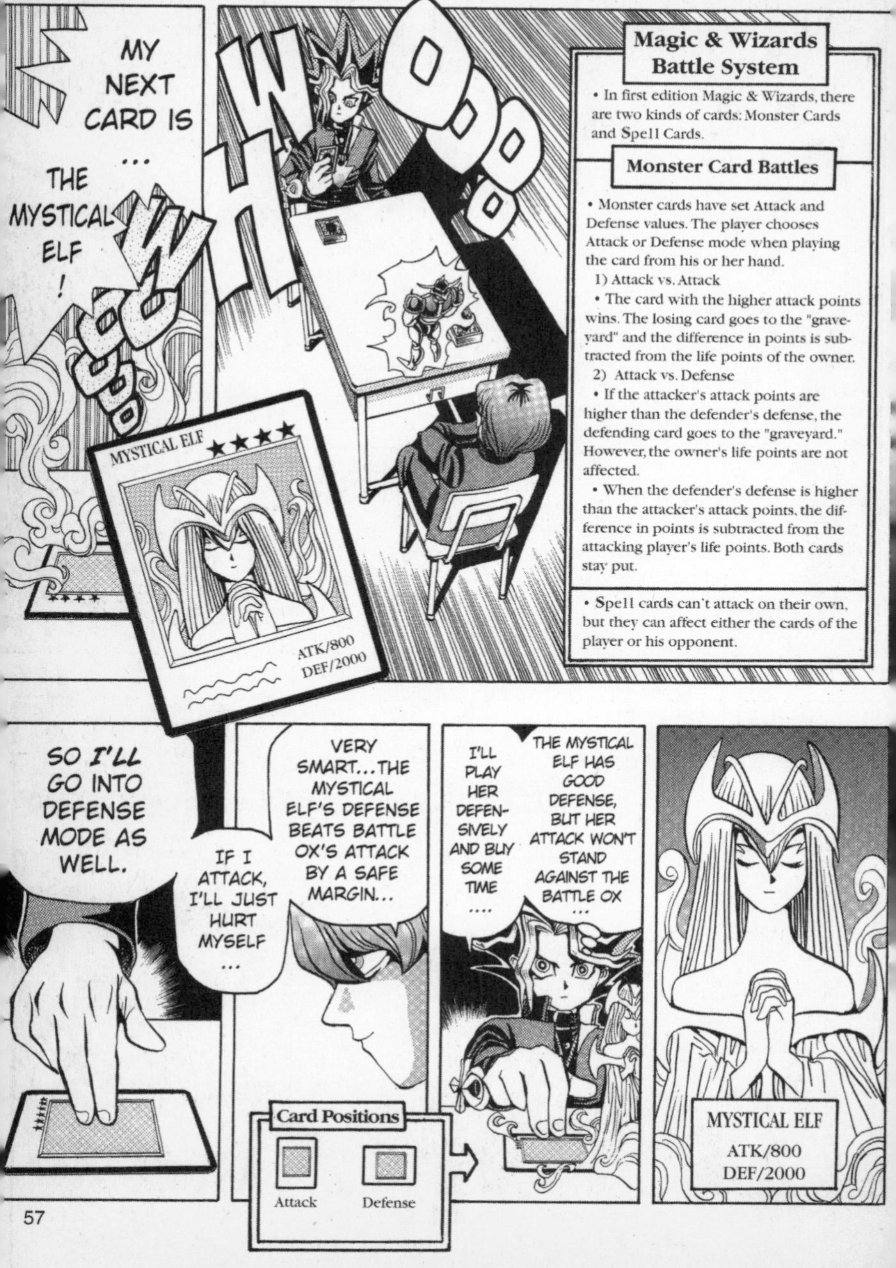
WHOOOOO
Magic & Wizards Battle System
• In first edition Magic & Wizards, there are two kinds of cards: Monster Cards and Spell Cards.
Monster Card Battles
• Monster cards have set Attack and Defense values. The player chooses Attack or Defense mode when playing the card from his or her hand.
1) Attack vs. Attack
• The card with the higher attack points wins. The losing card goes to the "graveyard" and the difference in points is subtracted from the life points of the owner.
2) Attack vs. Defense
• If the attacker's attack points are higher than the defender's defense, the defending card goes to the "graveyard." However, the owner's life points are not affected.
• When the defender's defense is higher than the attacker's attack points, the difference in points is subtracted from the attacking player's life points. Both cards stay put.
• Spell cards can't attack on their own, but they can affect either the cards of the player or his opponent.
MY NEXT CARD IS ... THE MYSTICAL ELF !
WHOOOO
MYSTICAL ELF
ATK/800
DEF/2000
MYSTICAL ELF
ATK/800
DEF/2000
THE MYSTICAL ELF HAS GOOD DEFENSE, BUT HER ATTACK WON'T STAND AGAINST THE BATTLE OX ...
I'LL PLAY HER DEFENSIVELY AND BUY SOME TIME ....
Card Positions
Attack
Defense
VERY SMART...THE MYSTICAL ELF'S DEFENSE BEATS BATTLE OX'S ATTACK BY A SAFE MARGIN...
IF I ATTACK, I'LL JUST HURT MYSELF ...
SO I'LL GO INTO DEFENSE MODE AS WELL.

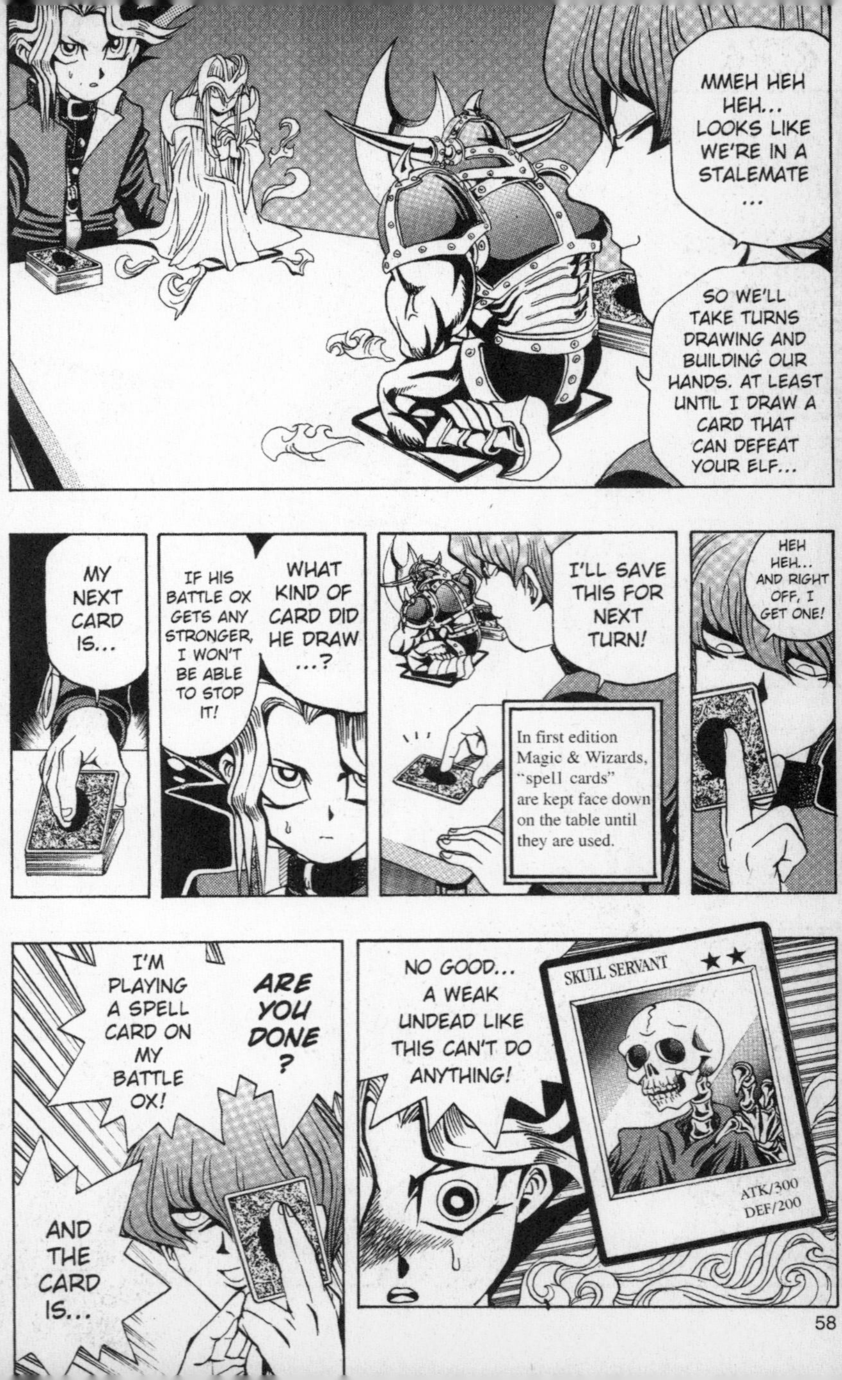
MMEH HEH HEH... LOOKS LIKE WE'RE IN A STALEMATE ...
SO WE'LL TAKE TURNS DRAWING AND BUILDING OUR HANDS. AT LEAST UNTIL I DRAW A CARD THAT CAN DEFEAT YOUR ELF...
MY NEXT CARD IS...
WHAT KIND OF CARD DID HE DRAW ...?
IF HIS BATTLE OX GETS ANY STRONGER, I WON'T BE ABLE TO STOP IT!
I'LL SAVE THIS FOR NEXT TURN!
In first edition Magic & Wizards, "spell cards" are kept face down on the table until they are used.
HEH HEH... AND RIGHT OFF, I GET ONE!
I'M PLAYING A SPELL CARD ON MY BATTLE OX!
ARE YOU DONE ?
AND THE CARD IS...
NO GOOD... A WEAK UNDEAD LIKE THIS CAN'T DO ANYTHING!
SKULL SERVANT
ATK/300
DEF/200

READ THIS WAY

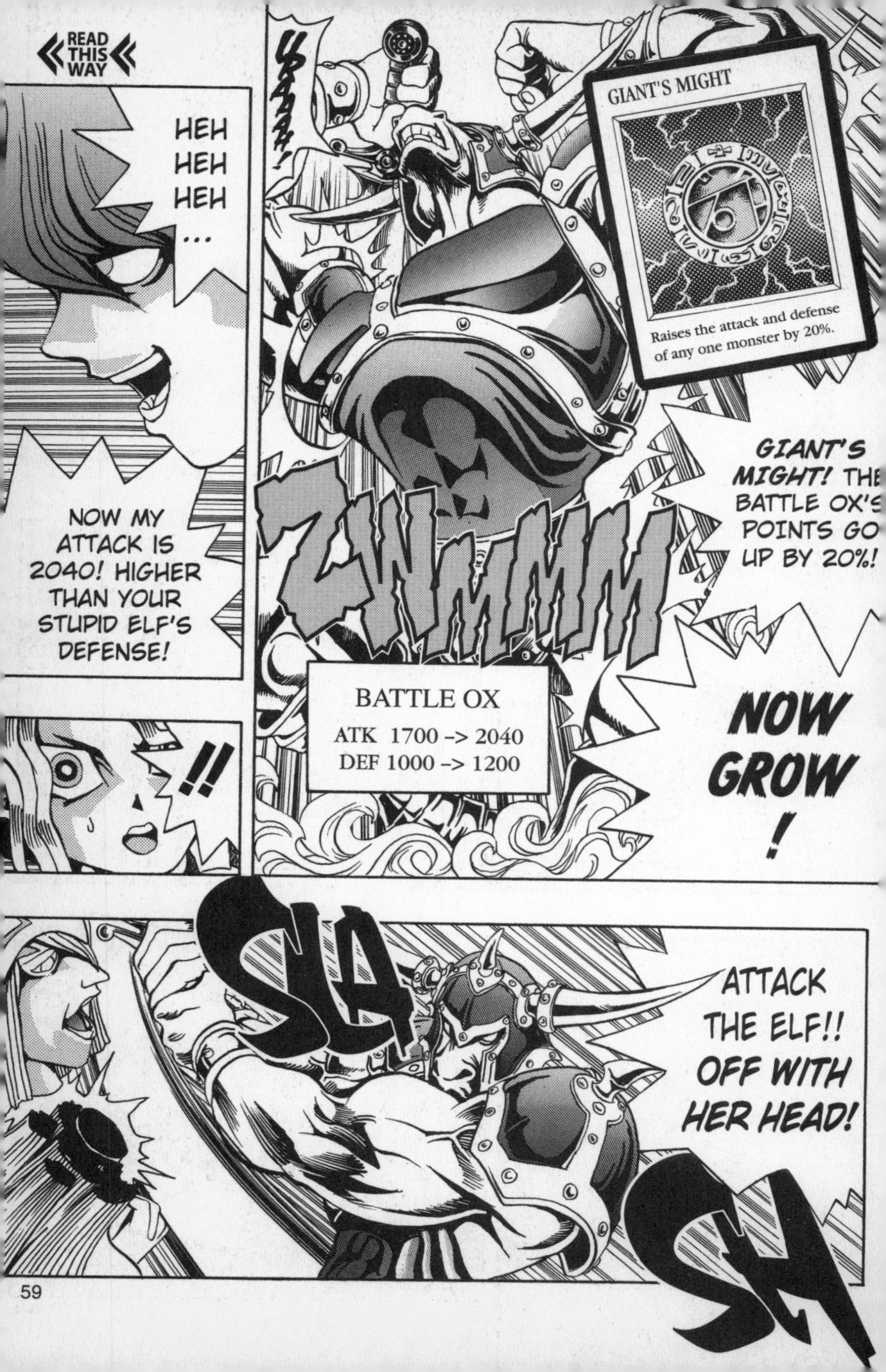

GIANT'S MIGHT
Raises the attack and defense of any one monster by 20%.
GIANT'S MIGHT! THE BATTLE OX'S POINTS GO UP BY 20%!
NOW GROW!
URAAAAH!
ZWMMM
BATTLE OX
ATK 1700 -> 2040
DEF 1000 -> 1200
HEH HEH HEH ...
NOW MY ATTACK IS 2040! HIGHER THAN YOUR STUPID ELF'S DEFENSE!
!!
ATTACK THE ELF!! OFF WITH HER HEAD!
SLA
SH

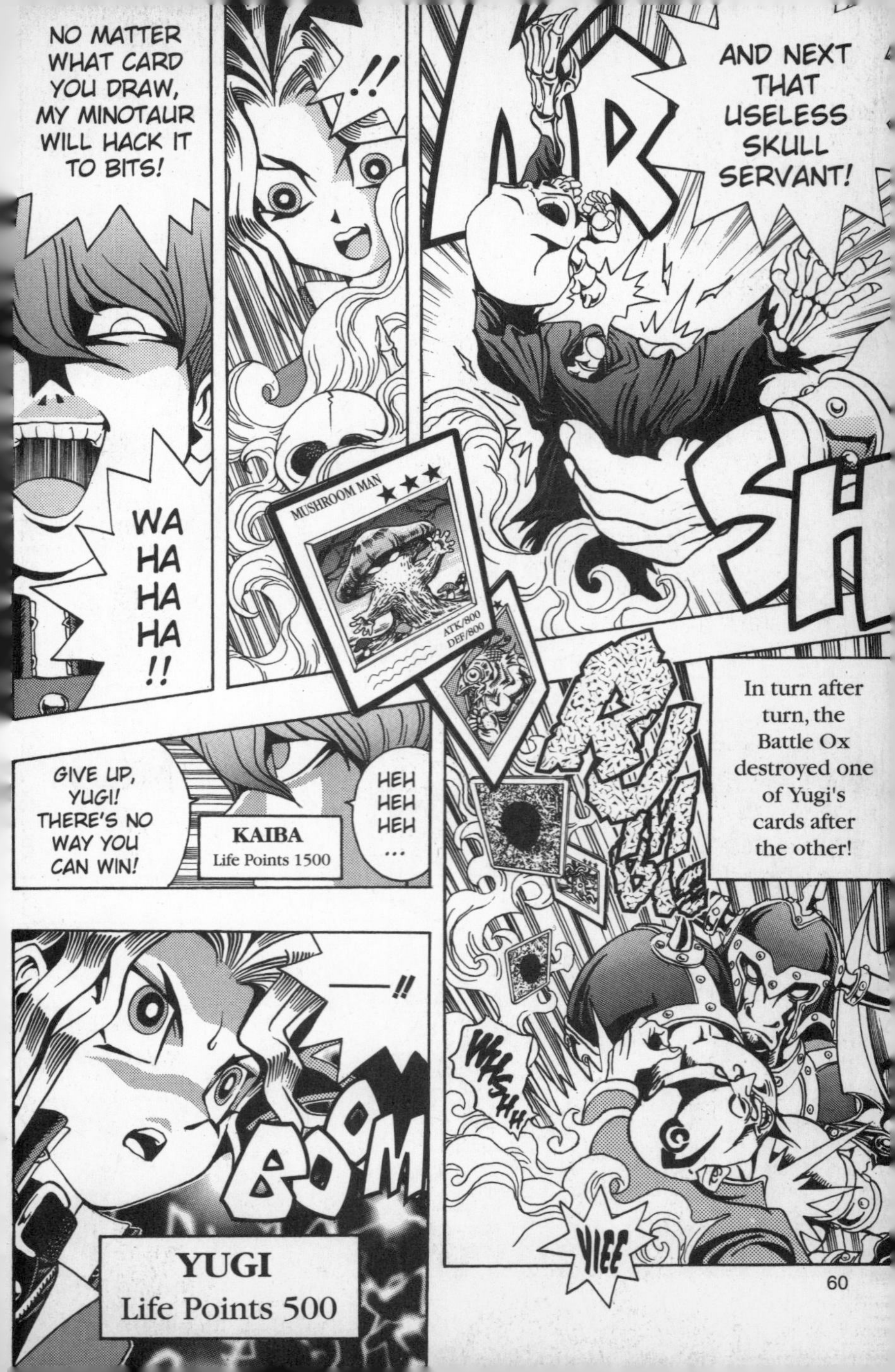
AND NEXT THAT USELESS SKULL SERVANT!
!!
NO MATTER WHAT CARD YOU DRAW, MY MINOTAUR WILL HACK IT TO BITS!
WA HA HA HA !!
MUSHROOM MAN
ATK/800 DEF/800
In turn after turn, the Battle Ox destroyed one of Yugi's cards after the other!
WHSHH
YIEE
HEH HEH HEH ...
GIVE UP, YUGI! THERE'S NO WAY YOU CAN WIN!
KAIBA
Life Points 1500
——!!
BOOM
YUGI
Life Points 500

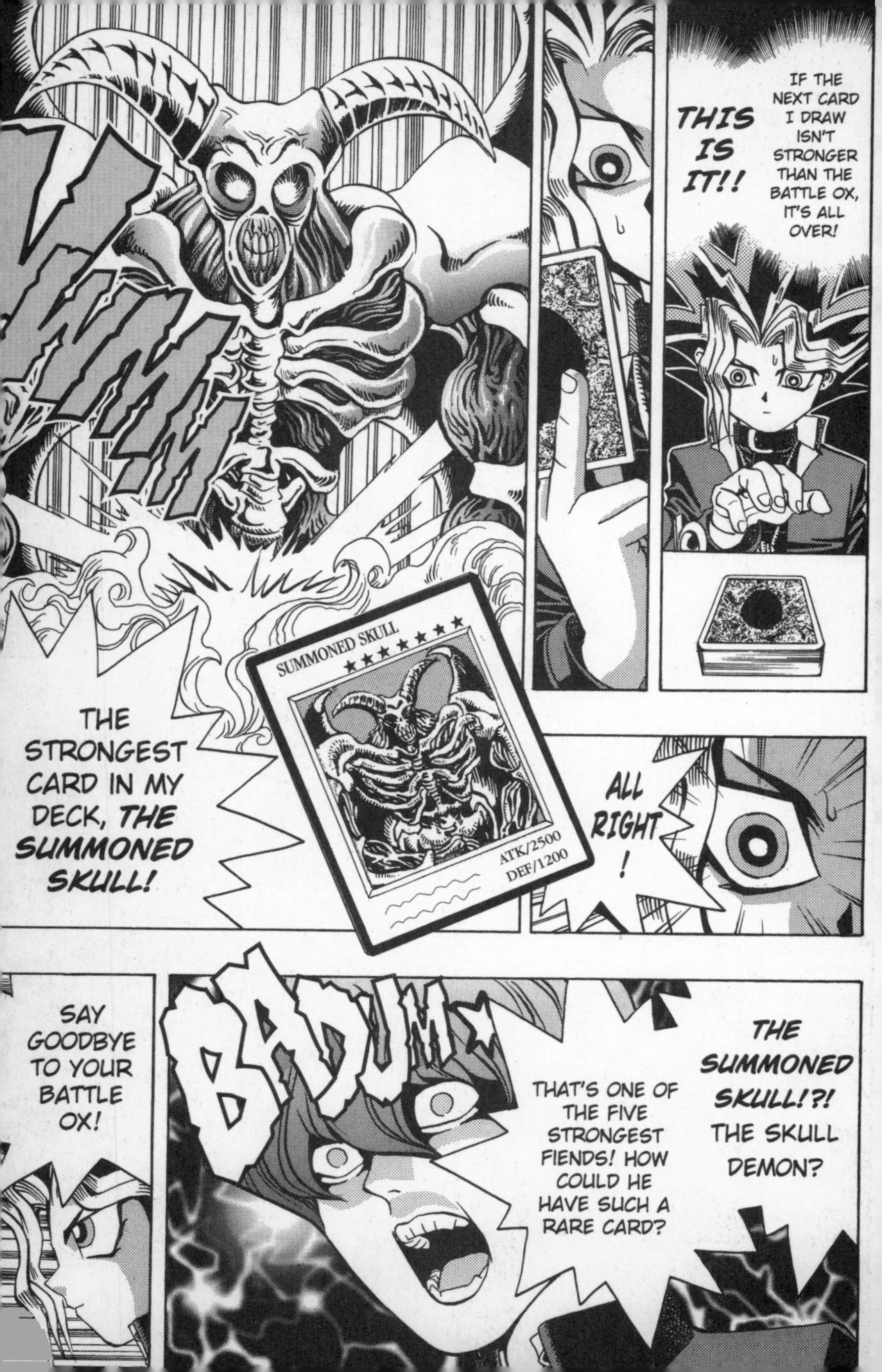
IF THE NEXT CARD I DRAW ISN'T STRONGER THAN THE BATTLE OX, IT'S ALL OVER!
THIS IS IT!!
ALL RIGHT!
THE STRONGEST CARD IN MY DECK, THE SUMMONED SKULL!
SUMMONED SKULL
ATK/2500
DEF/1200
THE SUMMONED SKULL!?! THE SKULL DEMON?
THAT'S ONE OF THE FIVE STRONGEST FIENDS! HOW COULD HE HAVE SUCH A RARE CARD?
BADUM
SAY GOODBYE TO YOUR BATTLE OX!

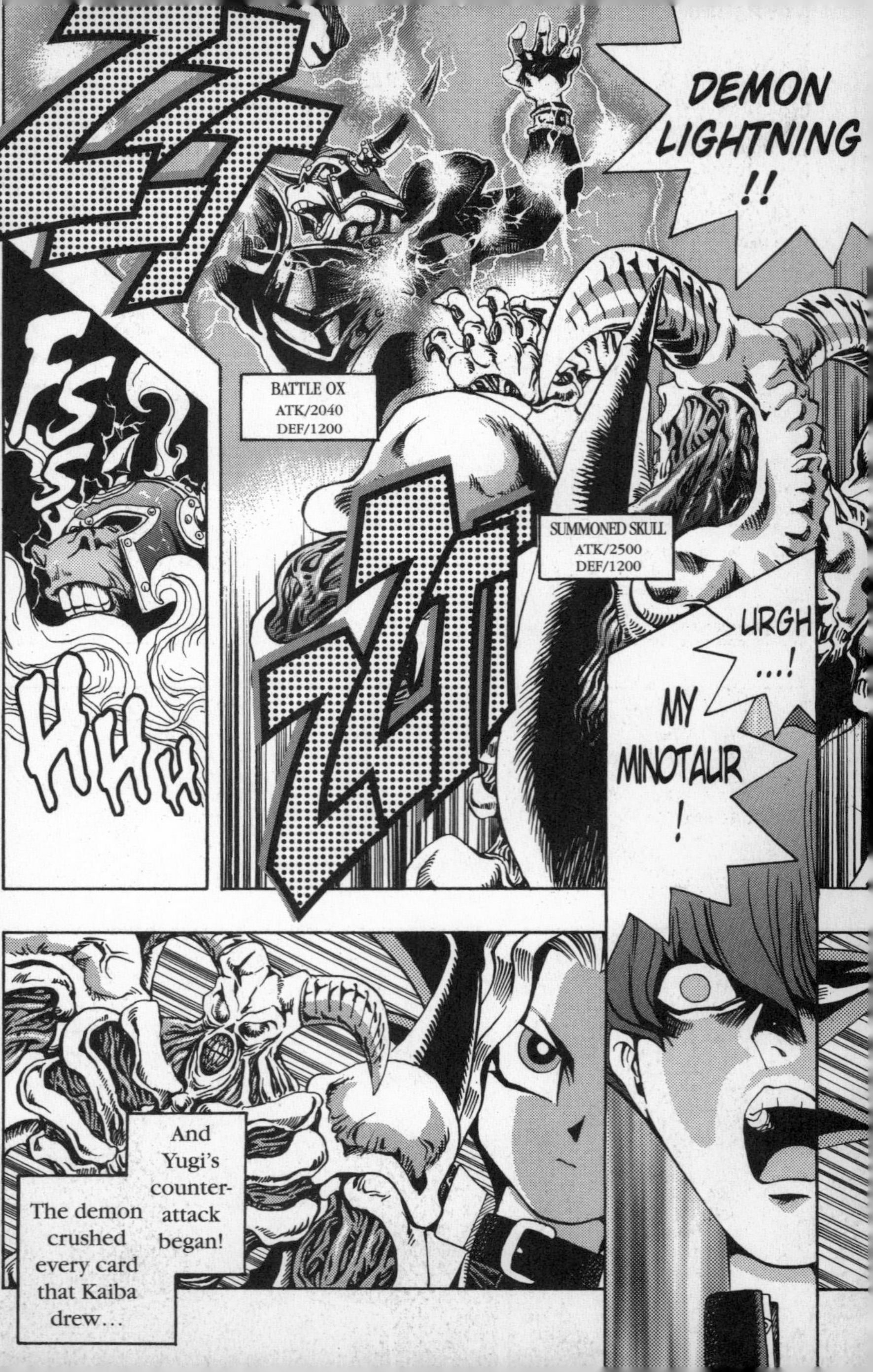
DEMON LIGHTNING !!
BATTLE OX ATK/2040 DEF/1200
SUMMONED SKULL ATK/2500 DEF/1200
URGH ...!
MY MINOTAUR !
The demon crushed every card that Kaiba drew...
And Yugi's counter-attack began!

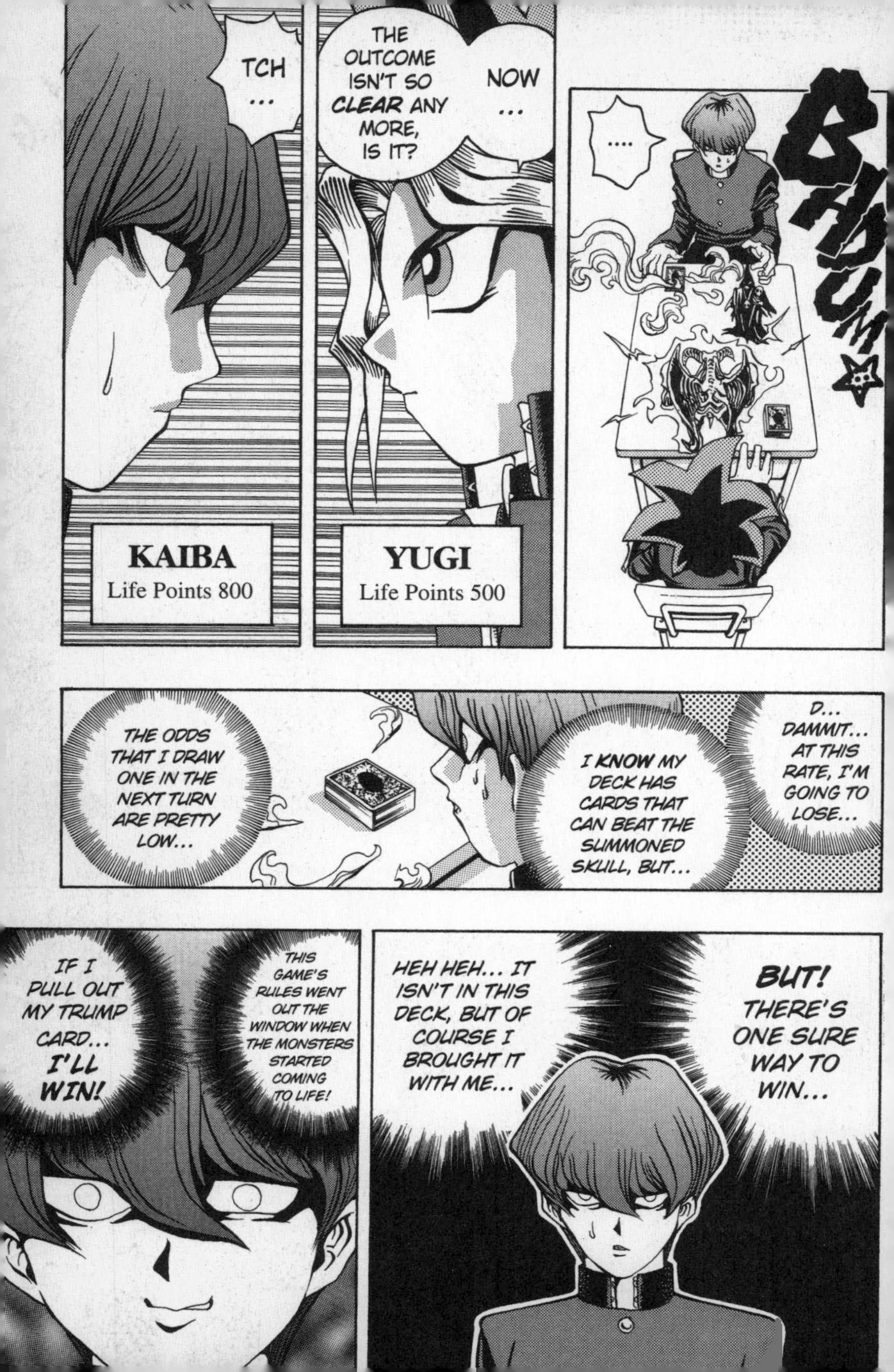
BADUM
....
THE OUTCOME ISN'T SO CLEAR ANY MORE, IS IT?
NOW ...
YUGI
Life Points 500
TCH ...
KAIBA
Life Points 800
D... DAMMIT... AT THIS RATE, I'M GOING TO LOSE...
I KNOW MY DECK HAS CARDS THAT CAN BEAT THE SUMMONED SKULL, BUT...
THE ODDS THAT I DRAW ONE IN THE NEXT TURN ARE PRETTY LOW...
BUT! THERE'S ONE SURE WAY TO WIN...
HEH HEH... IT ISN'T IN THIS DECK, BUT OF COURSE I BROUGHT IT WITH ME...
THIS GAME'S RULES WENT OUT THE WINDOW WHEN THE MONSTERS STARTED COMING TO LIFE!
IF I PULL OUT MY TRUMP CARD... I'LL WIN!

READ THIS WAY

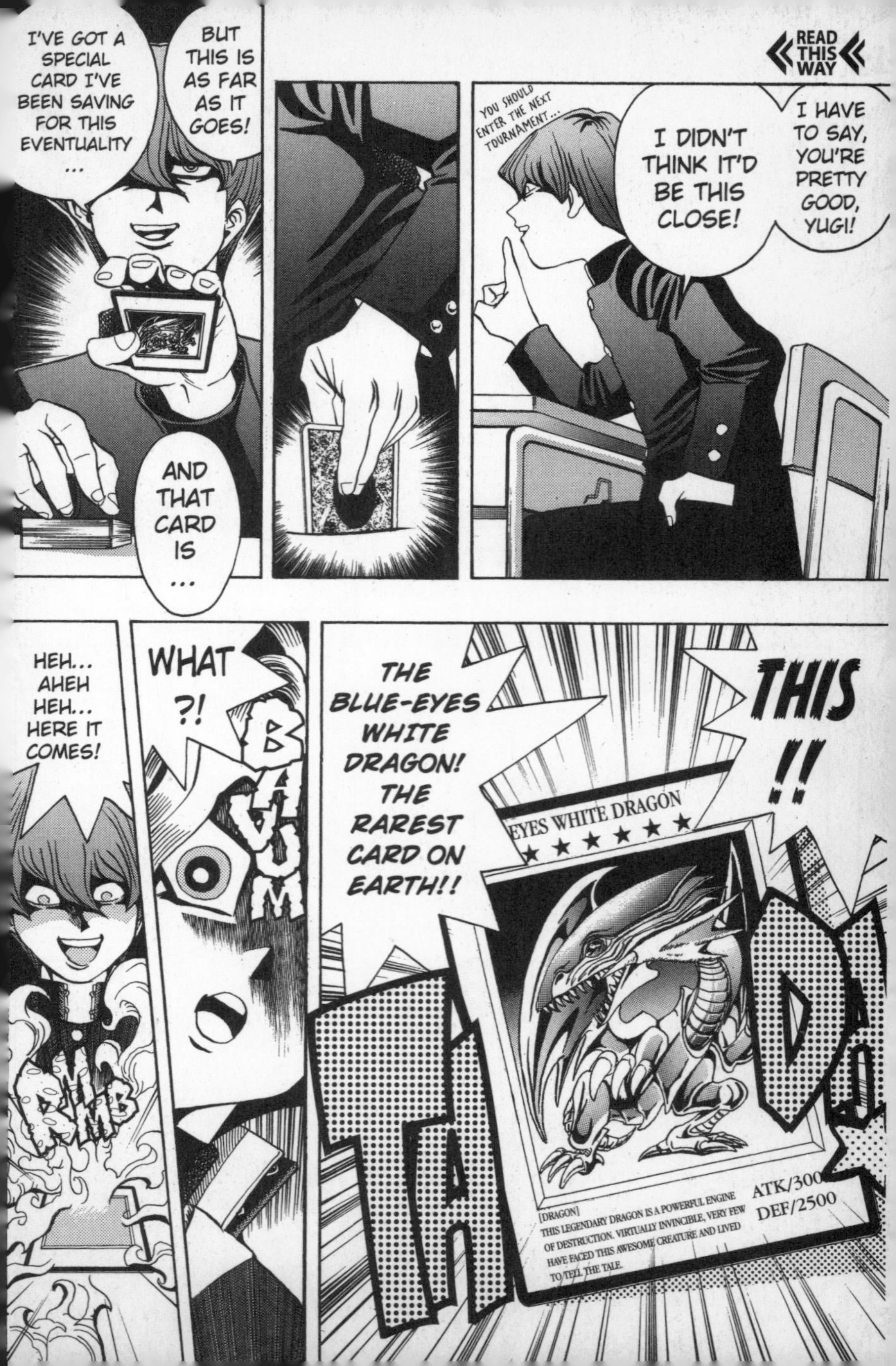

I HAVE TO SAY, YOU'RE PRETTY GOOD, YUGI!
I DIDN'T THINK IT'D BE THIS CLOSE!
YOU SHOULD ENTER THE NEXT TOURNAMENT...
BUT THIS IS AS FAR AS IT GOES!
I'VE GOT A SPECIAL CARD I'VE BEEN SAVING FOR THIS EVENTUALITY ...
AND THAT CARD IS ...
THIS !!
THE BLUE-EYES WHITE DRAGON! THE RAREST CARD ON EARTH!!
EYES WHITE DRAGON
ATK/300
DEF/2500
[DRAGON]
THIS LEGENDARY DRAGON IS A POWERFUL ENGINE OF DESTRUCTION. VIRTUALLY INVINCIBLE, VERY FEW HAVE FACED THIS AWESOME CREATURE AND LIVED TO TELL THE TALE.
WHAT ?!
HEH... AHEH HEH... HERE IT COMES!

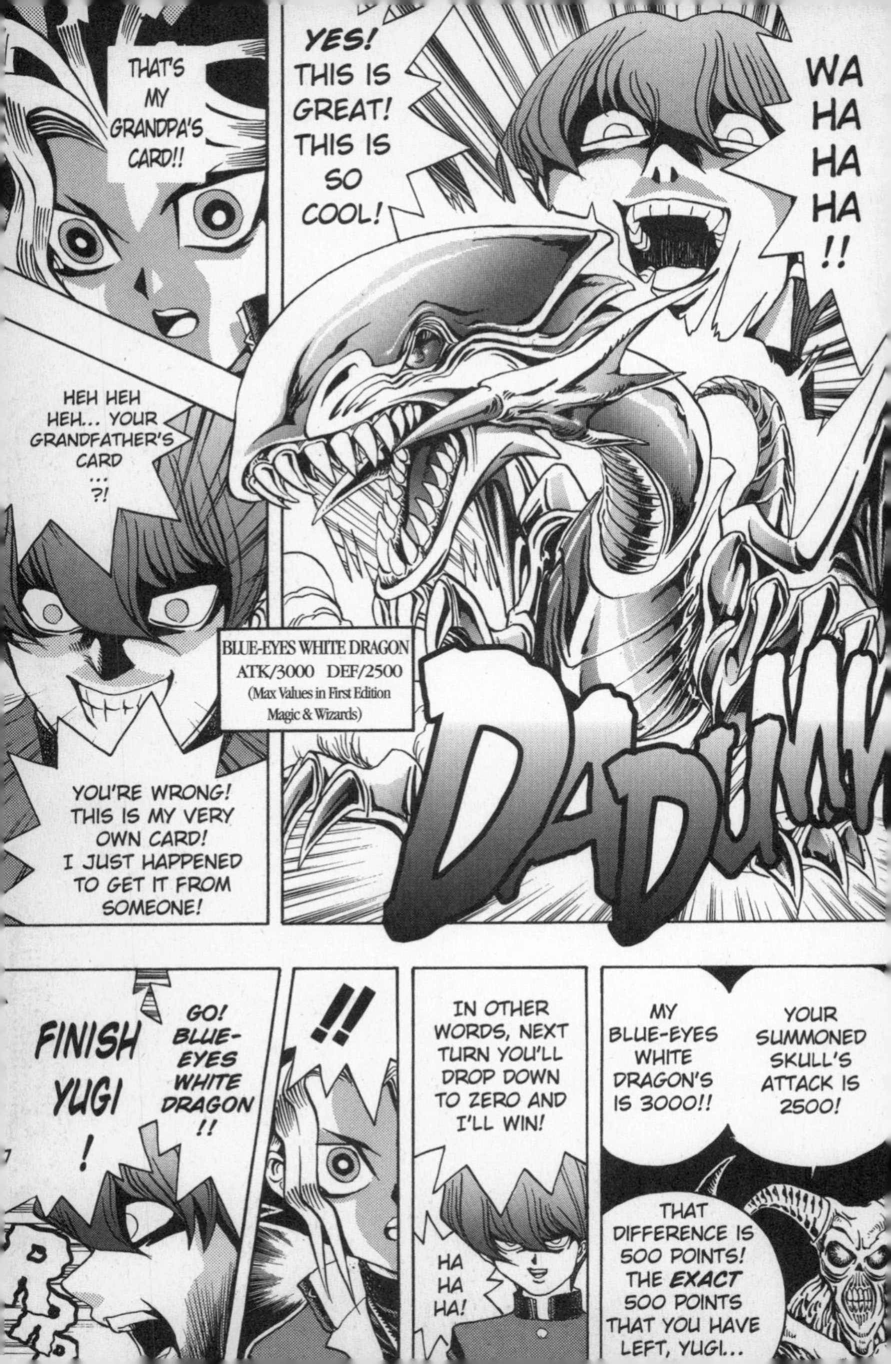
WA HA HA HA !!
YES! THIS IS GREAT! THIS IS SO COOL!
BLUE-EYES WHITE DRAGON ATK/3000 DEF/2500 (Max Values in First Edition Magic & Wizards)
DADUM
THAT'S MY GRANDPA'S CARD!!
HEH HEH HEH... YOUR GRANDFATHER'S CARD ...?!
YOU'RE WRONG! THIS IS MY VERY OWN CARD! I JUST HAPPENED TO GET IT FROM SOMEONE!
YOUR SUMMONED SKULL'S ATTACK IS 2500!
MY BLUE-EYES WHITE DRAGON'S IS 3000!!
THAT DIFFERENCE IS 500 POINTS! THE EXACT 500 POINTS THAT YOU HAVE LEFT, YUGI...
IN OTHER WORDS, NEXT TURN YOU'LL DROP DOWN TO ZERO AND I'LL WIN!
HA HA HA!
!!
GO! BLUE-EYES WHITE DRAGON !!
FINISH YUGI !

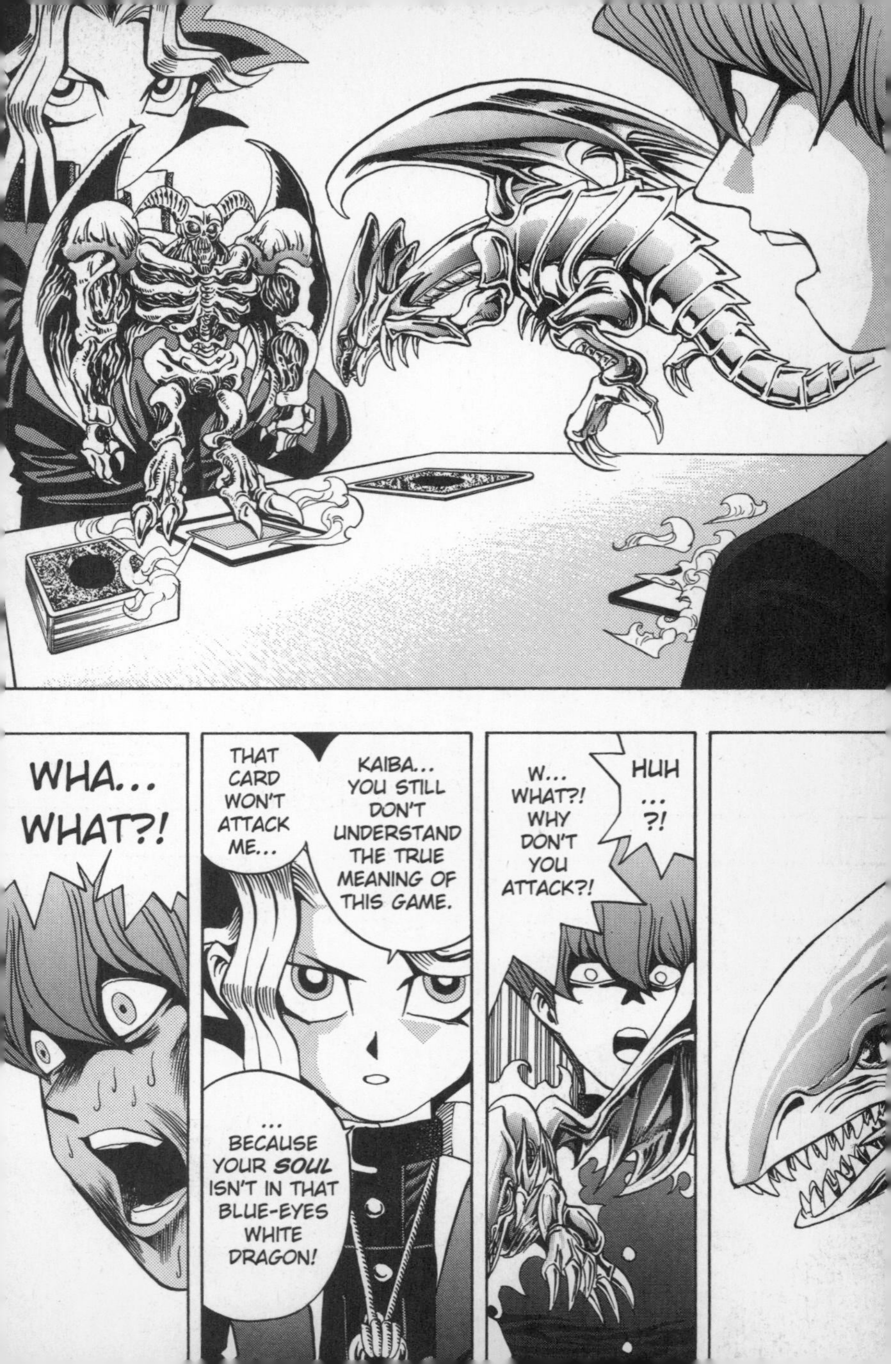
HUH ...?!
W... WHAT?! WHY DON'T YOU ATTACK?!
KAIBA... YOU STILL DON'T UNDERSTAND THE TRUE MEANING OF THIS GAME.
THAT CARD WON'T ATTACK ME...
... BECAUSE YOUR SOUL ISN'T IN THAT BLUE-EYES WHITE DRAGON!
WHA... WHAT?!

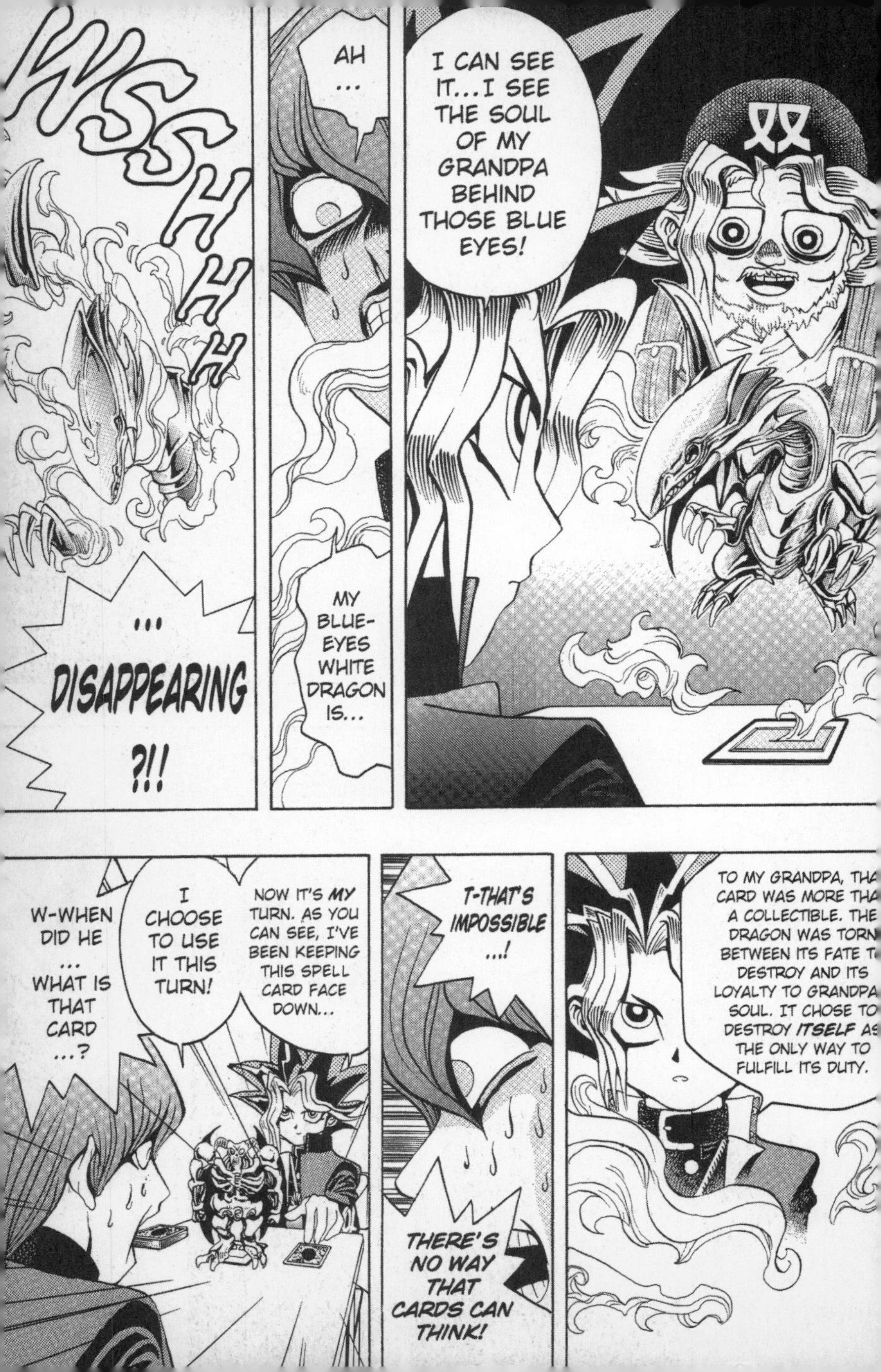
I CAN SEE IT...I SEE THE SOUL OF MY GRANDPA BEHIND THOSE BLUE EYES!
AH ...
MY BLUE-EYES WHITE DRAGON IS...
WSSHHH
... DISAPPEARING ?!!
TO MY GRANDPA, THA CARD WAS MORE THA A COLLECTIBLE. THE DRAGON WAS TORN BETWEEN ITS FATE T DESTROY AND ITS LOYALTY TO GRANDPA SOUL. IT CHOSE TO DESTROY ITSELF AS THE ONLY WAY TO FULFILL ITS DUTY.
T-THAT'S IMPOSSIBLE ...!
THERE'S NO WAY THAT CARDS CAN THINK!
NOW IT'S MY TURN. AS YOU CAN SEE, I'VE BEEN KEEPING THIS SPELL CARD FACE DOWN...
I CHOOSE TO USE IT THIS TURN!
W-WHEN DID HE ... WHAT IS THAT CARD ...?

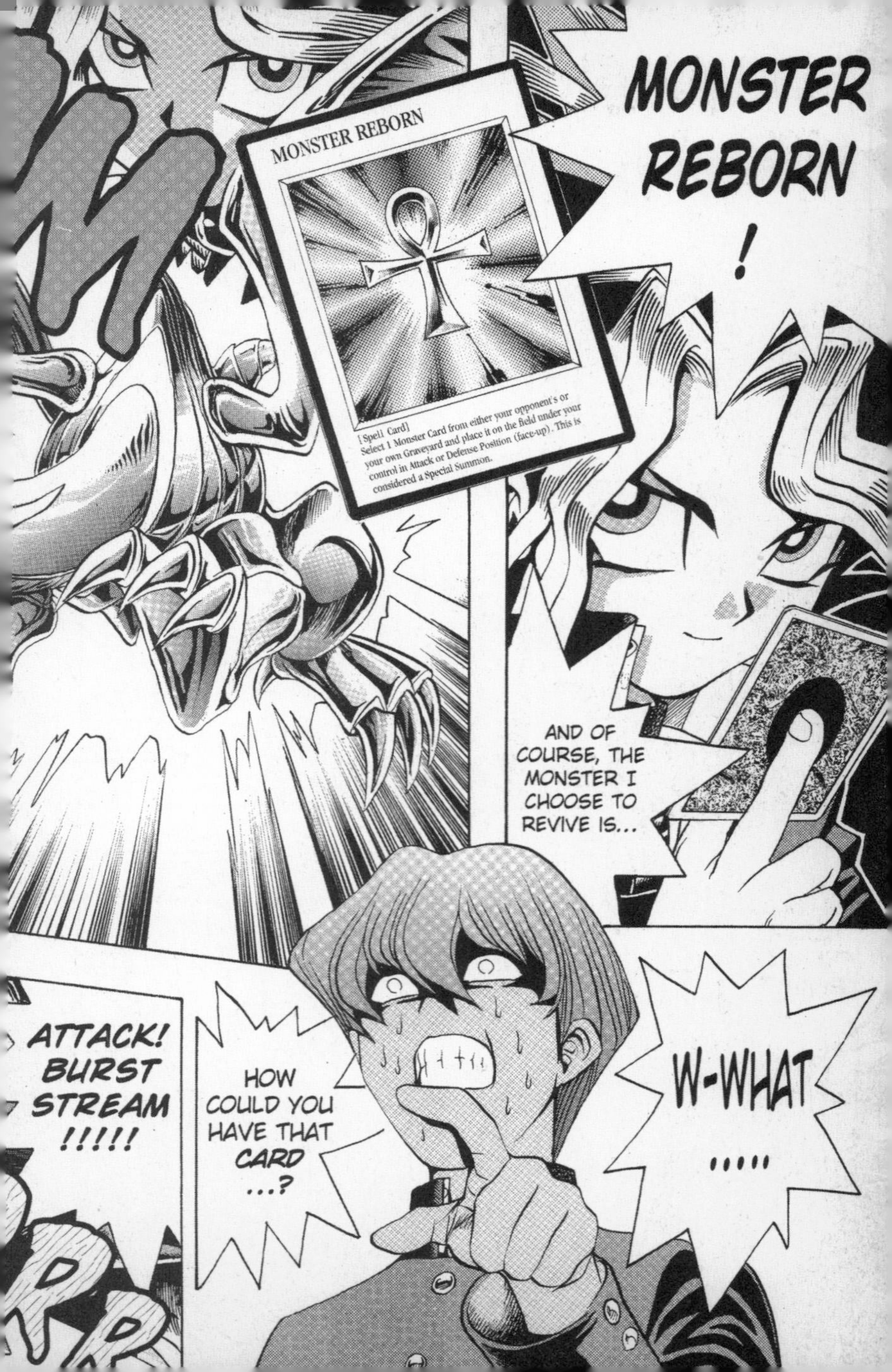
MONSTER REBORN !
MONSTER REBORN
[Spell Card]
Select 1 Monster Card from either your opponent's or your own Graveyard and place it on the field under your control in Attack or Defense Position (face-up). This is considered a Special Summon.
AND OF COURSE, THE MONSTER I CHOOSE TO REVIVE IS...
W-WHAT .....
HOW COULD YOU HAVE THAT CARD ...?
ATTACK! BURST STREAM !!!!!

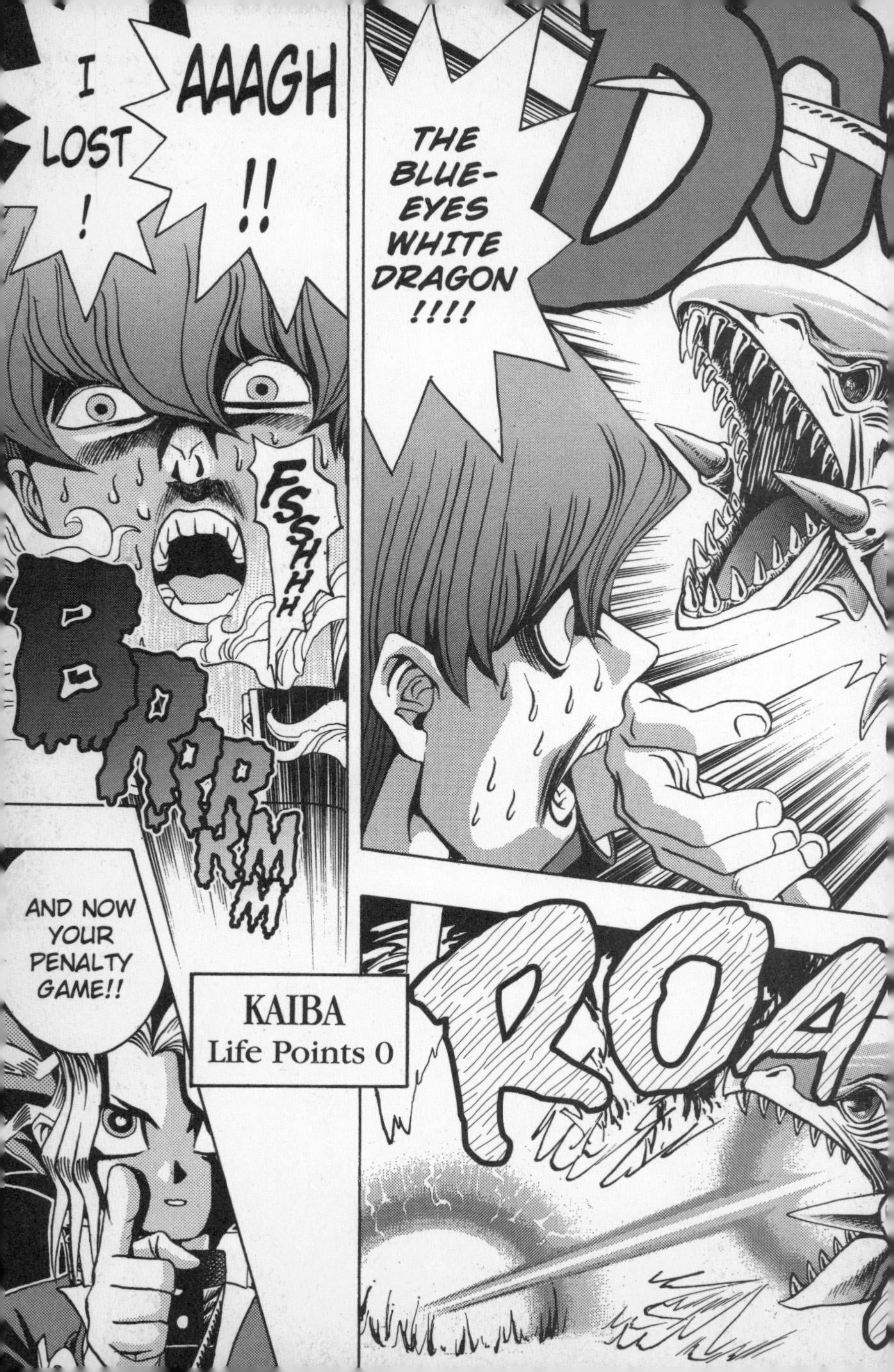
THE BLUE-EYES WHITE DRAGON!!!!
I LOST!
AAAGH!!
FSSHHHH
BRRRM
ROA
KAIBA
Life Points 0
AND NOW YOUR PENALTY GAME!!

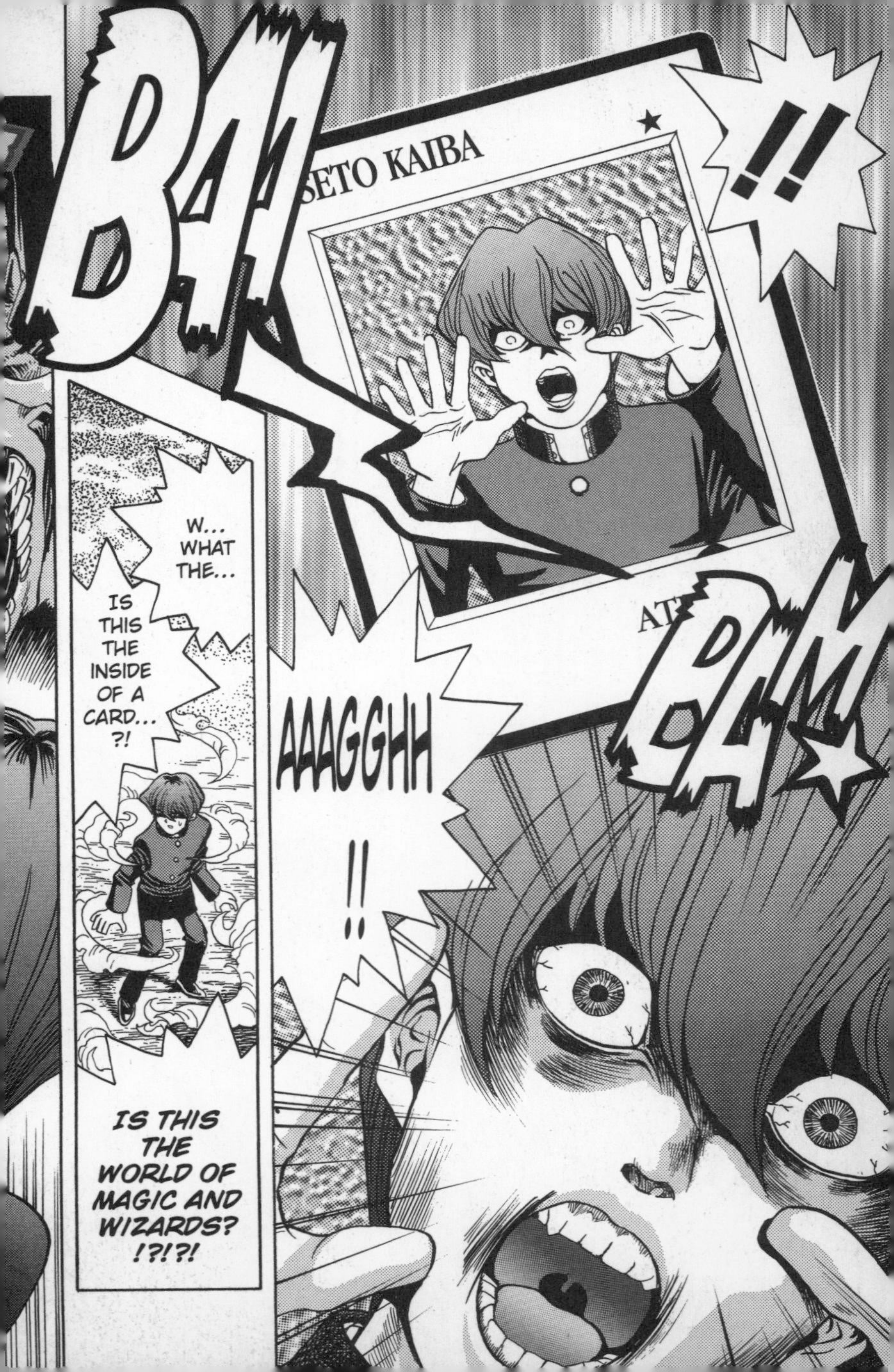
BA!
!!
SETO KAIBA
AT
BAM
AAAGGHH !!
W... WHAT THE...
IS THIS THE INSIDE OF A CARD...?!
IS THIS THE WORLD OF MAGIC AND WIZARDS? !?!?!

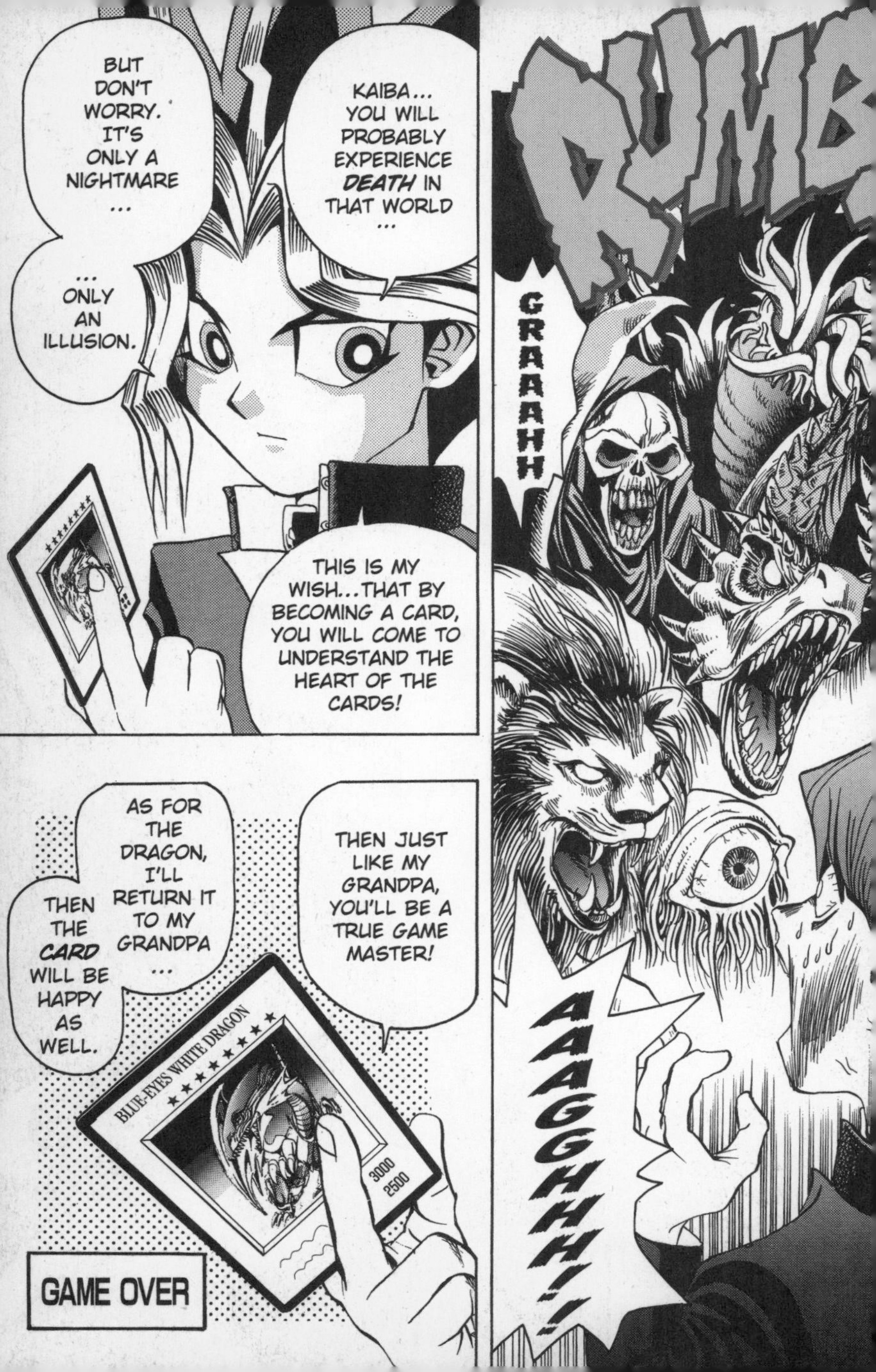
DUMB
GRAAAHH
AAAAGGHHHH!!
KAIBA... YOU WILL PROBABLY EXPERIENCE *DEATH* IN THAT WORLD ...
BUT DON'T WORRY. IT'S ONLY A NIGHTMARE ...
... ONLY AN ILLUSION.
THIS IS MY WISH...THAT BY BECOMING A CARD, YOU WILL COME TO UNDERSTAND THE HEART OF THE CARDS!
THEN JUST LIKE MY GRANDPA, YOU'LL BE A TRUE GAME MASTER!
AS FOR THE DRAGON, I'LL RETURN IT TO MY GRANDPA ...
THEN THE *CARD* WILL BE HAPPY AS WELL.
BLUE-EYES WHITE DRAGON
3000
2500
GAME OVER

Duel 11: The Wild Gang (Part 1)

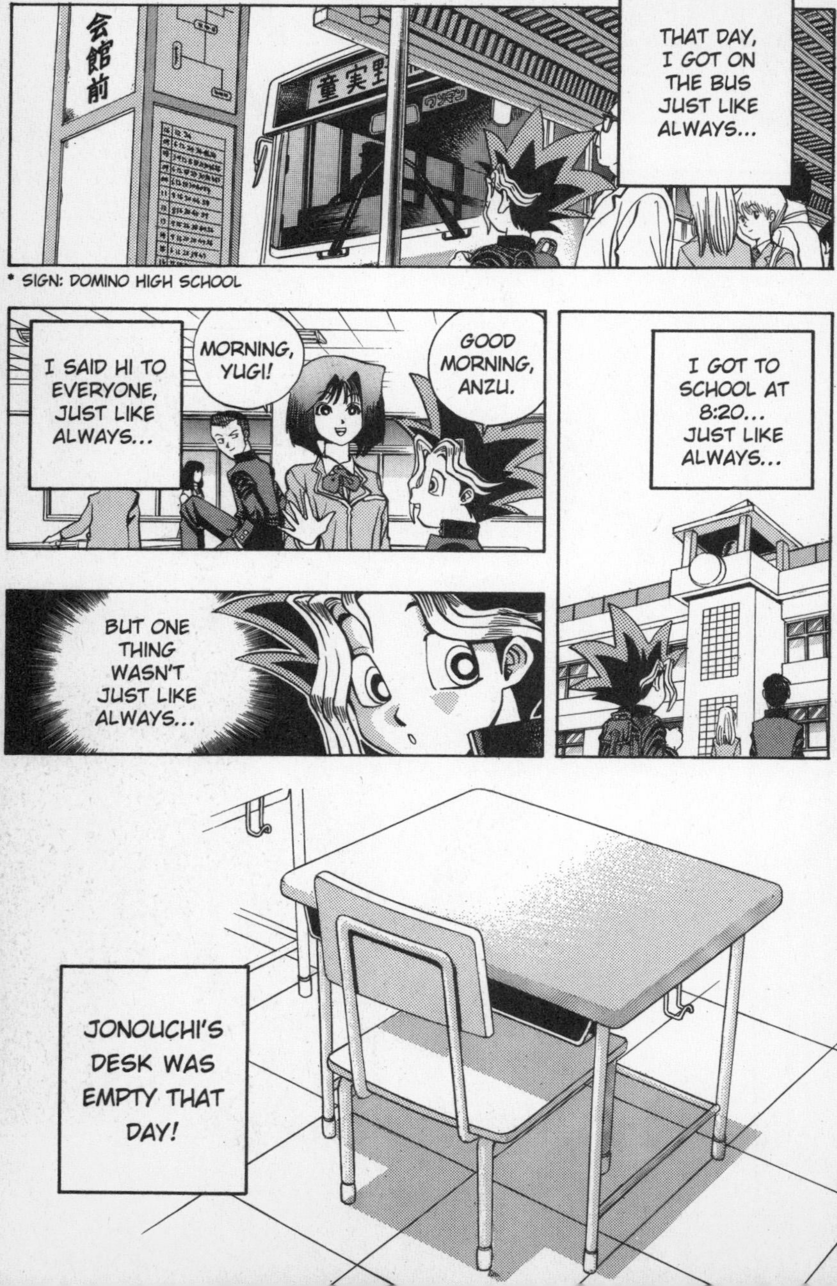
THAT DAY, I GOT ON THE BUS JUST LIKE ALWAYS...
会館前
童実野
I GOT TO SCHOOL AT 8:20... JUST LIKE ALWAYS...
I SAID HI TO EVERYONE, JUST LIKE ALWAYS...
MORNING, YUGI!
GOOD MORNING, ANZU.
BUT ONE THING WASN'T JUST LIKE ALWAYS...
JONOUCHI'S DESK WAS EMPTY THAT DAY!

* SIGN: DOMINO HIGH SCHOOL

Duel 11: The Wild Gang (Part 1)

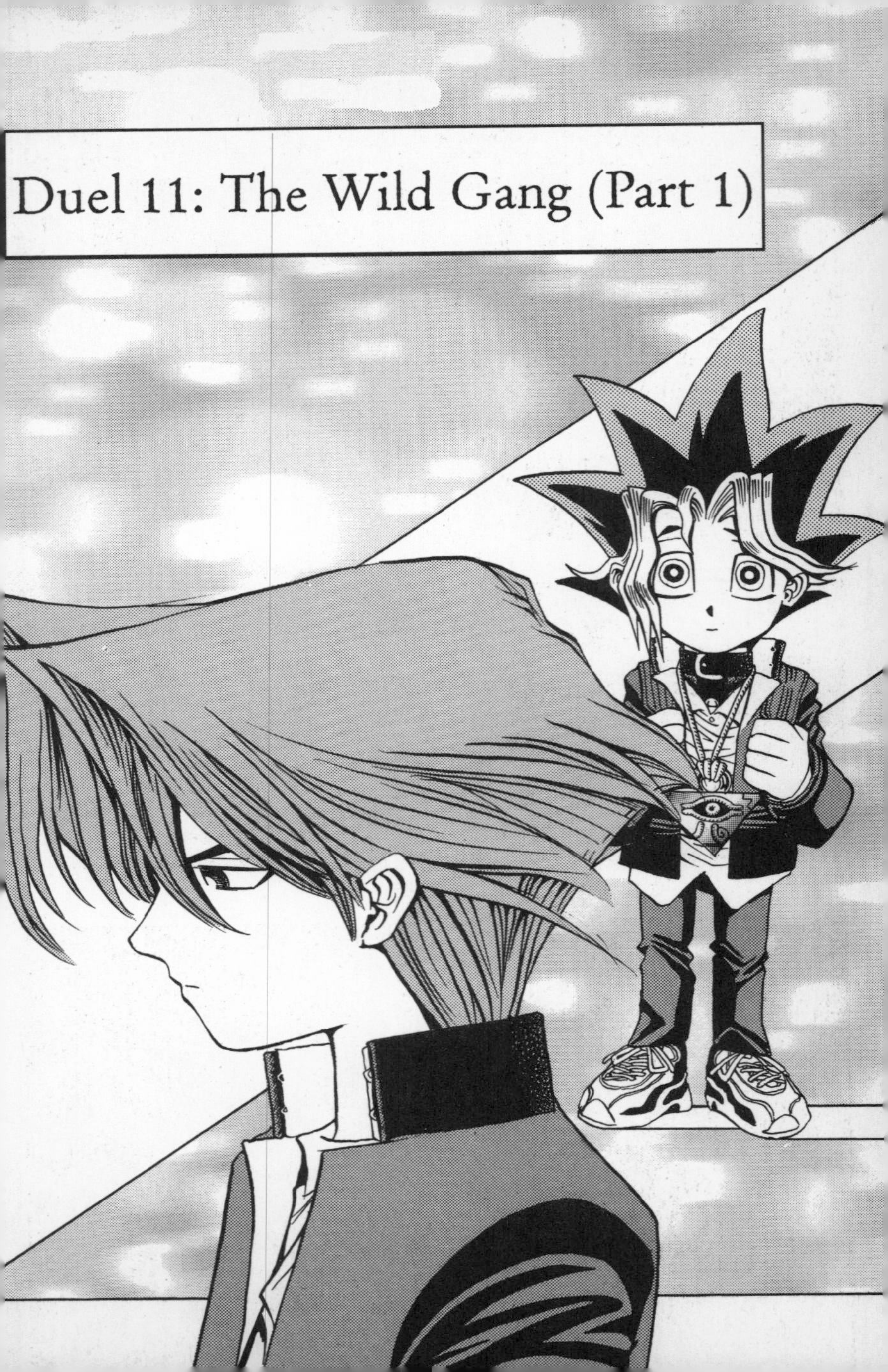

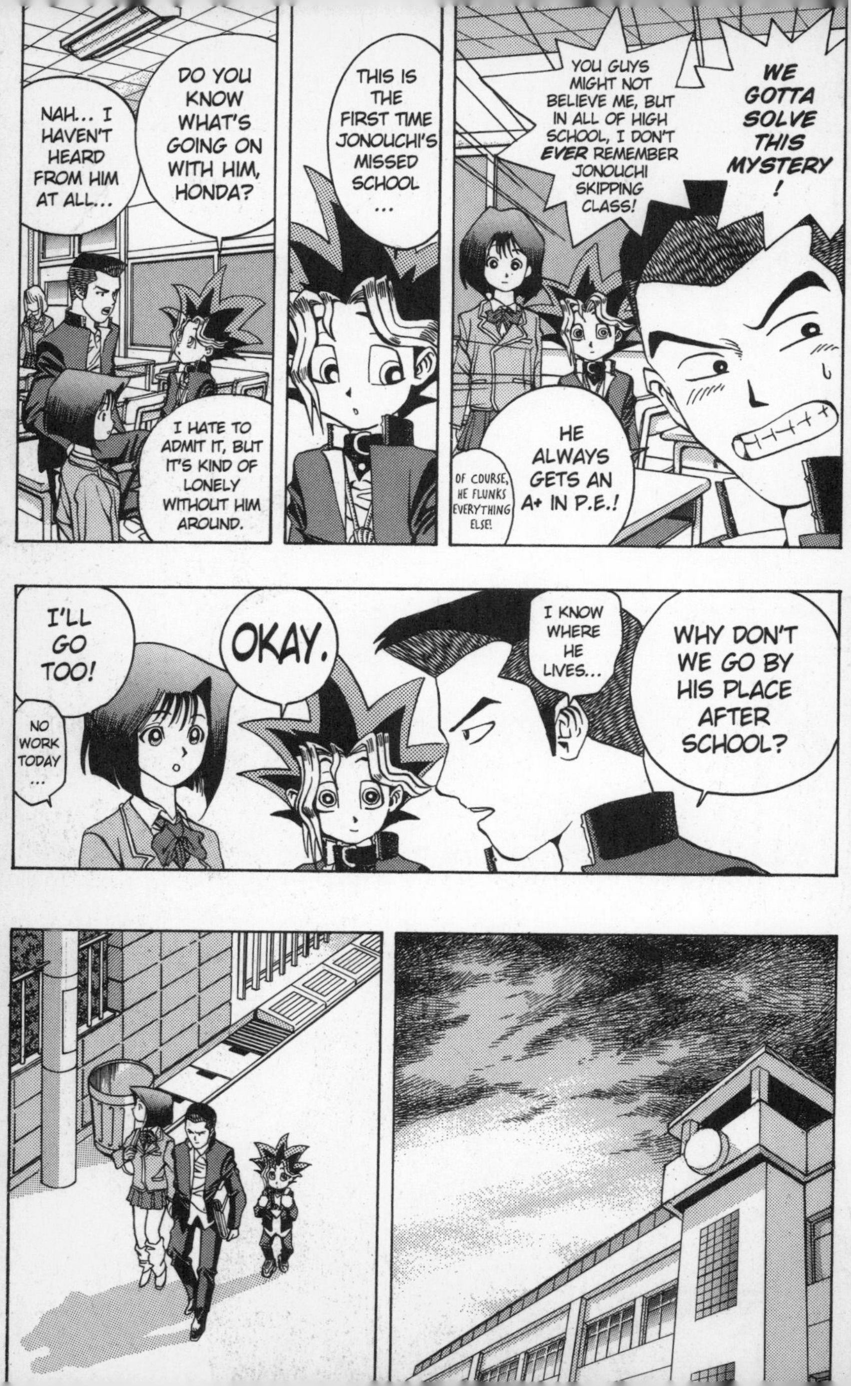
WE GOTTA SOLVE THIS MYSTERY!
YOU GUYS MIGHT NOT BELIEVE ME, BUT IN ALL OF HIGH SCHOOL, I DON'T EVER REMEMBER JONOUCHI SKIPPING CLASS!
HE ALWAYS GETS AN A+ IN P.E.!
OF COURSE, HE FLUNKS EVERYTHING ELSE!
THIS IS THE FIRST TIME JONOUCHI'S MISSED SCHOOL ...
DO YOU KNOW WHAT'S GOING ON WITH HIM, HONDA?
NAH... I HAVEN'T HEARD FROM HIM AT ALL...
I HATE TO ADMIT IT, BUT IT'S KIND OF LONELY WITHOUT HIM AROUND.
WHY DON'T WE GO BY HIS PLACE AFTER SCHOOL?
I KNOW WHERE HE LIVES...
OKAY.
I'LL GO TOO!
NO WORK TODAY ...

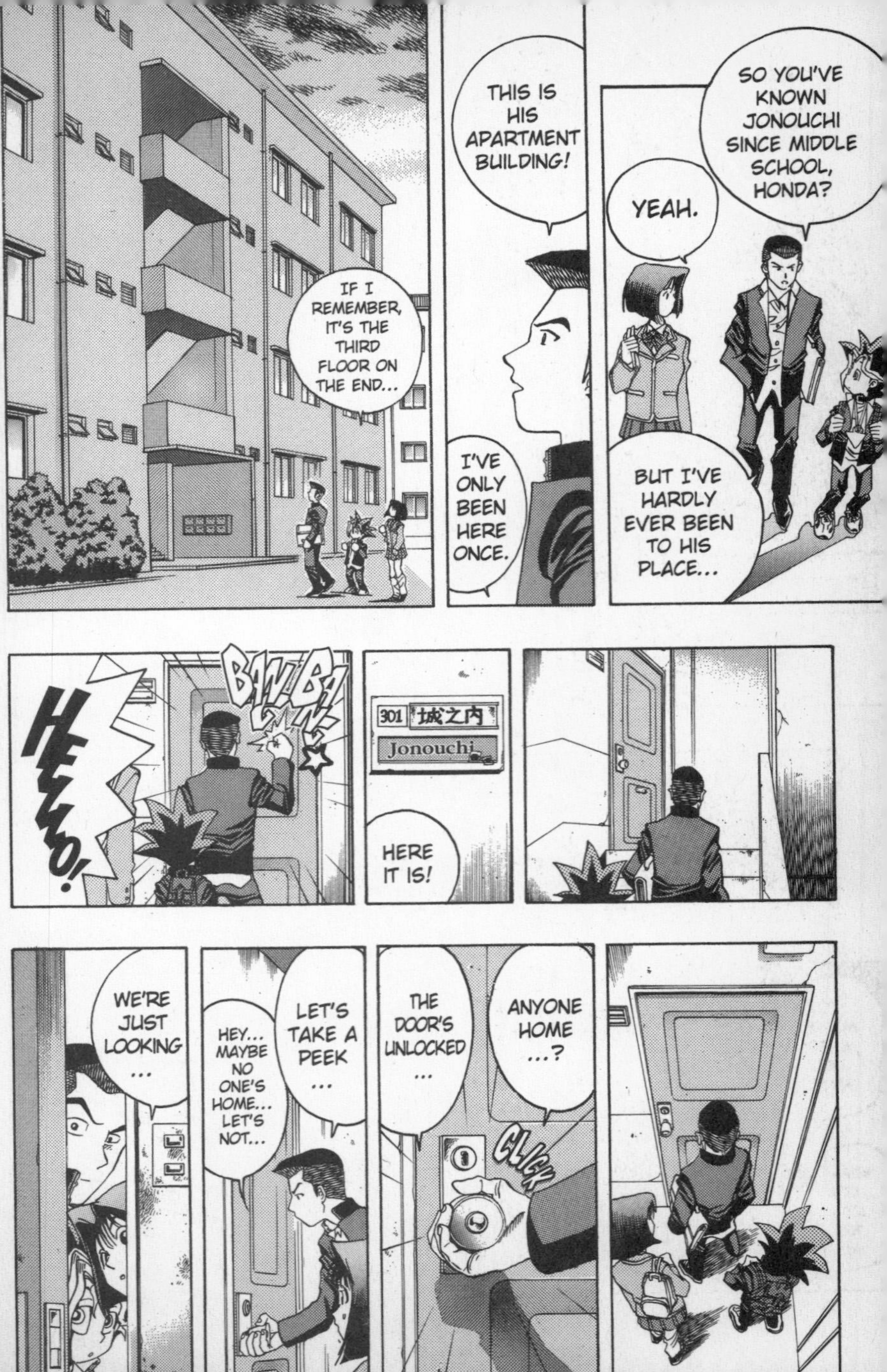
SO YOU'VE KNOWN JONOUCHI SINCE MIDDLE SCHOOL, HONDA?
YEAH.
BUT I'VE HARDLY EVER BEEN TO HIS PLACE...
THIS IS HIS APARTMENT BUILDING!
I'VE ONLY BEEN HERE ONCE.
IF I REMEMBER, IT'S THE THIRD FLOOR ON THE END...
301 城之内
Jonouchi
HERE IT IS!
BAN BAN
HELLO!
ANYONE HOME ...?
CLICK
THE DOOR'S UNLOCKED ...
LET'S TAKE A PEEK ...
HEY... MAYBE NO ONE'S HOME... LET'S NOT...
WE'RE JUST LOOKING ...

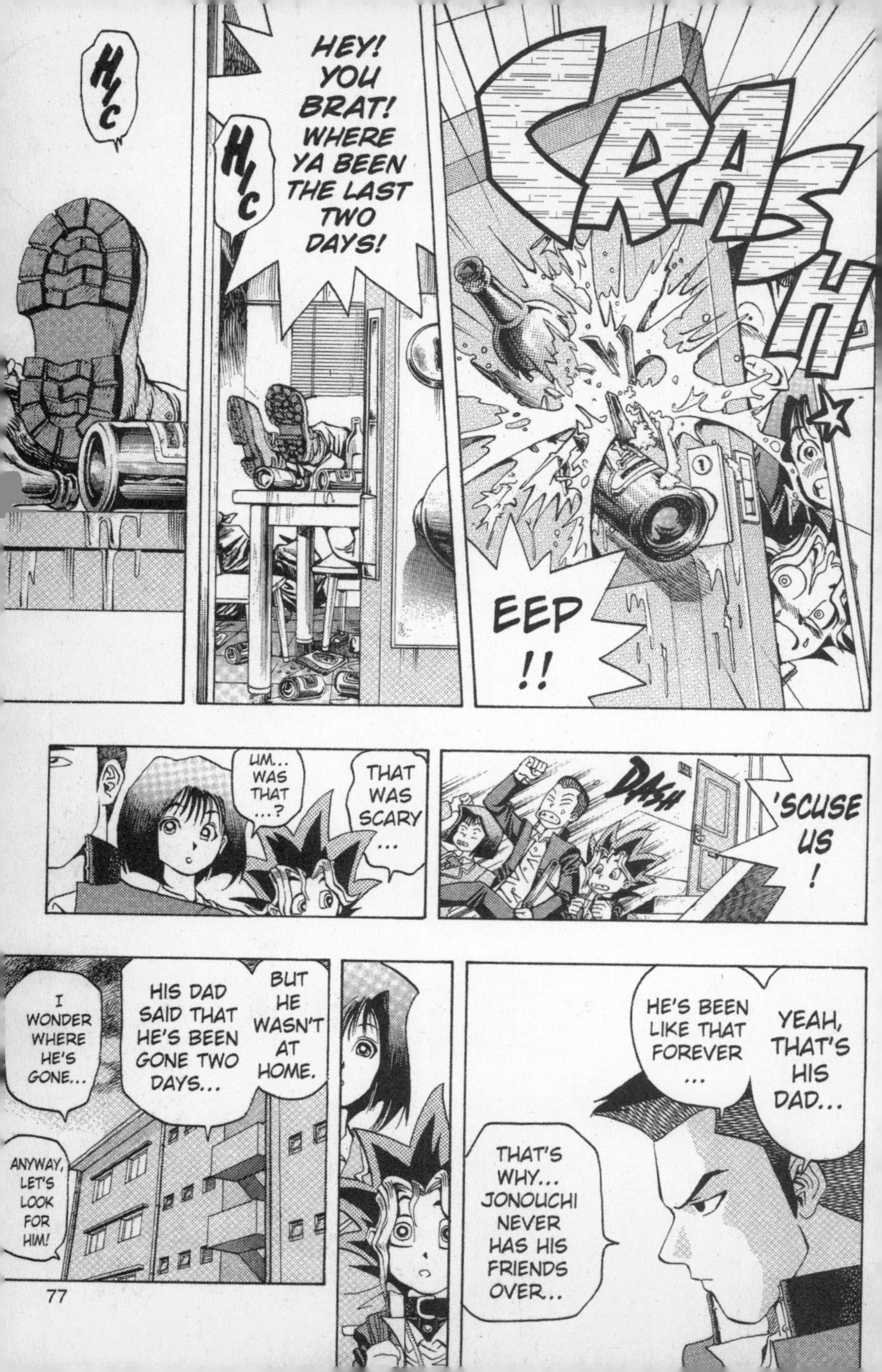
CRASH
EEP!!
HEY! YOU BRAT! WHERE YA BEEN THE LAST TWO DAYS!
HIC
HIC
'SCUSE US!
DASH
THAT WAS SCARY...
UM... WAS THAT...?
YEAH, THAT'S HIS DAD...
HE'S BEEN LIKE THAT FOREVER...
THAT'S WHY... JONOUCHI NEVER HAS HIS FRIENDS OVER...
BUT HE WASN'T AT HOME.
HIS DAD SAID THAT HE'S BEEN GONE TWO DAYS...
I WONDER WHERE HE'S GONE...
ANYWAY, LET'S LOOK FOR HIM!

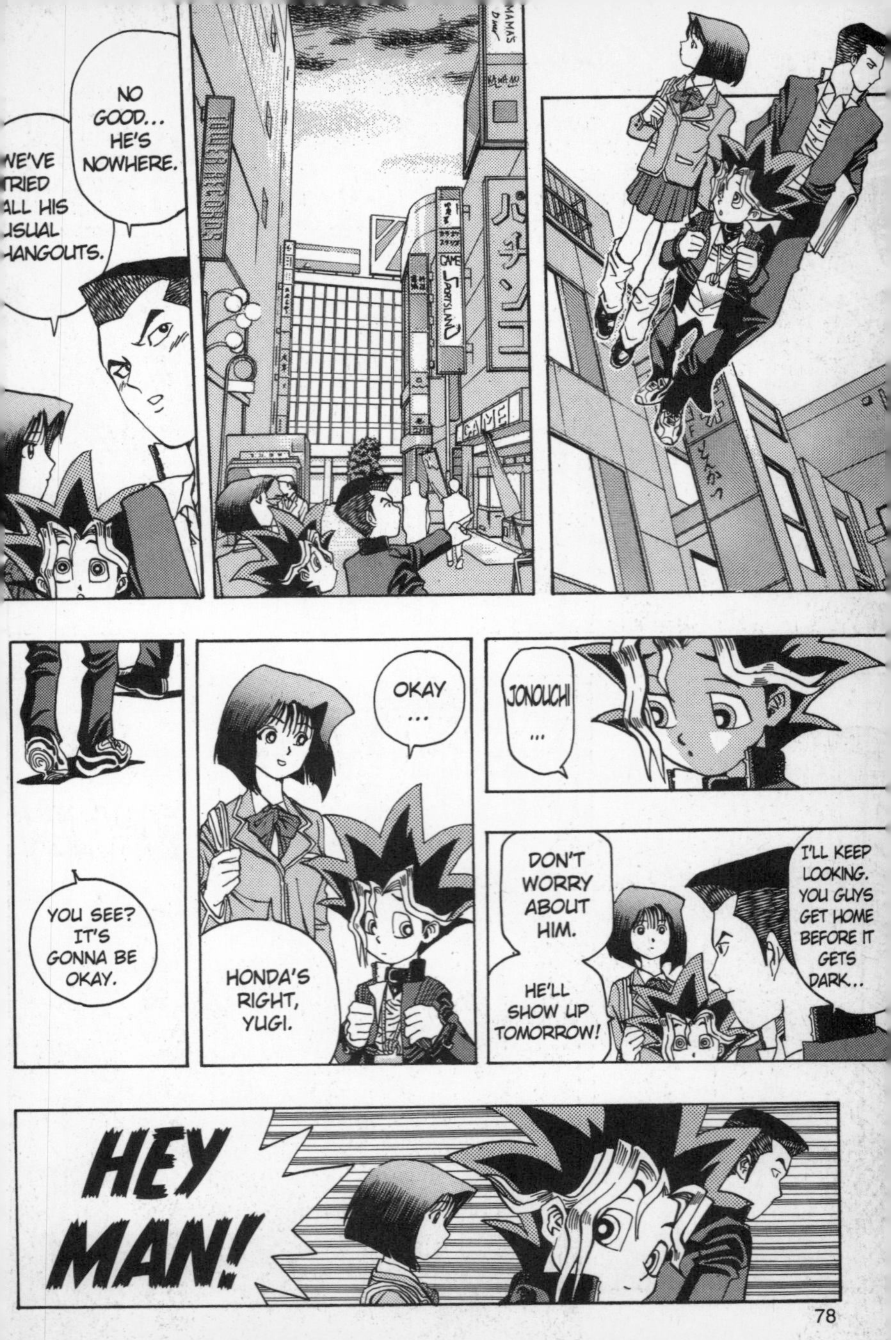
NO GOOD... HE'S NOWHERE.
WE'VE TRIED ALL HIS USUAL HANGOUTS.
JONOUCHI ...
I'LL KEEP LOOKING. YOU GUYS GET HOME BEFORE IT GETS DARK...
DON'T WORRY ABOUT HIM.
HE'LL SHOW UP TOMORROW!
OKAY ...
HONDA'S RIGHT, YUGI.
YOU SEE? IT'S GONNA BE OKAY.
HEY MAN!

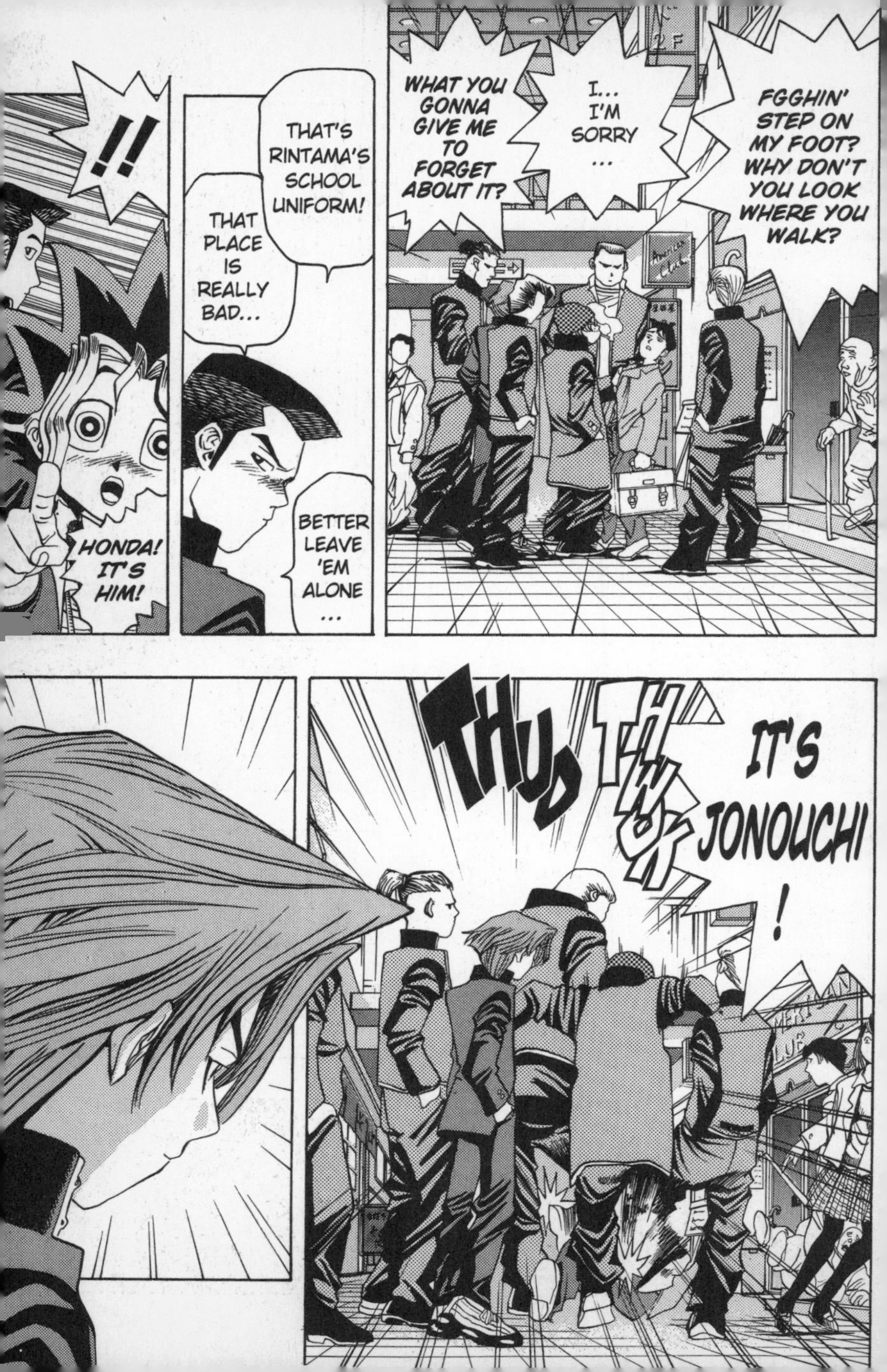

FGGHIN' STEP ON MY FOOT? WHY DON'T YOU LOOK WHERE YOU WALK?
I... I'M SORRY ...
WHAT YOU GONNA GIVE ME TO FORGET ABOUT IT?
THAT'S RINTAMA'S SCHOOL UNIFORM!
THAT PLACE IS REALLY BAD...
BETTER LEAVE 'EM ALONE ...
!!
HONDA! IT'S HIM!
IT'S JONOUCHI !
THUNK
THUD

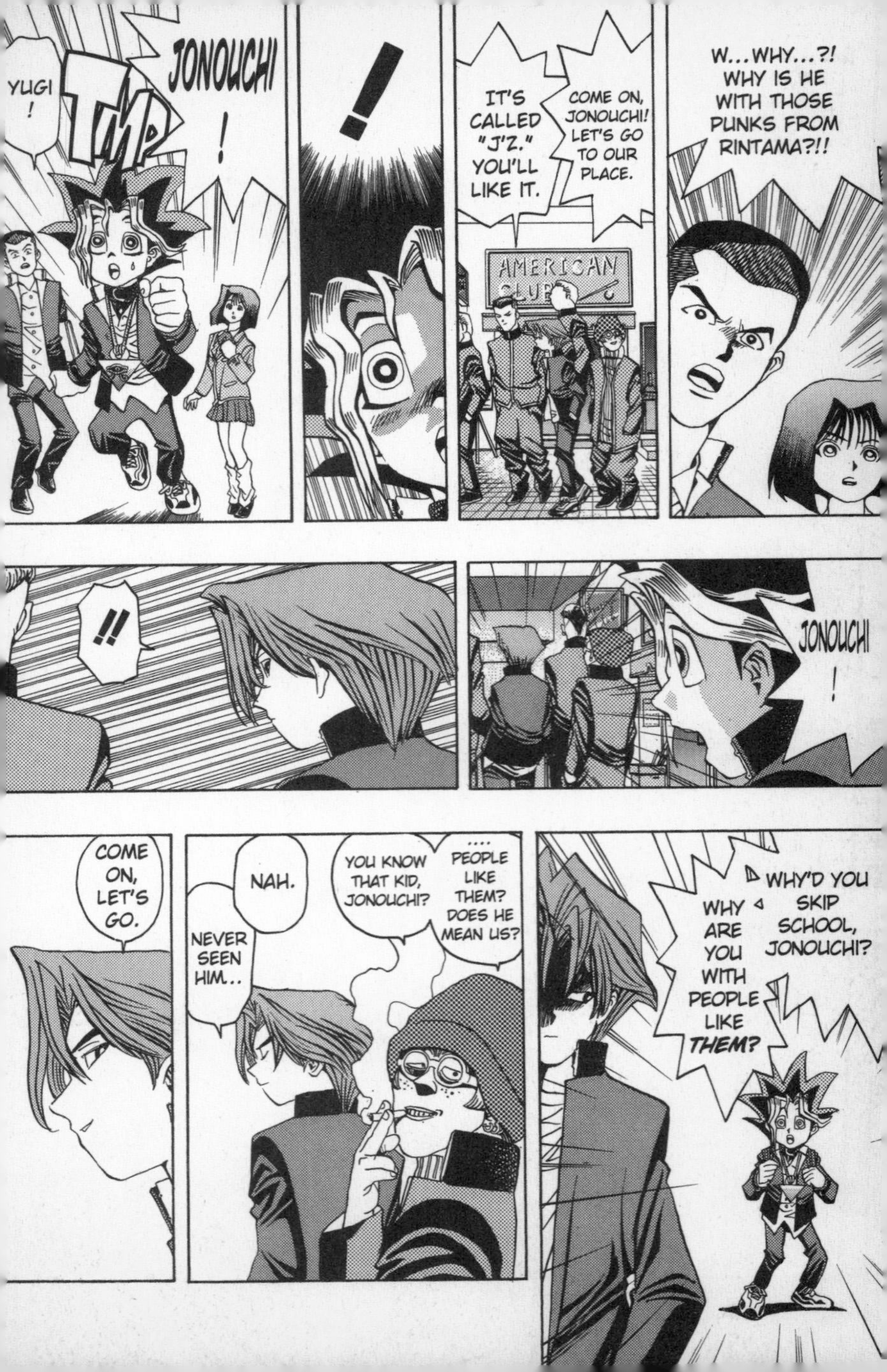
W...WHY...?! WHY IS HE WITH THOSE PUNKS FROM RINTAMA?!!
COME ON, JONOUCHI! LET'S GO TO OUR PLACE.
IT'S CALLED "J'Z." YOU'LL LIKE IT.
AMERICAN CLUB
!
JONOUCHI !
TMP
YUGI !
JONOUCHI !
!!
WHY'D YOU SKIP SCHOOL, JONOUCHI?
WHY ARE YOU WITH PEOPLE LIKE *THEM?*
.... PEOPLE LIKE THEM? DOES HE MEAN US?
YOU KNOW THAT KID, JONOUCHI?
NAH.
NEVER SEEN HIM...
COME ON, LET'S GO.

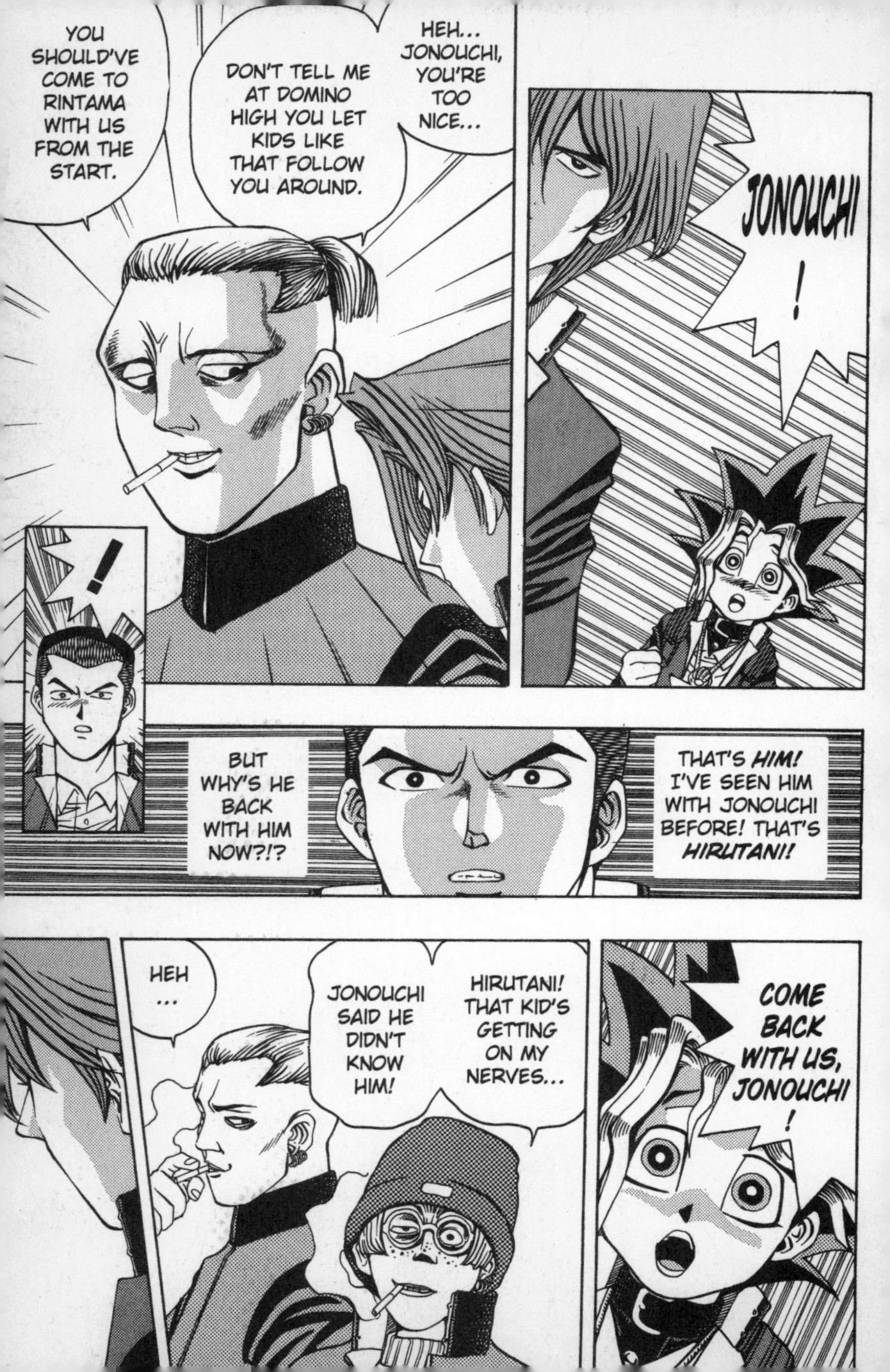
JONOUCHI !
HEH... JONOUCHI, YOU'RE TOO NICE...
DON'T TELL ME AT DOMINO HIGH YOU LET KIDS LIKE THAT FOLLOW YOU AROUND.
YOU SHOULD'VE COME TO RINTAMA WITH US FROM THE START.
!
THAT'S *HIM!* I'VE SEEN HIM WITH JONOUCHI BEFORE! THAT'S *HIRUTANI!*
BUT WHY'S HE BACK WITH HIM NOW?!?
COME BACK WITH US, JONOUCHI !
HIRUTANI! THAT KID'S GETTING ON MY NERVES...
JONOUCHI SAID HE DIDN'T KNOW HIM!
HEH ...

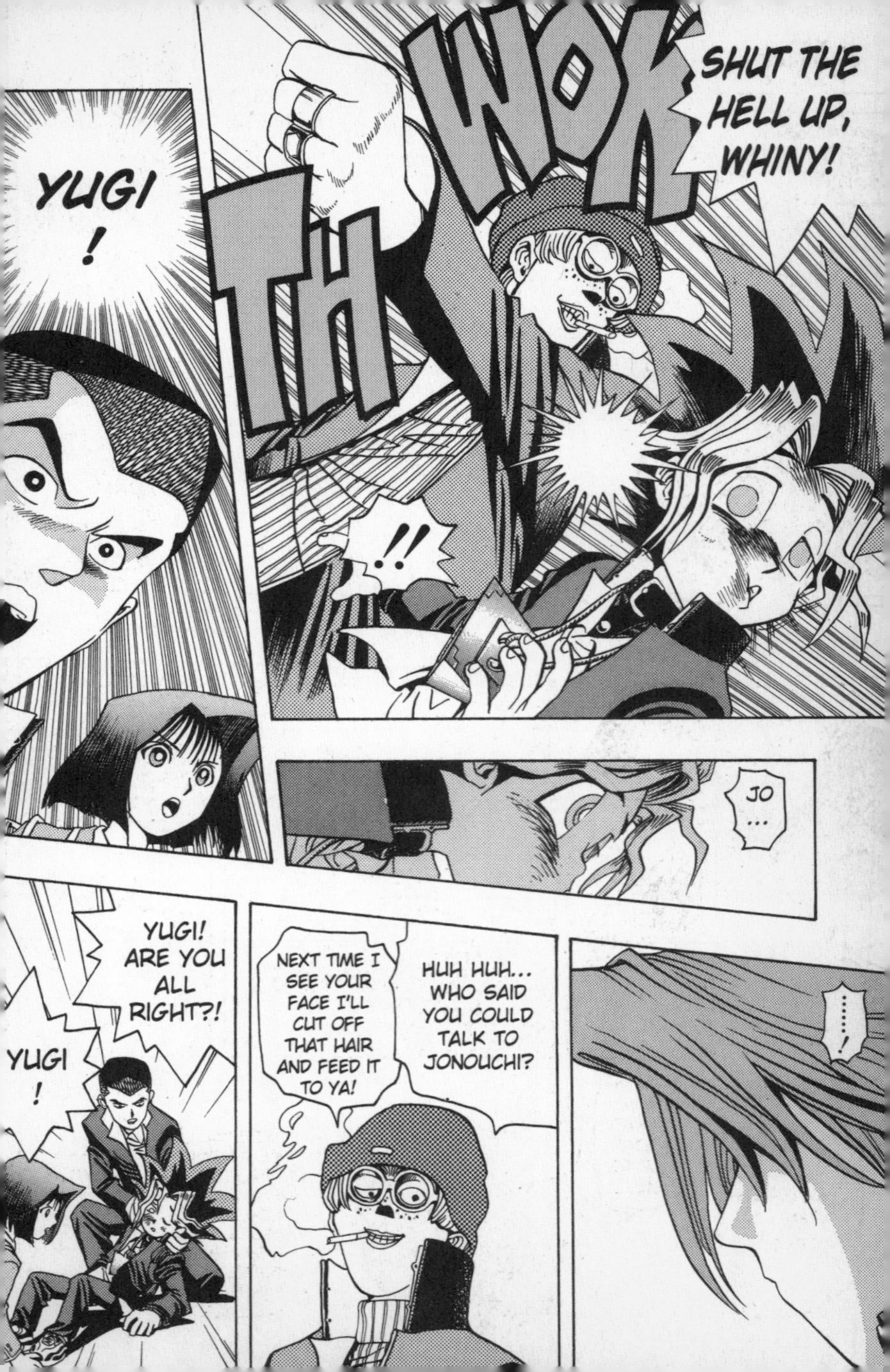
THWOK
SHUT THE HELL UP, WHINY!
!!
JO ...
YUGI !
......!
HUH HUH... WHO SAID YOU COULD TALK TO JONOUCHI?
NEXT TIME I SEE YOUR FACE I'LL CUT OFF THAT HAIR AND FEED IT TO YA!
YUGI! ARE YOU ALL RIGHT?!
YUGI !

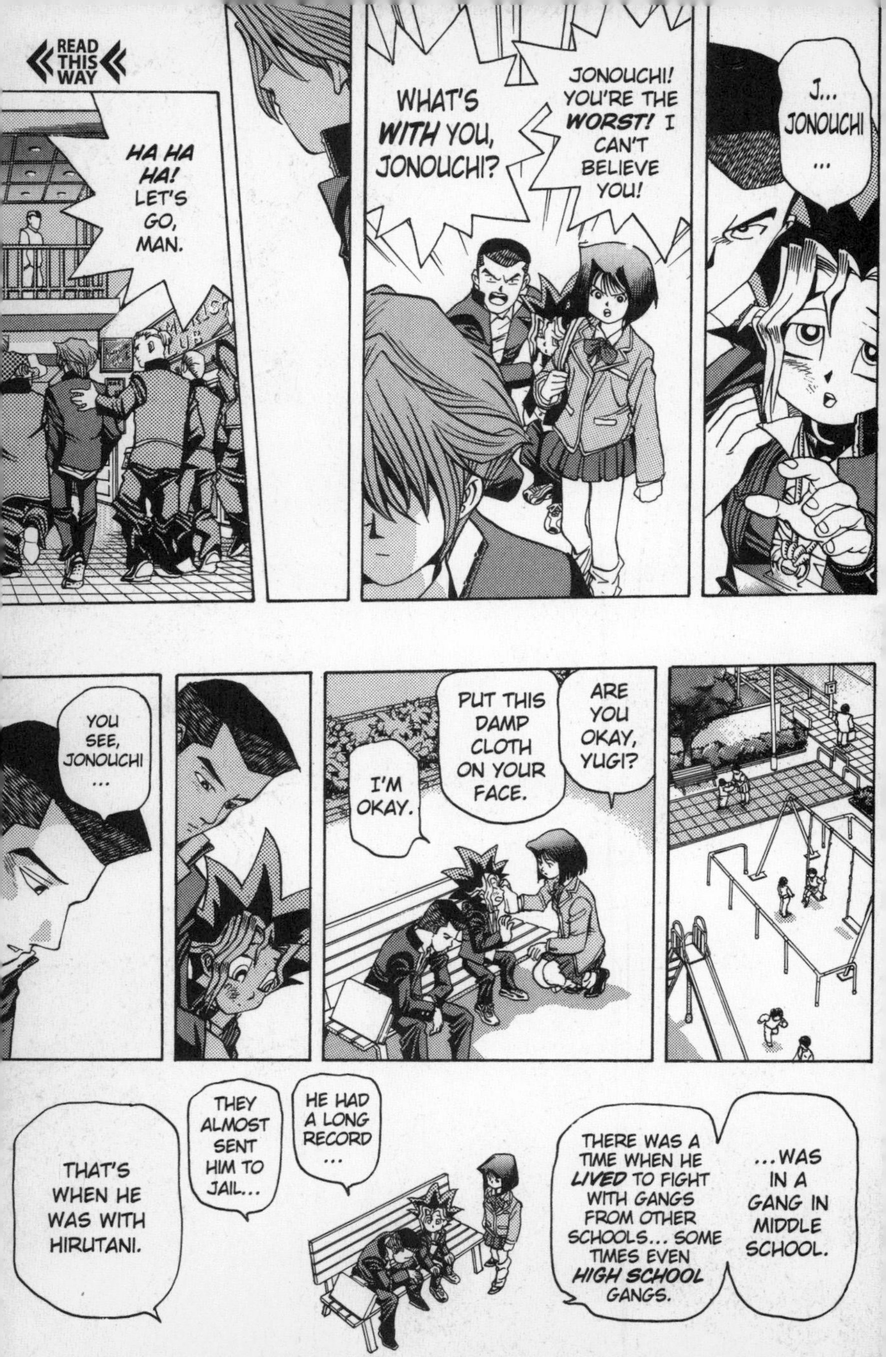
READ THIS WAY
J... JONOUCHI ...
JONOUCHI! YOU'RE THE WORST! I CAN'T BELIEVE YOU!
WHAT'S WITH YOU, JONOUCHI?
HA HA HA! LET'S GO, MAN.
ARE YOU OKAY, YUGI?
PUT THIS DAMP CLOTH ON YOUR FACE.
I'M OKAY.
YOU SEE, JONOUCHI ...
...WAS IN A GANG IN MIDDLE SCHOOL.
THERE WAS A TIME WHEN HE LIVED TO FIGHT WITH GANGS FROM OTHER SCHOOLS... SOME TIMES EVEN HIGH SCHOOL GANGS.
HE HAD A LONG RECORD ...
THEY ALMOST SENT HIM TO JAIL...
THAT'S WHEN HE WAS WITH HIRUTANI.

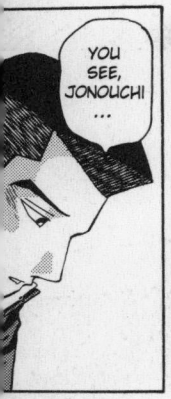

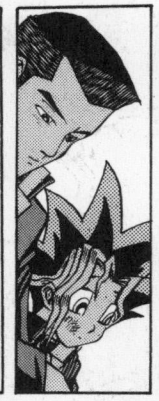

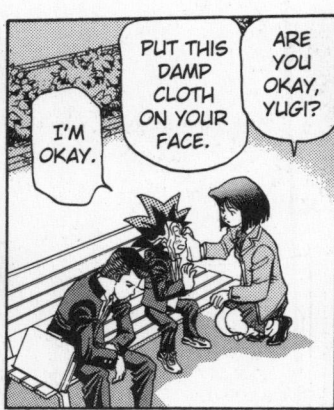

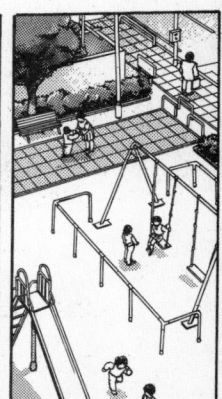

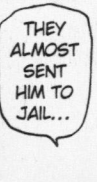

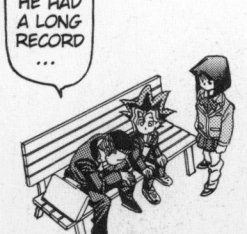

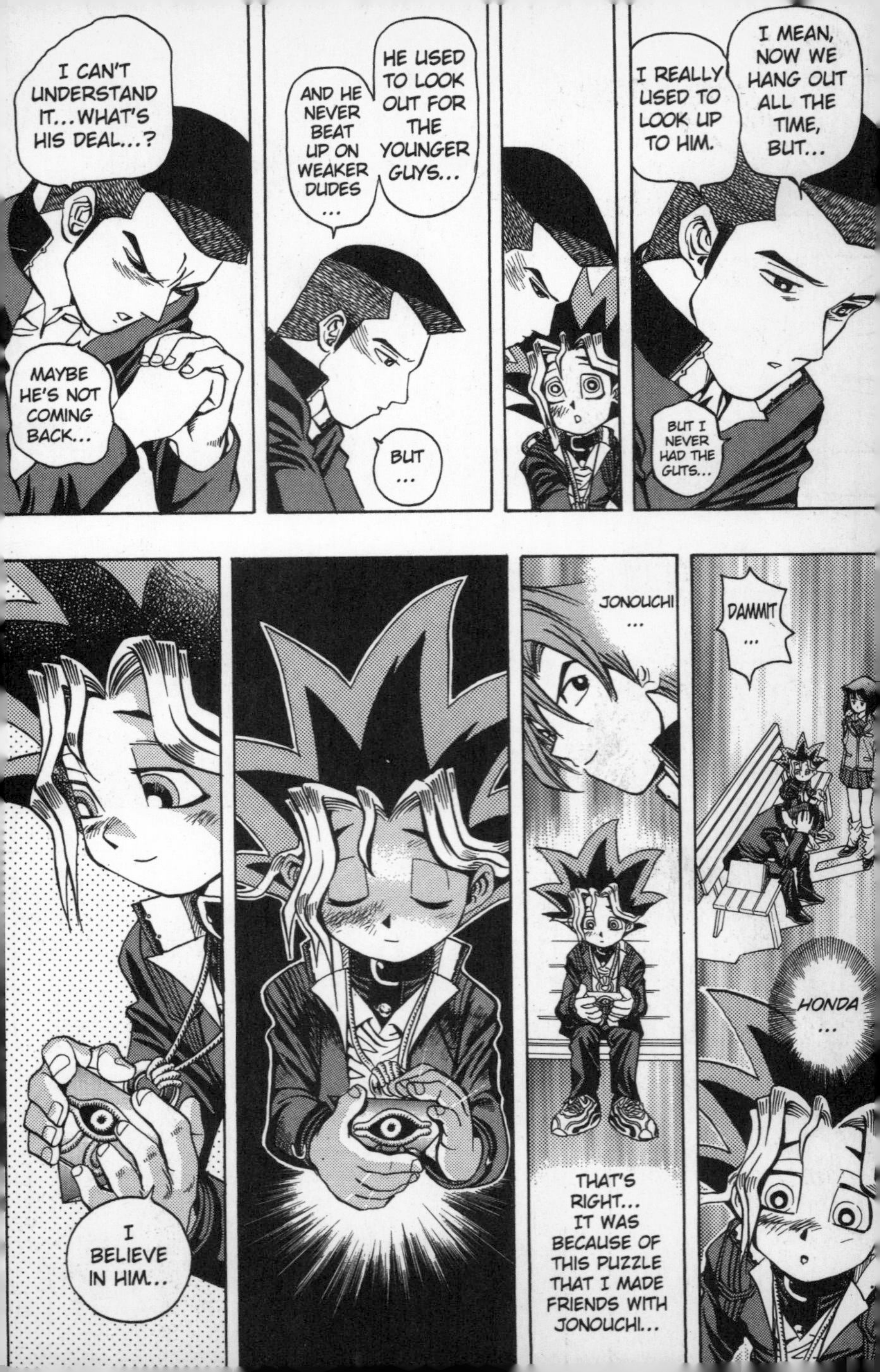
I MEAN, NOW WE HANG OUT ALL THE TIME, BUT...
I REALLY USED TO LOOK UP TO HIM.
BUT I NEVER HAD THE GUTS...
HE USED TO LOOK OUT FOR THE YOUNGER GUYS...
AND HE NEVER BEAT UP ON WEAKER DUDES ...
BUT ...
I CAN'T UNDERSTAND IT...WHAT'S HIS DEAL...?
MAYBE HE'S NOT COMING BACK...
DAMMIT ...
HONDA ...
JONOUCHI ...
THAT'S RIGHT... IT WAS BECAUSE OF THIS PUZZLE THAT I MADE FRIENDS WITH JONOUCHI...
I BELIEVE IN HIM...

READ THIS WAY

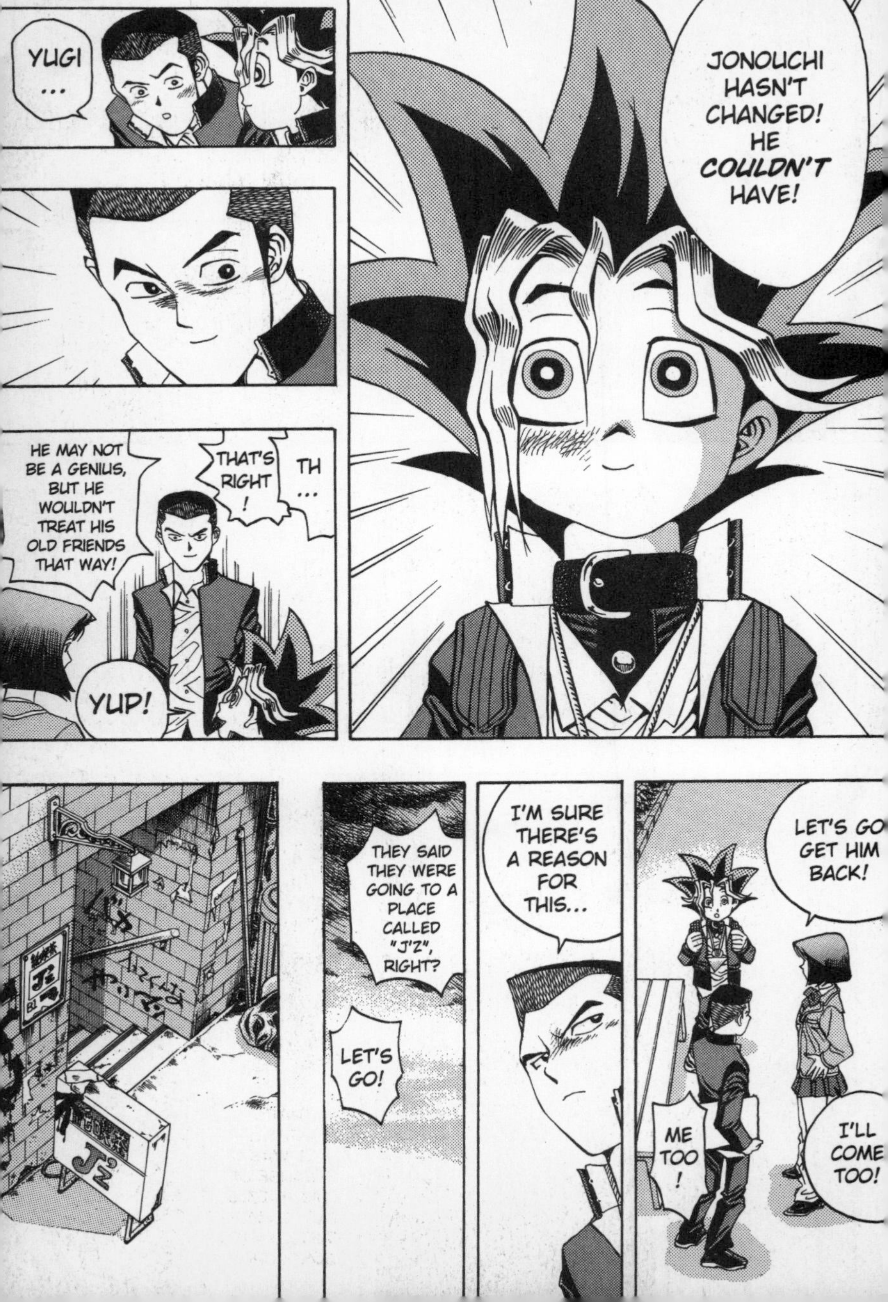
JONOUCHI HASN'T CHANGED! HE COULDN'T HAVE!
YUGI ...
TH ...
THAT'S RIGHT !
HE MAY NOT BE A GENIUS, BUT HE WOULDN'T TREAT HIS OLD FRIENDS THAT WAY!
YUP!
LET'S GO GET HIM BACK!
I'LL COME TOO!
ME TOO !
I'M SURE THERE'S A REASON FOR THIS...
THEY SAID THEY WERE GOING TO A PLACE CALLED "J'Z", RIGHT?
LET'S GO!

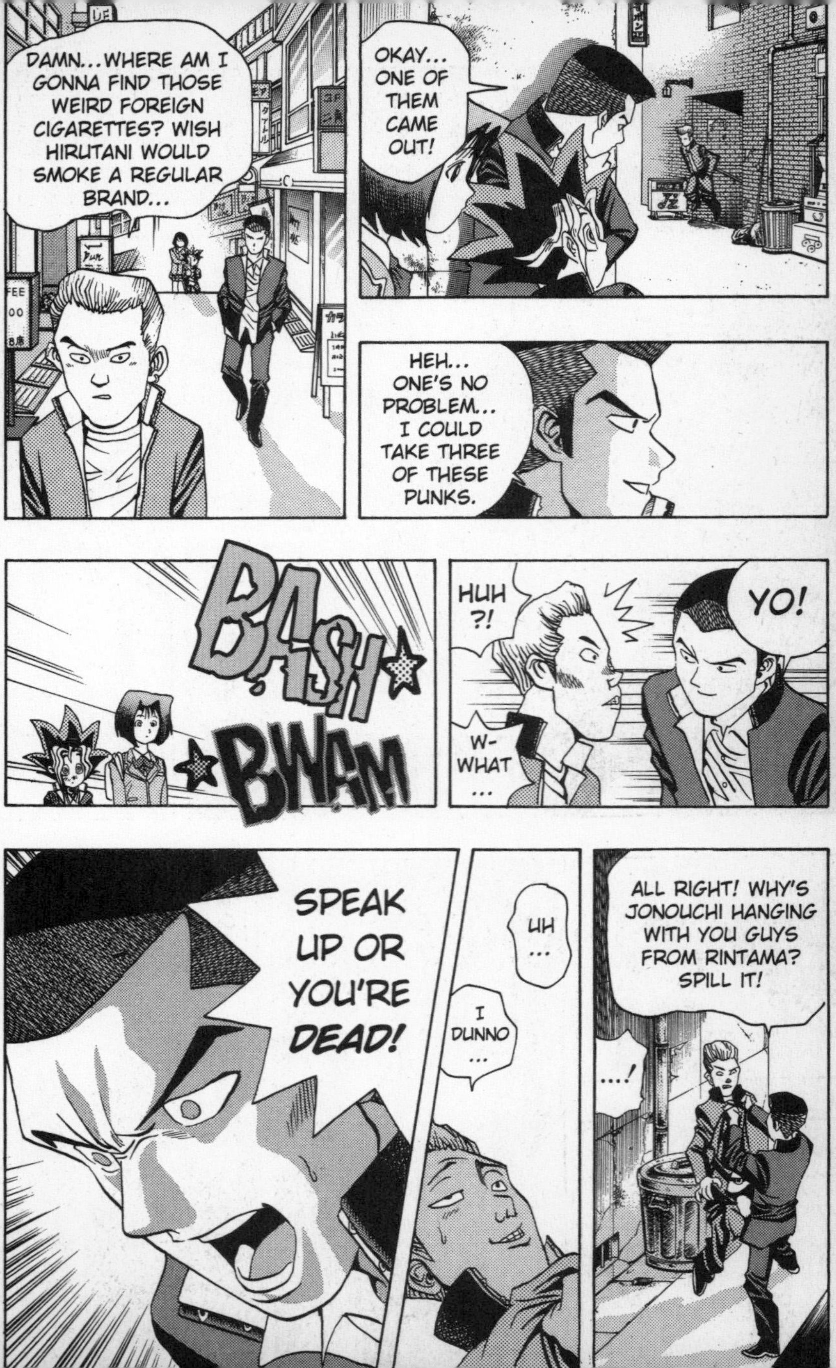
OKAY... ONE OF THEM CAME OUT!
HEH... ONE'S NO PROBLEM... I COULD TAKE THREE OF THESE PUNKS.
DAMN...WHERE AM I GONNA FIND THOSE WEIRD FOREIGN CIGARETTES? WISH HIRUTANI WOULD SMOKE A REGULAR BRAND...
YO!
HUH ?!
W- WHAT ...
BASH
BWAM
ALL RIGHT! WHY'S JONOUCHI HANGING WITH YOU GUYS FROM RINTAMA? SPILL IT!
...!
UH ...
I DUNNO ...
SPEAK UP OR YOU'RE *DEAD!*

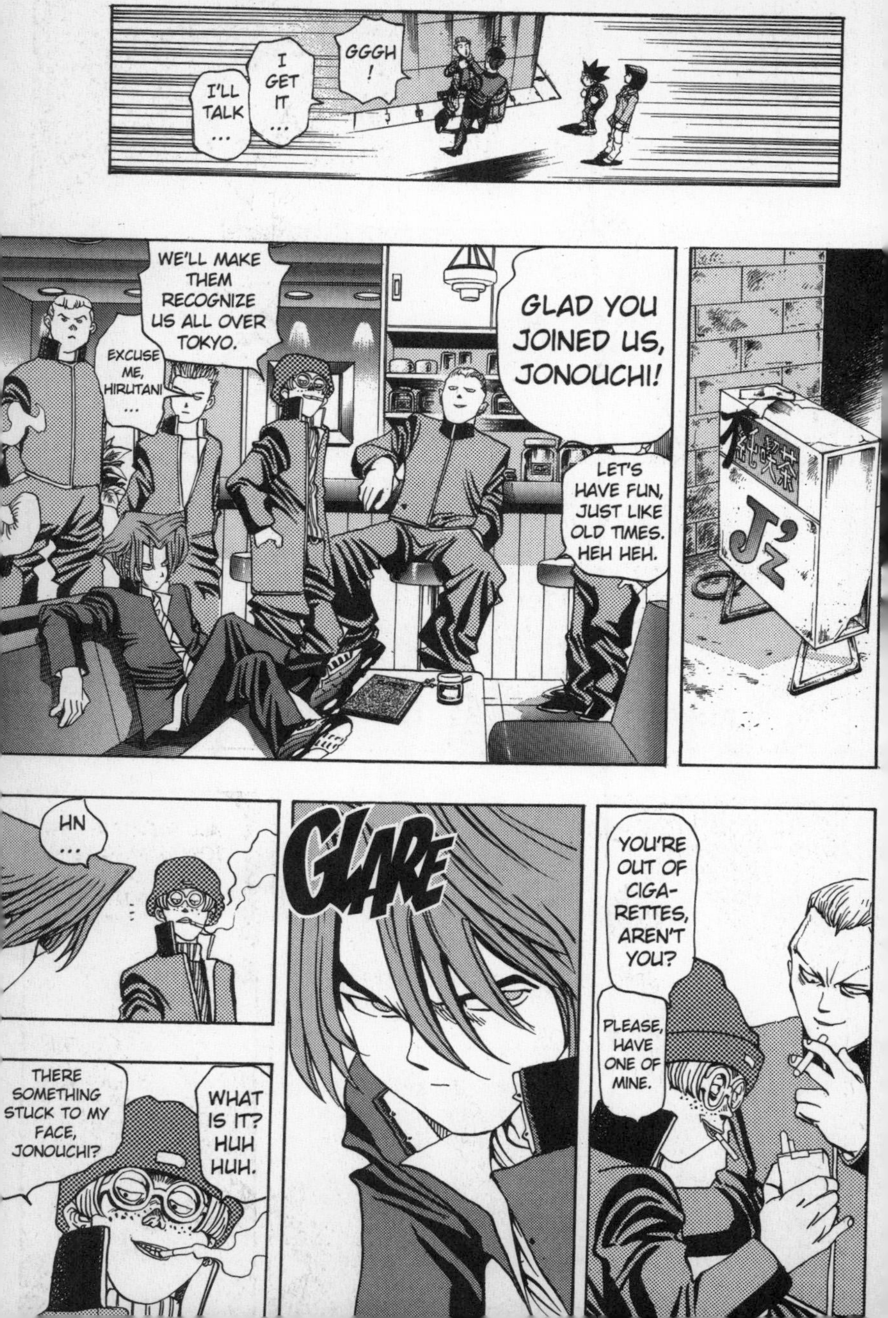
GGGH !
I GET IT ...
I'LL TALK ...
J'z
GLAD YOU JOINED US, JONOUCHI!
LET'S HAVE FUN, JUST LIKE OLD TIMES. HEH HEH.
WE'LL MAKE THEM RECOGNIZE US ALL OVER TOKYO.
EXCUSE ME, HIRUTANI ...
YOU'RE OUT OF CIGA-RETTES, AREN'T YOU?
PLEASE, HAVE ONE OF MINE.
GLARE
HN ...
WHAT IS IT? HUH HUH.
THERE SOMETHING STUCK TO MY FACE, JONOUCHI?

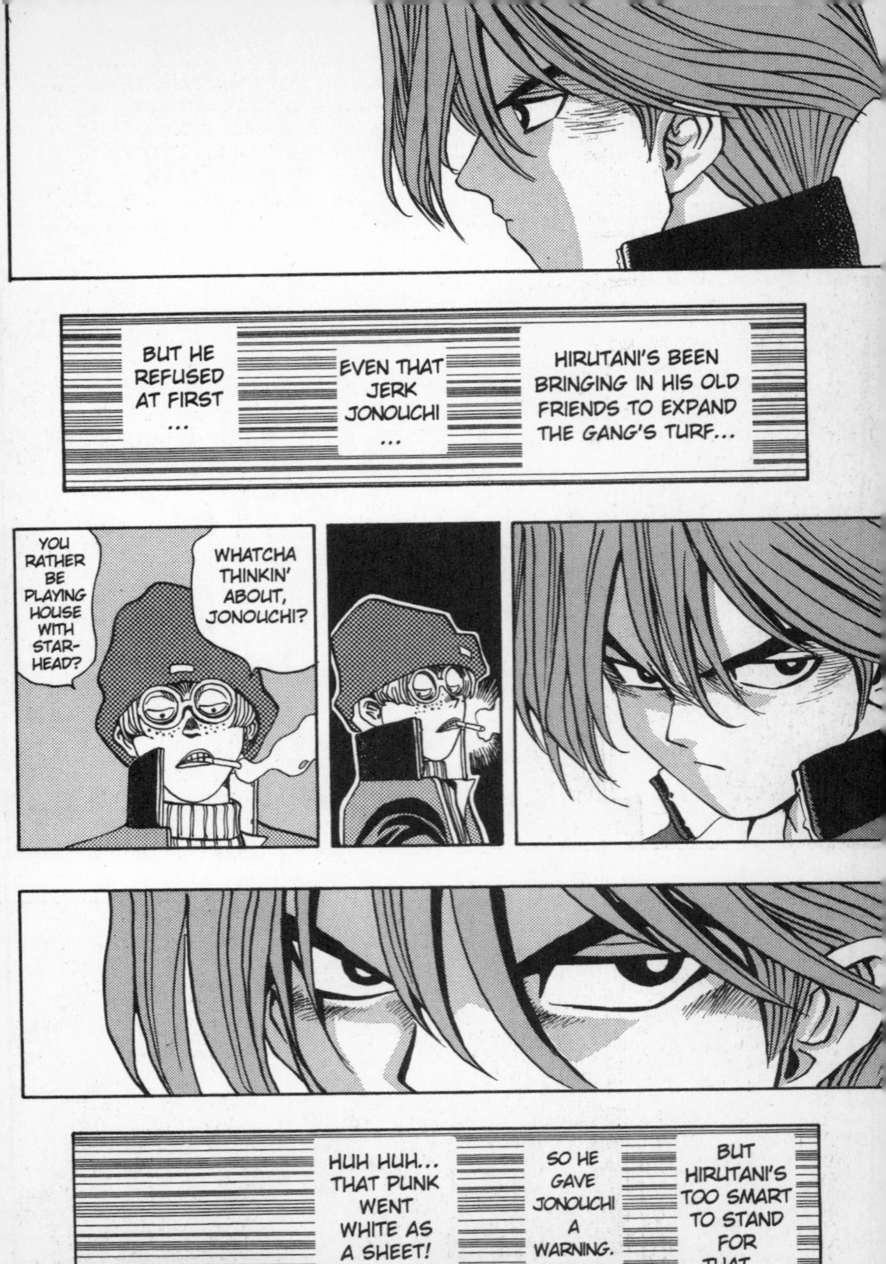
HIRUTANI'S BEEN BRINGING IN HIS OLD FRIENDS TO EXPAND THE GANG'S TURF...
EVEN THAT JERK JONOUCHI ...
BUT HE REFUSED AT FIRST ...
WHATCHA THINKIN' ABOUT, JONOUCHI?
YOU RATHER BE PLAYING HOUSE WITH STAR-HEAD?
BUT HIRUTANI'S TOO SMART TO STAND FOR THAT...
SO HE GAVE JONOUCHI A WARNING.
HUH HUH... THAT PUNK WENT WHITE AS A SHEET!

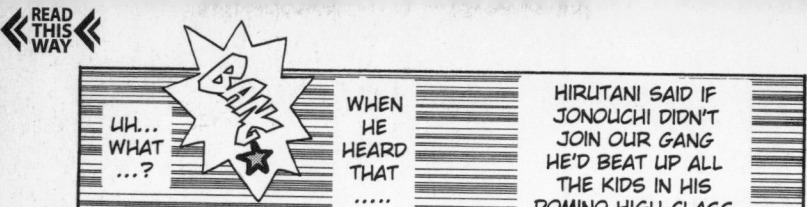

READ THIS WAY

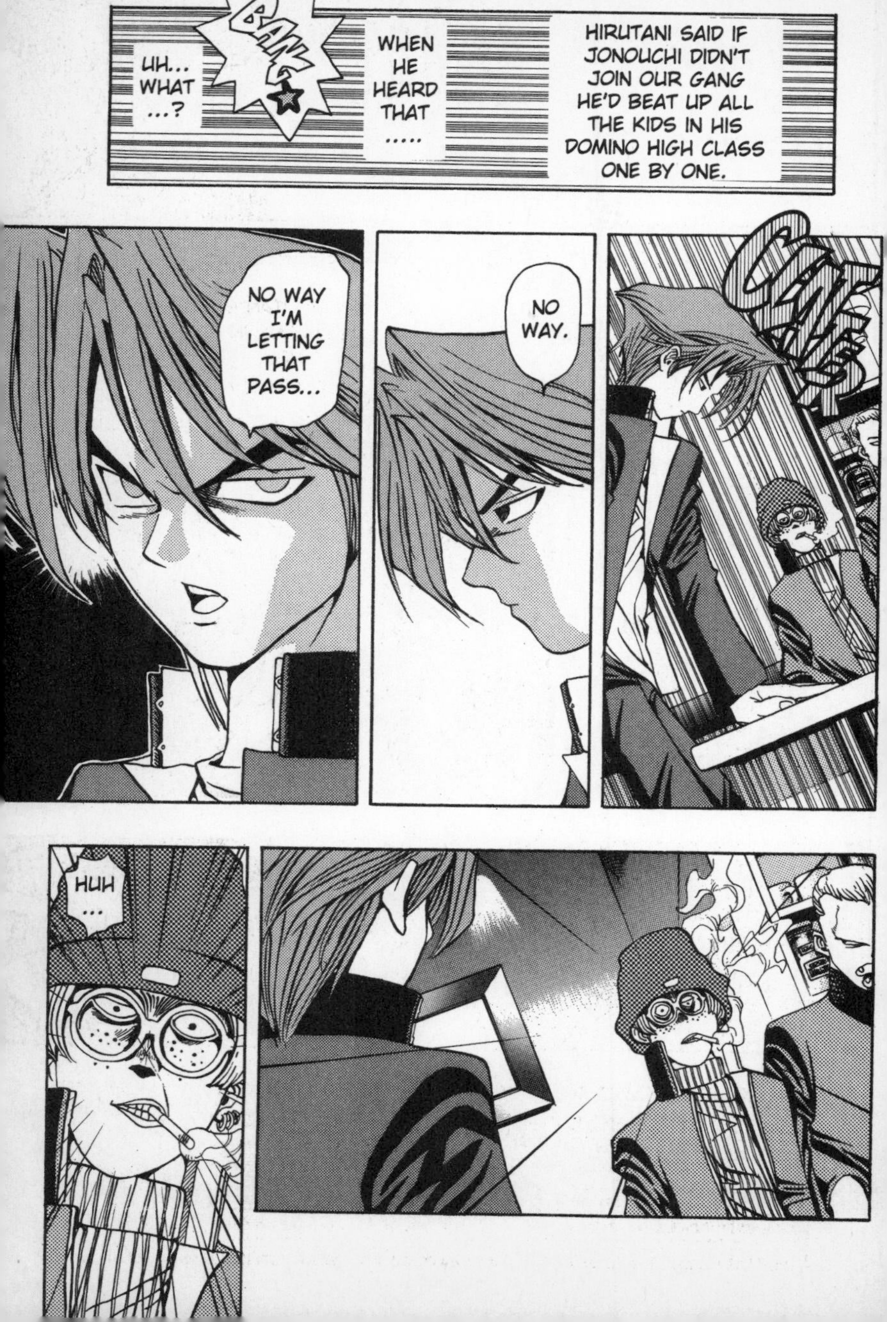
HIRUTANI SAID IF JONOUCHI DIDN'T JOIN OUR GANG HE'D BEAT UP ALL THE KIDS IN HIS DOMINO HIGH CLASS ONE BY ONE.
WHEN HE HEARD THAT .....
BANG
UH... WHAT ...?
NO WAY.
NO WAY I'M LETTING THAT PASS...
HUH ...

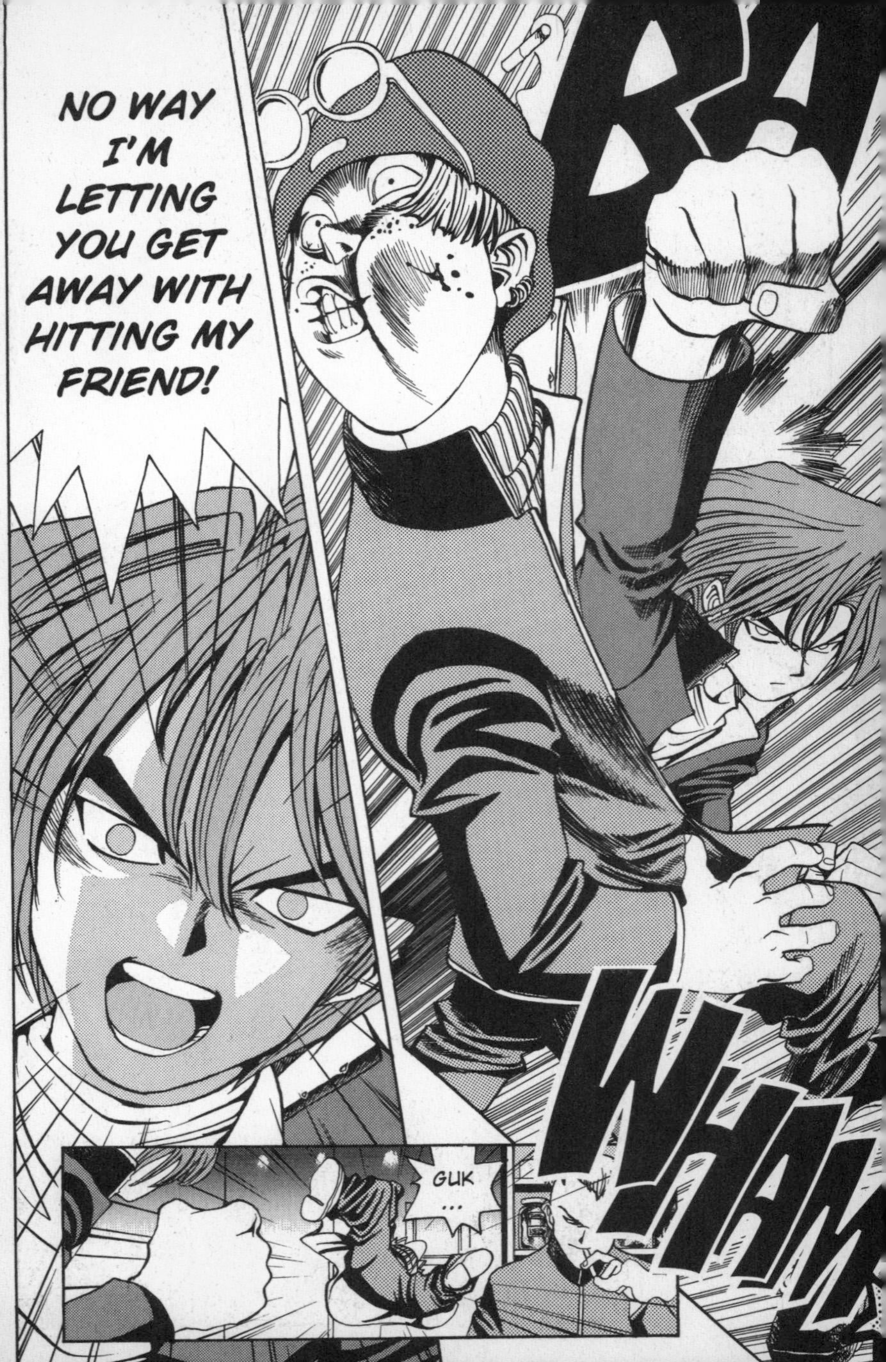
NO WAY I'M LETTING YOU GET AWAY WITH HITTING MY FRIEND!
GUK ...

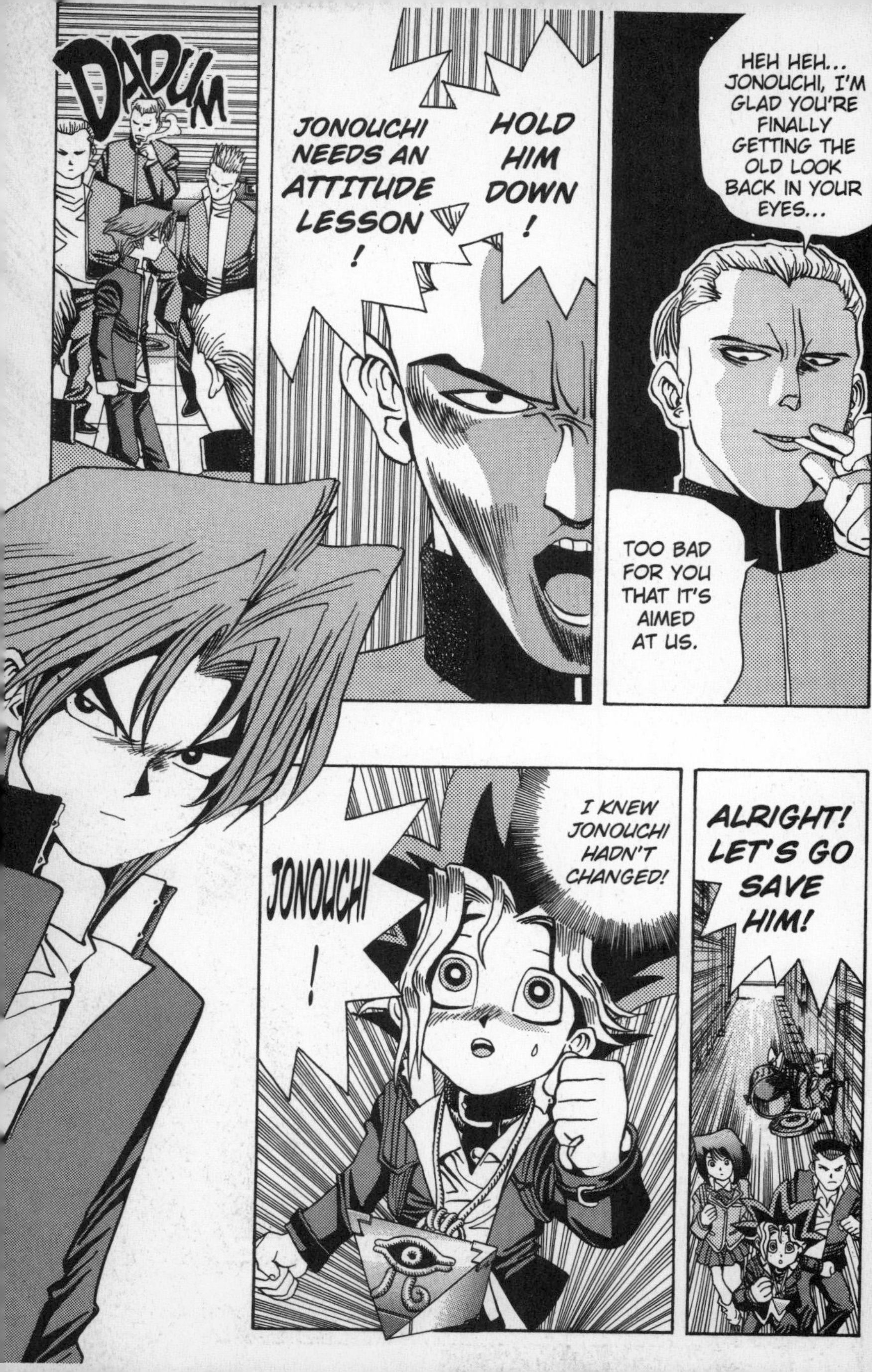
HEH HEH... JONOUCHI, I'M GLAD YOU'RE FINALLY GETTING THE OLD LOOK BACK IN YOUR EYES...
TOO BAD FOR YOU THAT IT'S AIMED AT US.
HOLD HIM DOWN!
JONOUCHI NEEDS AN ATTITUDE LESSON!
DADUM
ALRIGHT! LET'S GO SAVE HIM!
I KNEW JONOUCHI HADN'T CHANGED!
JONOUCHI!

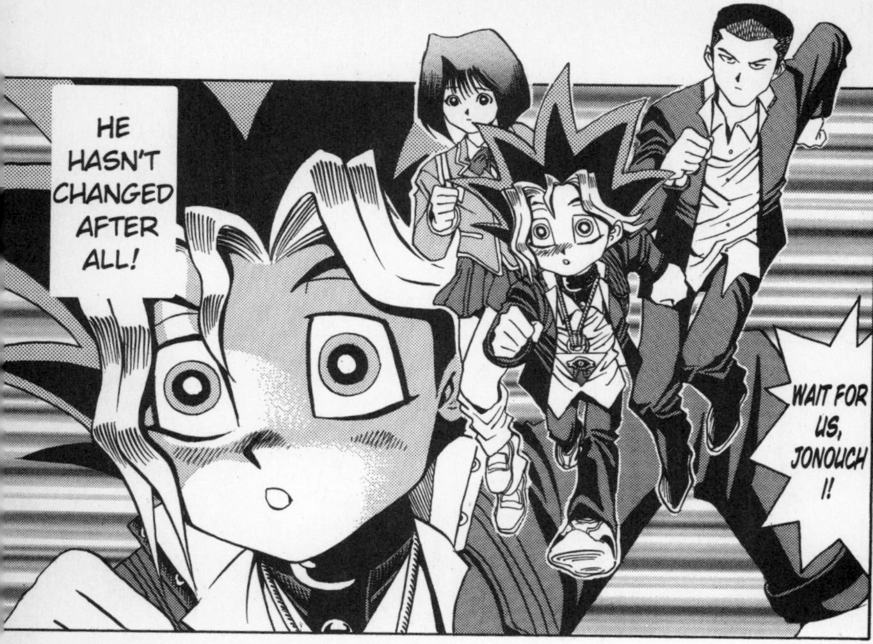
HE HASN'T CHANGED AFTER ALL!
WAIT FOR US, JONOUCHI!

Duel 12: The Wild Gang (Part 2)

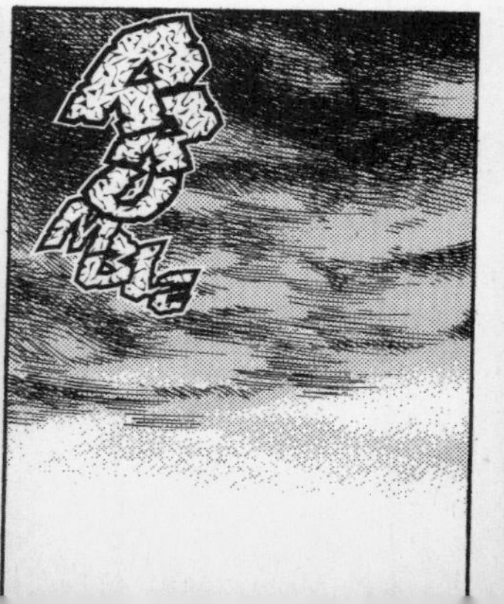

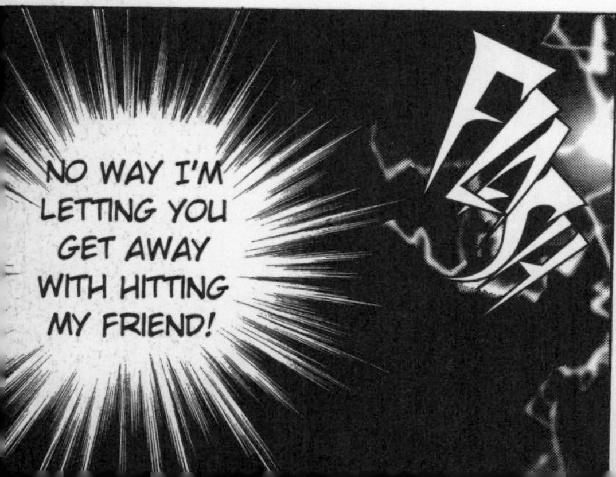
FLASH
NO WAY I'M LETTING YOU GET AWAY WITH HITTING MY FRIEND!

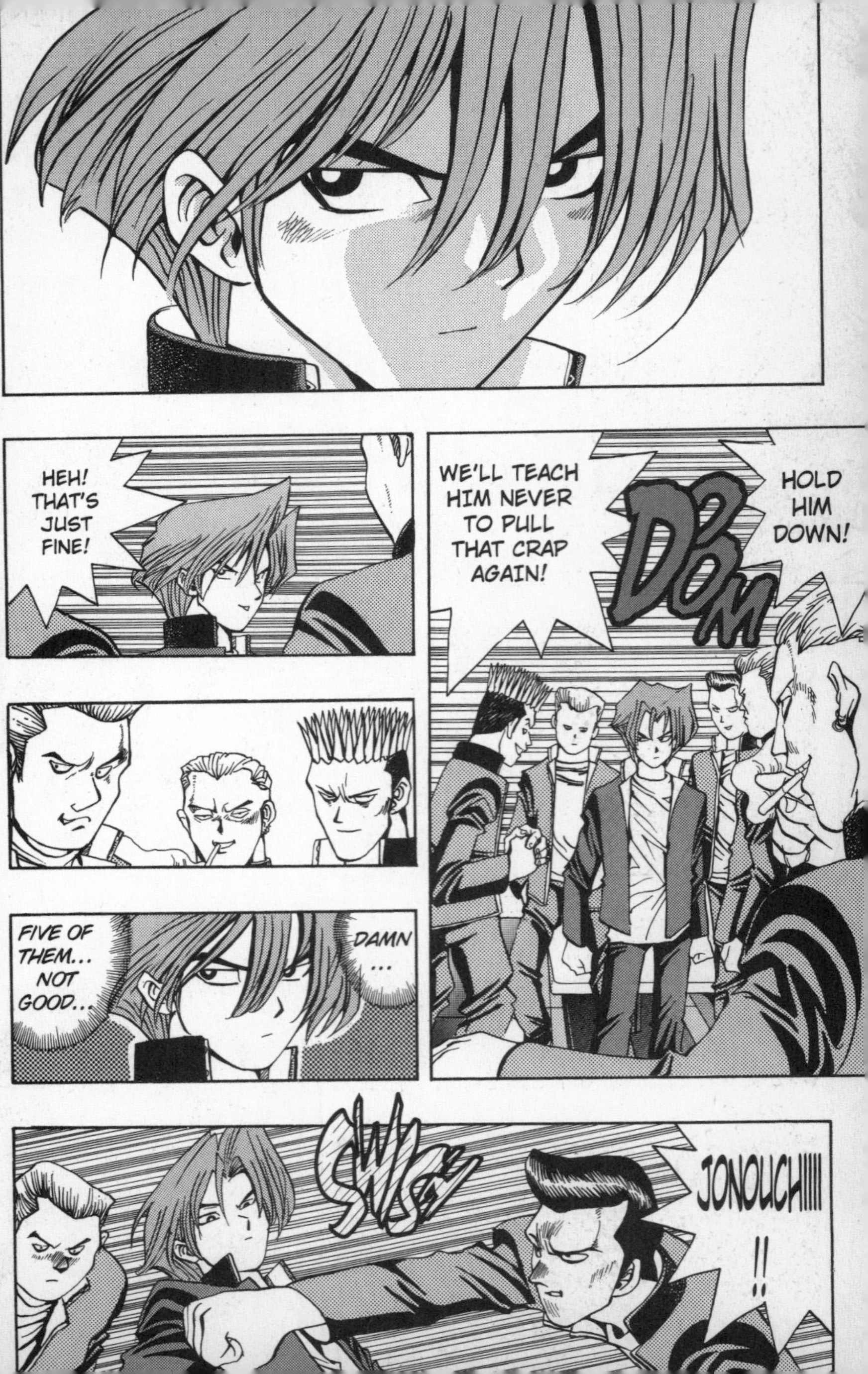
HEH! THAT'S JUST FINE!
FIVE OF THEM... NOT GOOD...
DAMN...
WE'LL TEACH HIM NEVER TO PULL THAT CRAP AGAIN!
DOOM
HOLD HIM DOWN!
JONOUCHIIIII!!

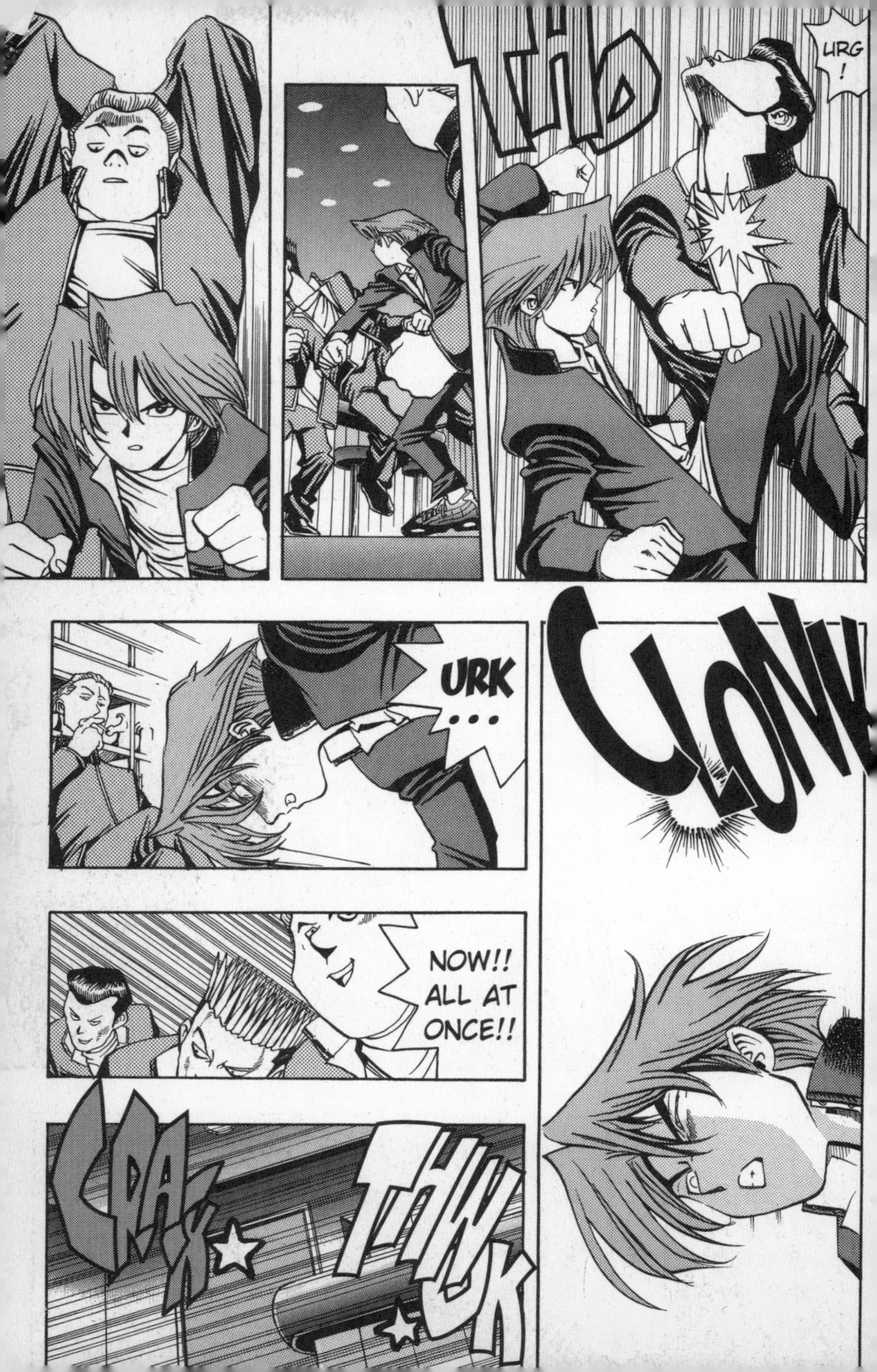
URG!
CLONK
URK...
NOW!! ALL AT ONCE!!

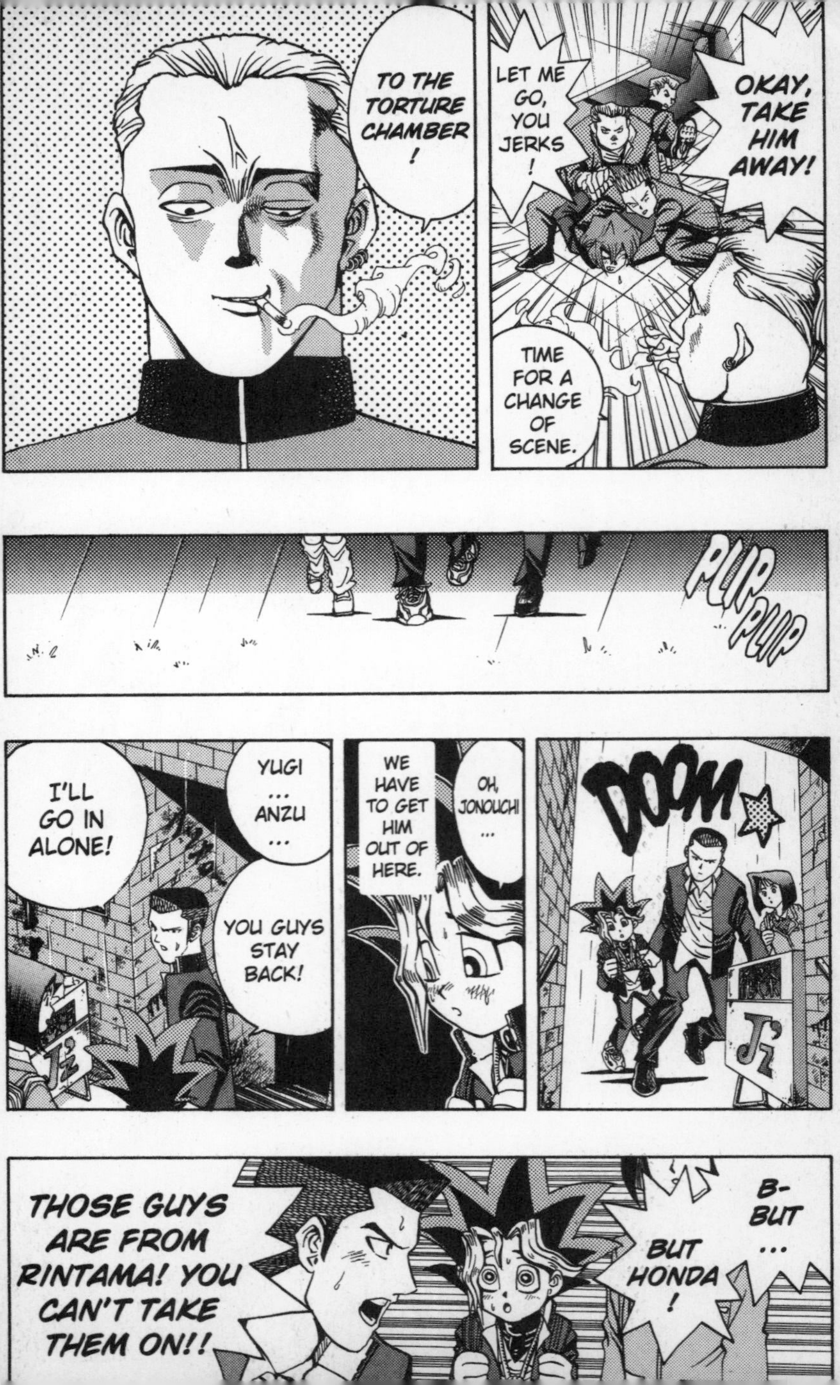
OKAY, TAKE HIM AWAY!
LET ME GO, YOU JERKS!
TIME FOR A CHANGE OF SCENE.
TO THE TORTURE CHAMBER!
PLIP PLIP
DOOM
OH, JONOUCHI...
WE HAVE TO GET HIM OUT OF HERE.
YUGI... ANZU...
I'LL GO IN ALONE!
YOU GUYS STAY BACK!
B-BUT...
BUT HONDA!
THOSE GUYS ARE FROM RINTAMA! YOU CAN'T TAKE THEM ON!!

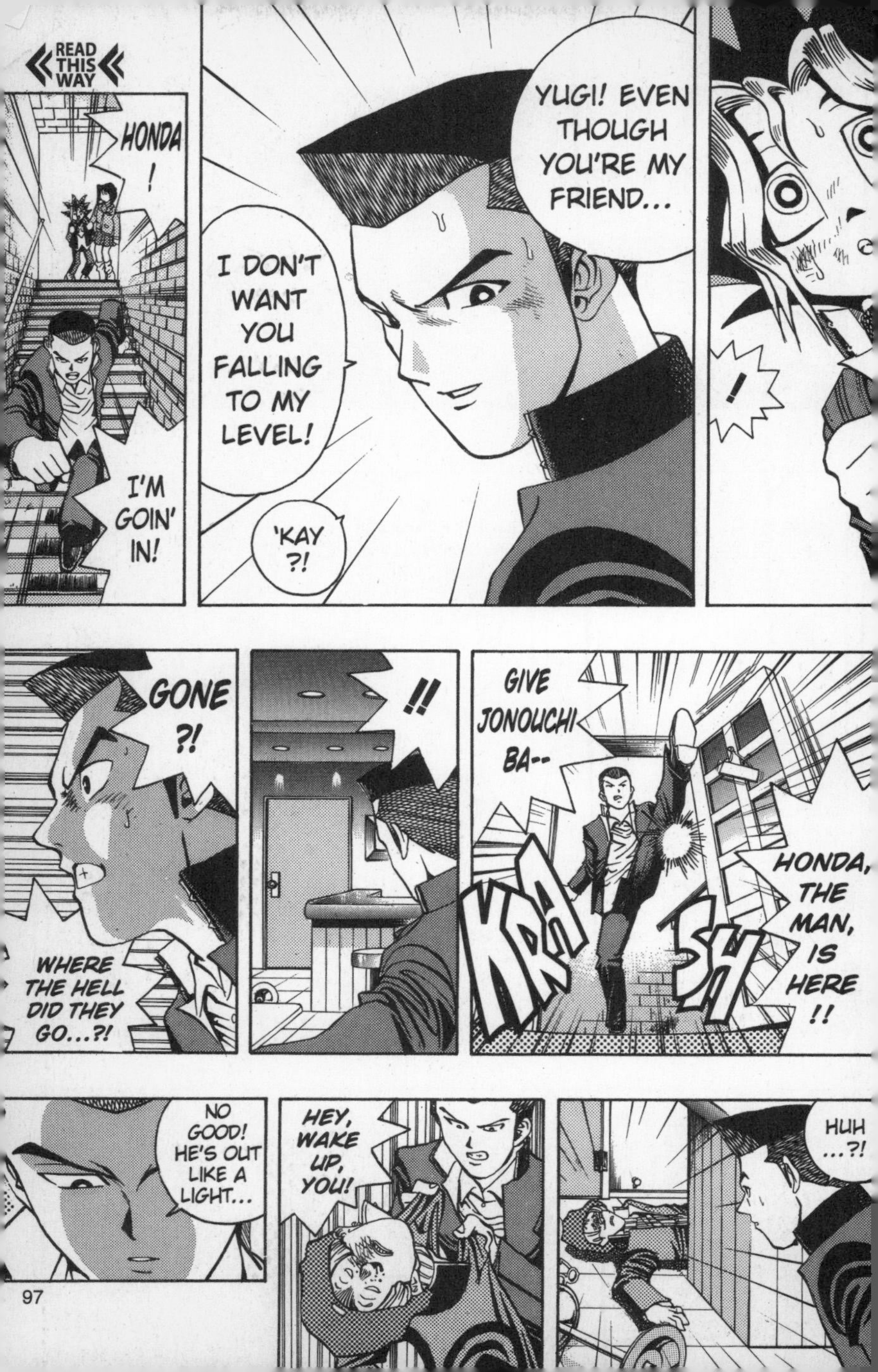
READ THIS WAY
!
YUGI! EVEN THOUGH YOU'RE MY FRIEND...
I DON'T WANT YOU FALLING TO MY LEVEL!
'KAY ?!
HONDA !
I'M GOIN' IN!
HONDA, THE MAN, IS HERE !!
GIVE JONOUCHI BA--
KRASH
!!
GONE ?!
WHERE THE HELL DID THEY GO...?!
HUH ...?!
HEY, WAKE UP, YOU!
NO GOOD! HE'S OUT LIKE A LIGHT...

READ THIS WAY

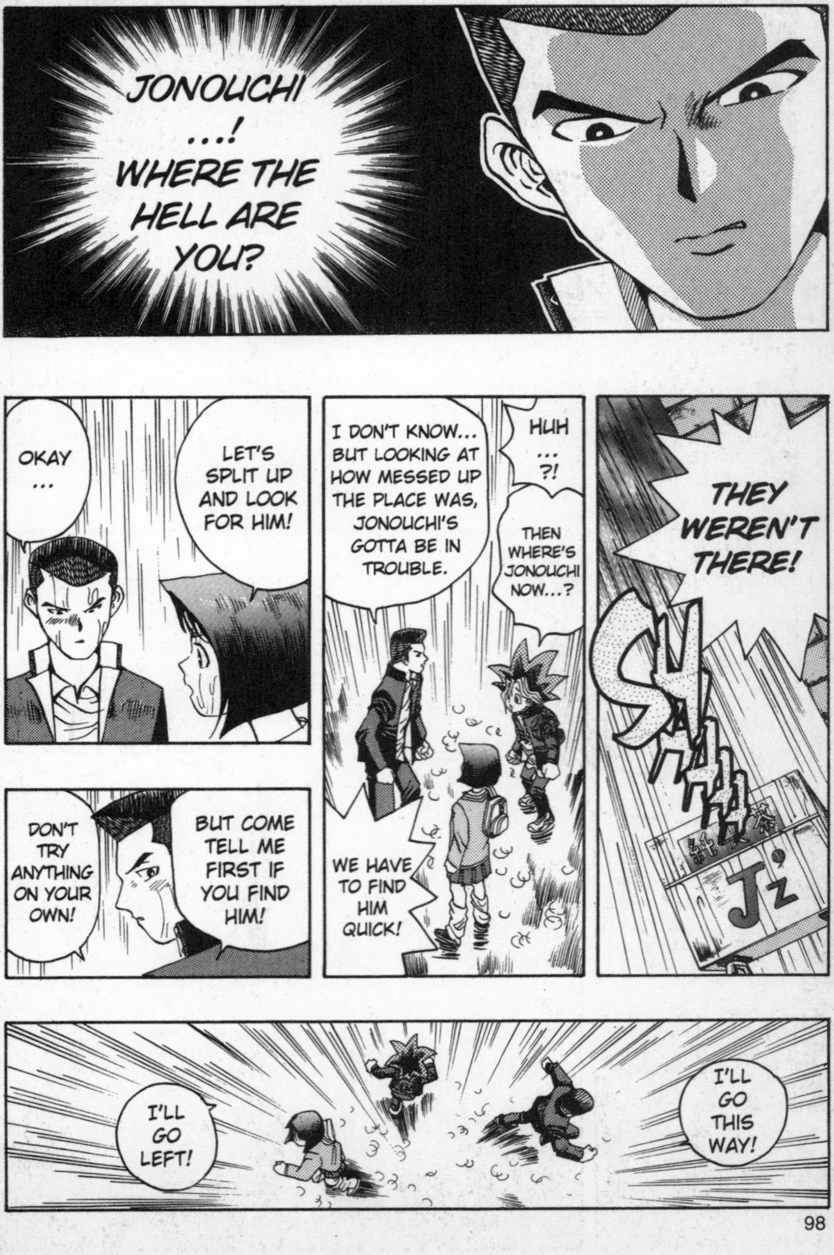

JONOUCHI ...! WHERE THE HELL ARE YOU?
THEY WEREN'T THERE!
HUH ...?!
THEN WHERE'S JONOUCHI NOW...?
I DON'T KNOW... BUT LOOKING AT HOW MESSED UP THE PLACE WAS, JONOUCHI'S GOTTA BE IN TROUBLE.
WE HAVE TO FIND HIM QUICK!
LET'S SPLIT UP AND LOOK FOR HIM!
OKAY ...
BUT COME TELL ME FIRST IF YOU FIND HIM!
DON'T TRY ANYTHING ON YOUR OWN!
I'LL GO THIS WAY!
I'LL GO LEFT!

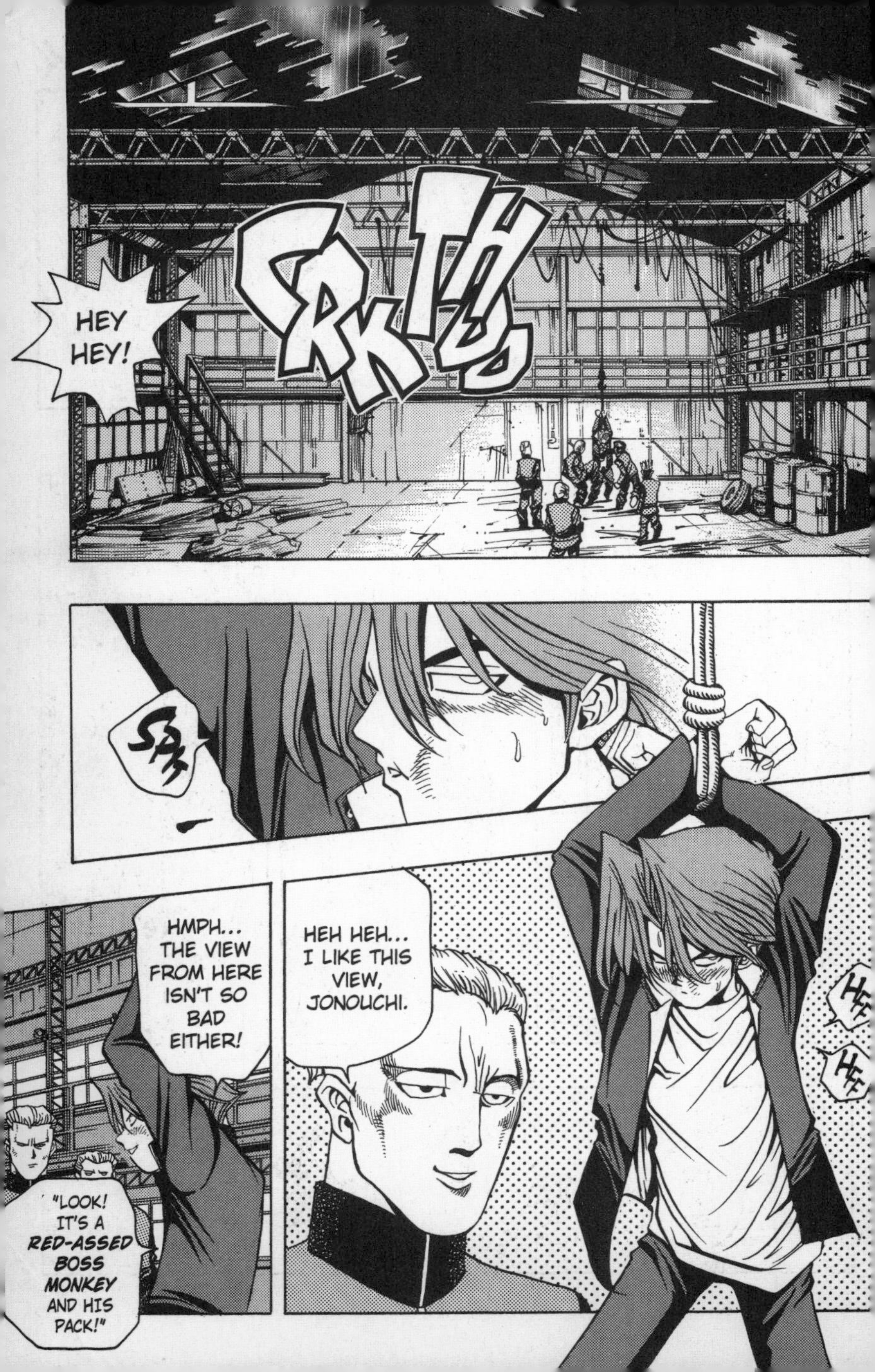
CRK THUD
HEY HEY!
HEF HEF
HEH HEH... I LIKE THIS VIEW, JONOUCHI.
HMPH... THE VIEW FROM HERE ISN'T SO BAD EITHER!
"LOOK! IT'S A *RED-ASSED* BOSS MONKEY AND HIS PACK!"

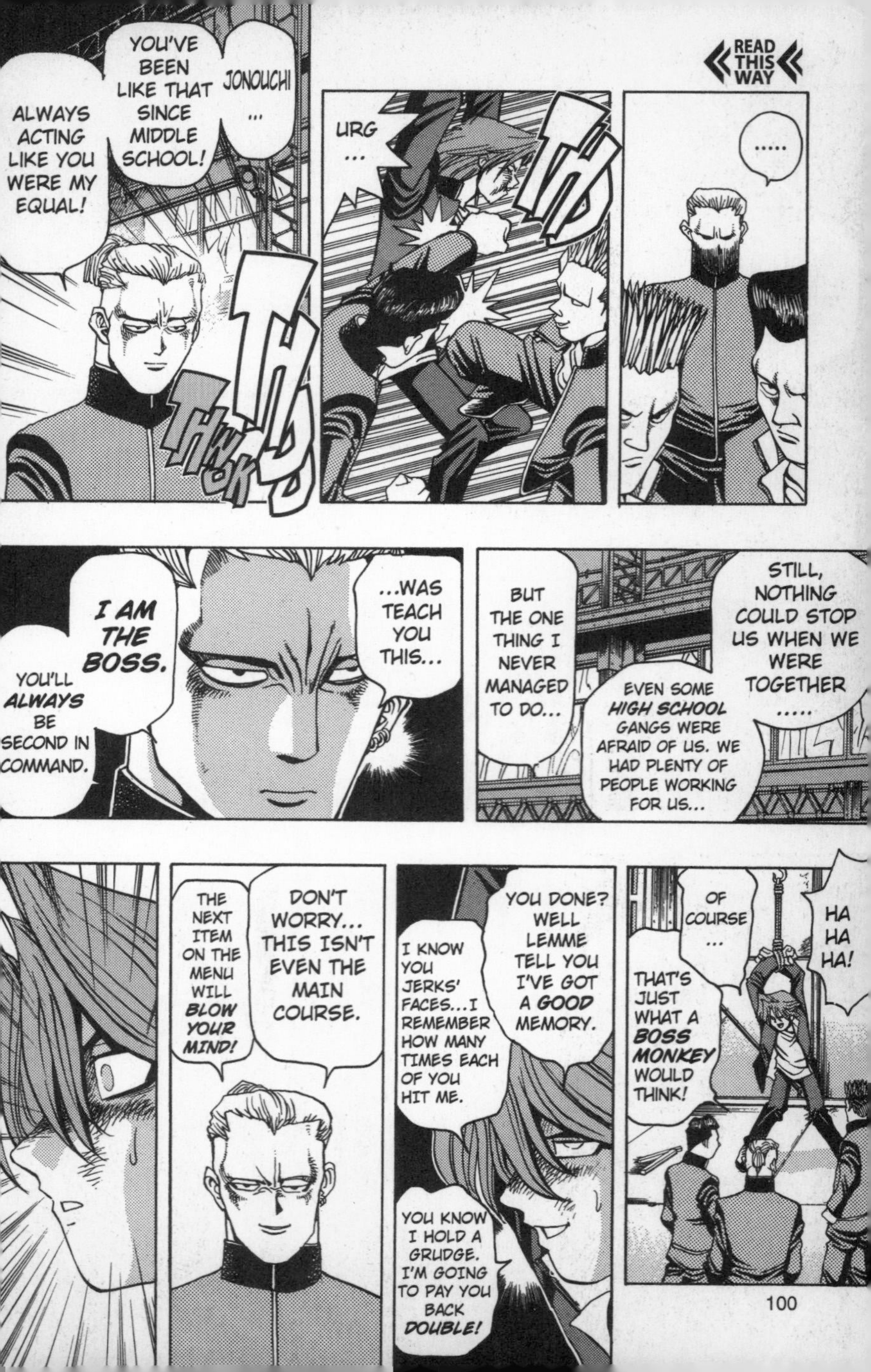
READ THIS WAY
.....
URG ...
JONOUCHI ...
YOU'VE BEEN LIKE THAT SINCE MIDDLE SCHOOL!
ALWAYS ACTING LIKE YOU WERE MY EQUAL!
STILL, NOTHING COULD STOP US WHEN WE WERE TOGETHER .....
EVEN SOME **HIGH SCHOOL** GANGS WERE AFRAID OF US. WE HAD PLENTY OF PEOPLE WORKING FOR US...
BUT THE ONE THING I NEVER MANAGED TO DO...
...WAS TEACH YOU THIS...
I AM THE BOSS.
YOU'LL ***ALWAYS*** BE SECOND IN COMMAND.
HA HA HA!
OF COURSE ...
THAT'S JUST WHAT A ***BOSS MONKEY*** WOULD THINK!
YOU DONE? WELL LEMME TELL YOU I'VE GOT A ***GOOD*** MEMORY.
I KNOW YOU JERKS' FACES...I REMEMBER HOW MANY TIMES EACH OF YOU HIT ME.
YOU KNOW I HOLD A GRUDGE. I'M GOING TO PAY YOU BACK ***DOUBLE!***
DON'T WORRY... THIS ISN'T EVEN THE MAIN COURSE.
THE NEXT ITEM ON THE MENU WILL ***BLOW YOUR MIND!***

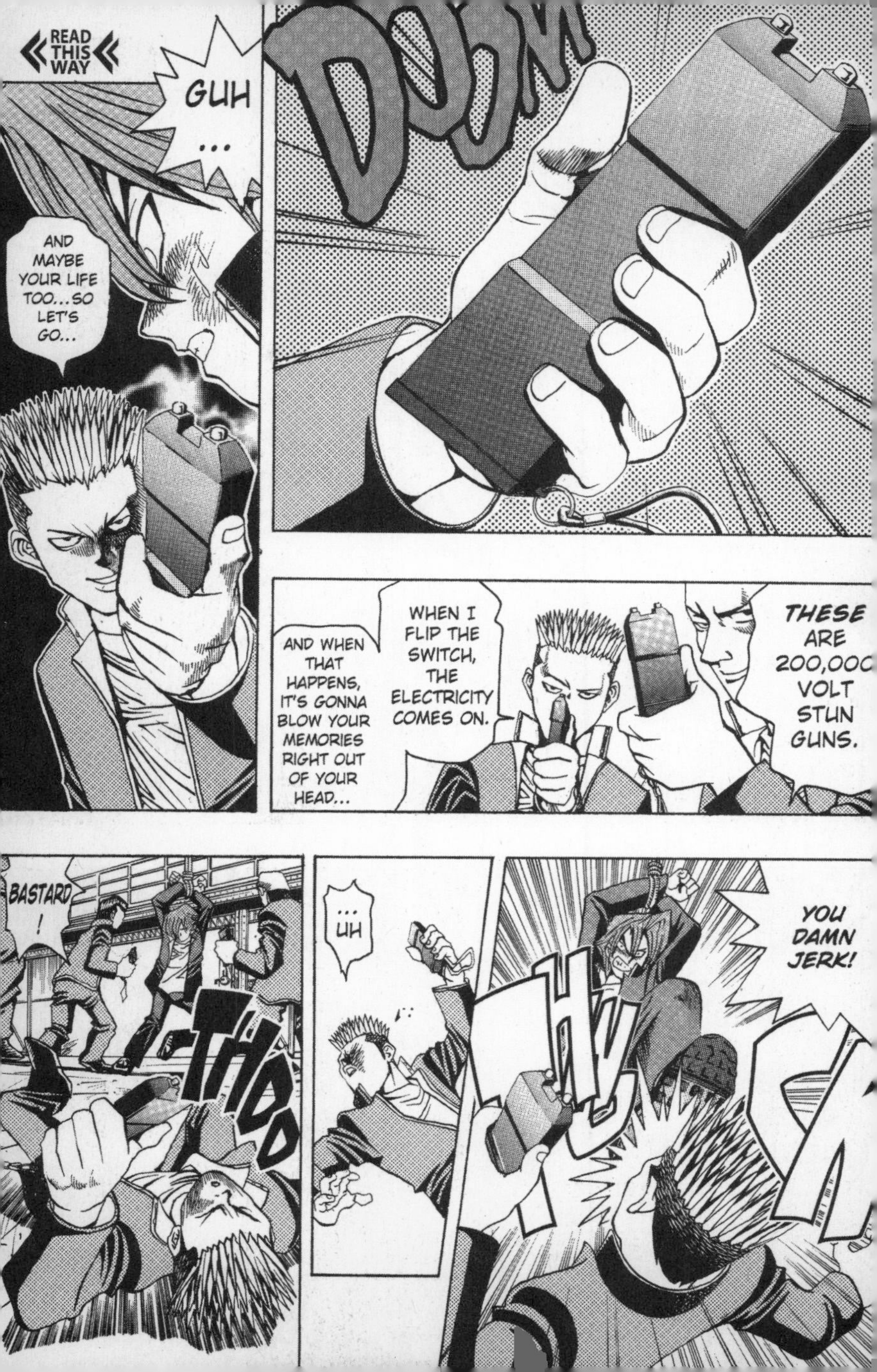
READ THIS WAY
DOOM
THESE ARE 200,000 VOLT STUN GUNS.
WHEN I FLIP THE SWITCH, THE ELECTRICITY COMES ON.
AND WHEN THAT HAPPENS, IT'S GONNA BLOW YOUR MEMORIES RIGHT OUT OF YOUR HEAD...
GUH...
AND MAYBE YOUR LIFE TOO...SO LET'S GO...
YOU DAMN JERK!
...UH
BASTARD!
THOD

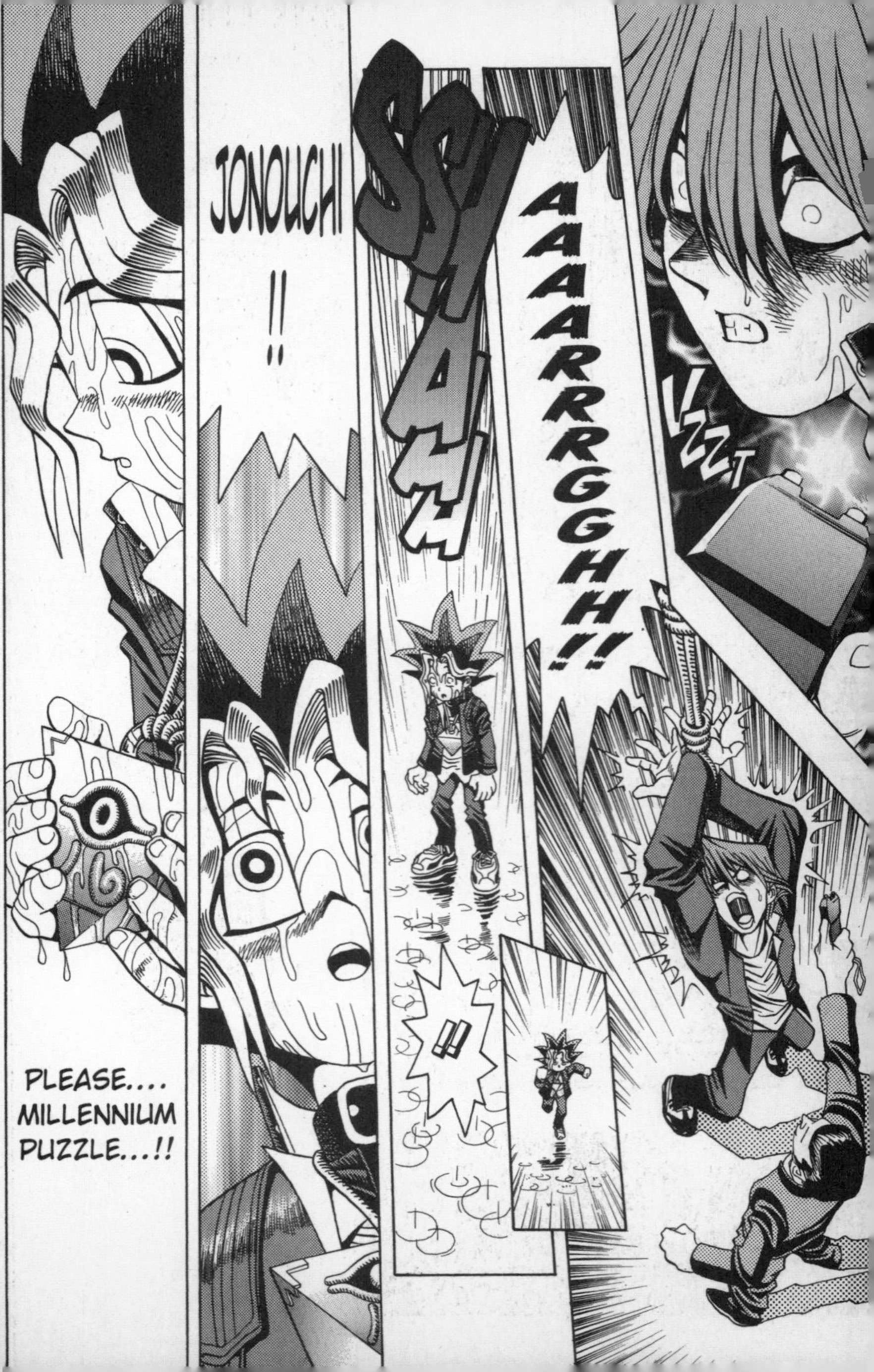

VZZT
AAAARRRGGHH!!
!!
JONOUCHI
!!
PLEASE....
MILLENNIUM
PUZZLE...!!

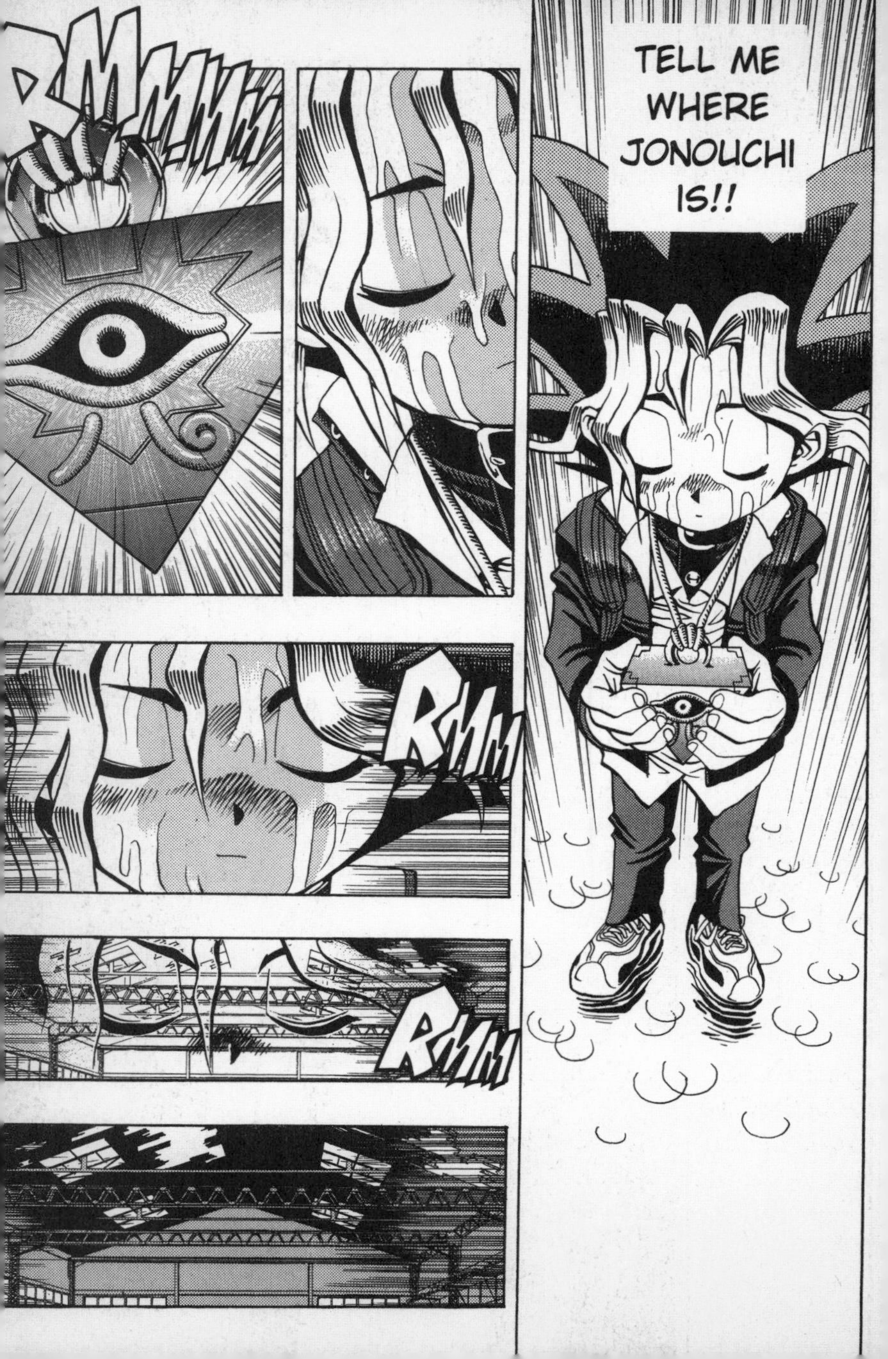

TELL ME WHERE JONOUCHI IS!!

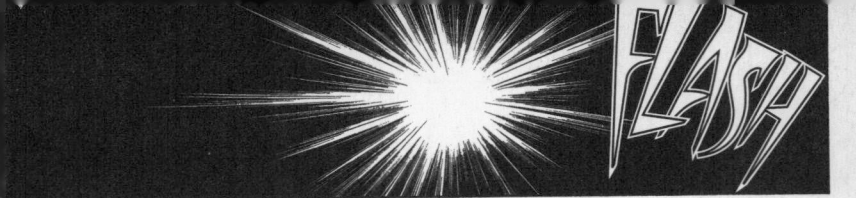

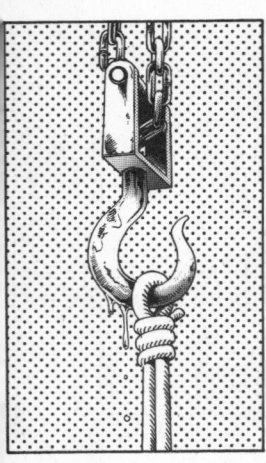

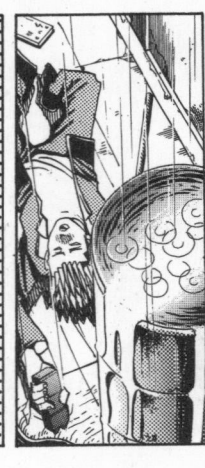

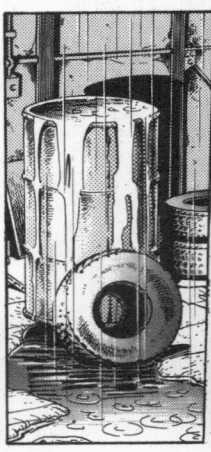

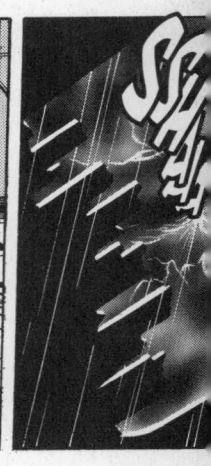

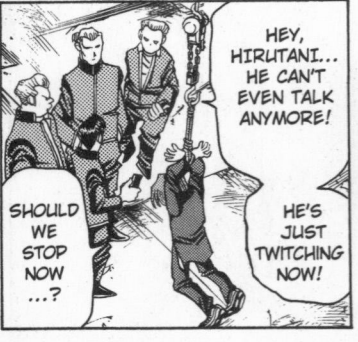

FLASH
VZZT
TWITCH TWITCH
HEY, HIRUTANI... HE CAN'T EVEN TALK ANYMORE!
HE'S JUST TWITCHING NOW!
SHOULD WE STOP NOW ...?
DO IT!
UH ...
BUT IF WE KEEP GOING HE'LL DIE...

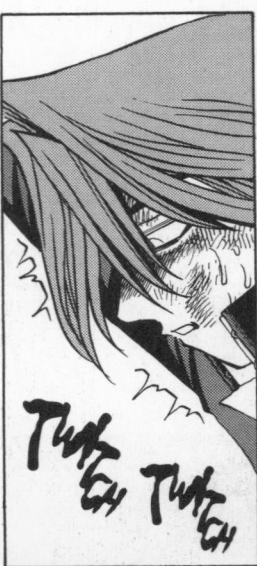

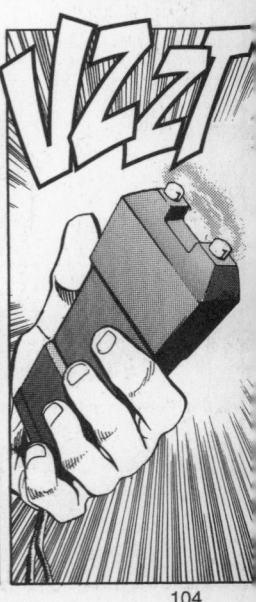

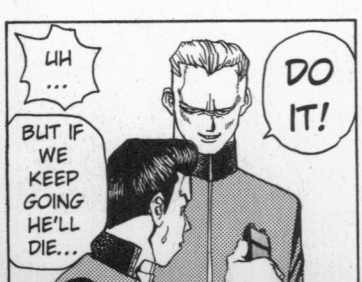

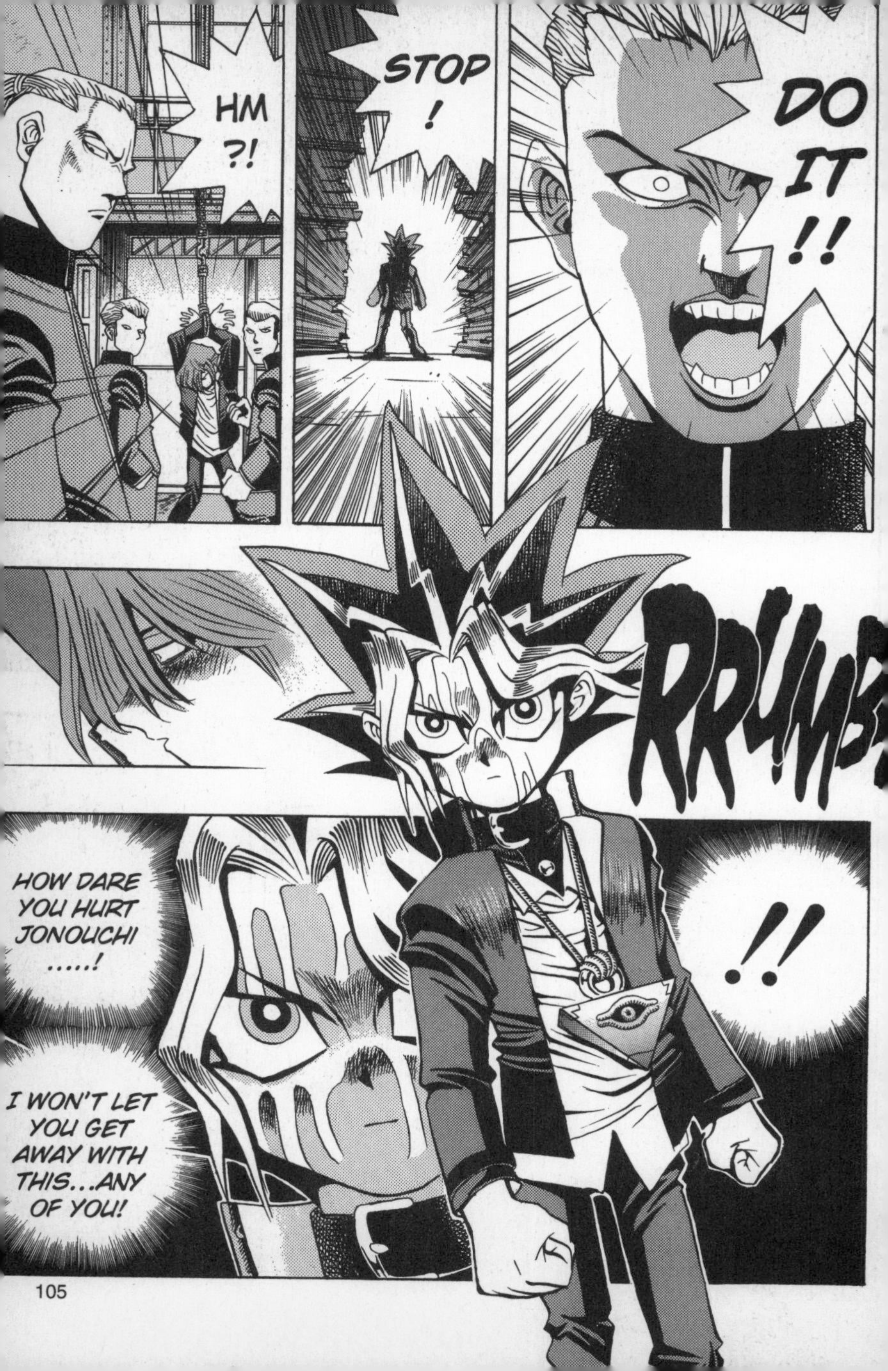
DO IT !!
STOP !
HM ?!
RRUMB
!!
HOW DARE YOU HURT JONOUCHI .....!
I WON'T LET YOU GET AWAY WITH THIS...ANY OF YOU!

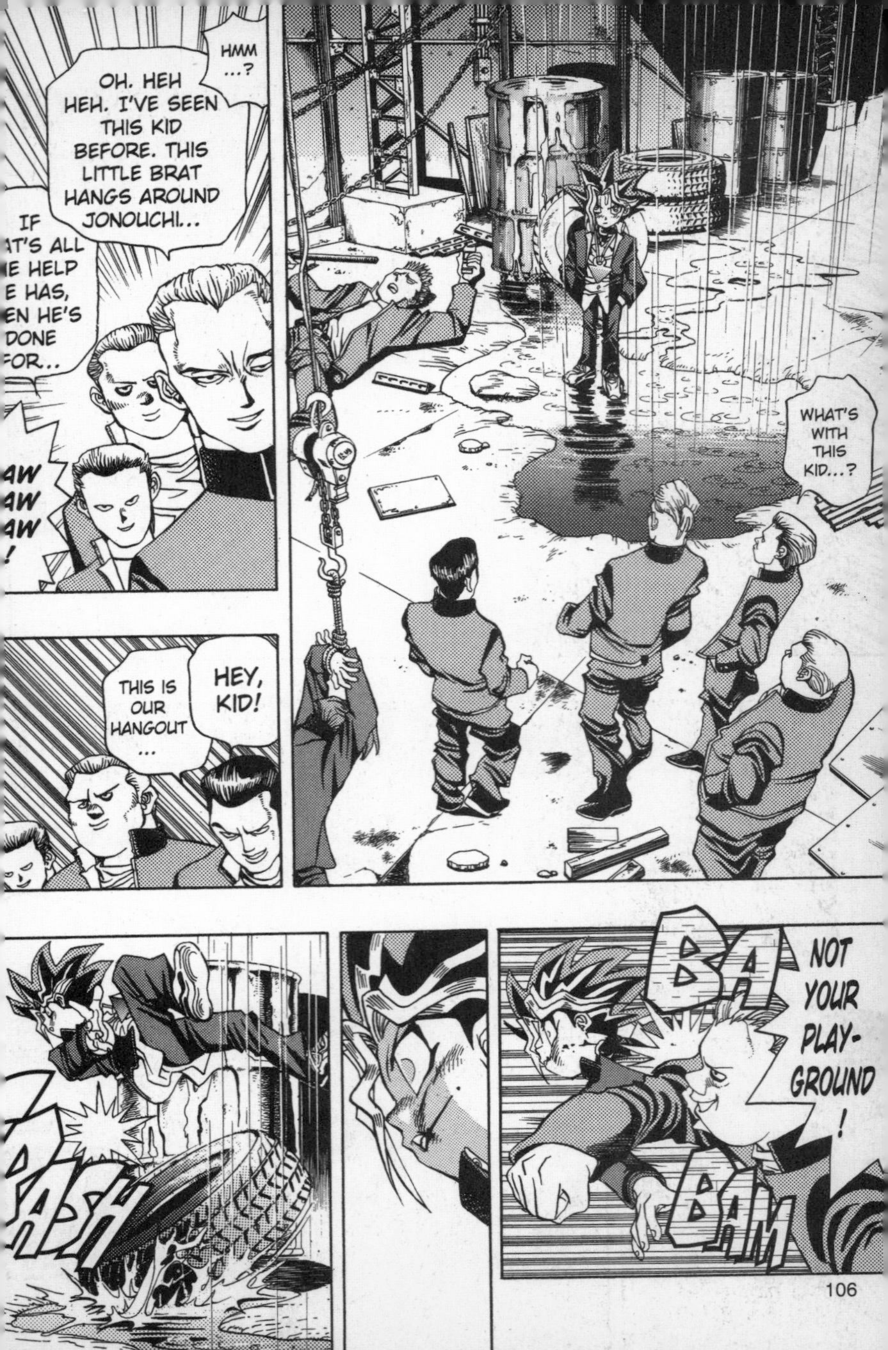
WHAT'S WITH THIS KID...?
HMM ...?
OH. HEH HEH. I'VE SEEN THIS KID BEFORE. THIS LITTLE BRAT HANGS AROUND JONOUCHI...
IF AT'S ALL E HELP E HAS, EN HE'S DONE FOR...
HEY, KID!
THIS IS OUR HANGOUT ...
BA
NOT YOUR PLAY-GROUND!
BAM

READ THIS WAY

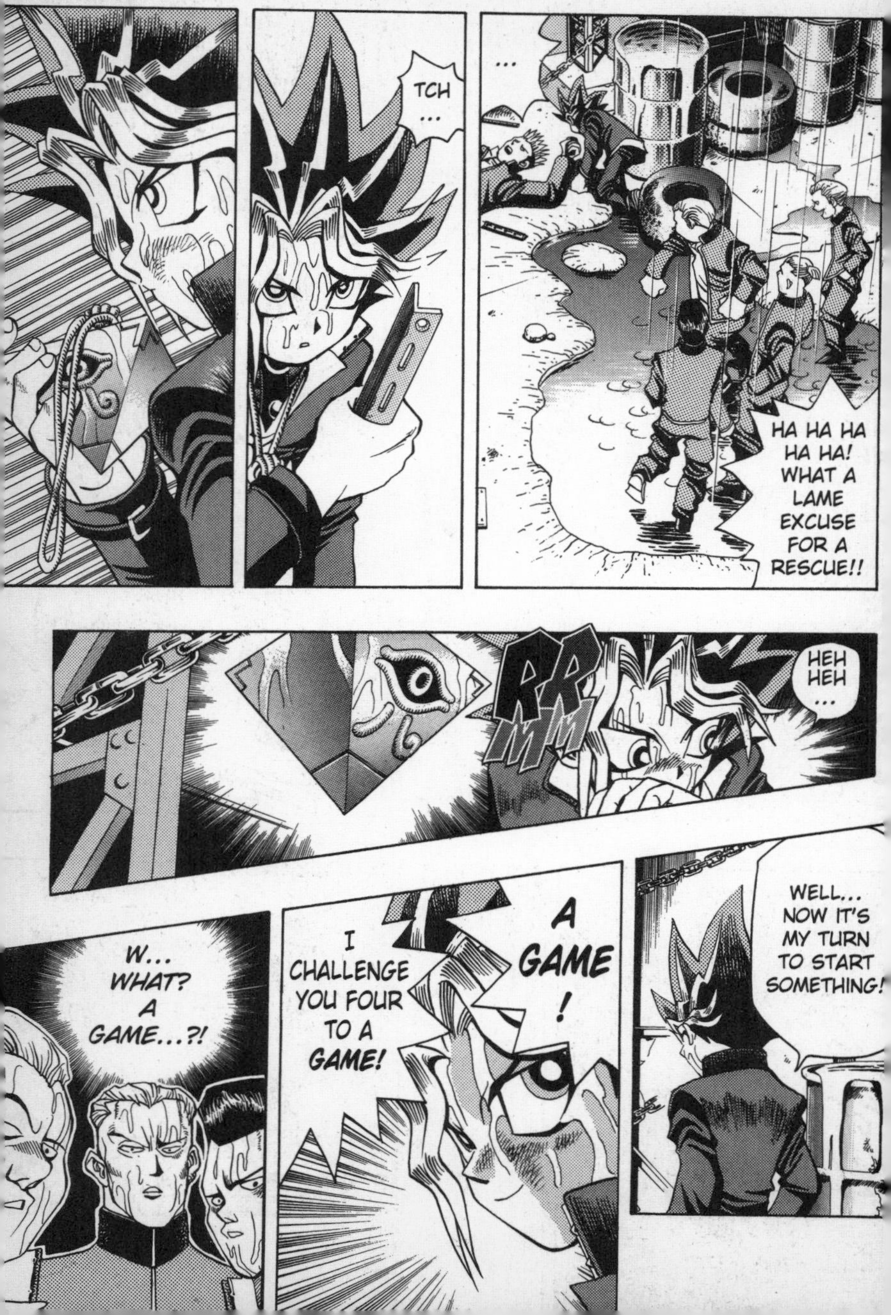
...
HA HA HA HA HA! WHAT A LAME EXCUSE FOR A RESCUE!!
TCH ...
HEH HEH ...
RR MM
WELL... NOW IT'S MY TURN TO START SOMETHING!
A GAME !
I CHALLENGE YOU FOUR TO A GAME!
W... WHAT? A GAME...?!

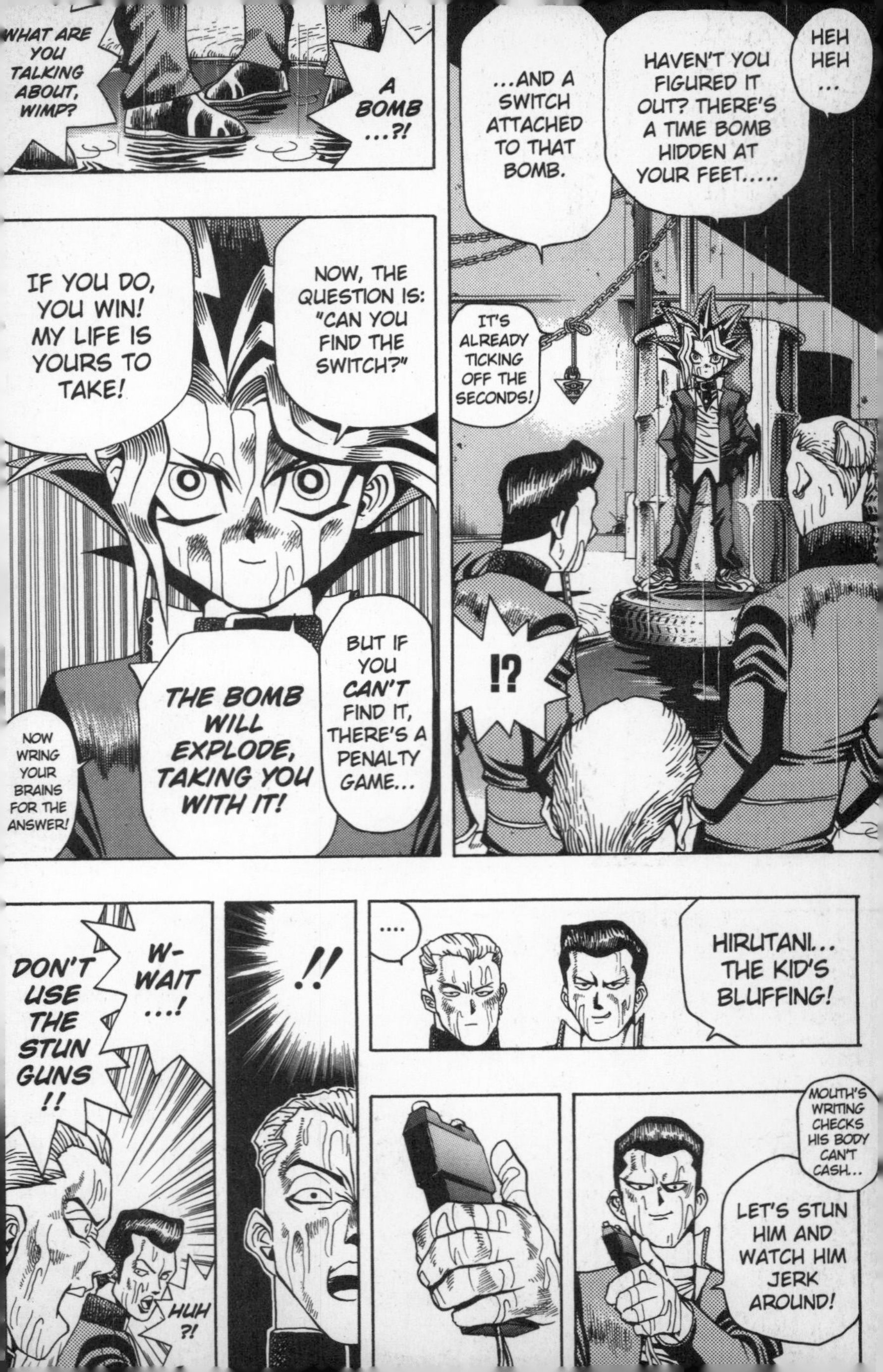
HEH HEH ...
HAVEN'T YOU FIGURED IT OUT? THERE'S A TIME BOMB HIDDEN AT YOUR FEET.....
...AND A SWITCH ATTACHED TO THAT BOMB.
IT'S ALREADY TICKING OFF THE SECONDS!
!?
A BOMB ...?!
WHAT ARE YOU TALKING ABOUT, WIMP?
NOW, THE QUESTION IS: "CAN YOU FIND THE SWITCH?"
IF YOU DO, YOU WIN! MY LIFE IS YOURS TO TAKE!
BUT IF YOU CAN'T FIND IT, THERE'S A PENALTY GAME...
THE BOMB WILL EXPLODE, TAKING YOU WITH IT!
NOW WRING YOUR BRAINS FOR THE ANSWER!
HIRUTANI... THE KID'S BLUFFING!
....
MOUTH'S WRITING CHECKS HIS BODY CAN'T CASH...
LET'S STUN HIM AND WATCH HIM JERK AROUND!
!!
W-WAIT ...!
DON'T USE THE STUN GUNS !!
HUH ?!

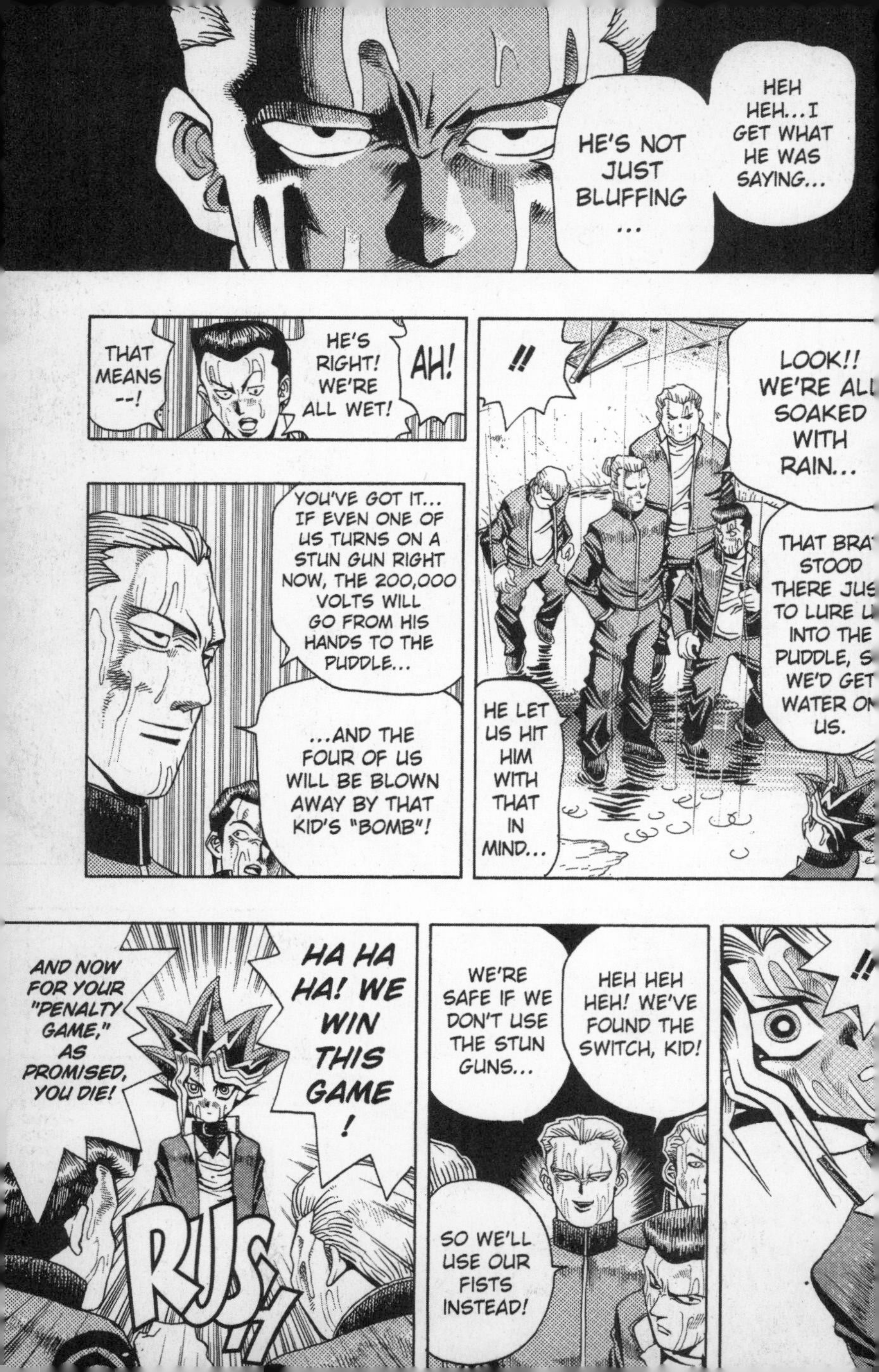
HEH HEH...I GET WHAT HE WAS SAYING...
HE'S NOT JUST BLUFFING ...
!!
LOOK!! WE'RE ALL SOAKED WITH RAIN...
THAT BRAT STOOD THERE JUST TO LURE US INTO THE PUDDLE, SO WE'D GET WATER ON US.
HE LET US HIT HIM WITH THAT IN MIND...
AH!
HE'S RIGHT! WE'RE ALL WET!
THAT MEANS --!
YOU'VE GOT IT... IF EVEN ONE OF US TURNS ON A STUN GUN RIGHT NOW, THE 200,000 VOLTS WILL GO FROM HIS HANDS TO THE PUDDLE...
...AND THE FOUR OF US WILL BE BLOWN AWAY BY THAT KID'S "BOMB"!
!!
HEH HEH HEH! WE'VE FOUND THE SWITCH, KID!
WE'RE SAFE IF WE DON'T USE THE STUN GUNS...
SO WE'LL USE OUR FISTS INSTEAD!
HA HA HA! WE WIN THIS GAME !
AND NOW FOR YOUR "PENALTY GAME," AS PROMISED, YOU DIE!
RUSH

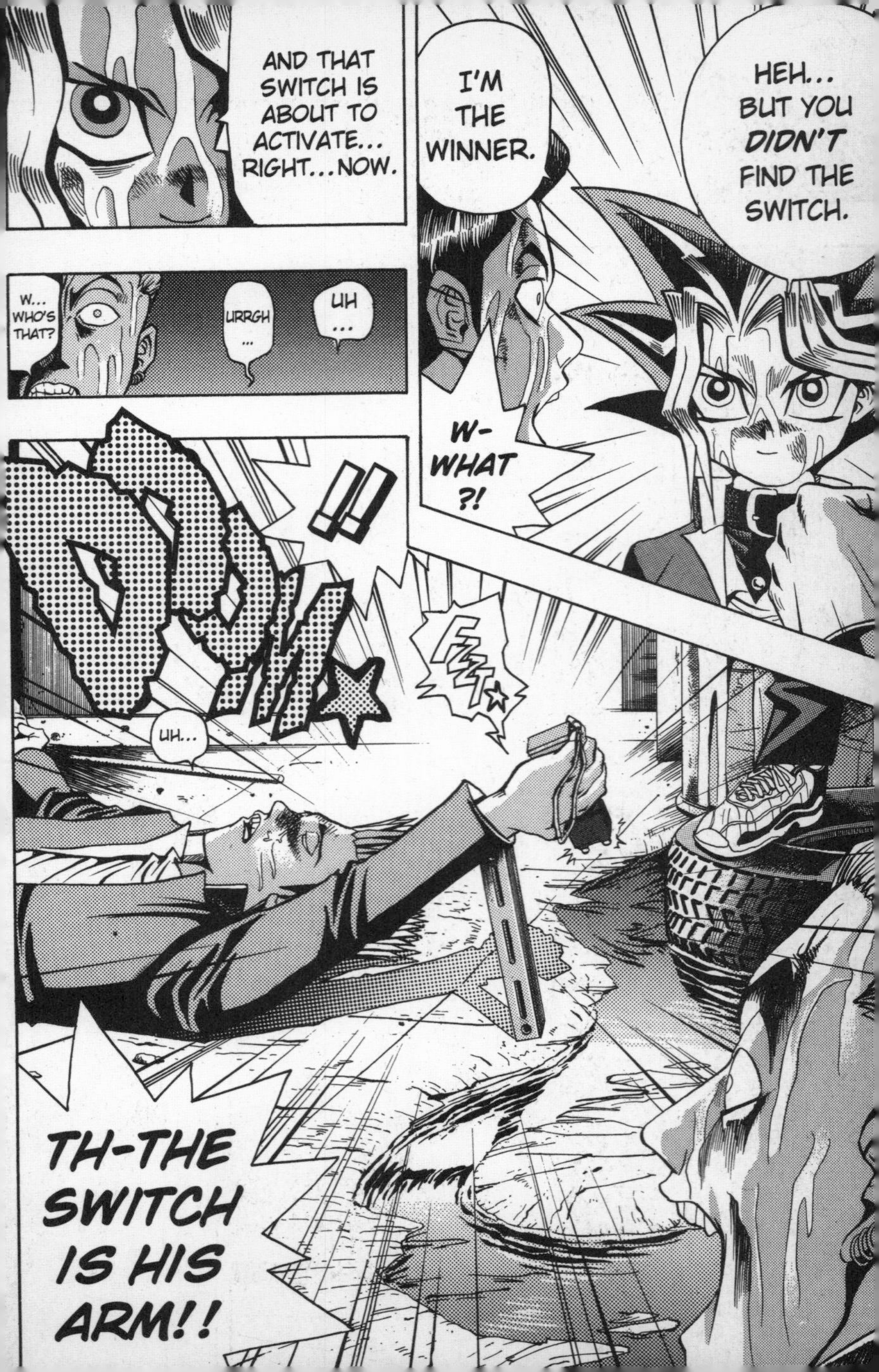
AND THAT SWITCH IS ABOUT TO ACTIVATE... RIGHT...NOW.
I'M THE WINNER.
HEH... BUT YOU DIDN'T FIND THE SWITCH.
W-WHAT?!
W... WHO'S THAT?
URRGH ...
UH ...
FZZT☆
UH...
TH-THE SWITCH IS HIS ARM!!

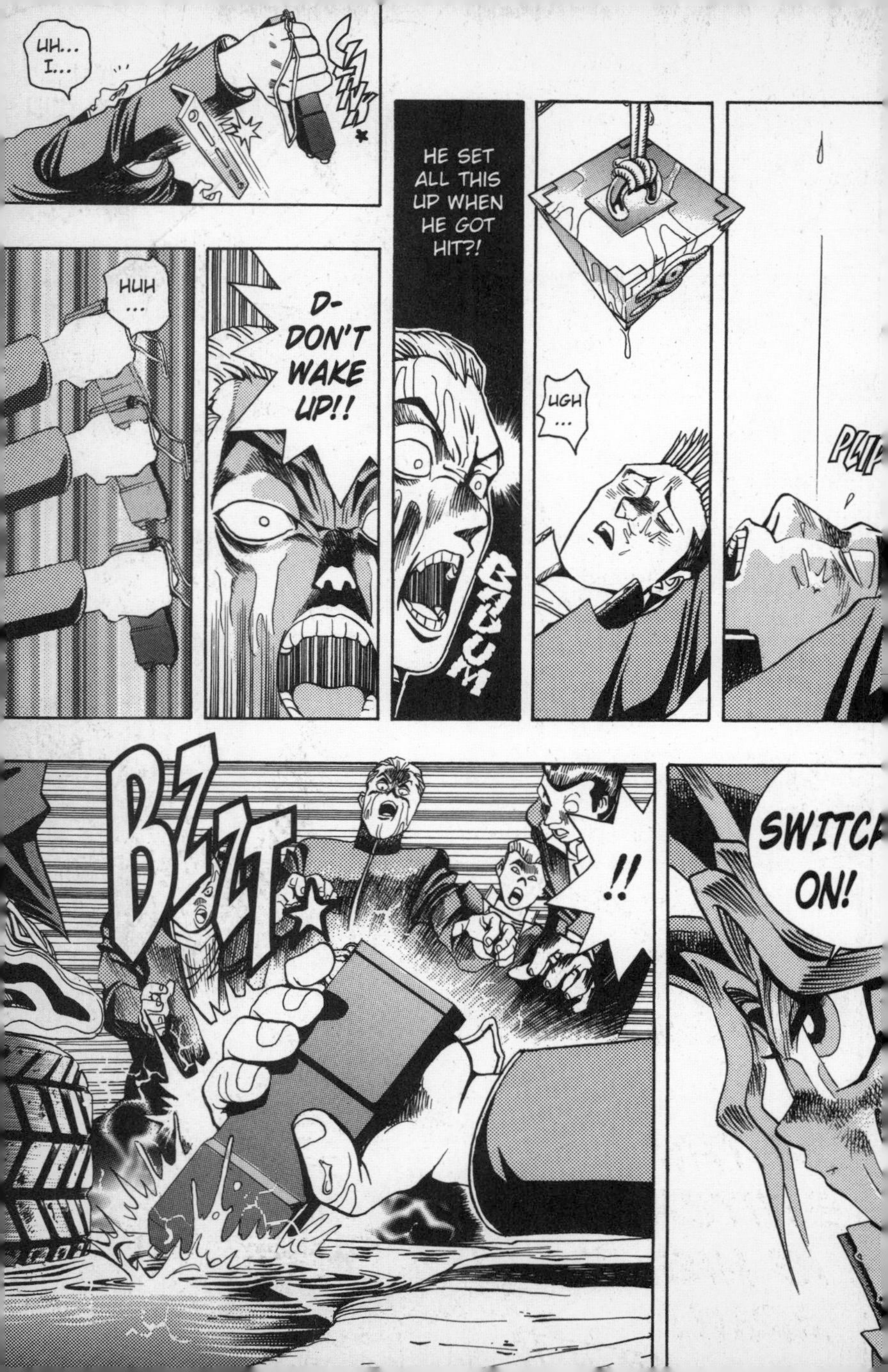
PLIP
UGH...
HE SET ALL THIS UP WHEN HE GOT HIT?!
BADUM
UH... I...
D-DON'T WAKE UP!!
HUH...
SWITCH ON!
!!
BZZT

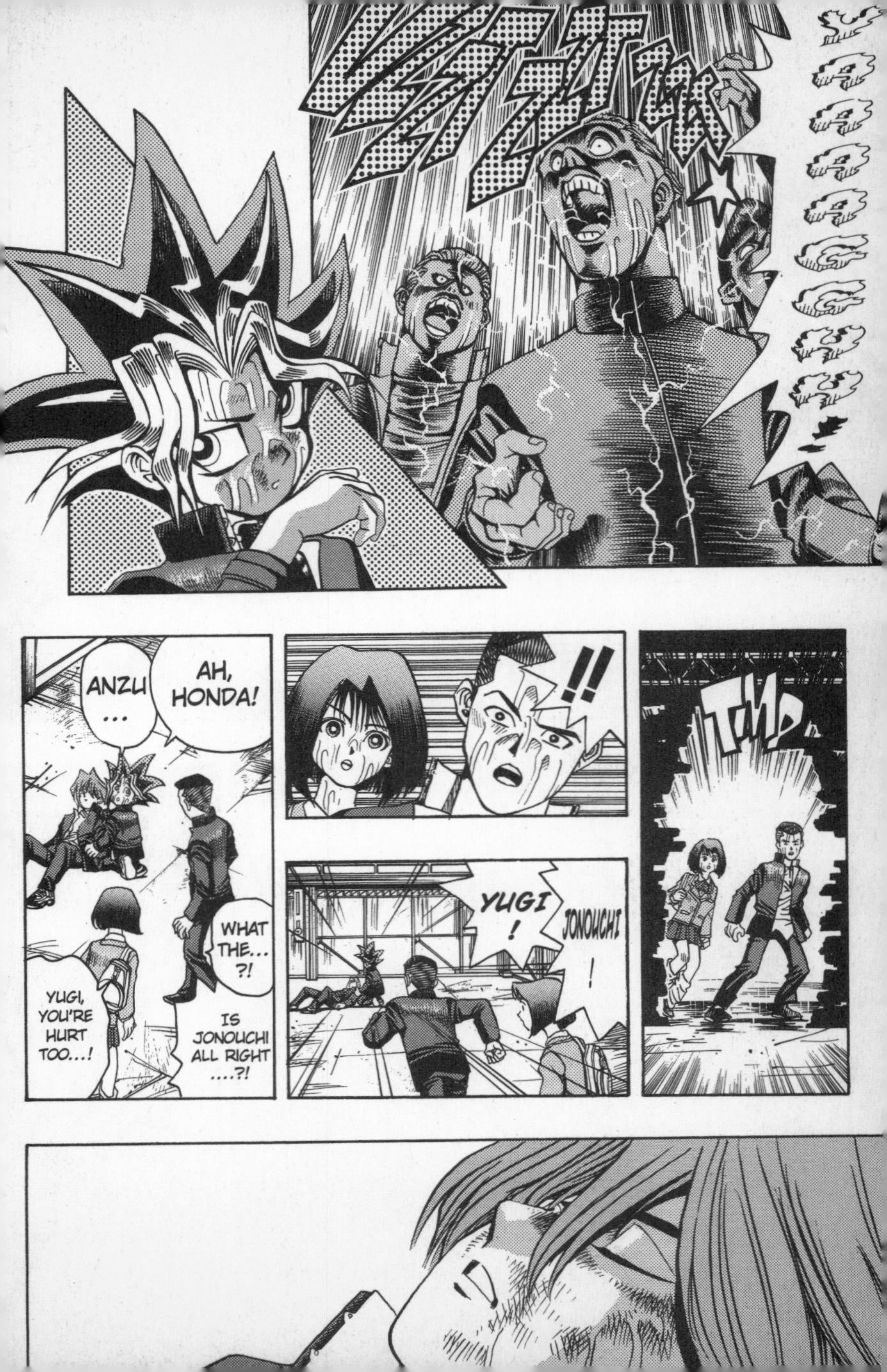

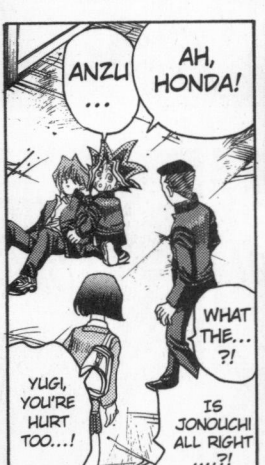

JONOUCHI !
YUGI !
!!
AH, HONDA!
ANZU ...
WHAT THE... ?!
IS JONOUCHI ALL RIGHT ....?!
YUGI, YOU'RE HURT TOO...!

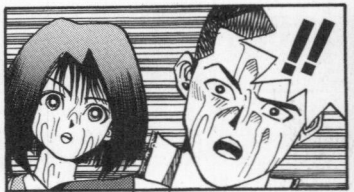

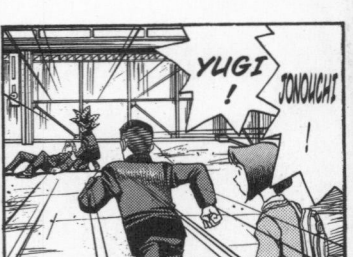

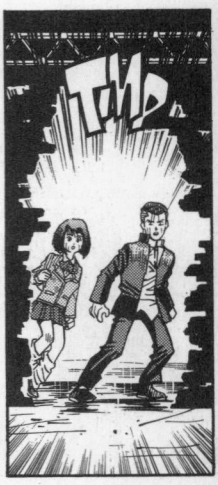

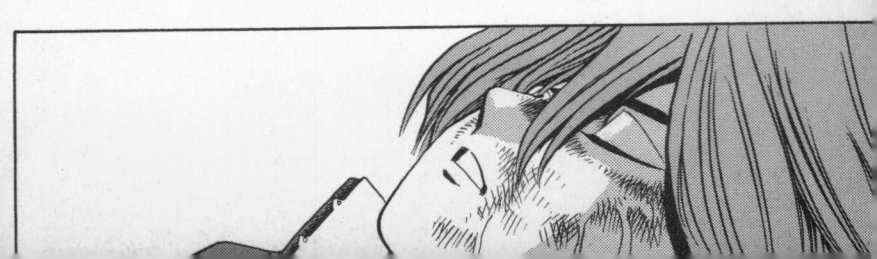

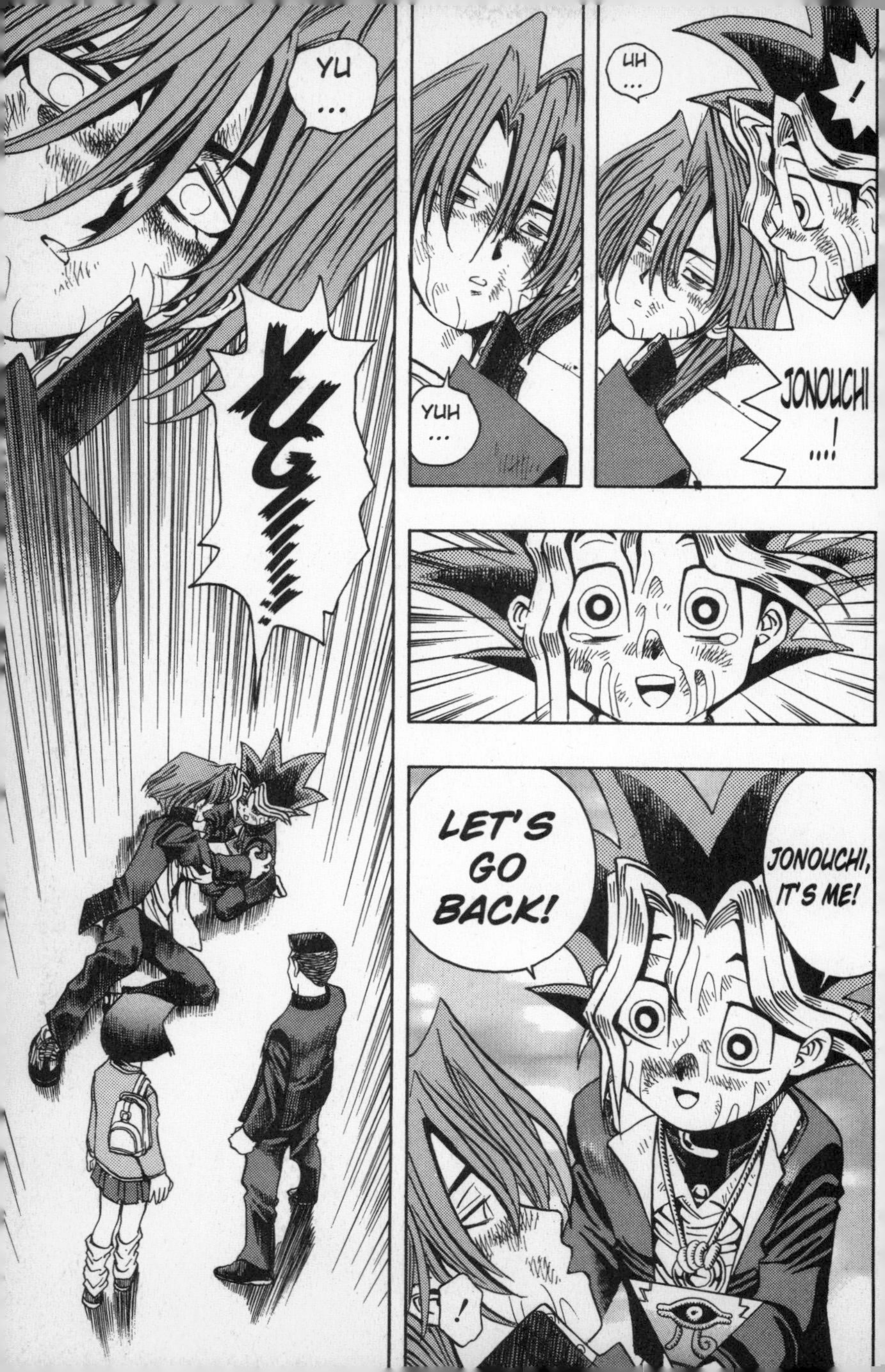
UH ...
!
JONOUCHI ...!
YUH ...
JONOUCHI, IT'S ME!
LET'S GO BACK!
!
YU ...
YUGI!!!!!!

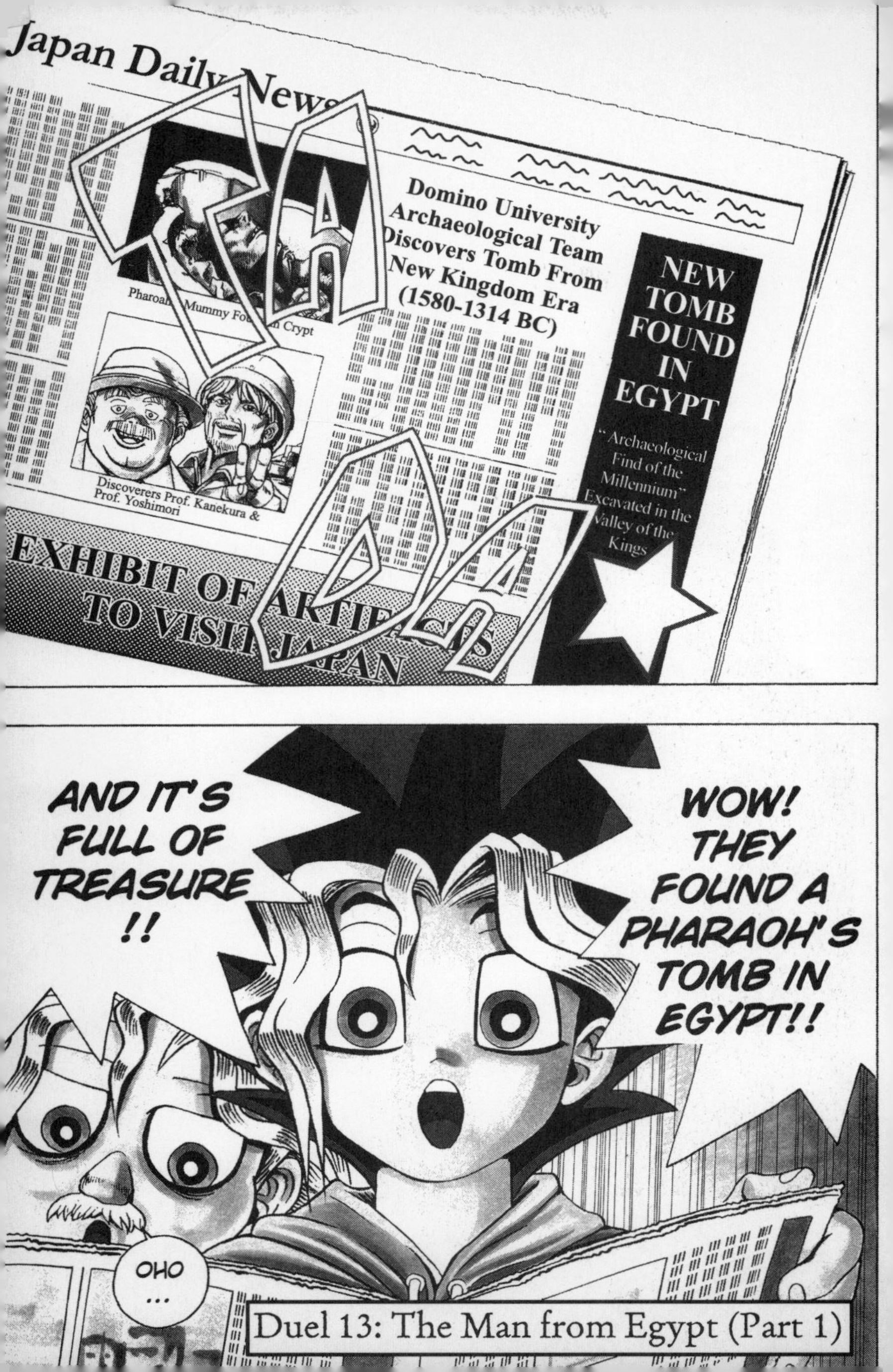
Japan Daily News
Domino University Archaeological Team Discovers Tomb From New Kingdom Era (1580-1314 BC)
NEW TOMB FOUND IN EGYPT
"Archaeological Find of the Millennium" Excavated in the Valley of the Kings
Discoverers Prof. Kanekura & Prof. Yoshimori
EXHIBIT OF ARTIFACTS TO VISIT JAPAN
WOW! THEY FOUND A PHARAOH'S TOMB IN EGYPT!!
AND IT'S FULL OF TREASURE!!
OHO...

Duel 13: The Man from Egypt (Part 1)

Duel 13: The Man from Egypt (Part 1)

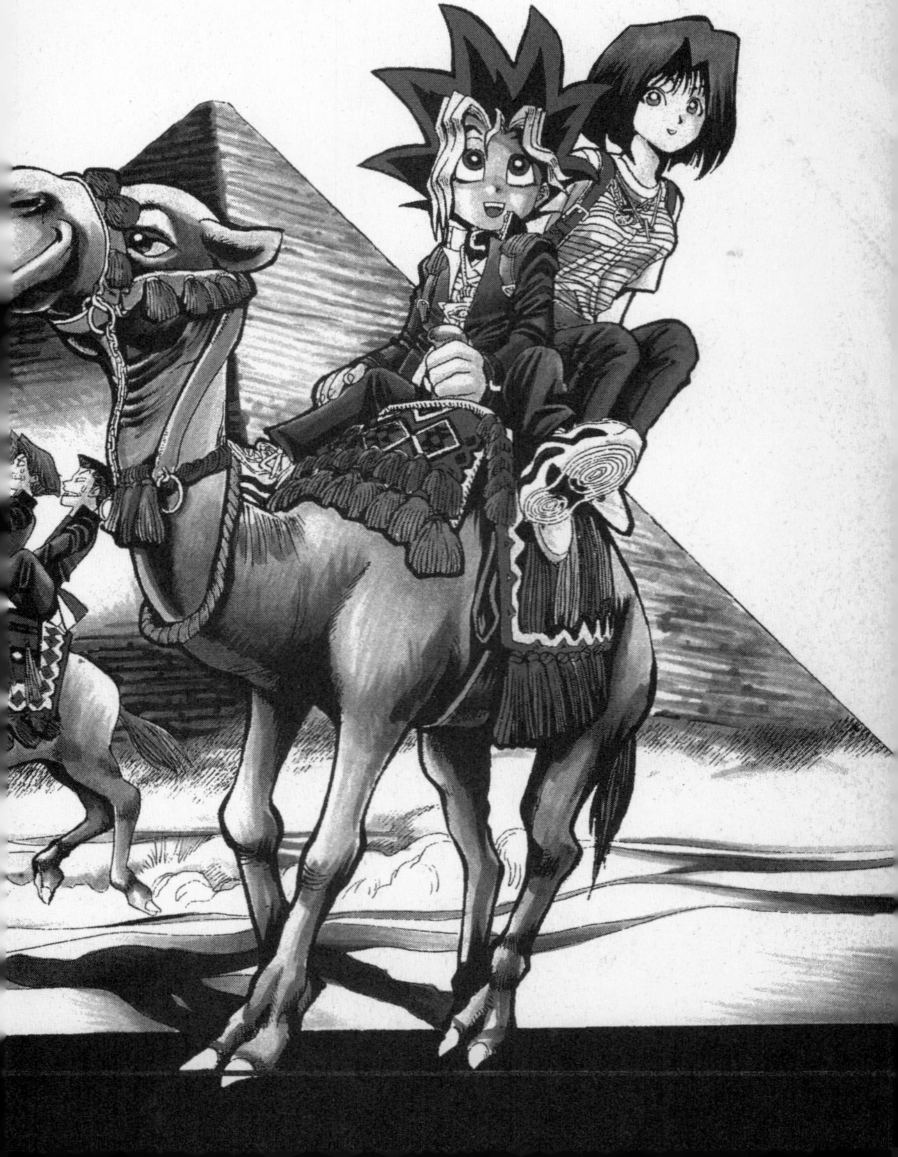

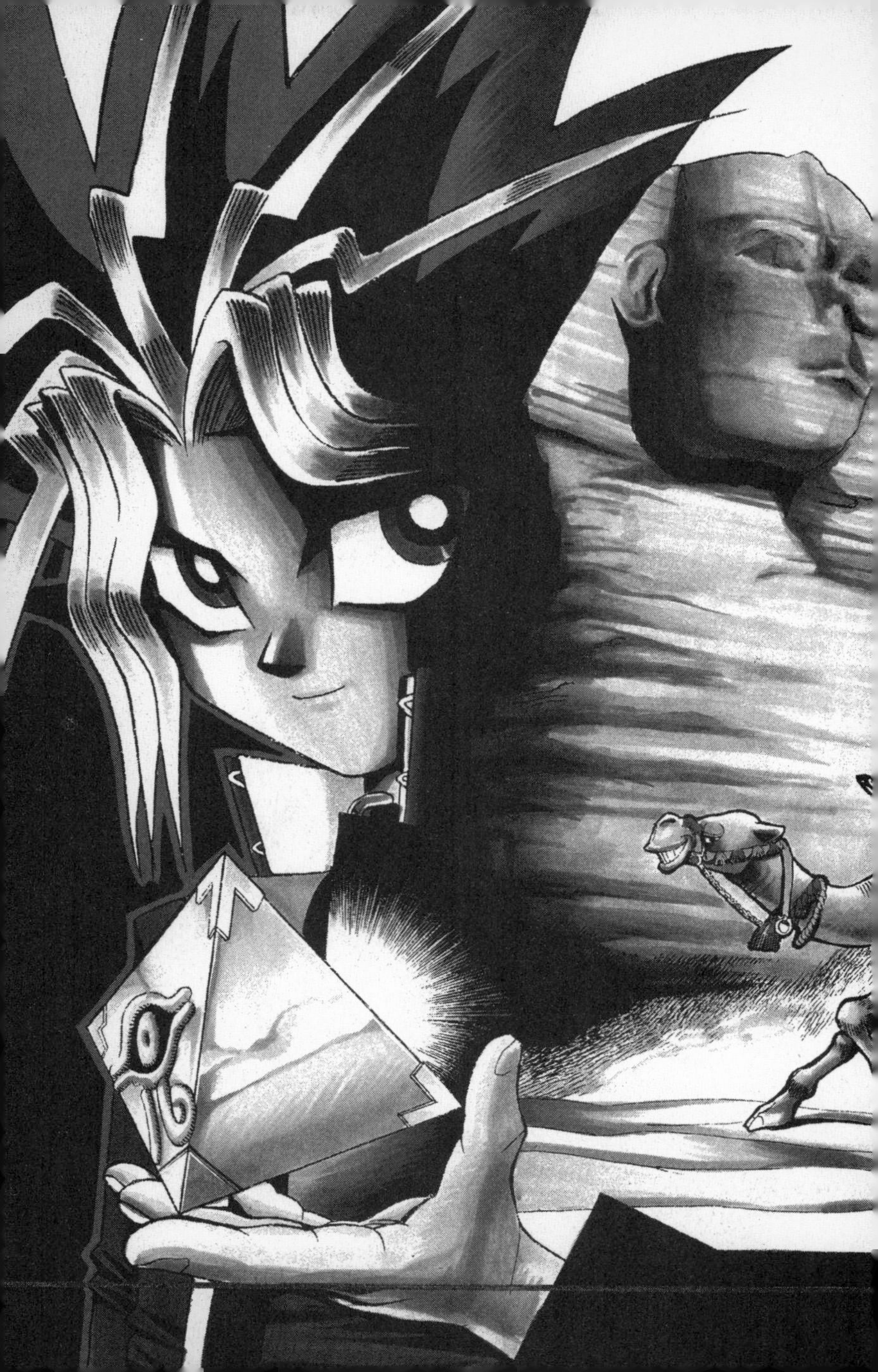

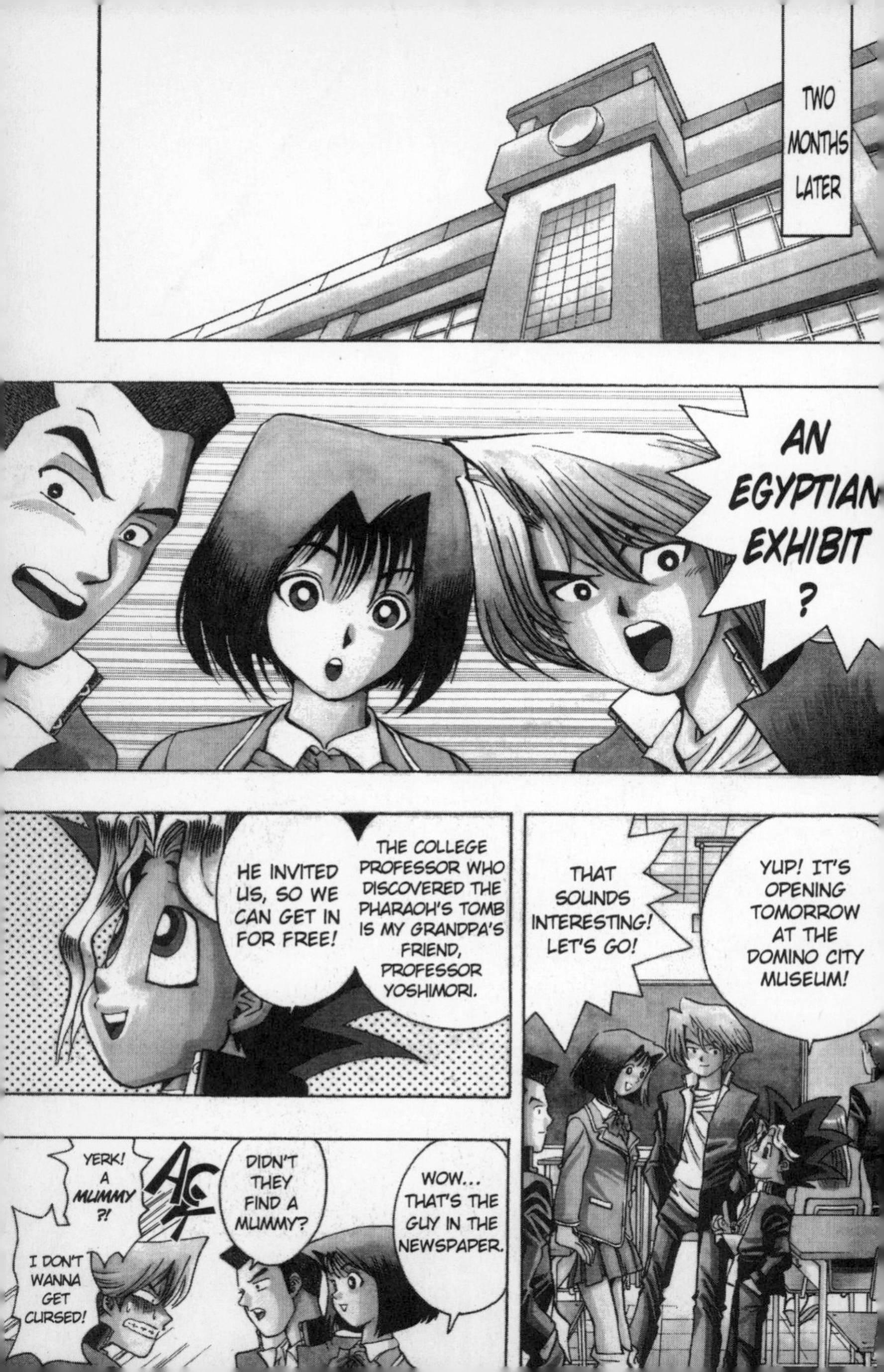

TWO MONTHS LATER
AN EGYPTIAN EXHIBIT?
YUP! IT'S OPENING TOMORROW AT THE DOMINO CITY MUSEUM!
THAT SOUNDS INTERESTING! LET'S GO!
THE COLLEGE PROFESSOR WHO DISCOVERED THE PHARAOH'S TOMB IS MY GRANDPA'S FRIEND, PROFESSOR YOSHIMORI.
HE INVITED US, SO WE CAN GET IN FOR FREE!
WOW... THAT'S THE GUY IN THE NEWSPAPER.
DIDN'T THEY FIND A MUMMY?
YERK! A *MUMMY* ?!
I DON'T WANNA GET CURSED!

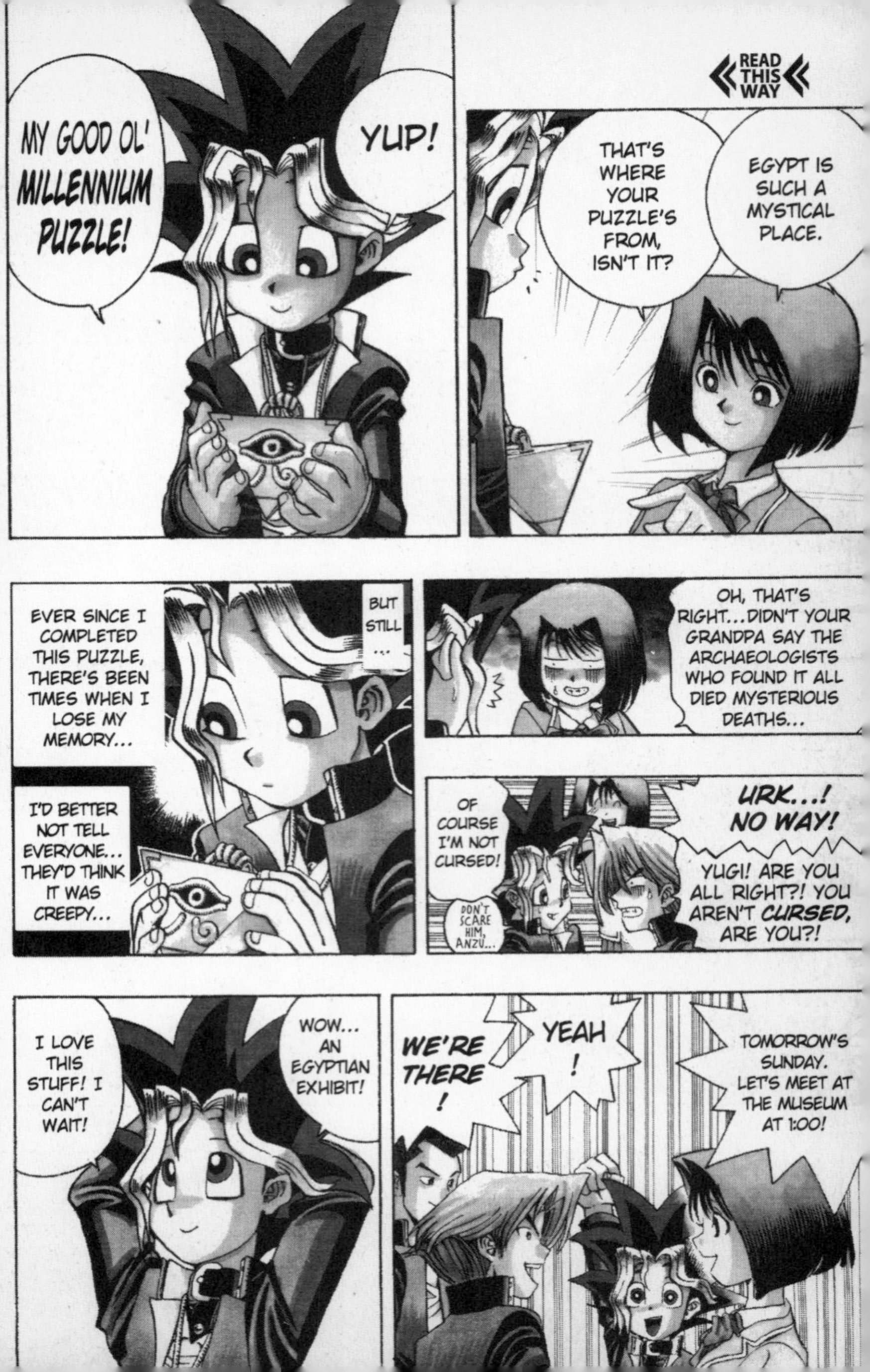
READ THIS WAY
EGYPT IS SUCH A MYSTICAL PLACE.
THAT'S WHERE YOUR PUZZLE'S FROM, ISN'T IT?
YUP!
MY GOOD OL' MILLENNIUM PUZZLE!
OH, THAT'S RIGHT...DIDN'T YOUR GRANDPA SAY THE ARCHAEOLOGISTS WHO FOUND IT ALL DIED MYSTERIOUS DEATHS...
URK...! NO WAY!
YUGI! ARE YOU ALL RIGHT?! YOU AREN'T CURSED, ARE YOU?!
OF COURSE I'M NOT CURSED!
DON'T SCARE HIM, ANZU...
BUT STILL ...
EVER SINCE I COMPLETED THIS PUZZLE, THERE'S BEEN TIMES WHEN I LOSE MY MEMORY...
I'D BETTER NOT TELL EVERYONE... THEY'D THINK IT WAS CREEPY...
TOMORROW'S SUNDAY. LET'S MEET AT THE MUSEUM AT 1:00!
YEAH!
WE'RE THERE!
WOW... AN EGYPTIAN EXHIBIT!
I LOVE THIS STUFF! I CAN'T WAIT!

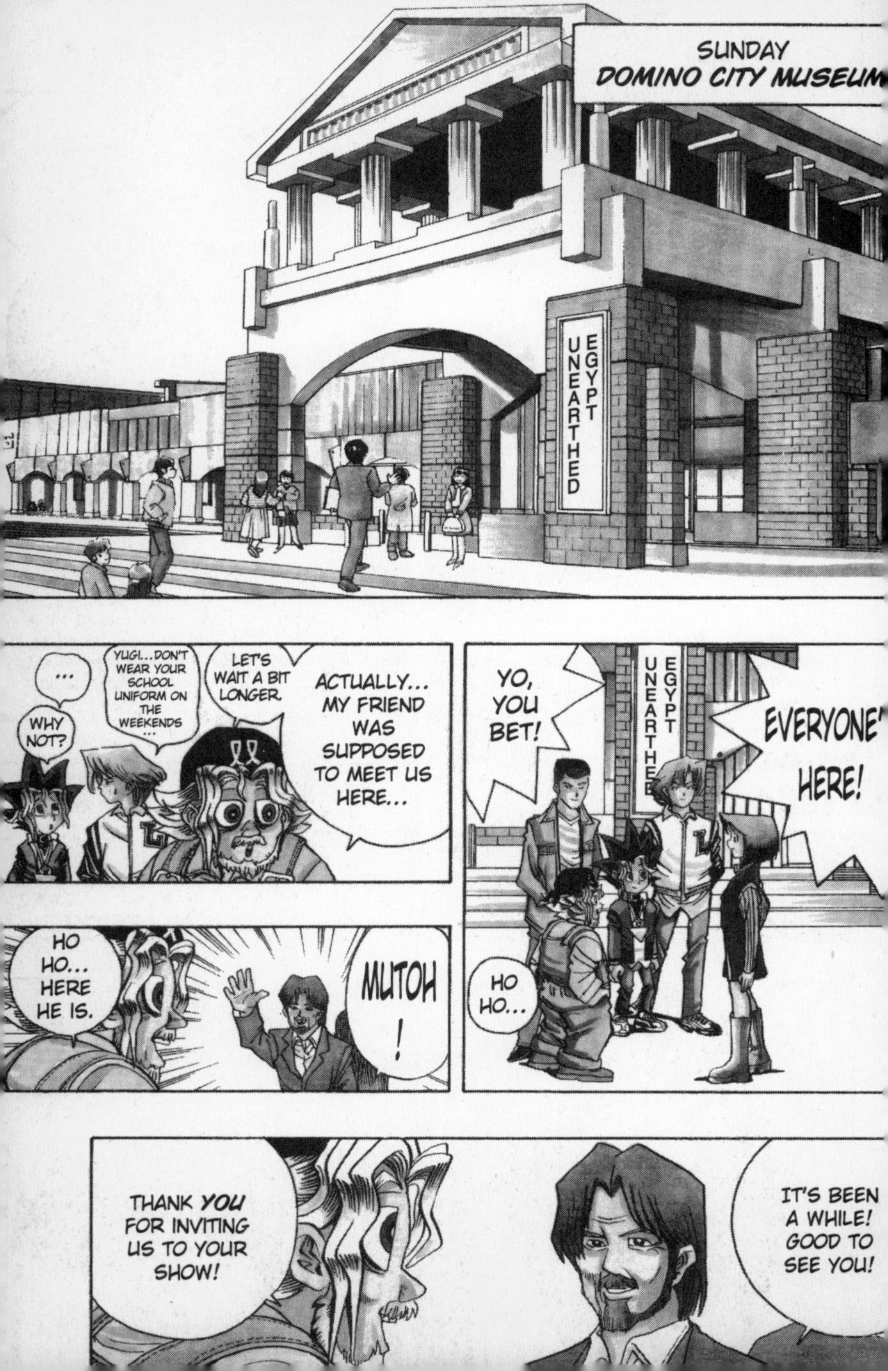
SUNDAY
DOMINO CITY MUSEUM
UNEARTHED EGYPT
EVERYONE' HERE!
YO, YOU BET!
UNEARTHED EGYPT
HO HO...
ACTUALLY... MY FRIEND WAS SUPPOSED TO MEET US HERE...
LET'S WAIT A BIT LONGER.
YUGI...DON'T WEAR YOUR SCHOOL UNIFORM ON THE WEEKENDS...
...
WHY NOT?
MUTOH!
HO HO... HERE HE IS.
IT'S BEEN A WHILE! GOOD TO SEE YOU!
THANK YOU FOR INVITING US TO YOUR SHOW!

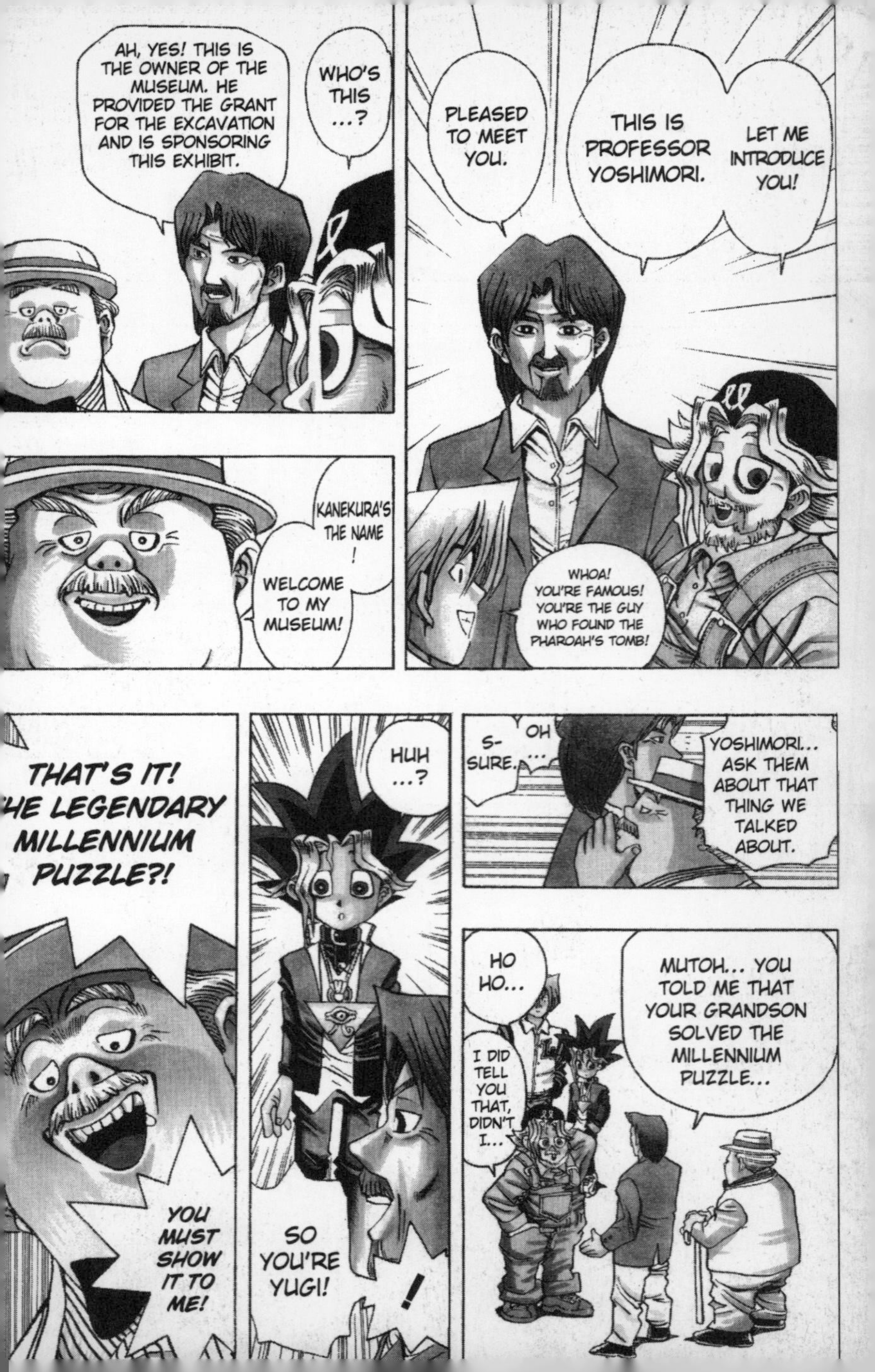
LET ME INTRODUCE YOU!
THIS IS PROFESSOR YOSHIMORI.
PLEASED TO MEET YOU.
WHOA! YOU'RE FAMOUS! YOU'RE THE GUY WHO FOUND THE PHAROAH'S TOMB!
WHO'S THIS ...?
AH, YES! THIS IS THE OWNER OF THE MUSEUM. HE PROVIDED THE GRANT FOR THE EXCAVATION AND IS SPONSORING THIS EXHIBIT.
KANEKURA'S THE NAME !
WELCOME TO MY MUSEUM!
YOSHIMORI... ASK THEM ABOUT THAT THING WE TALKED ABOUT.
OH ...
S-SURE.
MUTOH... YOU TOLD ME THAT YOUR GRANDSON SOLVED THE MILLENNIUM PUZZLE...
HO HO...
I DID TELL YOU THAT, DIDN'T I...
HUH ...?
SO YOU'RE YUGI!
!
THAT'S IT! HE LEGENDARY MILLENNIUM PUZZLE?!
YOU MUST SHOW IT TO ME!

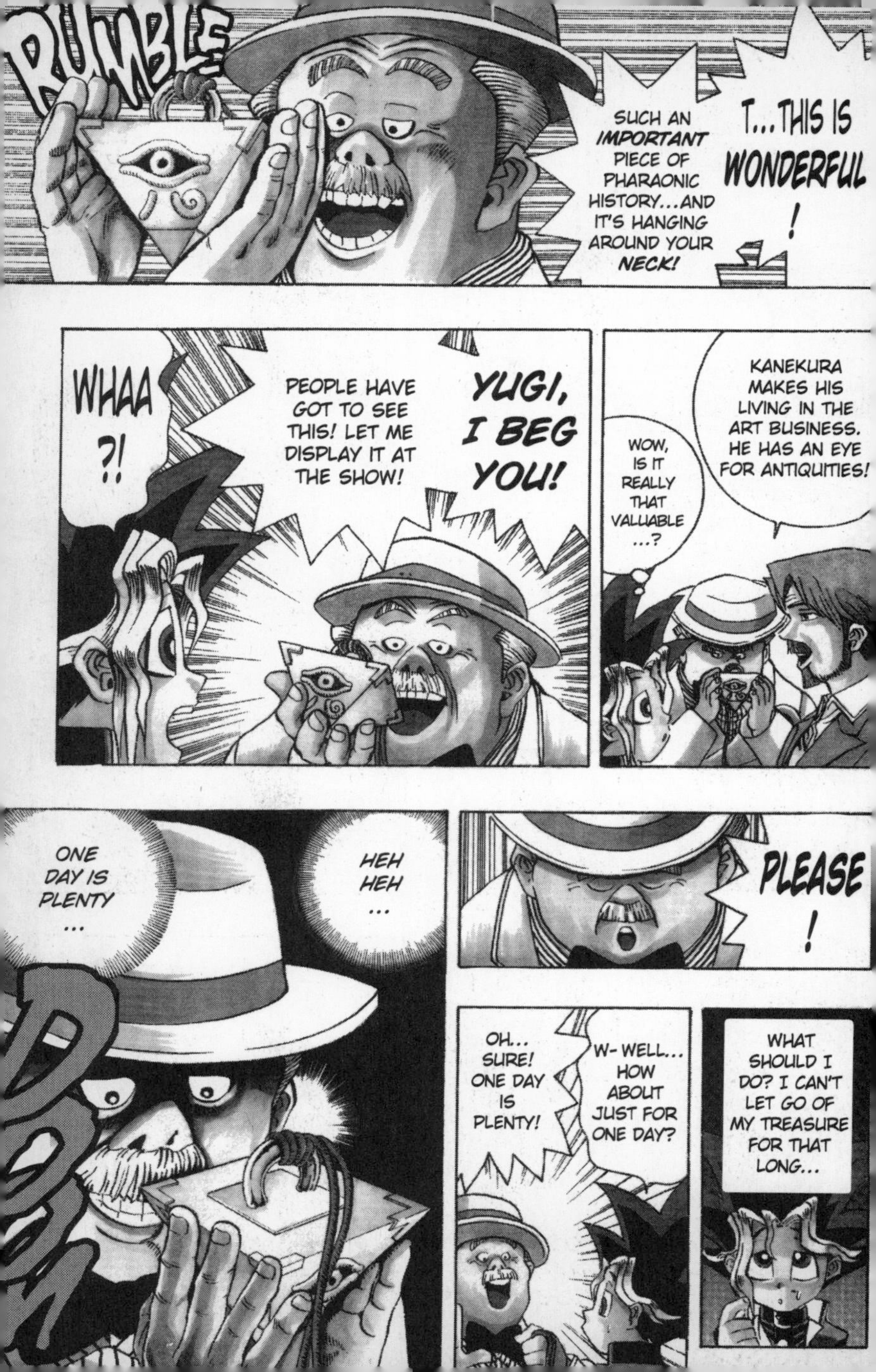
T...THIS IS WONDERFUL!
SUCH AN IMPORTANT PIECE OF PHARAONIC HISTORY...AND IT'S HANGING AROUND YOUR NECK!
RUMBLE
KANEKURA MAKES HIS LIVING IN THE ART BUSINESS. HE HAS AN EYE FOR ANTIQUITIES!
WOW, IS IT REALLY THAT VALUABLE ...?
YUGI, I BEG YOU!
PEOPLE HAVE GOT TO SEE THIS! LET ME DISPLAY IT AT THE SHOW!
WHAA ?!
PLEASE !
WHAT SHOULD I DO? I CAN'T LET GO OF MY TREASURE FOR THAT LONG...
W-WELL... HOW ABOUT JUST FOR ONE DAY?
OH... SURE! ONE DAY IS PLENTY!
HEH HEH ...
ONE DAY IS PLENTY ...

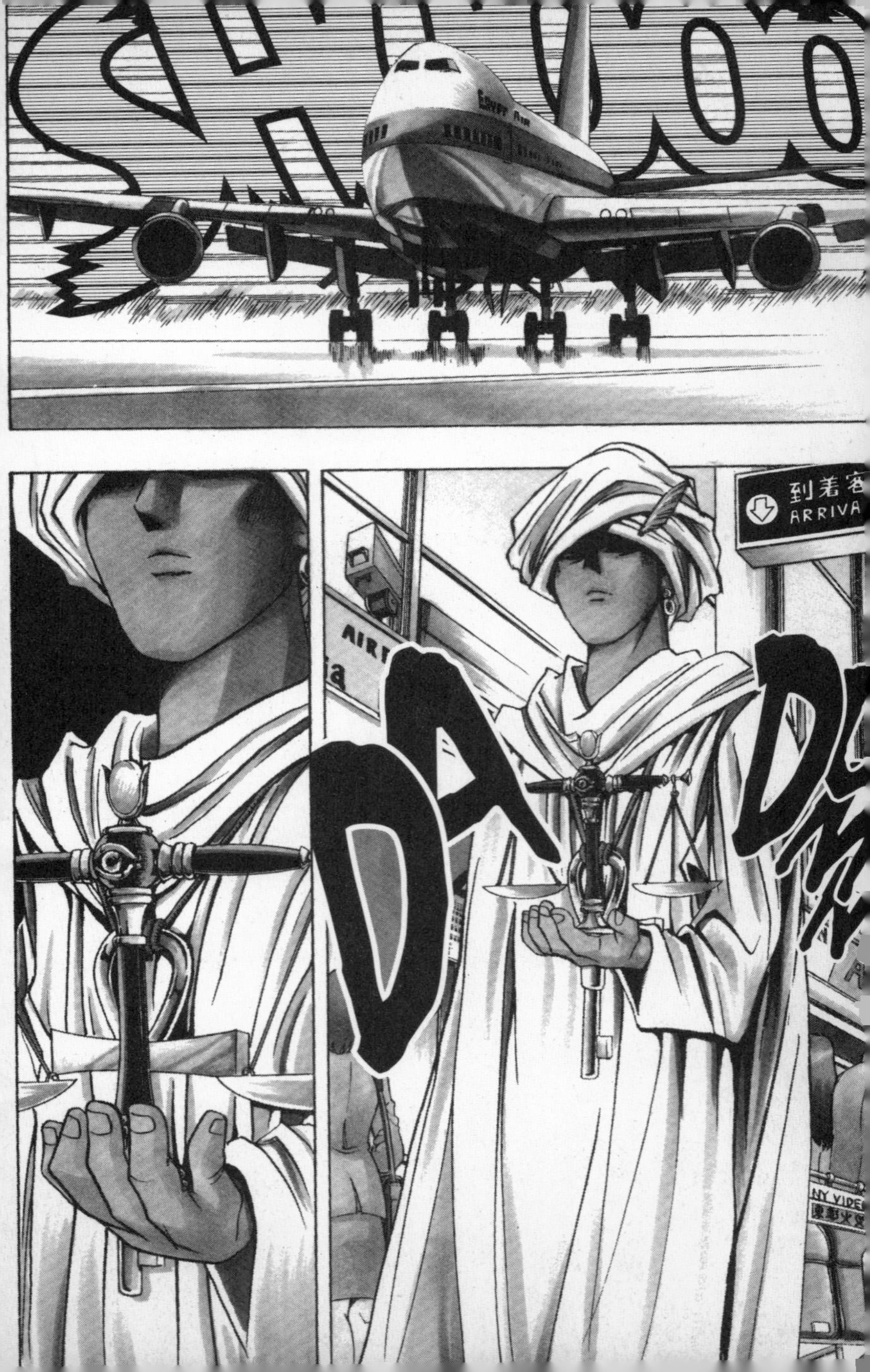
到着客
ARRIVA
DA

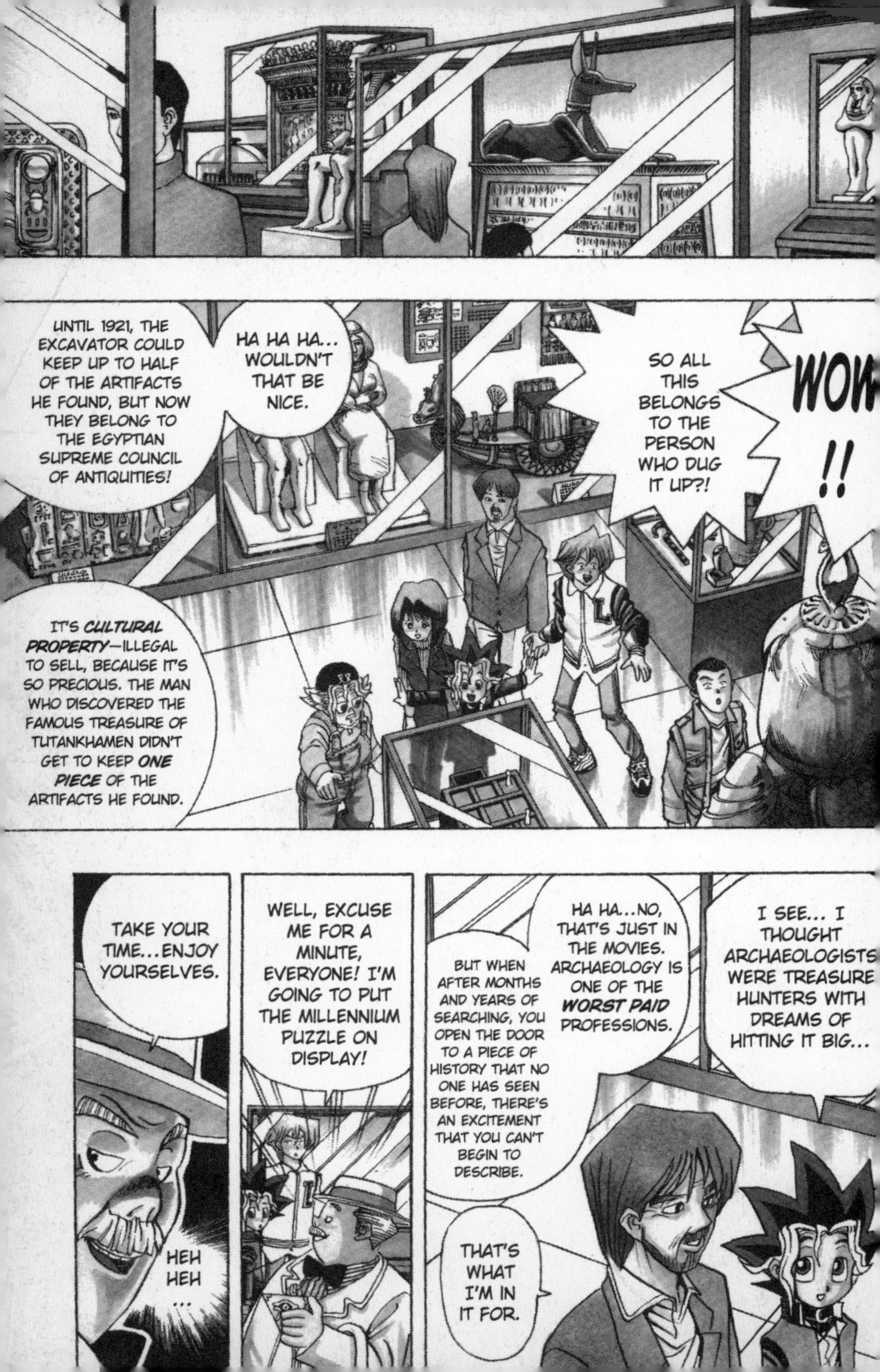
WOW!!
SO ALL THIS BELONGS TO THE PERSON WHO DUG IT UP?!
HA HA HA... WOULDN'T THAT BE NICE.
UNTIL 1921, THE EXCAVATOR COULD KEEP UP TO HALF OF THE ARTIFACTS HE FOUND, BUT NOW THEY BELONG TO THE EGYPTIAN SUPREME COUNCIL OF ANTIQUITIES!
IT'S *CULTURAL PROPERTY*—ILLEGAL TO SELL, BECAUSE IT'S SO PRECIOUS. THE MAN WHO DISCOVERED THE FAMOUS TREASURE OF TUTANKHAMEN DIDN'T GET TO KEEP *ONE PIECE* OF THE ARTIFACTS HE FOUND.
I SEE... I THOUGHT ARCHAEOLOGISTS WERE TREASURE HUNTERS WITH DREAMS OF HITTING IT BIG...
HA HA...NO, THAT'S JUST IN THE MOVIES. ARCHAEOLOGY IS ONE OF THE *WORST PAID* PROFESSIONS.
BUT WHEN AFTER MONTHS AND YEARS OF SEARCHING, YOU OPEN THE DOOR TO A PIECE OF HISTORY THAT NO ONE HAS SEEN BEFORE, THERE'S AN EXCITEMENT THAT YOU CAN'T BEGIN TO DESCRIBE.
THAT'S WHAT I'M IN IT FOR.
WELL, EXCUSE ME FOR A MINUTE, EVERYONE! I'M GOING TO PUT THE MILLENNIUM PUZZLE ON DISPLAY!
TAKE YOUR TIME...ENJOY YOURSELVES.
HEH HEH ...

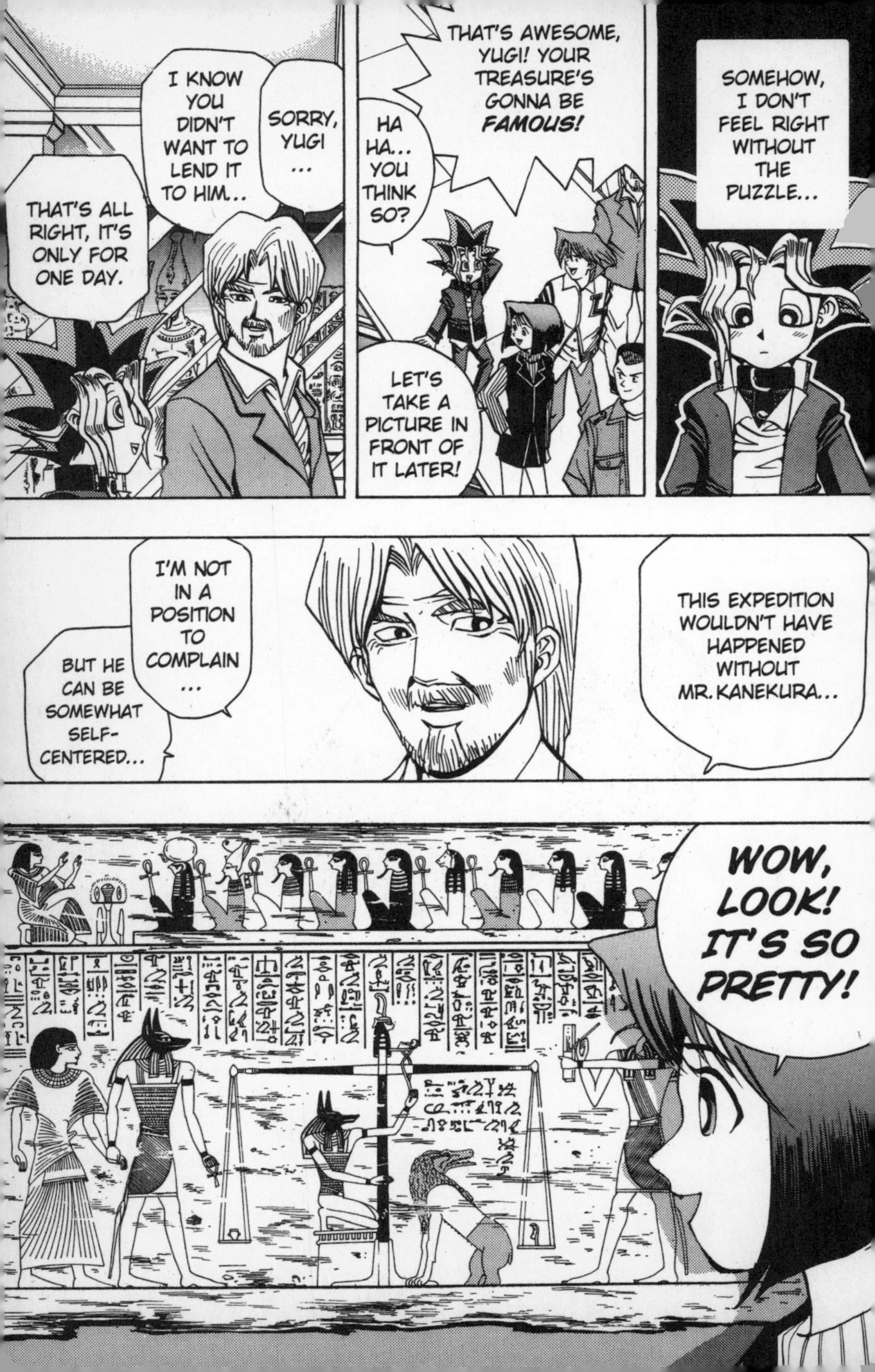
I KNOW YOU DIDN'T WANT TO LEND IT TO HIM...
SORRY, YUGI ...
THAT'S ALL RIGHT, IT'S ONLY FOR ONE DAY.
THAT'S AWESOME, YUGI! YOUR TREASURE'S GONNA BE *FAMOUS!*
HA HA... YOU THINK SO?
LET'S TAKE A PICTURE IN FRONT OF IT LATER!
SOMEHOW, I DON'T FEEL RIGHT WITHOUT THE PUZZLE...
I'M NOT IN A POSITION TO COMPLAIN ...
BUT HE CAN BE SOMEWHAT SELF-CENTERED...
THIS EXPEDITION WOULDN'T HAVE HAPPENED WITHOUT MR. KANEKURA...
WOW, LOOK! IT'S SO PRETTY!

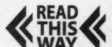

READ THIS WAY

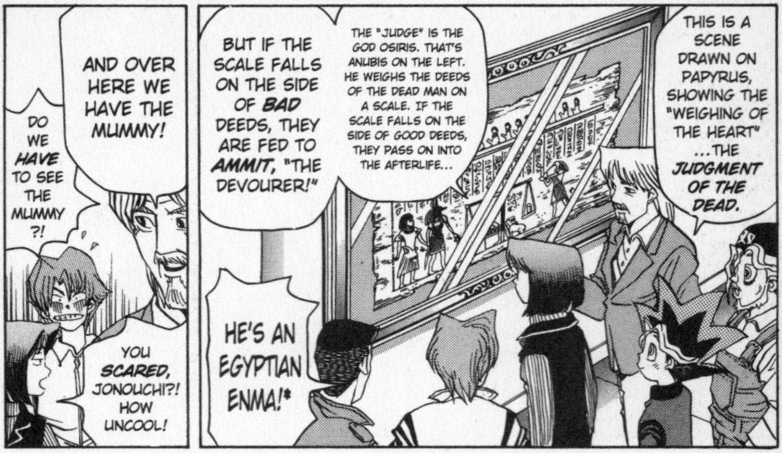
THIS IS A SCENE DRAWN ON PAPYRUS, SHOWING THE "WEIGHING OF THE HEART" ...THE JUDGMENT OF THE DEAD.
THE "JUDGE" IS THE GOD OSIRIS. THAT'S ANUBIS ON THE LEFT. HE WEIGHS THE DEEDS OF THE DEAD MAN ON A SCALE. IF THE SCALE FALLS ON THE SIDE OF GOOD DEEDS, THEY PASS ON INTO THE AFTERLIFE...
BUT IF THE SCALE FALLS ON THE SIDE OF BAD DEEDS, THEY ARE FED TO AMMIT, "THE DEVOURER!"
HE'S AN EGYPTIAN ENMA!*
AND OVER HERE WE HAVE THE MUMMY!
DO WE HAVE TO SEE THE MUMMY ?!
YOU SCARED, JONOUCHI?! HOW UNCOOL!

* ENMA=THE JUDGE OF THE DEAD IN JAPANESE MYTHOLOGY (LIKE KOENMA IN *YUYU HAKUSHO*)

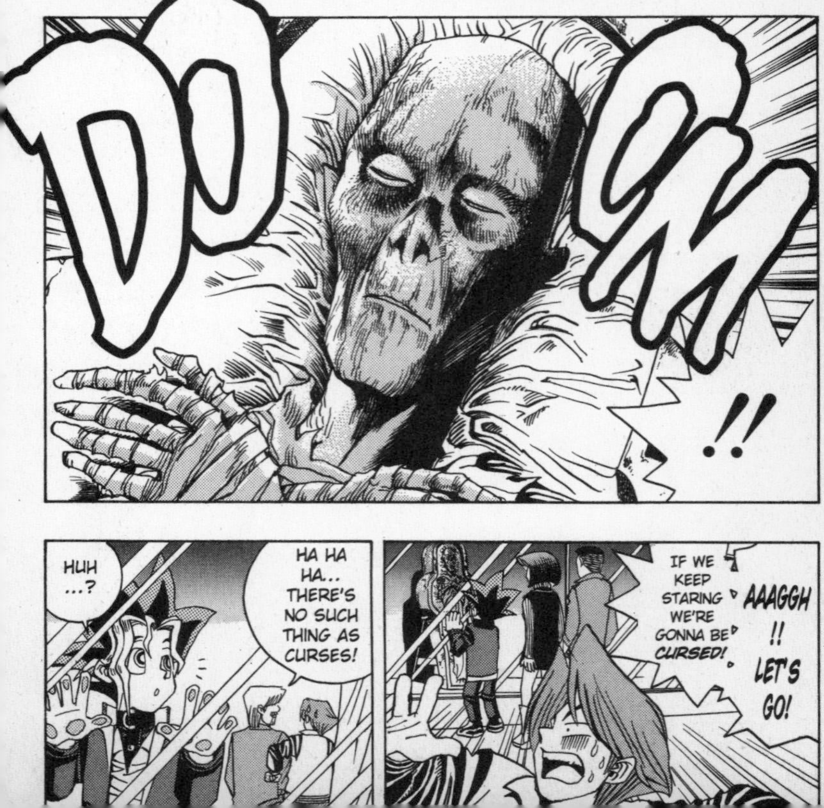
DOOM
!!
IF WE KEEP STARING WE'RE GONNA BE CURSED!
AAAGGH!! LET'S GO!
HA HA HA... THERE'S NO SUCH THING AS CURSES!
HUH ...?

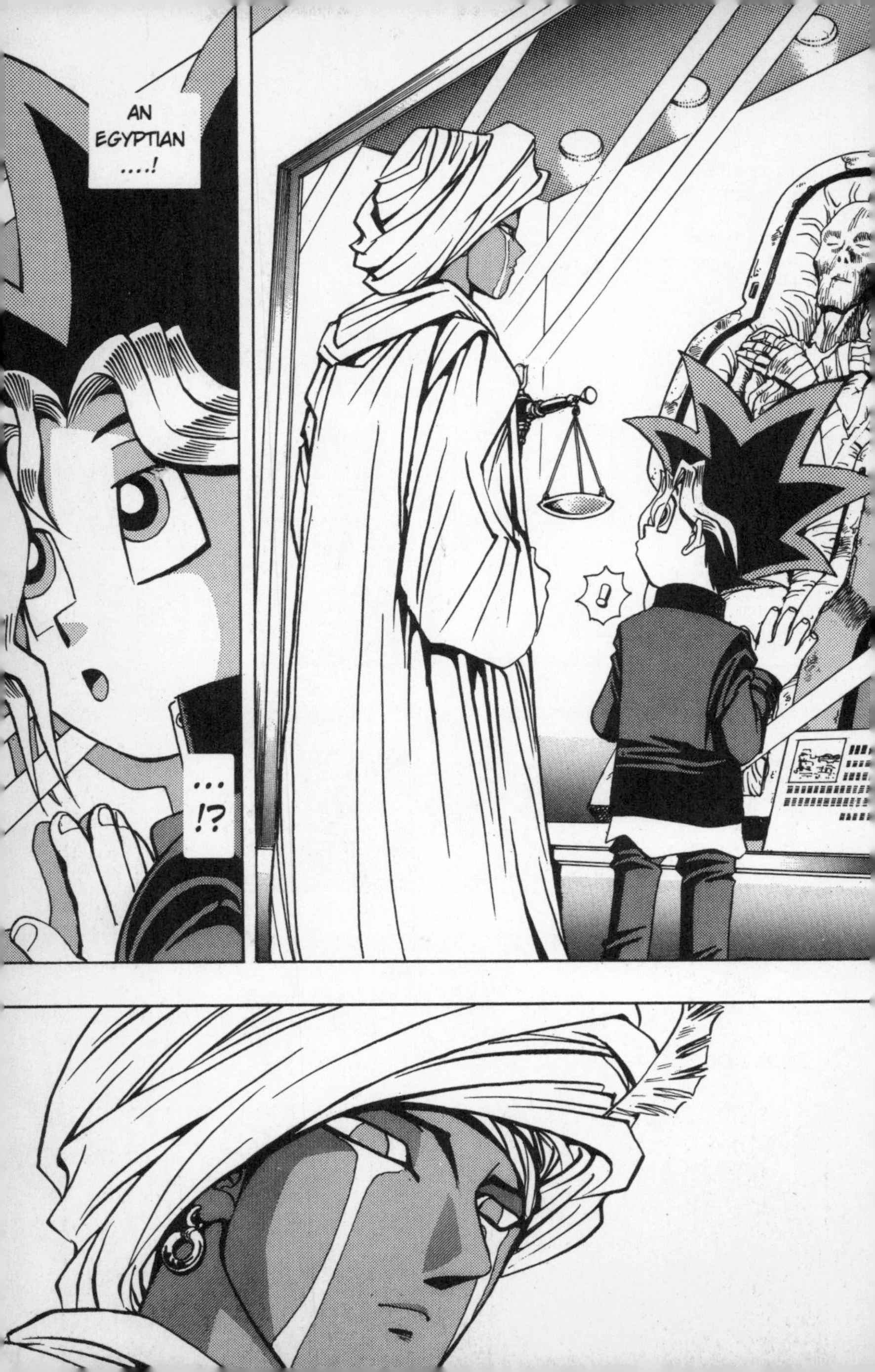
!
AN EGYPTIAN ....!
... !?

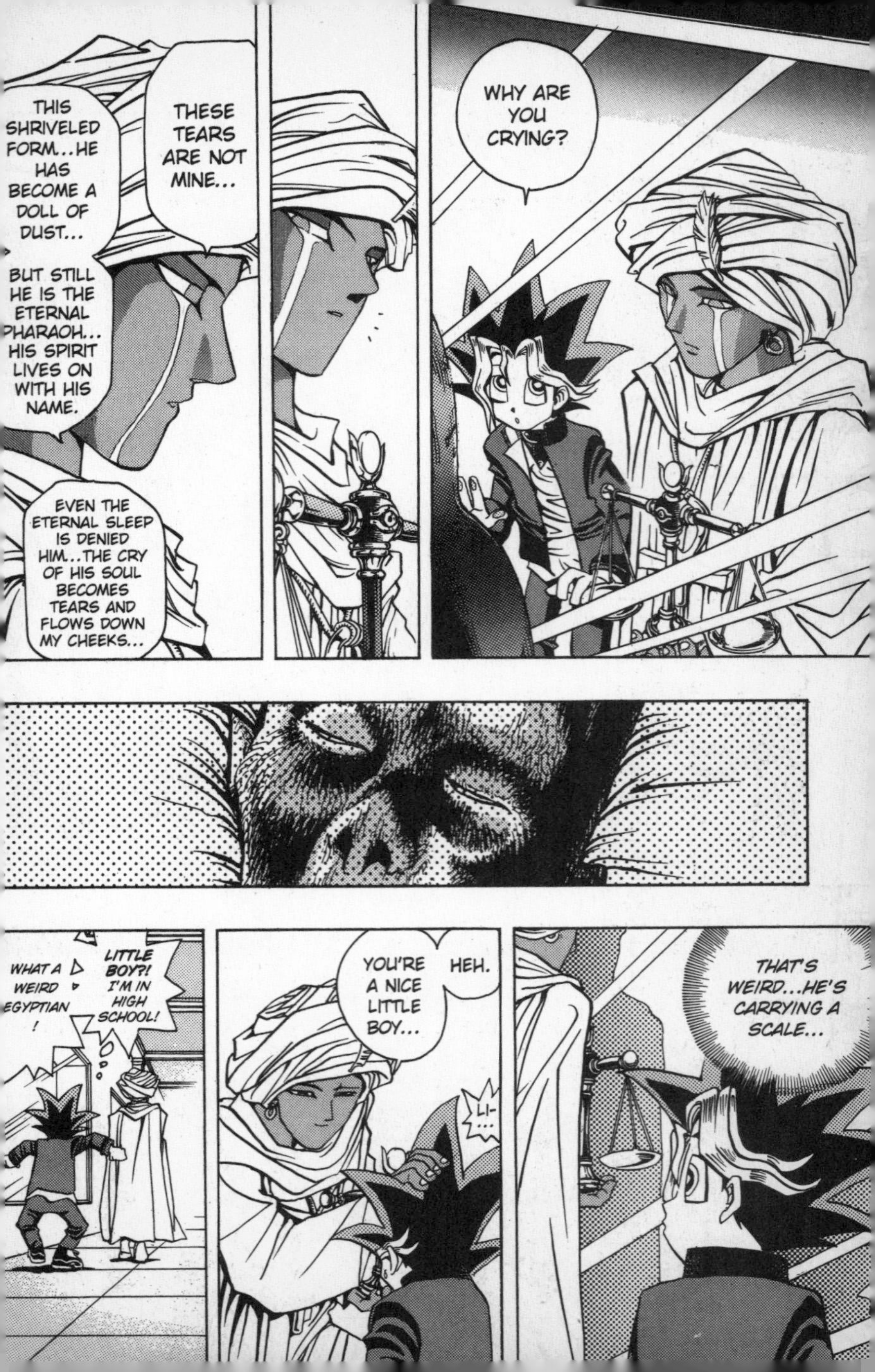
WHY ARE YOU CRYING?
THESE TEARS ARE NOT MINE...
THIS SHRIVELED FORM...HE HAS BECOME A DOLL OF DUST...
BUT STILL HE IS THE ETERNAL PHARAOH... HIS SPIRIT LIVES ON WITH HIS NAME.
EVEN THE ETERNAL SLEEP IS DENIED HIM...THE CRY OF HIS SOUL BECOMES TEARS AND FLOWS DOWN MY CHEEKS...
THAT'S WEIRD...HE'S CARRYING A SCALE...
HEH.
YOU'RE A NICE LITTLE BOY...
LI-...
LITTLE BOY?! I'M IN HIGH SCHOOL!
WHAT A WEIRD EGYPTIAN!

READ THIS WAY

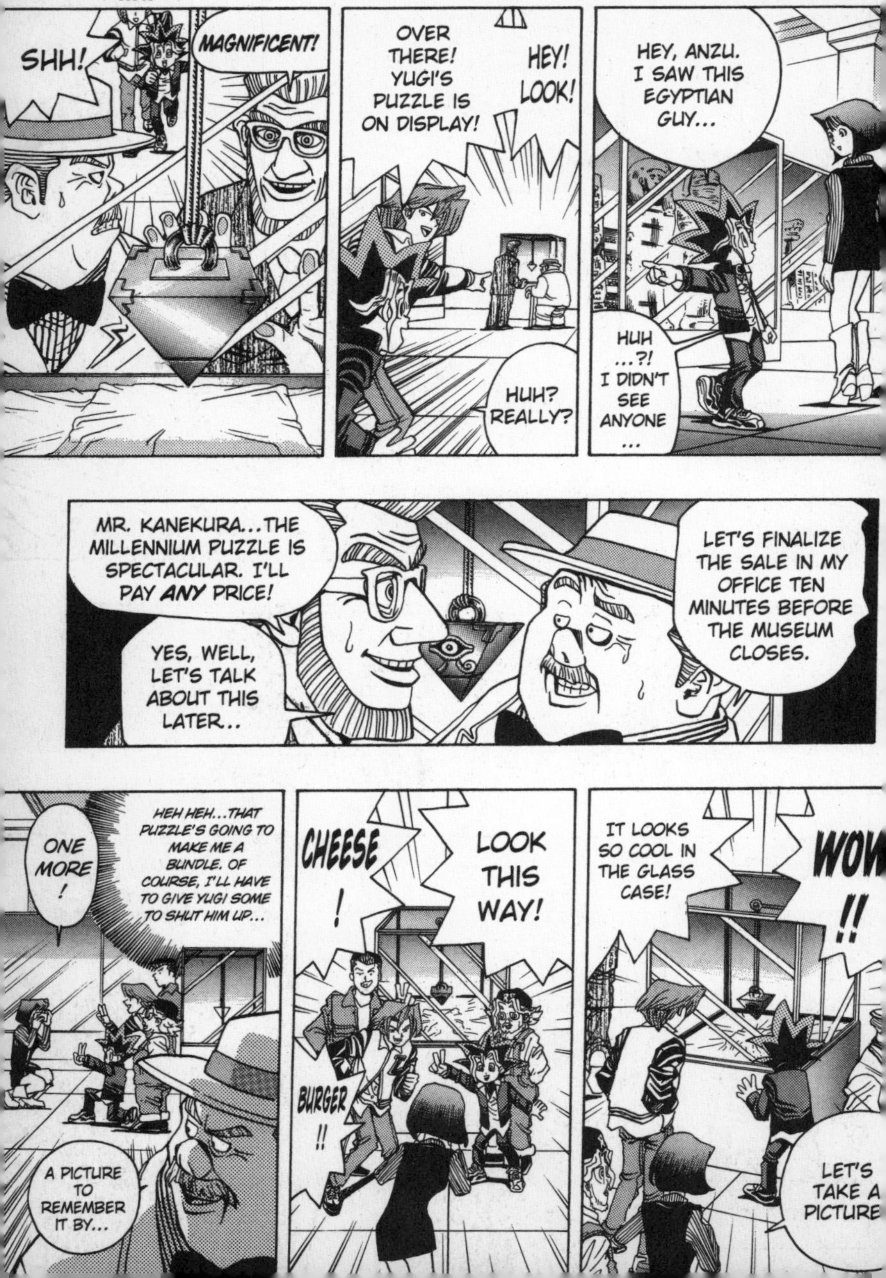
HEY, ANZU. I SAW THIS EGYPTIAN GUY...
HUH ...?! I DIDN'T SEE ANYONE ...
HEY! LOOK!
OVER THERE! YUGI'S PUZZLE IS ON DISPLAY!
HUH? REALLY?
MAGNIFICENT!
SHH!
MR. KANEKURA...THE MILLENNIUM PUZZLE IS SPECTACULAR. I'LL PAY *ANY* PRICE!
YES, WELL, LET'S TALK ABOUT THIS LATER...
LET'S FINALIZE THE SALE IN MY OFFICE TEN MINUTES BEFORE THE MUSEUM CLOSES.
WOW !!
IT LOOKS SO COOL IN THE GLASS CASE!
LET'S TAKE A PICTURE
LOOK THIS WAY!
CHEESE !
BURGER !!
HEH HEH...THAT PUZZLE'S GOING TO MAKE ME A BUNDLE. OF COURSE, I'LL HAVE TO GIVE YUGI SOME TO SHUT HIM UP...
ONE MORE !
A PICTURE TO REMEMBER IT BY...

READ THIS WAY

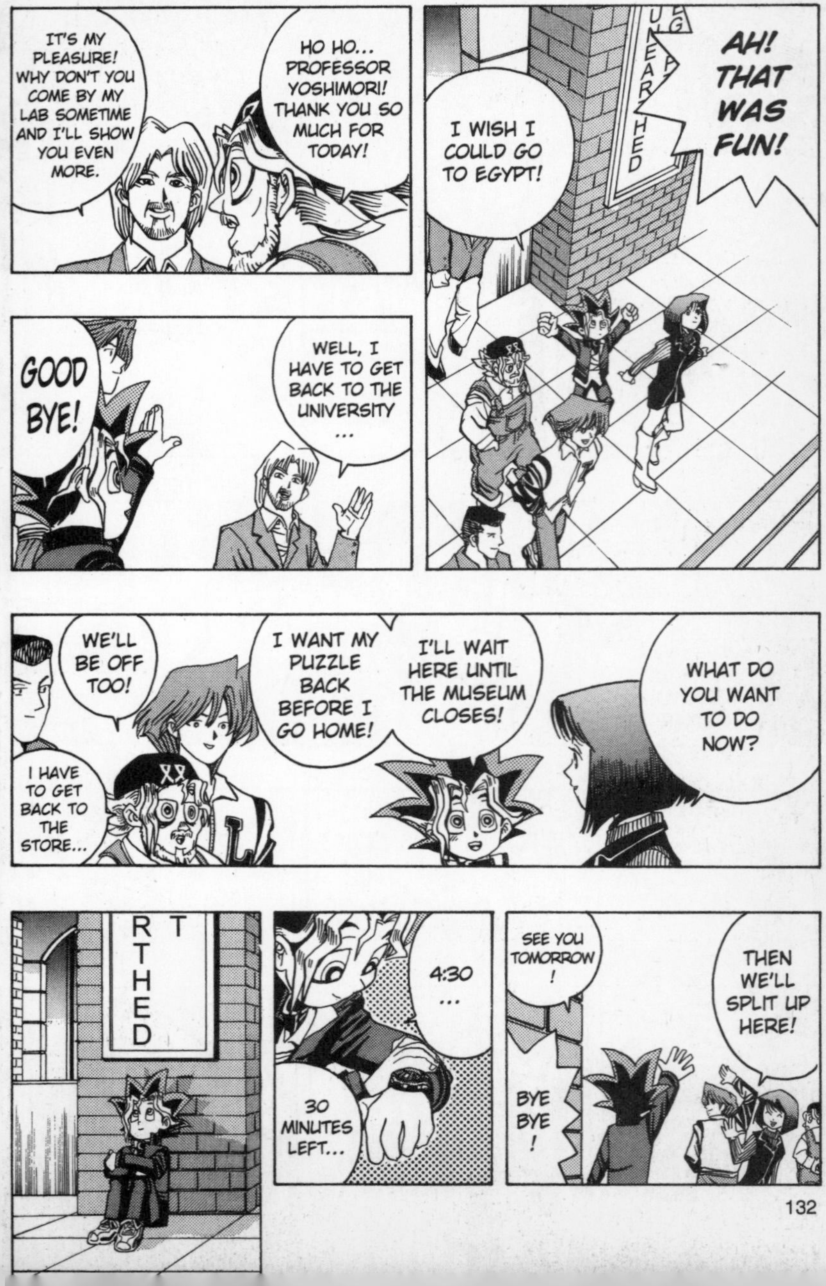
AH! THAT WAS FUN!
I WISH I COULD GO TO EGYPT!
HO HO... PROFESSOR YOSHIMORI! THANK YOU SO MUCH FOR TODAY!
IT'S MY PLEASURE! WHY DON'T YOU COME BY MY LAB SOMETIME AND I'LL SHOW YOU EVEN MORE.
WELL, I HAVE TO GET BACK TO THE UNIVERSITY ...
GOOD BYE!
WHAT DO YOU WANT TO DO NOW?
I'LL WAIT HERE UNTIL THE MUSEUM CLOSES!
I WANT MY PUZZLE BACK BEFORE I GO HOME!
WE'LL BE OFF TOO!
I HAVE TO GET BACK TO THE STORE...
THEN WE'LL SPLIT UP HERE!
SEE YOU TOMORROW!
BYE BYE!
4:30 ...
30 MINUTES LEFT...

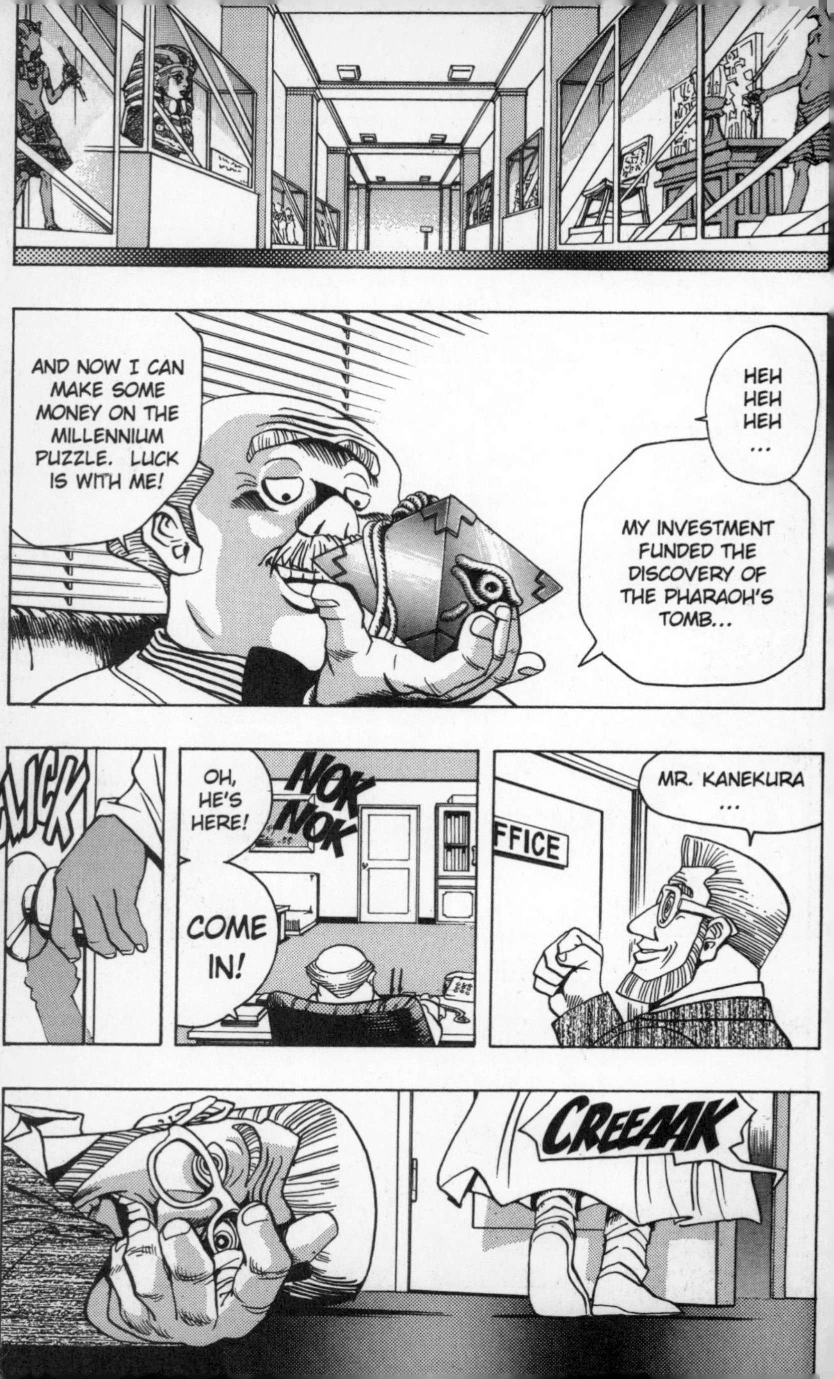
HEH HEH HEH ...
MY INVESTMENT FUNDED THE DISCOVERY OF THE PHARAOH'S TOMB...
AND NOW I CAN MAKE SOME MONEY ON THE MILLENNIUM PUZZLE. LUCK IS WITH ME!
MR. KANEKURA ...
FFICE
NOK NOK
OH, HE'S HERE!
COME IN!
CLICK
CREEAAK

READ THIS WAY

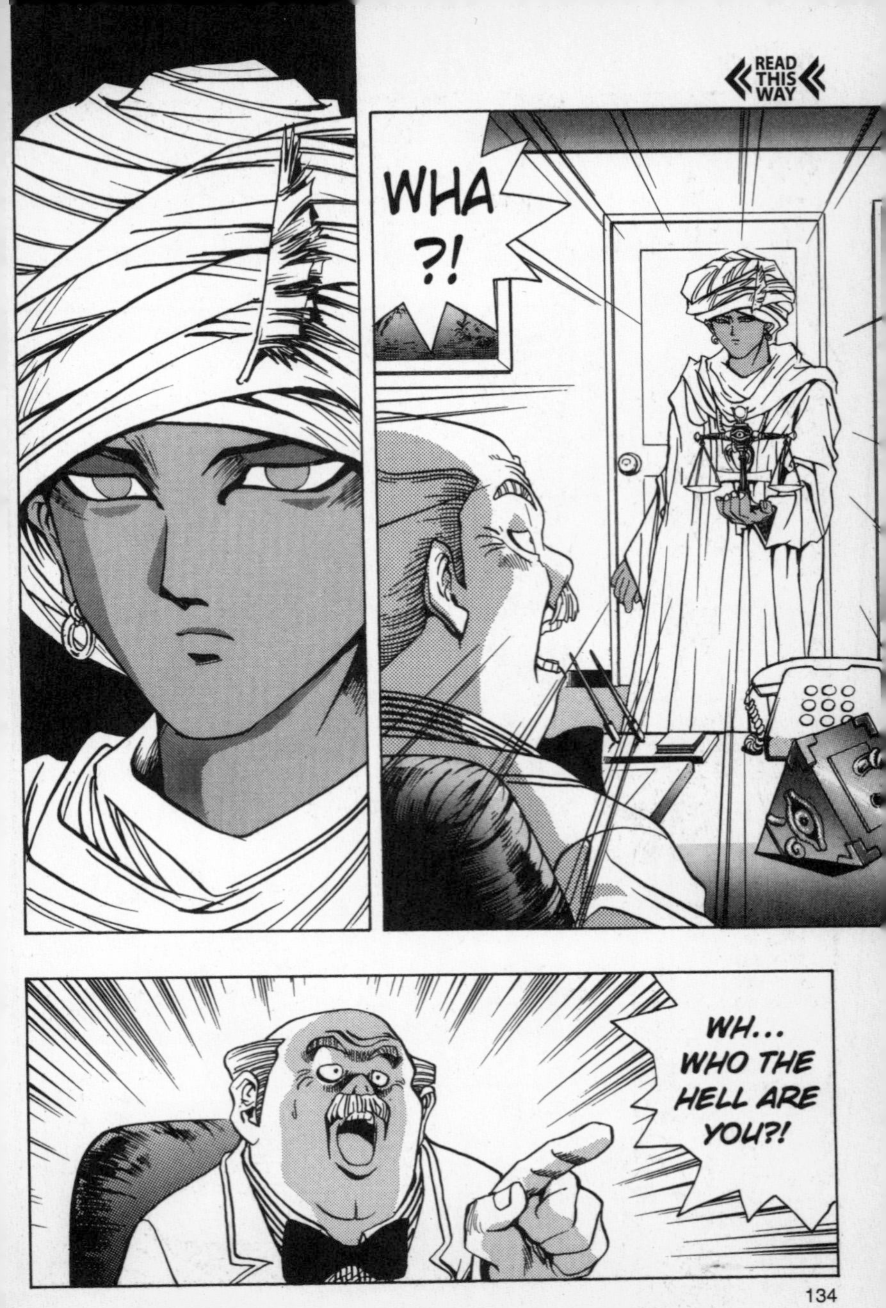
WHA ?!
WH... WHO THE HELL ARE YOU?!

READ THIS WAY

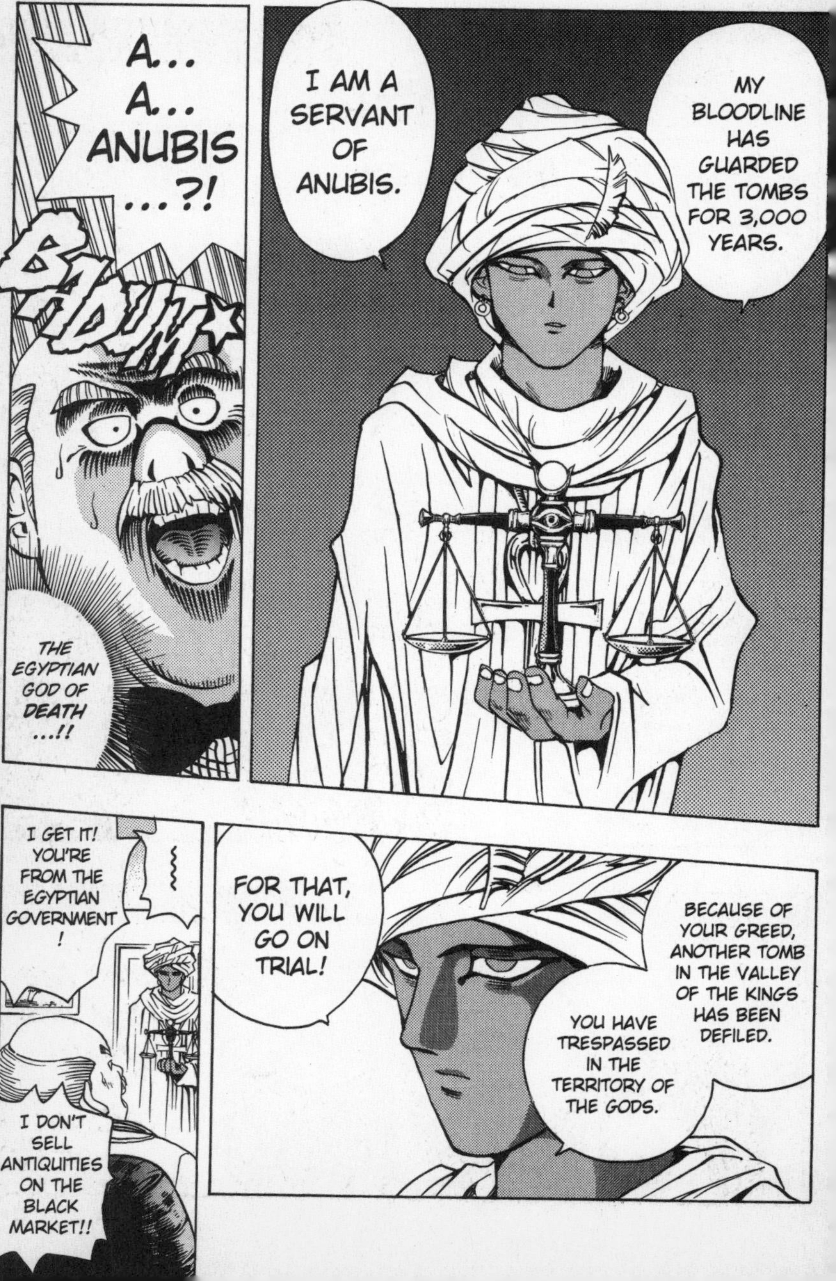

I AM A SERVANT OF ANUBIS.
MY BLOODLINE HAS GUARDED THE TOMBS FOR 3,000 YEARS.
A... A... ANUBIS ...?!
BADUM★
THE EGYPTIAN GOD OF DEATH ...!!
BECAUSE OF YOUR GREED, ANOTHER TOMB IN THE VALLEY OF THE KINGS HAS BEEN DEFILED.
YOU HAVE TRESPASSED IN THE TERRITORY OF THE GODS.
FOR THAT, YOU WILL GO ON TRIAL!
...
I GET IT! YOU'RE FROM THE EGYPTIAN GOVERNMENT!
I DON'T SELL ANTIQUITIES ON THE BLACK MARKET!!

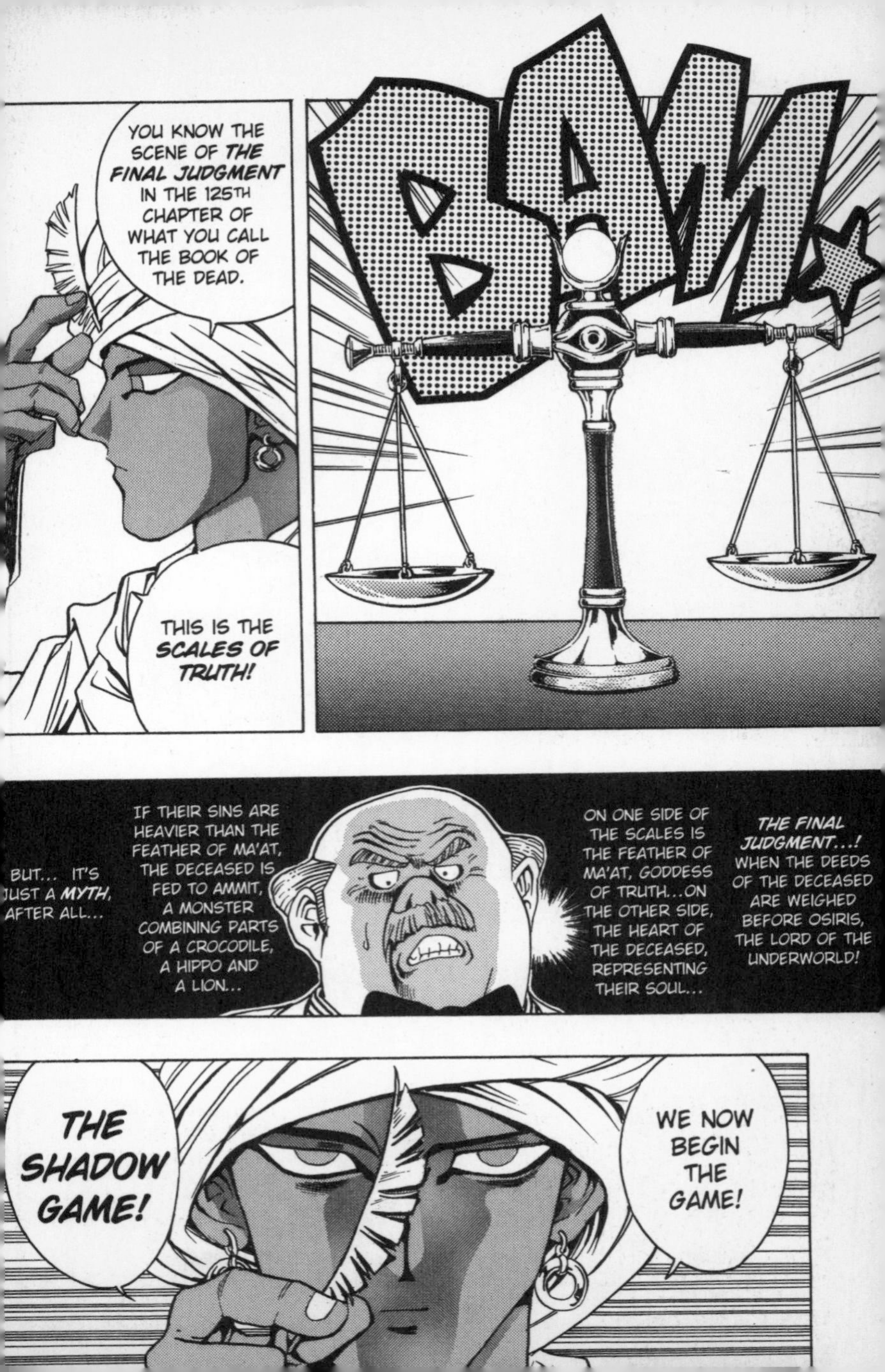
BAM
YOU KNOW THE SCENE OF THE FINAL JUDGMENT IN THE 125TH CHAPTER OF WHAT YOU CALL THE BOOK OF THE DEAD.
THIS IS THE SCALES OF TRUTH!
THE FINAL JUDGMENT...! WHEN THE DEEDS OF THE DECEASED ARE WEIGHED BEFORE OSIRIS, THE LORD OF THE UNDERWORLD!
ON ONE SIDE OF THE SCALES IS THE FEATHER OF MA'AT, GODDESS OF TRUTH...ON THE OTHER SIDE, THE HEART OF THE DECEASED, REPRESENTING THEIR SOUL...
IF THEIR SINS ARE HEAVIER THAN THE FEATHER OF MA'AT, THE DECEASED IS FED TO AMMIT, A MONSTER COMBINING PARTS OF A CROCODILE, A HIPPO AND A LION...
BUT... IT'S JUST A MYTH, AFTER ALL...
WE NOW BEGIN THE GAME!
THE SHADOW GAME!

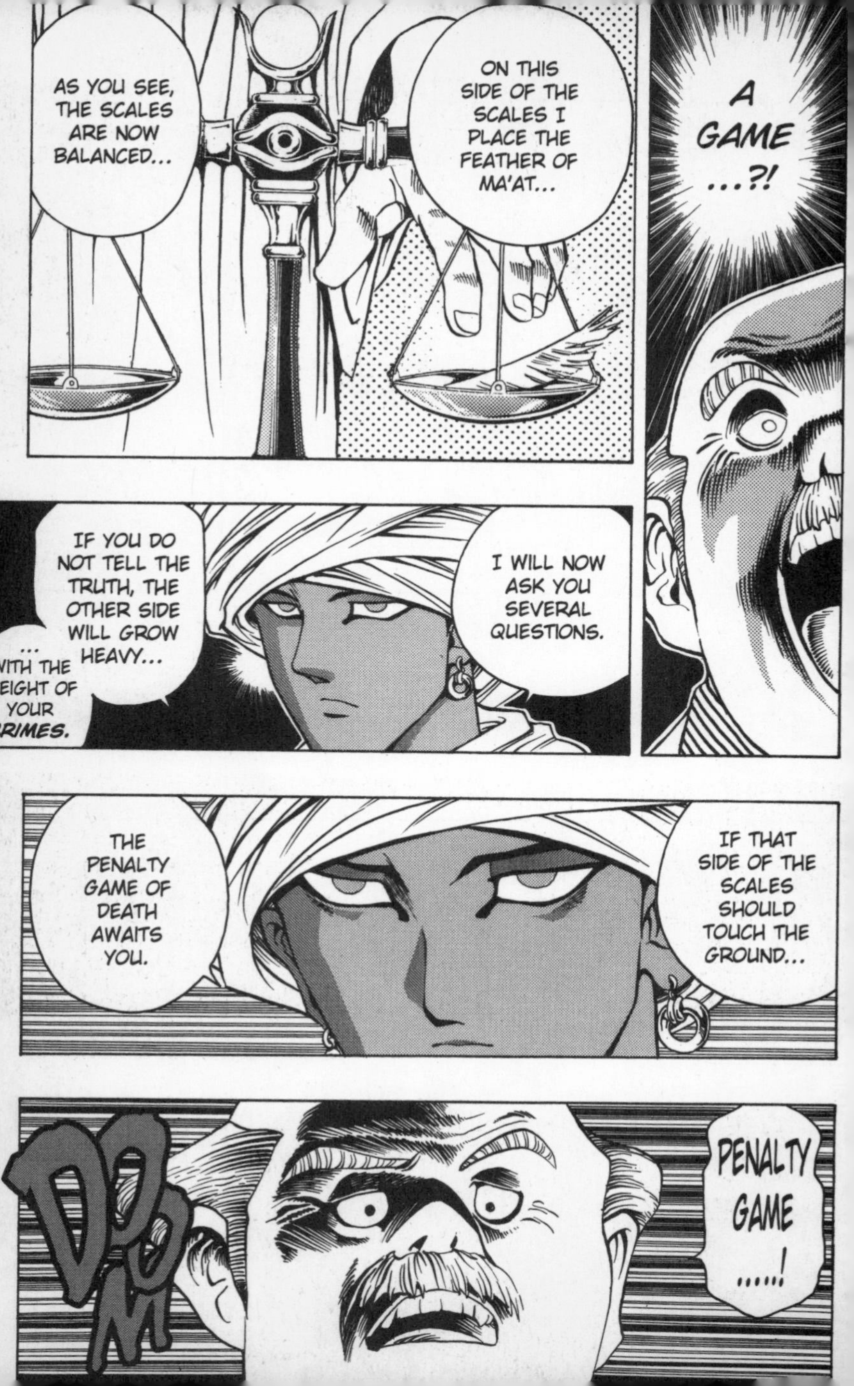
A GAME ...?!
ON THIS SIDE OF THE SCALES I PLACE THE FEATHER OF MA'AT...
AS YOU SEE, THE SCALES ARE NOW BALANCED...
I WILL NOW ASK YOU SEVERAL QUESTIONS.
IF YOU DO NOT TELL THE TRUTH, THE OTHER SIDE WILL GROW HEAVY...
... WITH THE WEIGHT OF YOUR CRIMES.
IF THAT SIDE OF THE SCALES SHOULD TOUCH THE GROUND...
THE PENALTY GAME OF DEATH AWAITS YOU.
PENALTY GAME ......!
DOOM

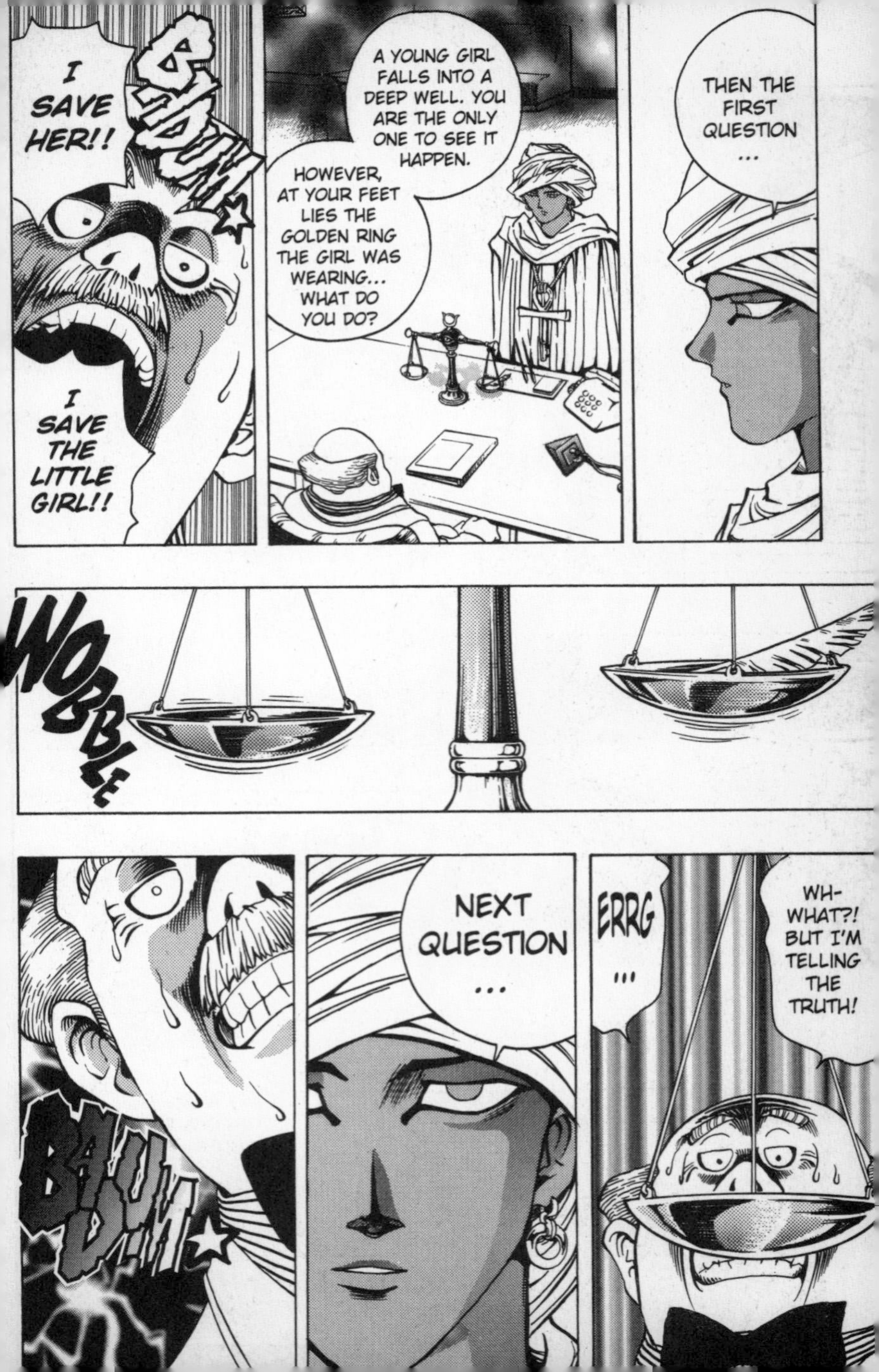
THEN THE FIRST QUESTION ...
A YOUNG GIRL FALLS INTO A DEEP WELL. YOU ARE THE ONLY ONE TO SEE IT HAPPEN.
HOWEVER, AT YOUR FEET LIES THE GOLDEN RING THE GIRL WAS WEARING... WHAT DO YOU DO?
I SAVE HER!!
I SAVE THE LITTLE GIRL!!
WOBBLE
WH- WHAT?! BUT I'M TELLING THE TRUTH!
ERRG ...
NEXT QUESTION ...

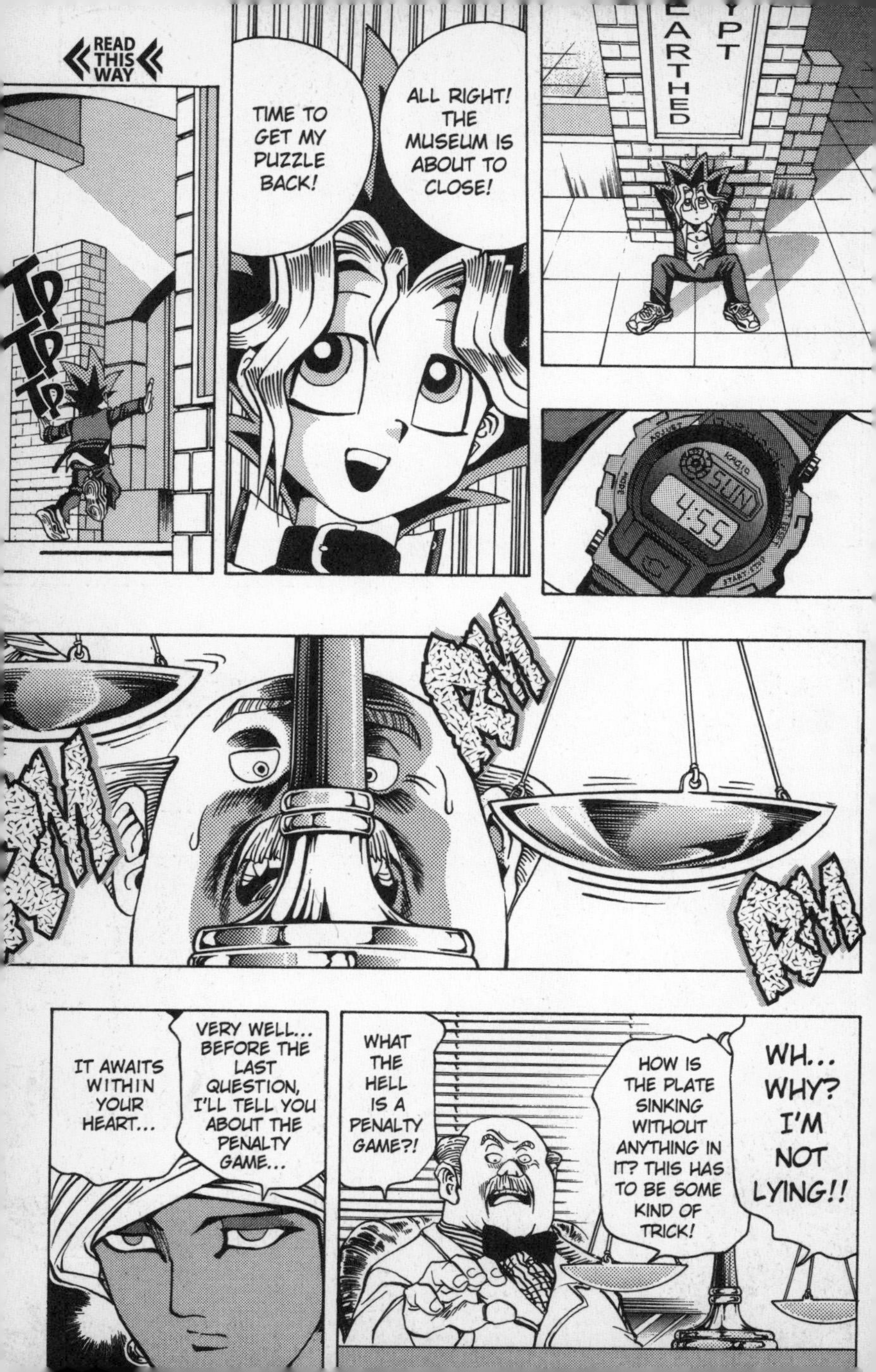
READ THIS WAY
EARTHED
SUN
4:55
ALL RIGHT! THE MUSEUM IS ABOUT TO CLOSE!
TIME TO GET MY PUZZLE BACK!
TP TP TP
WH... WHY? I'M NOT LYING!!
HOW IS THE PLATE SINKING WITHOUT ANYTHING IN IT? THIS HAS TO BE SOME KIND OF TRICK!
WHAT THE HELL IS A PENALTY GAME?!
VERY WELL... BEFORE THE LAST QUESTION, I'LL TELL YOU ABOUT THE PENALTY GAME...
IT AWAITS WITHIN YOUR HEART...

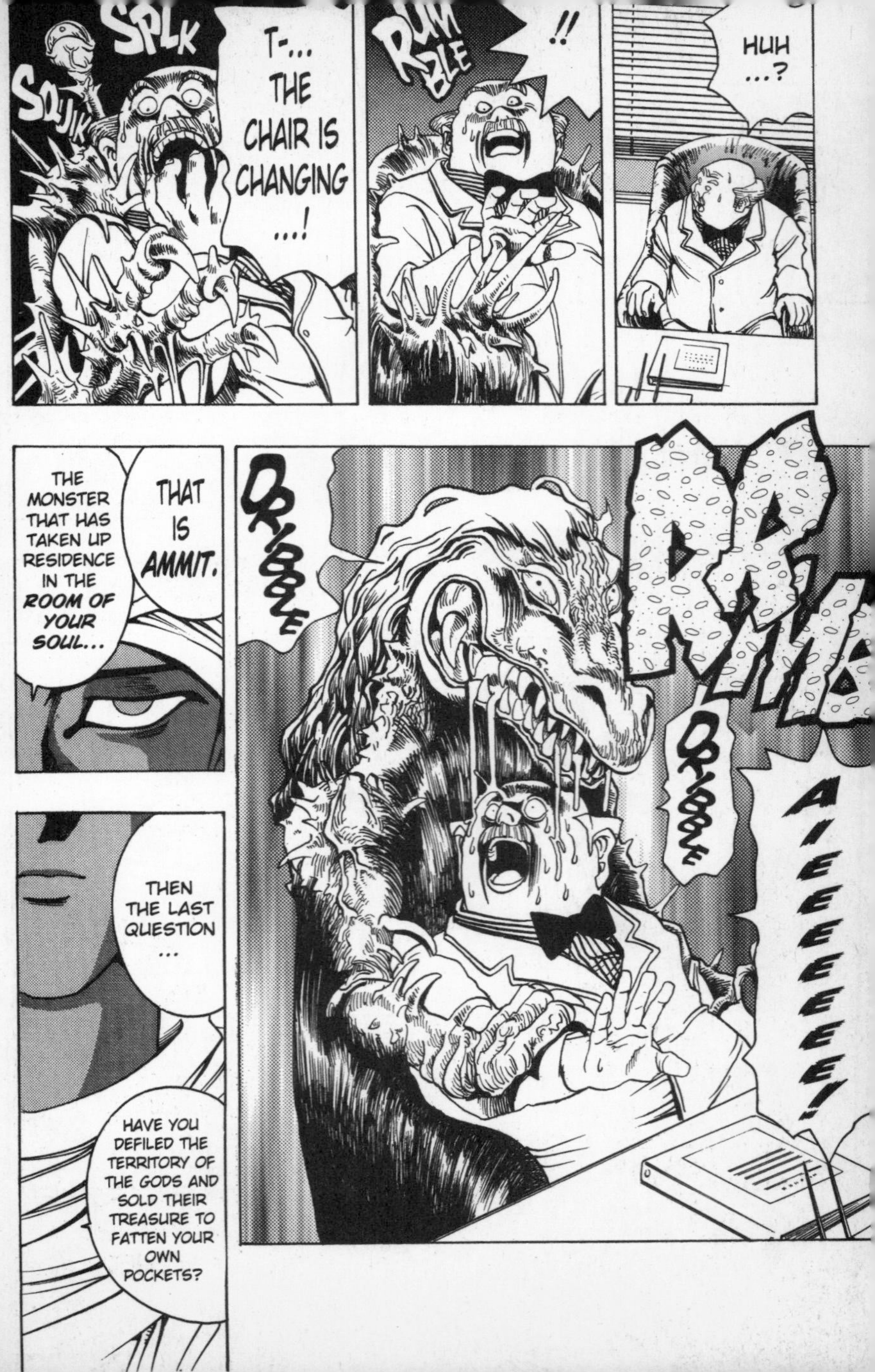
HUH ...?
RUMBLE
!!
SPLK
SQUJIK
T-... THE CHAIR IS CHANGING ...!
DRIBBLE
DRM
DRIBBLE
AIEEEEEEEEE!
THE MONSTER THAT HAS TAKEN UP RESIDENCE IN THE *ROOM OF YOUR SOUL...*
THAT IS *AMMIT.*
THEN THE LAST QUESTION ...
HAVE YOU DEFILED THE TERRITORY OF THE GODS AND SOLD THEIR TREASURE TO FATTEN YOUR OWN POCKETS?

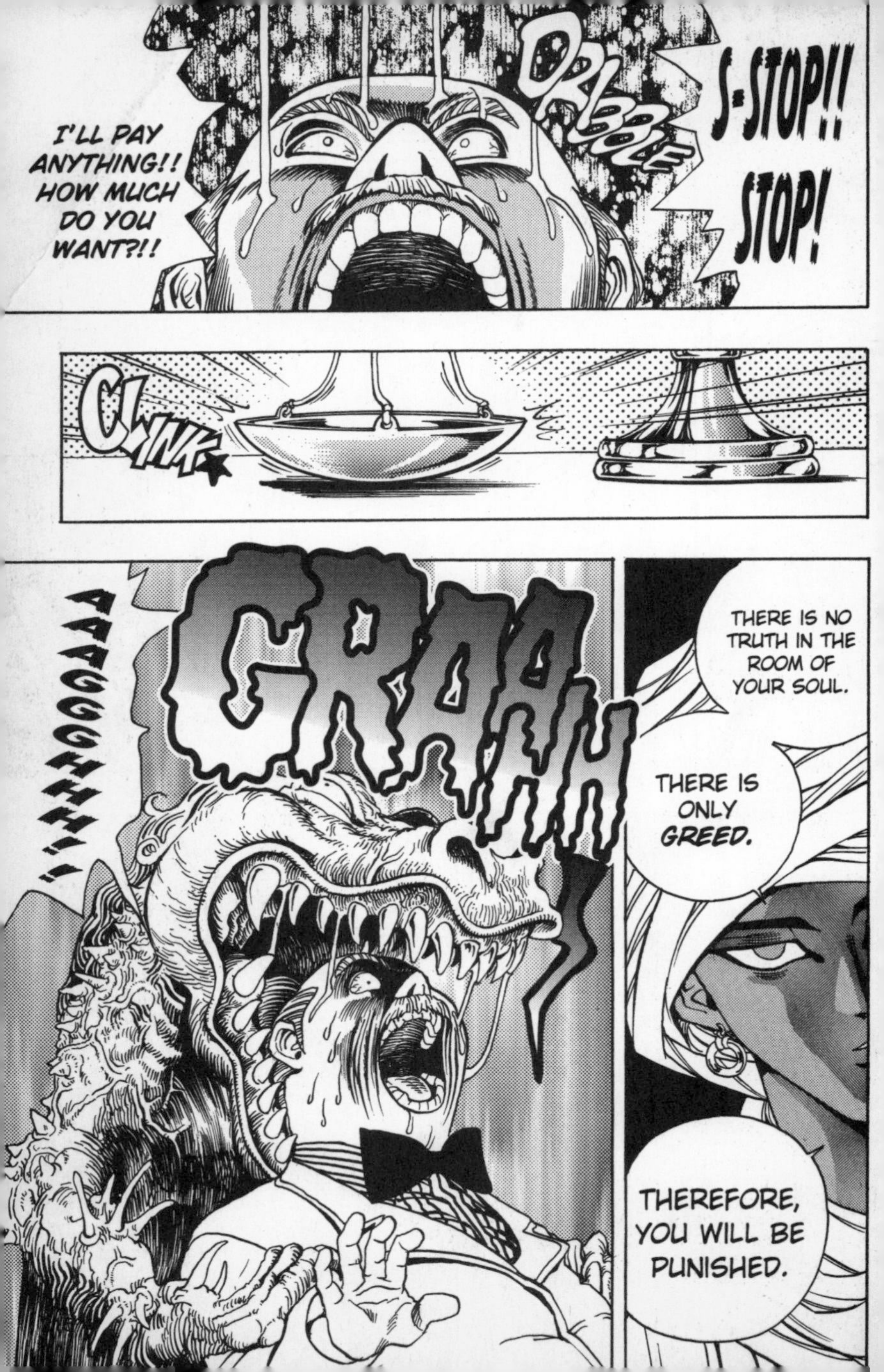
S-STOP!! STOP!
DRIBBLE
I'LL PAY ANYTHING!! HOW MUCH DO YOU WANT?!!
CLINK
THERE IS NO TRUTH IN THE ROOM OF YOUR SOUL.
THERE IS ONLY GREED.
THEREFORE, YOU WILL BE PUNISHED.
CRAAH
AAAAGGGHHHH!!

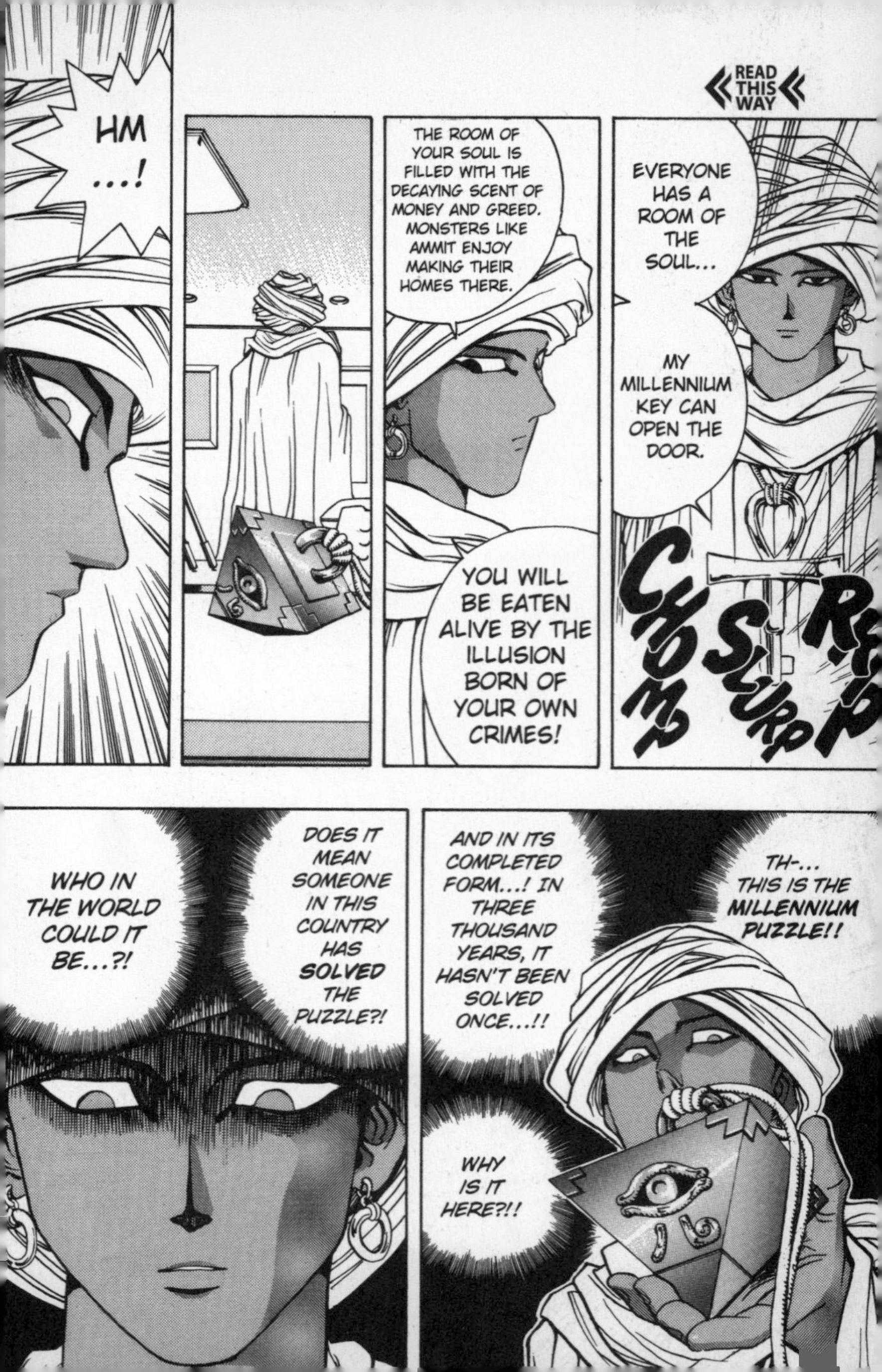
READ THIS WAY
EVERYONE HAS A ROOM OF THE SOUL...
MY MILLENNIUM KEY CAN OPEN THE DOOR.
SLURP
CHOMP
THE ROOM OF YOUR SOUL IS FILLED WITH THE DECAYING SCENT OF MONEY AND GREED. MONSTERS LIKE AMMIT ENJOY MAKING THEIR HOMES THERE.
YOU WILL BE EATEN ALIVE BY THE ILLUSION BORN OF YOUR OWN CRIMES!
HM ...!
TH-... THIS IS THE MILLENNIUM PUZZLE!!
AND IN ITS COMPLETED FORM...! IN THREE THOUSAND YEARS, IT HASN'T BEEN SOLVED ONCE...!!
WHY IS IT HERE?!!
DOES IT MEAN SOMEONE IN THIS COUNTRY HAS SOLVED THE PUZZLE?!
WHO IN THE WORLD COULD IT BE...?!

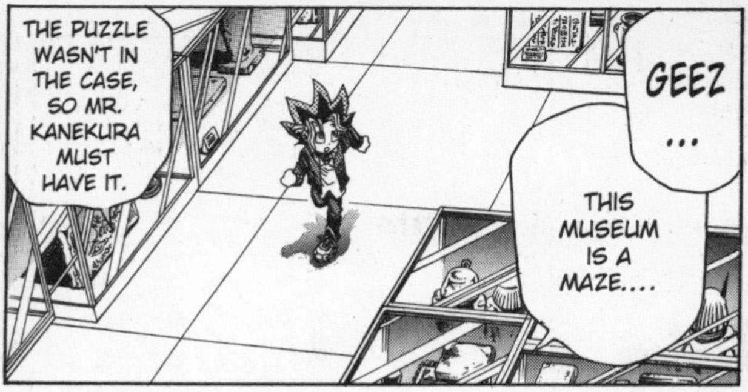
GEEZ ...
THIS MUSEUM IS A MAZE....
THE PUZZLE WASN'T IN THE CASE, SO MR. KANEKURA MUST HAVE IT.
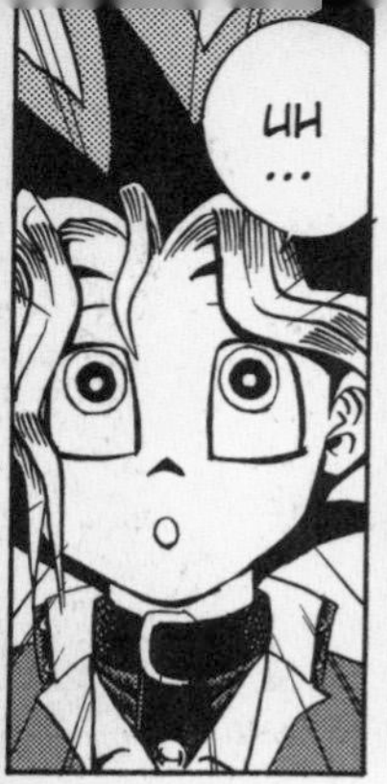
UH ...
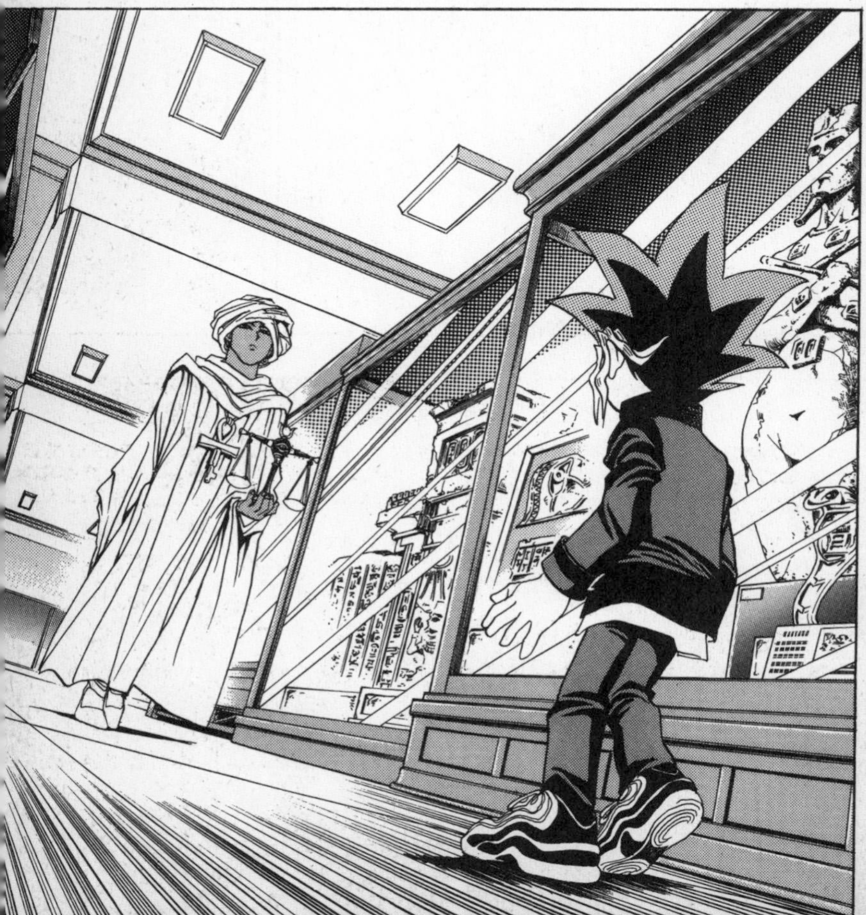

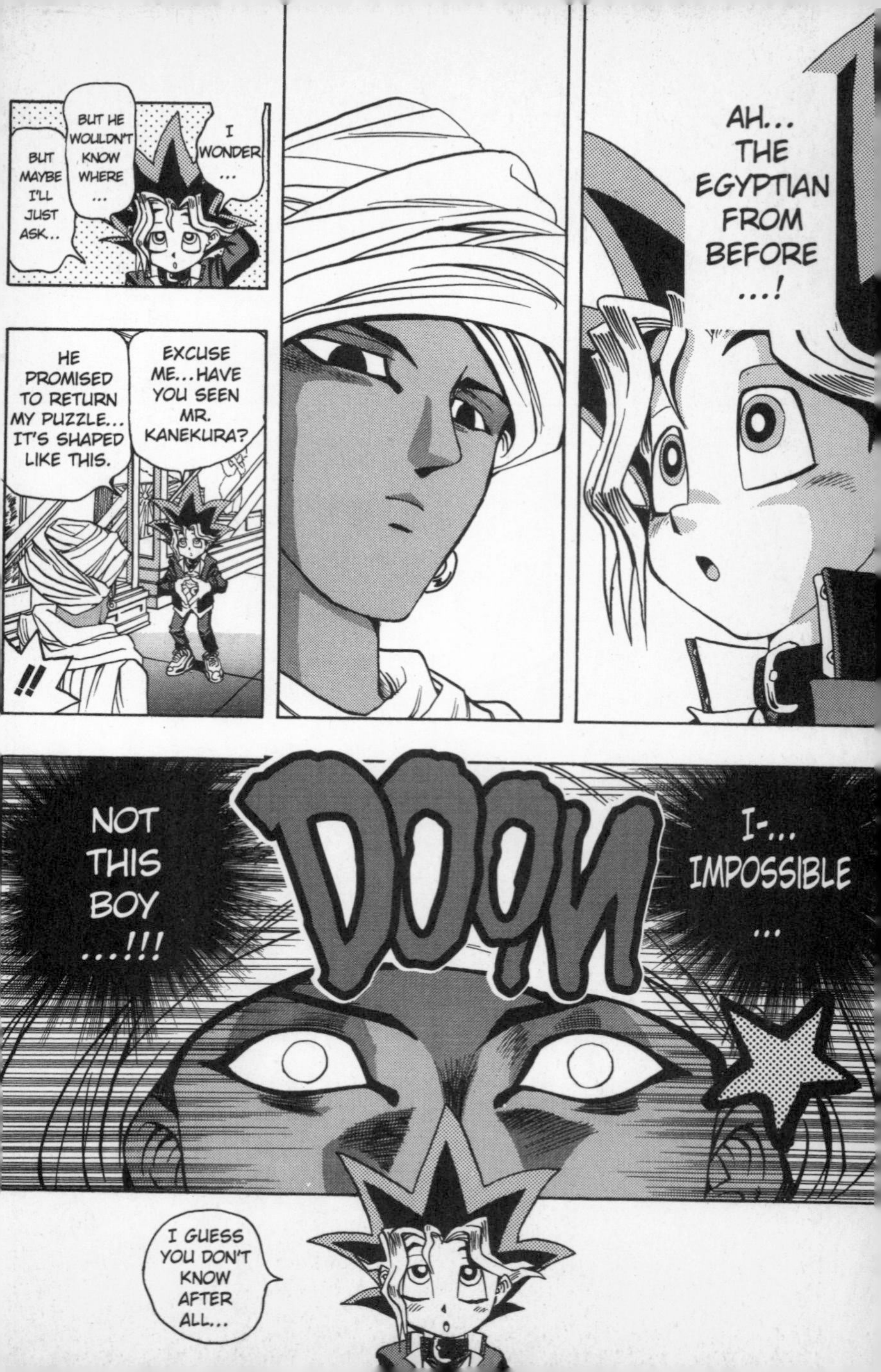
I WONDER ...
BUT HE WOULDN'T KNOW WHERE ...
BUT MAYBE I'LL JUST ASK...
EXCUSE ME...HAVE YOU SEEN MR. KANEKURA?
HE PROMISED TO RETURN MY PUZZLE... IT'S SHAPED LIKE THIS.
!!
AH... THE EGYPTIAN FROM BEFORE ...!
DOOON
NOT THIS BOY ...!!!
I-... IMPOSSIBLE ...
I GUESS YOU DON'T KNOW AFTER ALL...

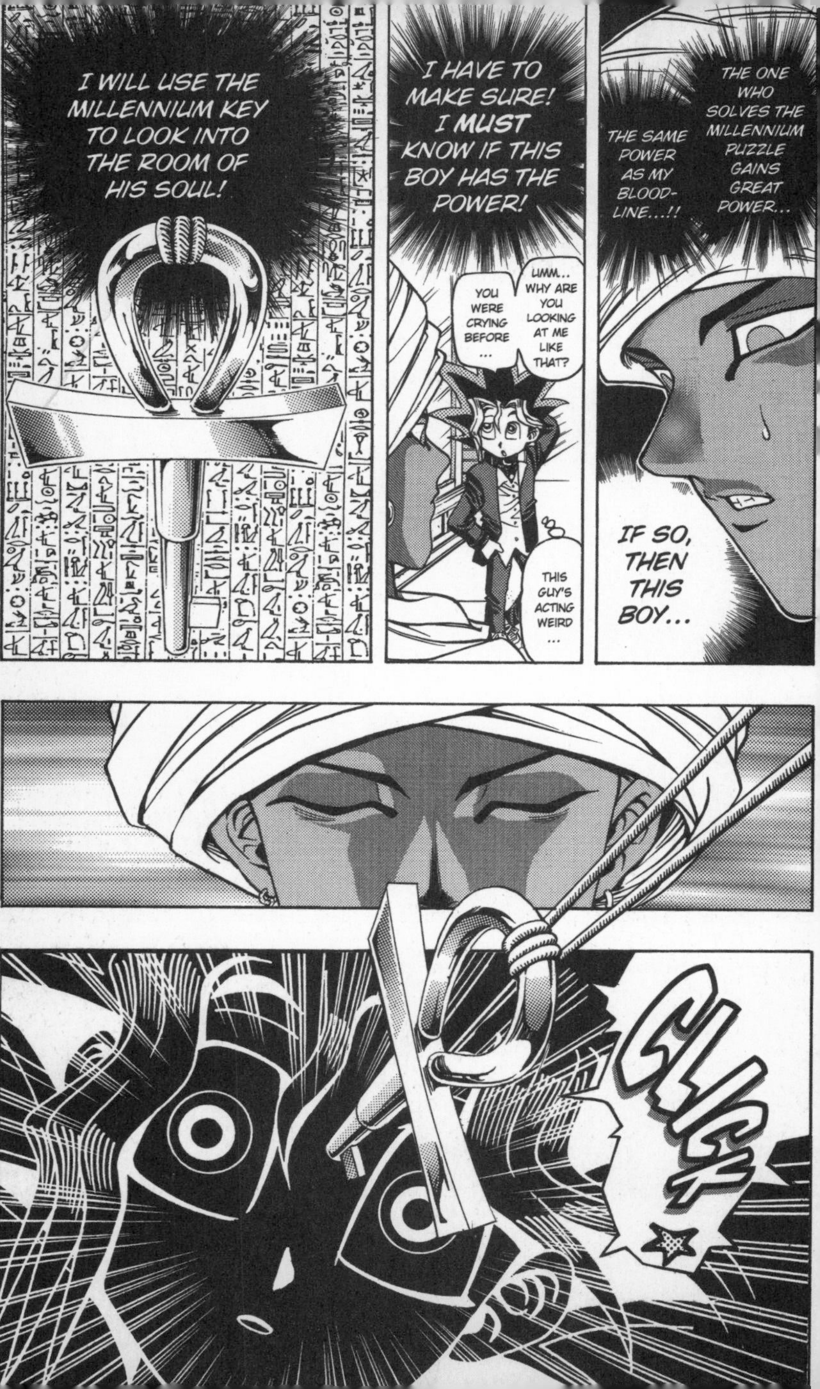
THE ONE WHO SOLVES THE MILLENNIUM PUZZLE GAINS GREAT POWER...
THE SAME POWER AS MY BLOOD-LINE...!!
IF SO, THEN THIS BOY...
I HAVE TO MAKE SURE! I MUST KNOW IF THIS BOY HAS THE POWER!
UMM... WHY ARE YOU LOOKING AT ME LIKE THAT?
YOU WERE CRYING BEFORE...
THIS GUY'S ACTING WEIRD...
I WILL USE THE MILLENNIUM KEY TO LOOK INTO THE ROOM OF HIS SOUL!
CLICK

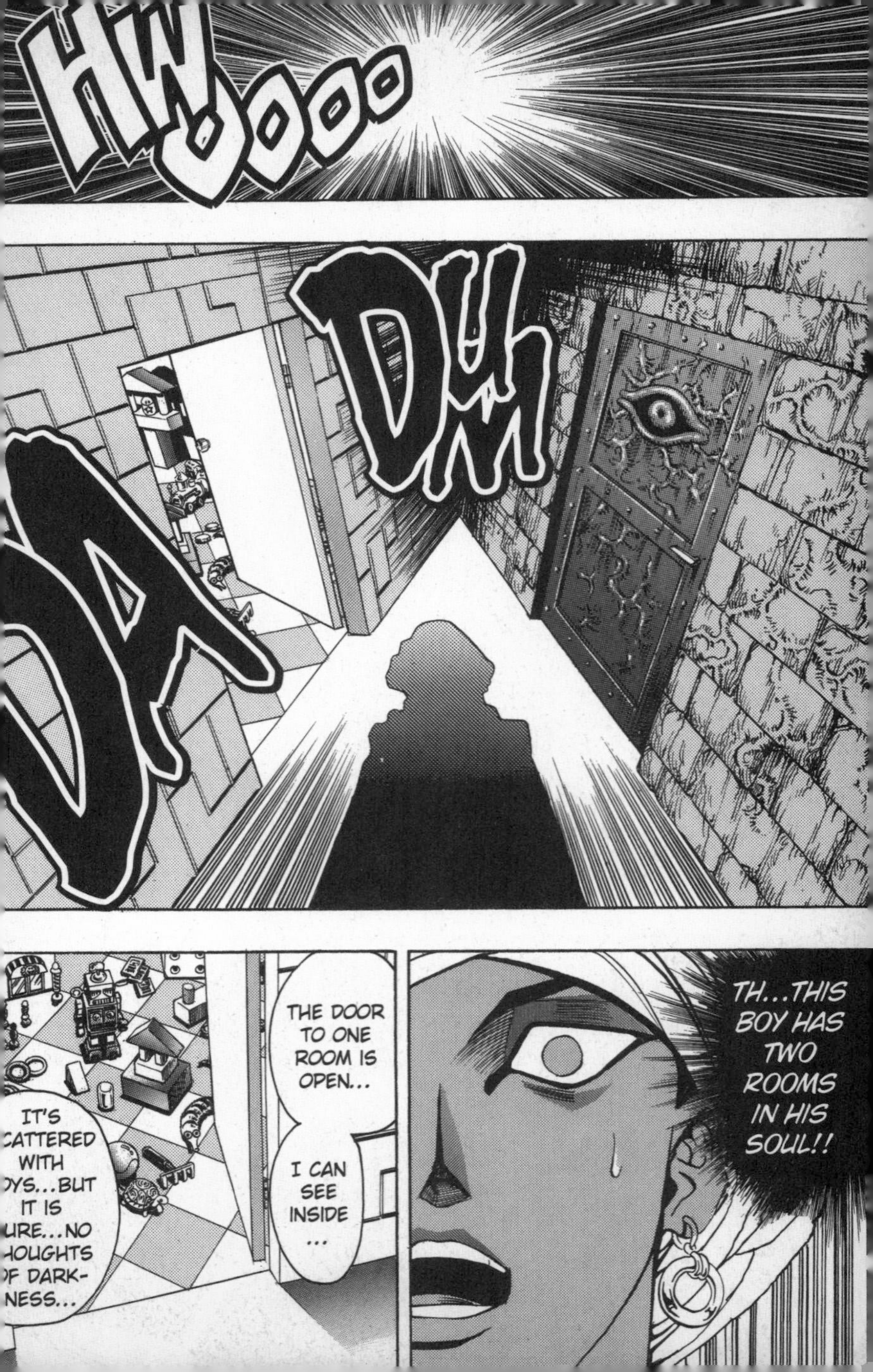

HWOOO
DA
TH...THIS BOY HAS TWO ROOMS IN HIS SOUL!!
THE DOOR TO ONE ROOM IS OPEN...
I CAN SEE INSIDE ...
IT'S CATTERED WITH OYS...BUT IT IS URE...NO HOUGHTS OF DARK-NESS...

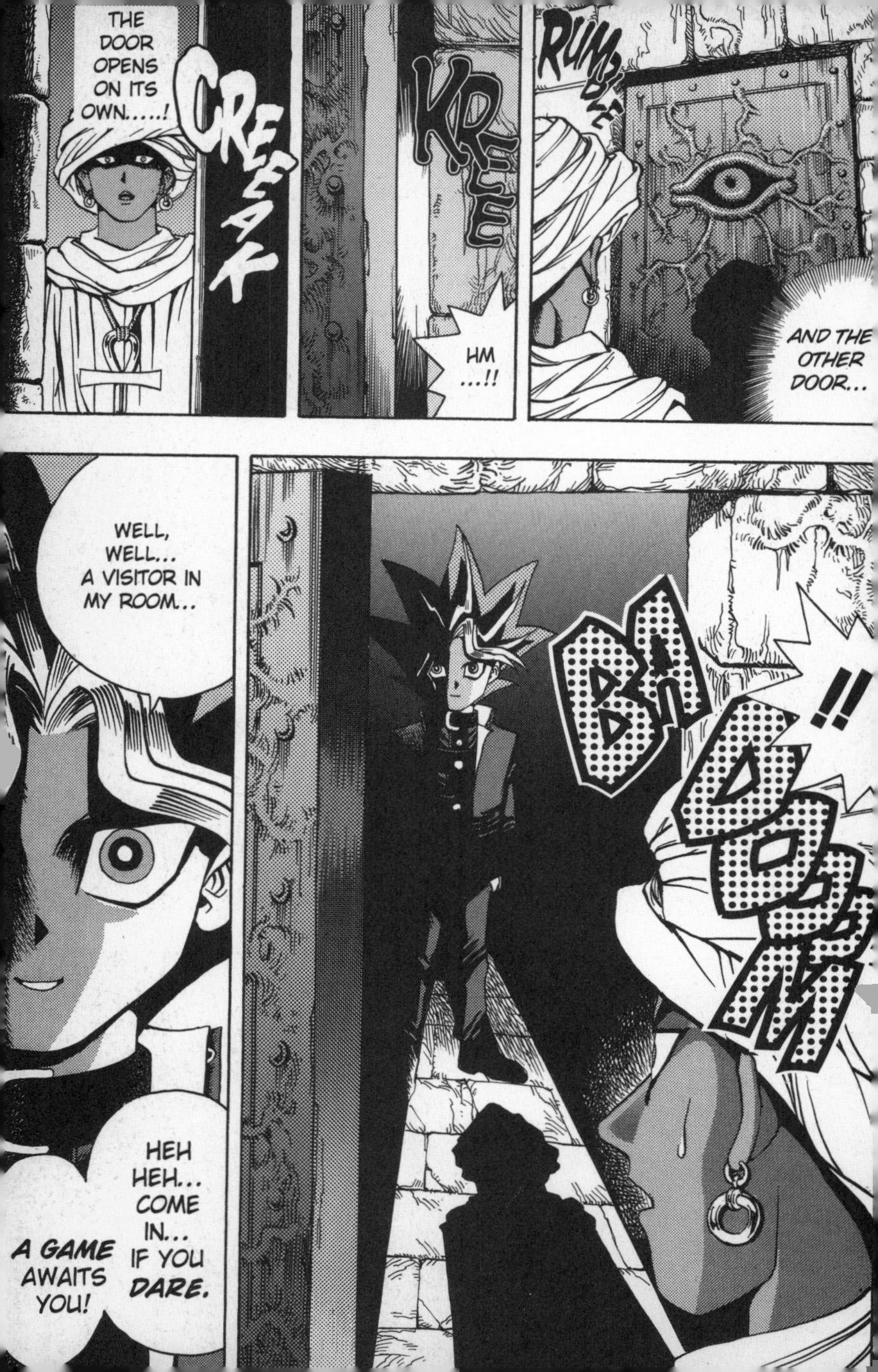
RUMBLE
AND THE OTHER DOOR...
KREEE
HM ...!!
THE DOOR OPENS ON ITS OWN.....!
CREEAK
BAN!!
DOOM
WELL, WELL... A VISITOR IN MY ROOM...
HEH HEH... COME IN... IF YOU DARE.
A GAME AWAITS YOU!

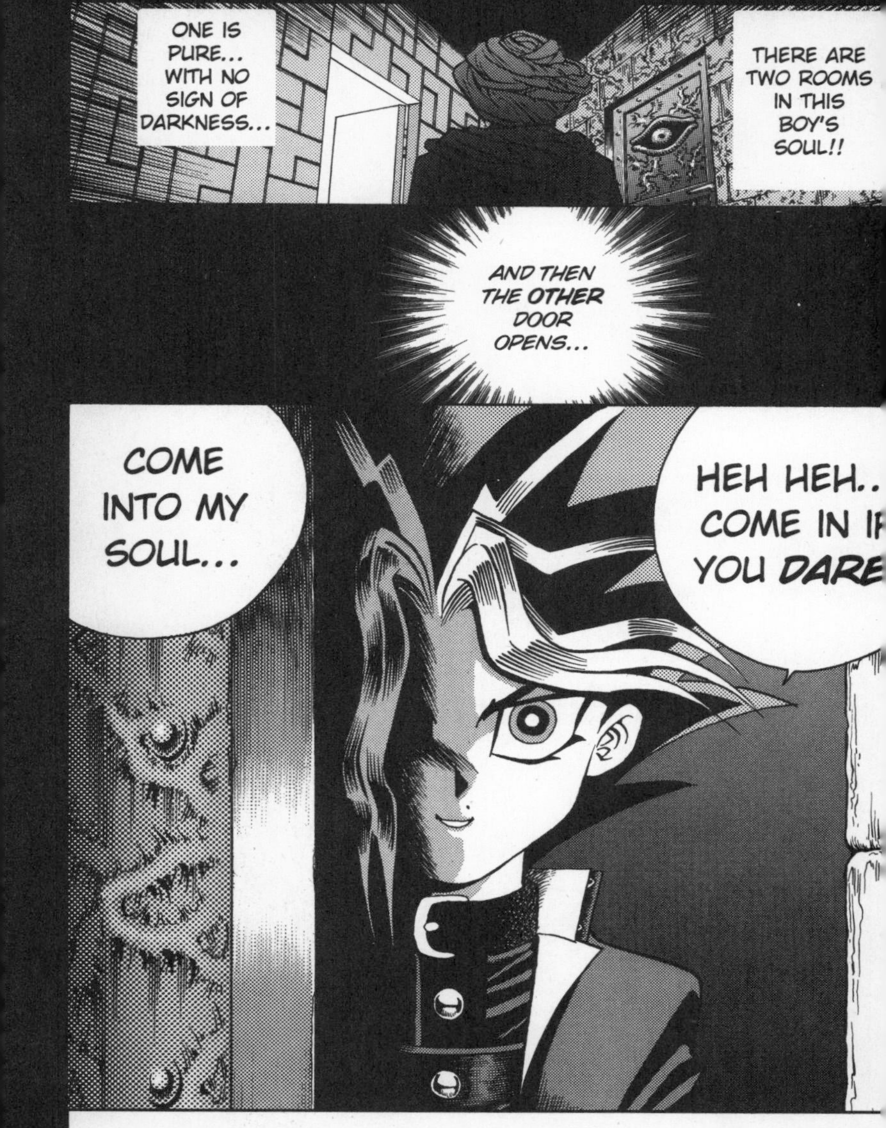
THERE ARE TWO ROOMS IN THIS BOY'S SOUL!!
ONE IS PURE... WITH NO SIGN OF DARKNESS...
AND THEN THE OTHER DOOR OPENS...
HEH HEH.. COME IN I YOU DARE
COME INTO MY SOUL...

Duel 14: The Man from Egypt (Part 2)

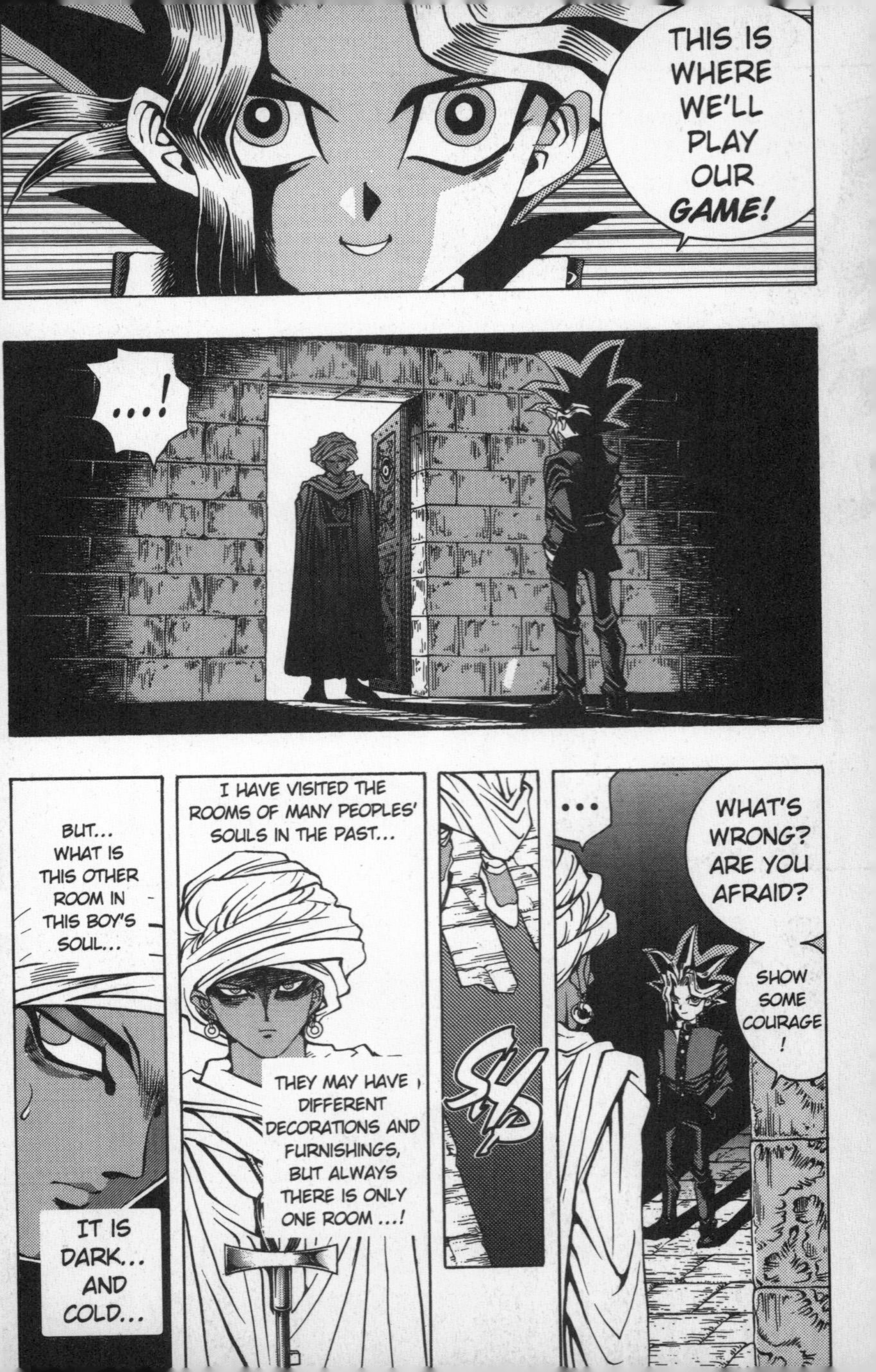
THIS IS WHERE WE'LL PLAY OUR GAME!
...!
...
WHAT'S WRONG? ARE YOU AFRAID?
SHOW SOME COURAGE!
I HAVE VISITED THE ROOMS OF MANY PEOPLES' SOULS IN THE PAST...
THEY MAY HAVE DIFFERENT DECORATIONS AND FURNISHINGS, BUT ALWAYS THERE IS ONLY ONE ROOM ...!
BUT... WHAT IS THIS OTHER ROOM IN THIS BOY'S SOUL...
IT IS DARK... AND COLD...

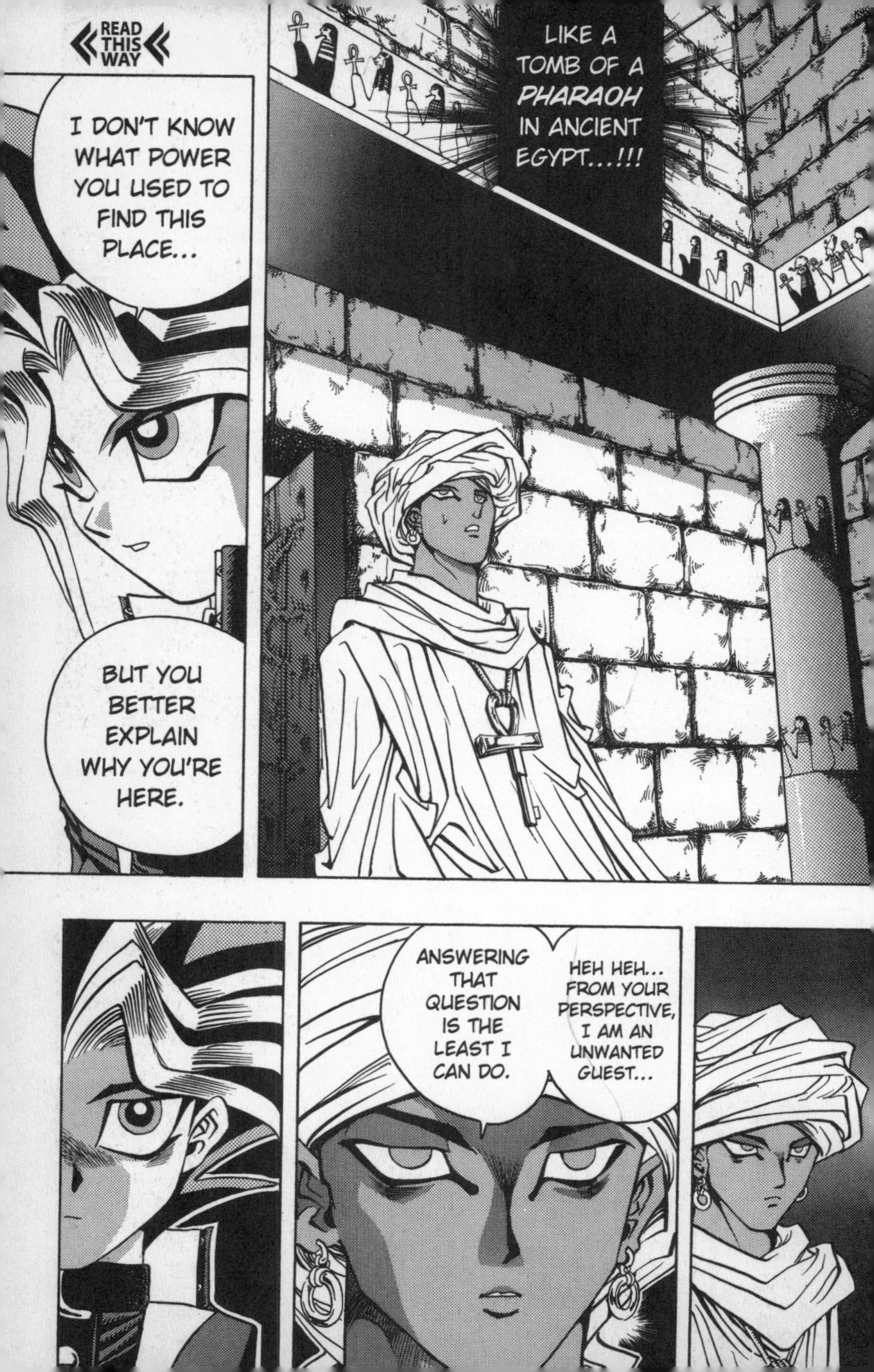
READ THIS WAY
LIKE A TOMB OF A *PHARAOH* IN ANCIENT EGYPT...!!!
I DON'T KNOW WHAT POWER YOU USED TO FIND THIS PLACE...
BUT YOU BETTER EXPLAIN WHY YOU'RE HERE.
HEH HEH... FROM YOUR PERSPECTIVE, I AM AN UNWANTED GUEST...
ANSWERING THAT QUESTION IS THE LEAST I CAN DO.

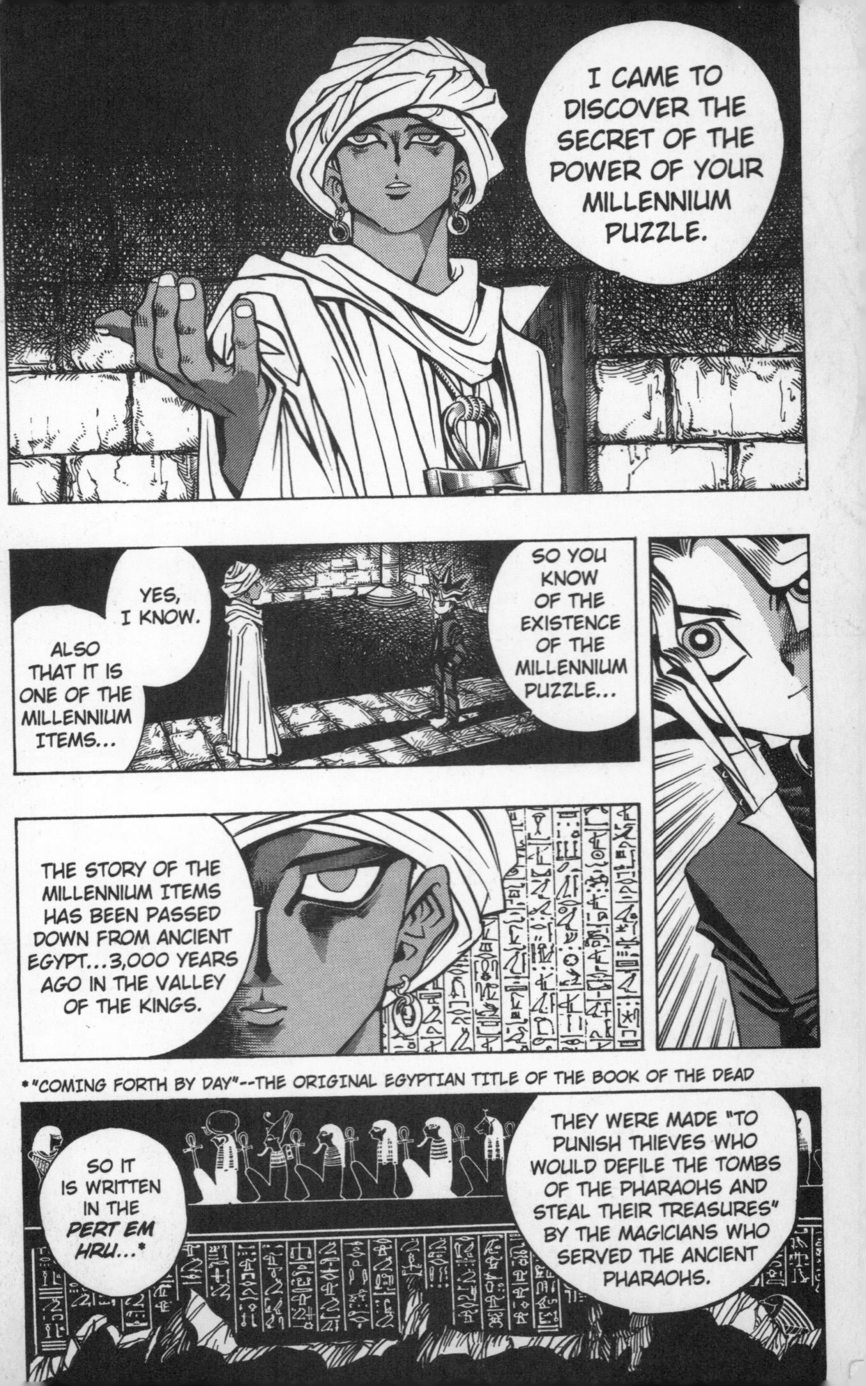
I CAME TO DISCOVER THE SECRET OF THE POWER OF YOUR MILLENNIUM PUZZLE.
SO YOU KNOW OF THE EXISTENCE OF THE MILLENNIUM PUZZLE...
YES, I KNOW.
ALSO THAT IT IS ONE OF THE MILLENNIUM ITEMS...
THE STORY OF THE MILLENNIUM ITEMS HAS BEEN PASSED DOWN FROM ANCIENT EGYPT...3,000 YEARS AGO IN THE VALLEY OF THE KINGS.
THEY WERE MADE "TO PUNISH THIEVES WHO WOULD DEFILE THE TOMBS OF THE PHARAOHS AND STEAL THEIR TREASURES" BY THE MAGICIANS WHO SERVED THE ANCIENT PHARAOHS.
SO IT IS WRITTEN IN THE *PERT EM HRU*...*

*"COMING FORTH BY DAY"--THE ORIGINAL EGYPTIAN TITLE OF THE BOOK OF THE DEAD

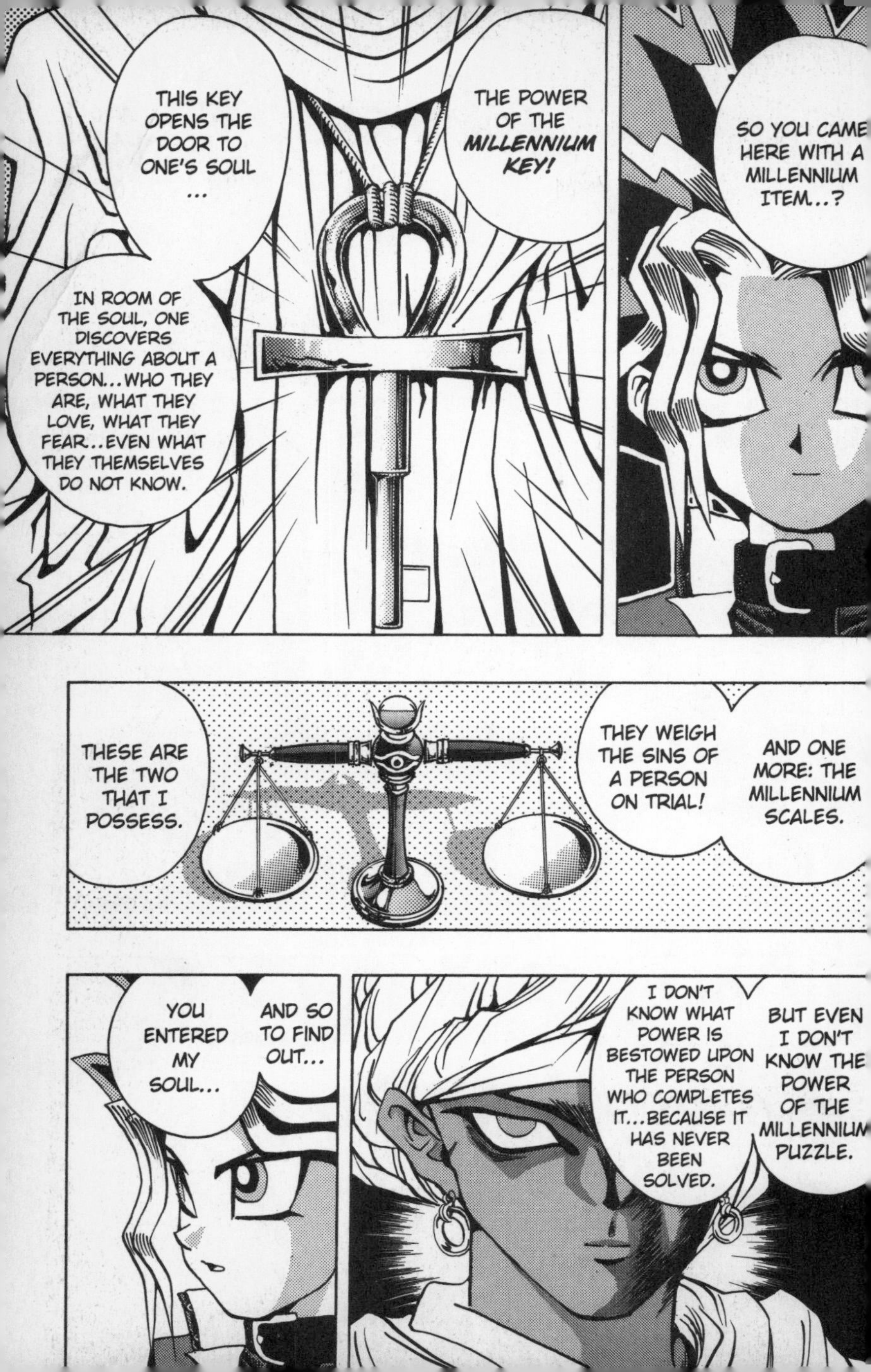

SO YOU CAME HERE WITH A MILLENNIUM ITEM...?
THE POWER OF THE *MILLENNIUM KEY!*
THIS KEY OPENS THE DOOR TO ONE'S SOUL ...
IN ROOM OF THE SOUL, ONE DISCOVERS EVERYTHING ABOUT A PERSON...WHO THEY ARE, WHAT THEY LOVE, WHAT THEY FEAR...EVEN WHAT THEY THEMSELVES DO NOT KNOW.
AND ONE MORE: THE MILLENNIUM SCALES.
THEY WEIGH THE SINS OF A PERSON ON TRIAL!
THESE ARE THE TWO THAT I POSSESS.
BUT EVEN I DON'T KNOW THE POWER OF THE MILLENNIUM PUZZLE.
I DON'T KNOW WHAT POWER IS BESTOWED UPON THE PERSON WHO COMPLETES IT...BECAUSE IT HAS NEVER BEEN SOLVED.
AND SO TO FIND OUT...
YOU ENTERED MY SOUL...

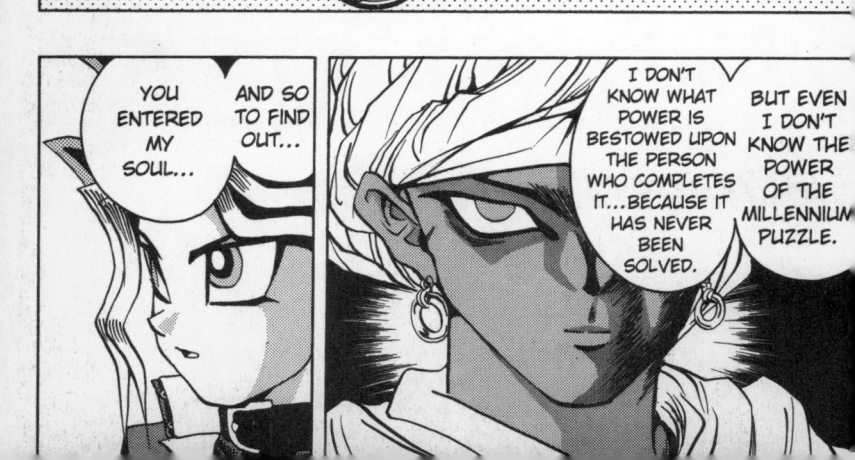

THAT IS WHAT I CAME TO DISCOVER.

...I CAN SEE WHAT KIND OF POWER THEY POSSESS.

IF I CAN SEE A PERSON'S "ROOM"...

THIS POWER YOU SPEAK OF *DOES* REST IN MY ROOM.

HOWEVER... I CAN'T LET YOU SEE IT THAT EASILY!

!

AND IF THAT POWER IS NEEDED... I WILL DRAW IT INTO MY BLOODLINE...

THIS IS A GAME!

A SHADOW GAME!!

YOU KNOW THE ROUTINE...

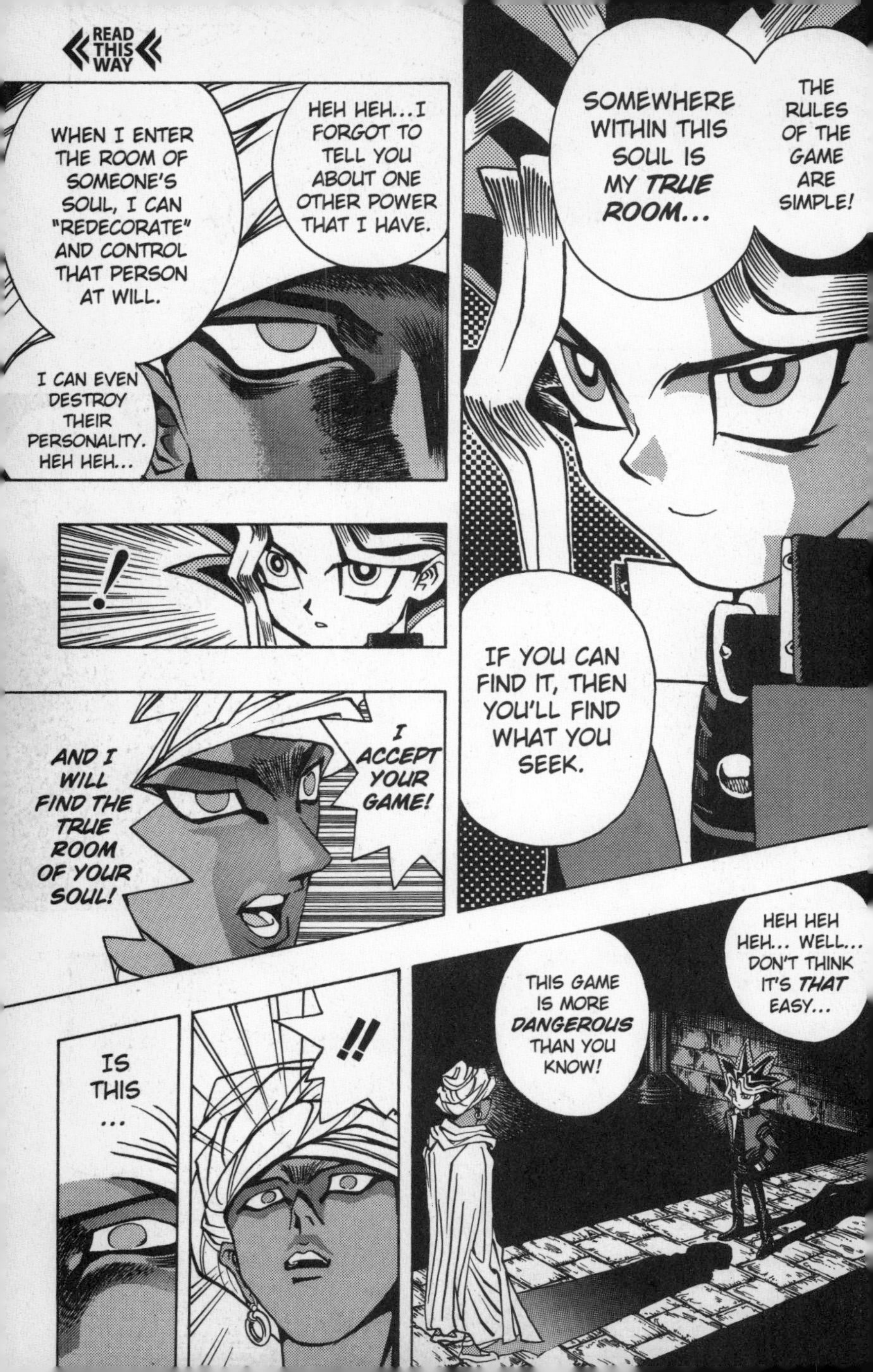
READ THIS WAY
THE RULES OF THE GAME ARE SIMPLE!
SOMEWHERE WITHIN THIS SOUL IS MY *TRUE ROOM...*
IF YOU CAN FIND IT, THEN YOU'LL FIND WHAT YOU SEEK.
HEH HEH...I FORGOT TO TELL YOU ABOUT ONE OTHER POWER THAT I HAVE.
WHEN I ENTER THE ROOM OF SOMEONE'S SOUL, I CAN "REDECORATE" AND CONTROL THAT PERSON AT WILL.
I CAN EVEN DESTROY THEIR PERSONALITY. HEH HEH...
!
I ACCEPT YOUR GAME!
AND I WILL FIND THE TRUE ROOM OF YOUR SOUL!
HEH HEH HEH... WELL... DON'T THINK IT'S *THAT* EASY...
THIS GAME IS MORE *DANGEROUS* THAN YOU KNOW!
!!
IS THIS ...

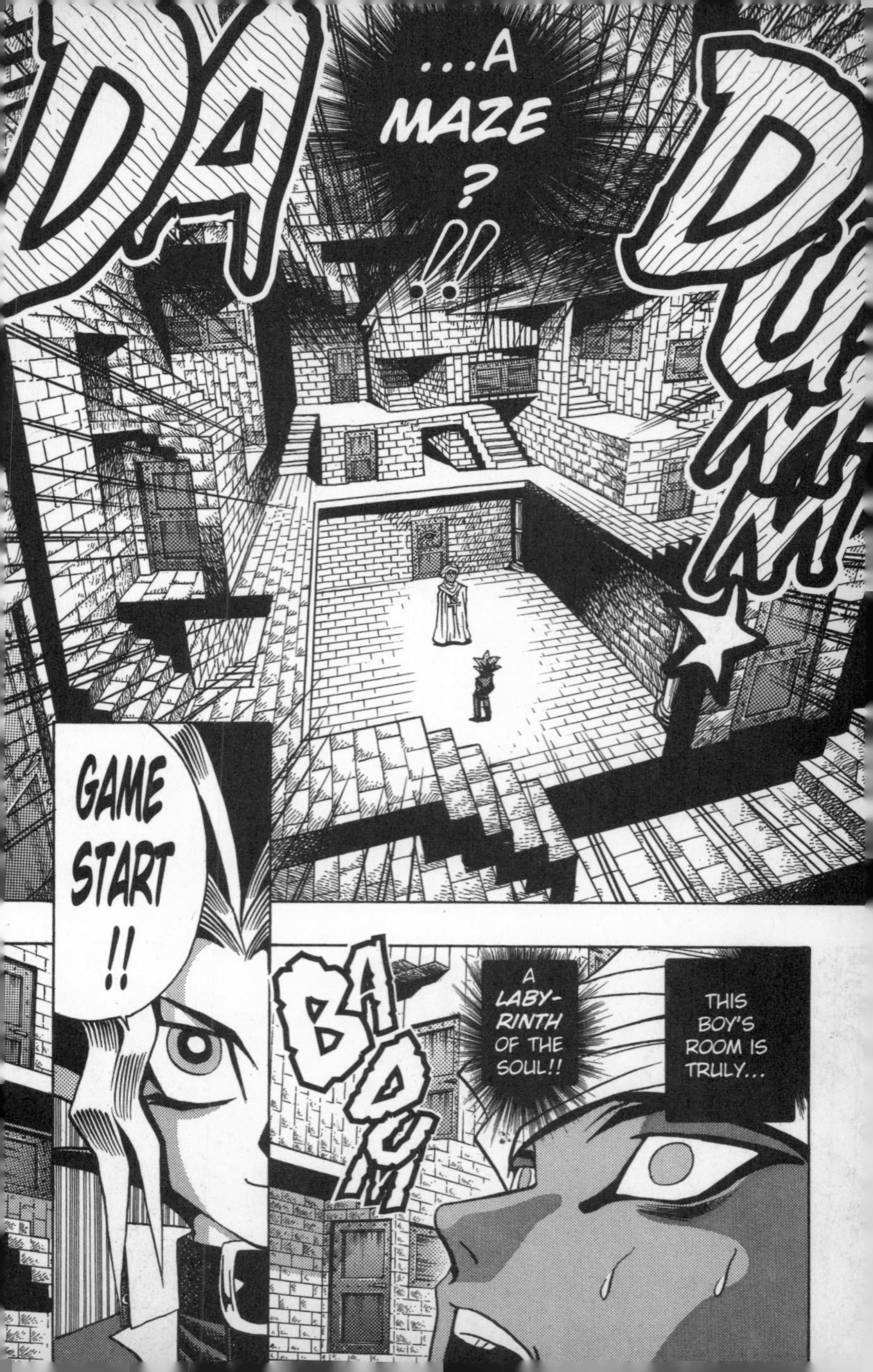
DA
...A MAZE ?!!
THIS BOY'S ROOM IS TRULY...
A LABYRINTH OF THE SOUL!!
GAME START !!

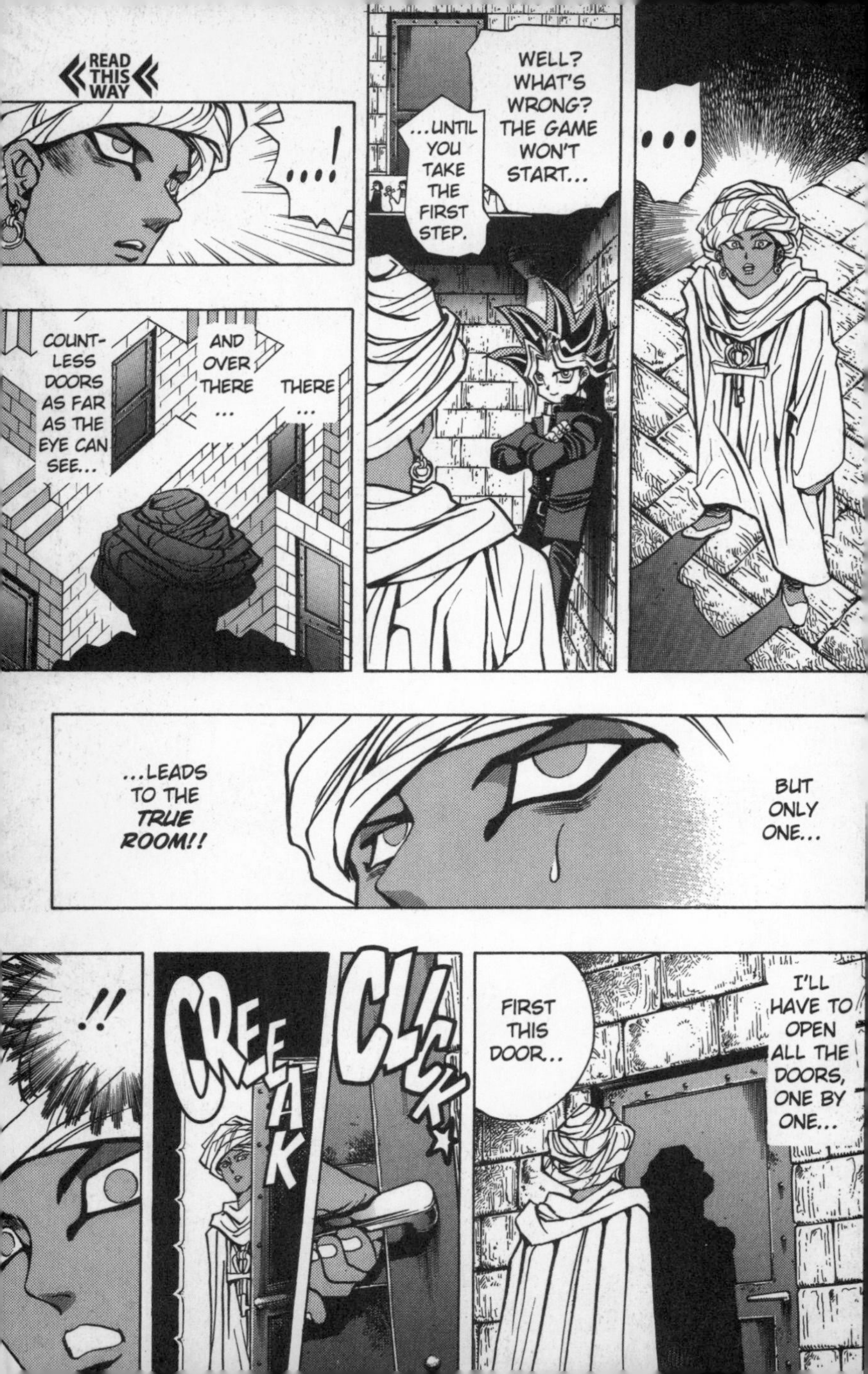
READ THIS WAY
...
WELL? WHAT'S WRONG? THE GAME WON'T START...
...UNTIL YOU TAKE THE FIRST STEP.
...!
THERE ...
AND OVER THERE ...
COUNTLESS DOORS AS FAR AS THE EYE CAN SEE...
BUT ONLY ONE...
...LEADS TO THE *TRUE ROOM!!*
I'LL HAVE TO OPEN ALL THE DOORS, ONE BY ONE...
FIRST THIS DOOR...
CLICK
CREEAK
!!

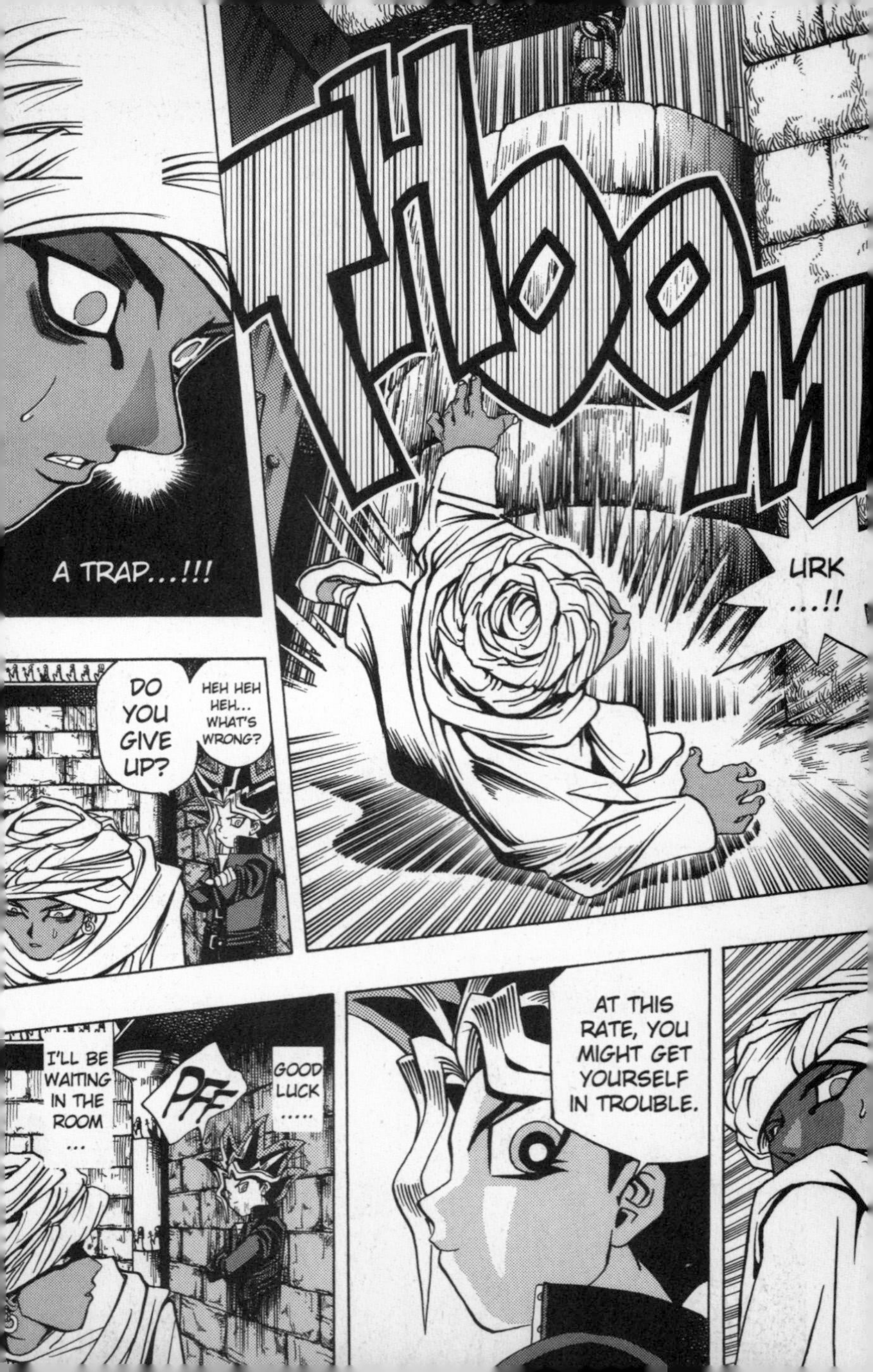
WHOOM
URK ...!!
A TRAP...!!!
HEH HEH HEH... WHAT'S WRONG?
DO YOU GIVE UP?
AT THIS RATE, YOU MIGHT GET YOURSELF IN TROUBLE.
GOOD LUCK ......
PFF
I'LL BE WAITING IN THE ROOM ...

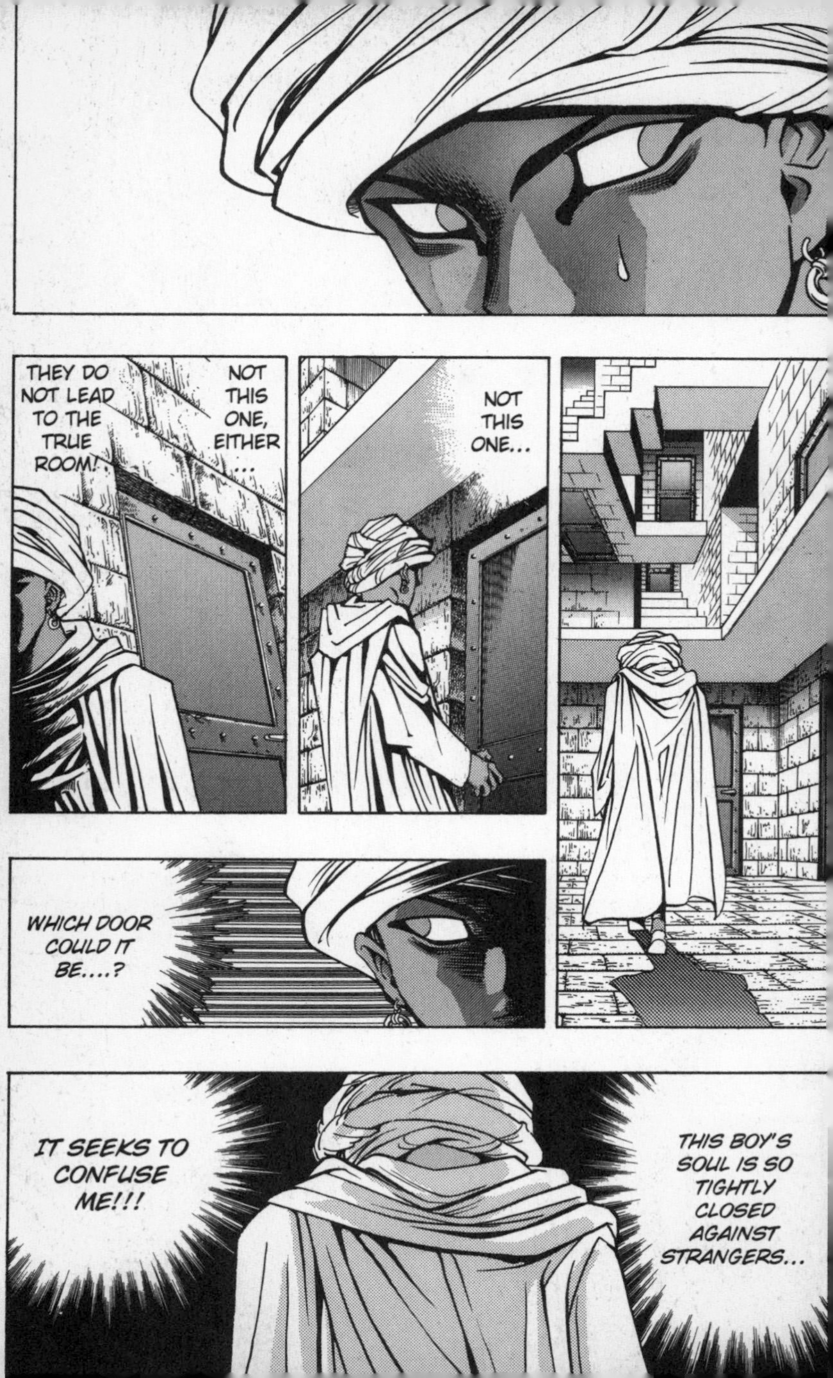
NOT THIS ONE...
NOT THIS ONE, EITHER...
THEY DO NOT LEAD TO THE TRUE ROOM!
WHICH DOOR COULD IT BE....?
THIS BOY'S SOUL IS SO TIGHTLY CLOSED AGAINST STRANGERS...
IT SEEKS TO CONFUSE ME!!!

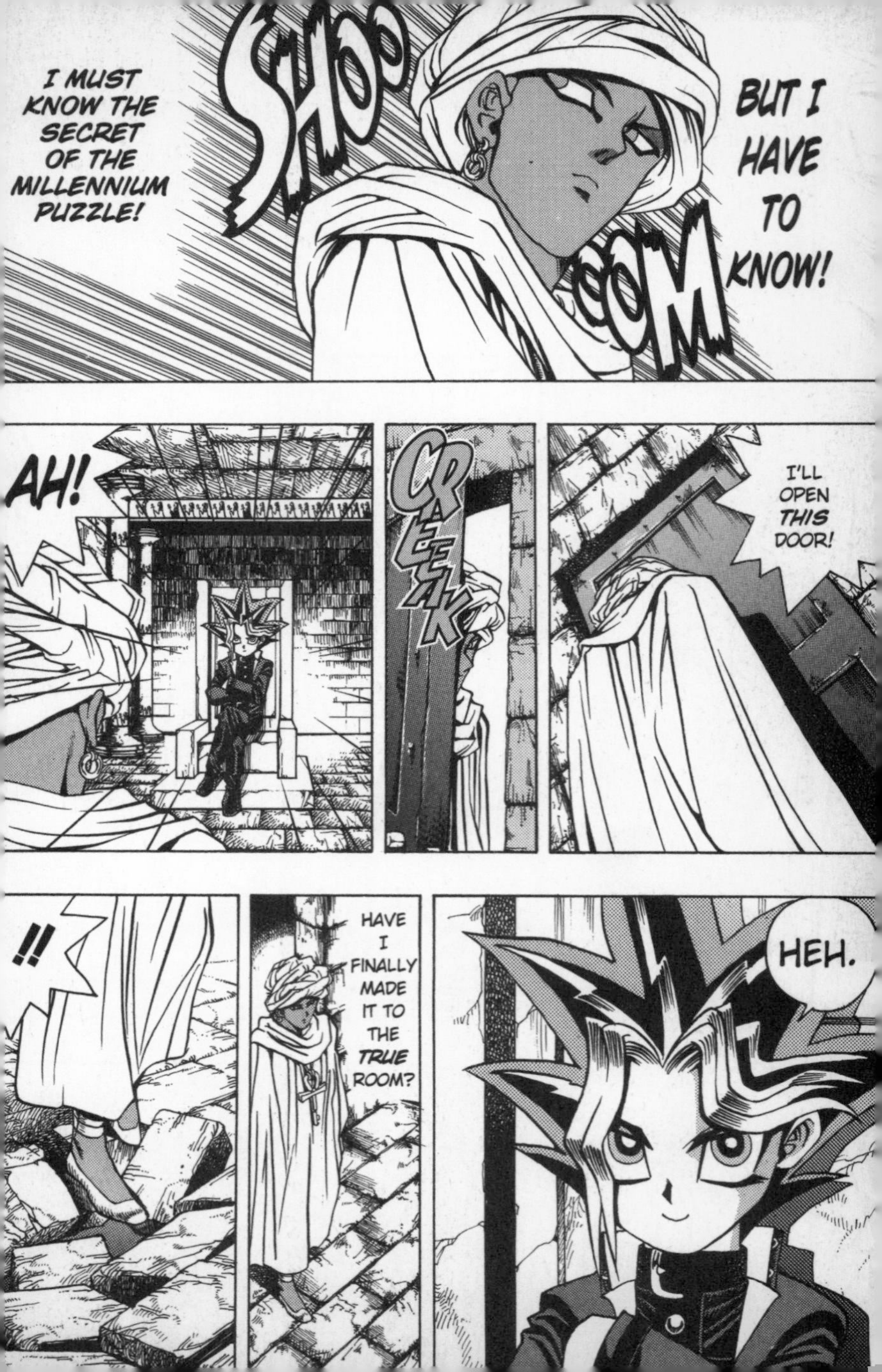
SHOOP
I MUST KNOW THE SECRET OF THE MILLENNIUM PUZZLE!
BUT I HAVE TO KNOW!
OOM
I'LL OPEN *THIS* DOOR!
CREEEAK
AH!
HEH.
HAVE I FINALLY MADE IT TO THE *TRUE* ROOM?
!!

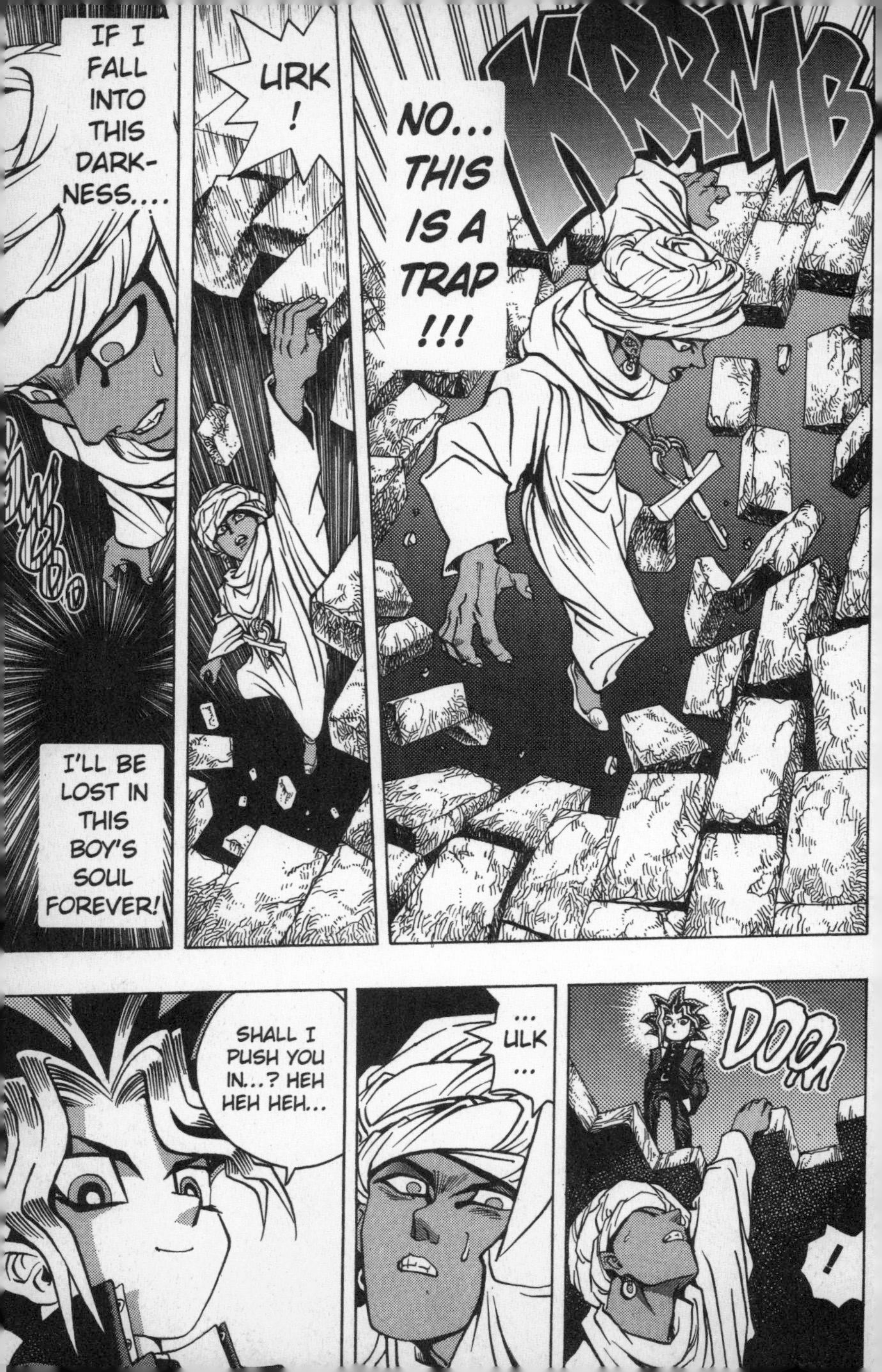
KRRMB
NO... THIS IS A TRAP!!!
URK!
IF I FALL INTO THIS DARKNESS....
I'LL BE LOST IN THIS BOY'S SOUL FOREVER!
DOON
!
... ULK ...
SHALL I PUSH YOU IN...? HEH HEH HEH...

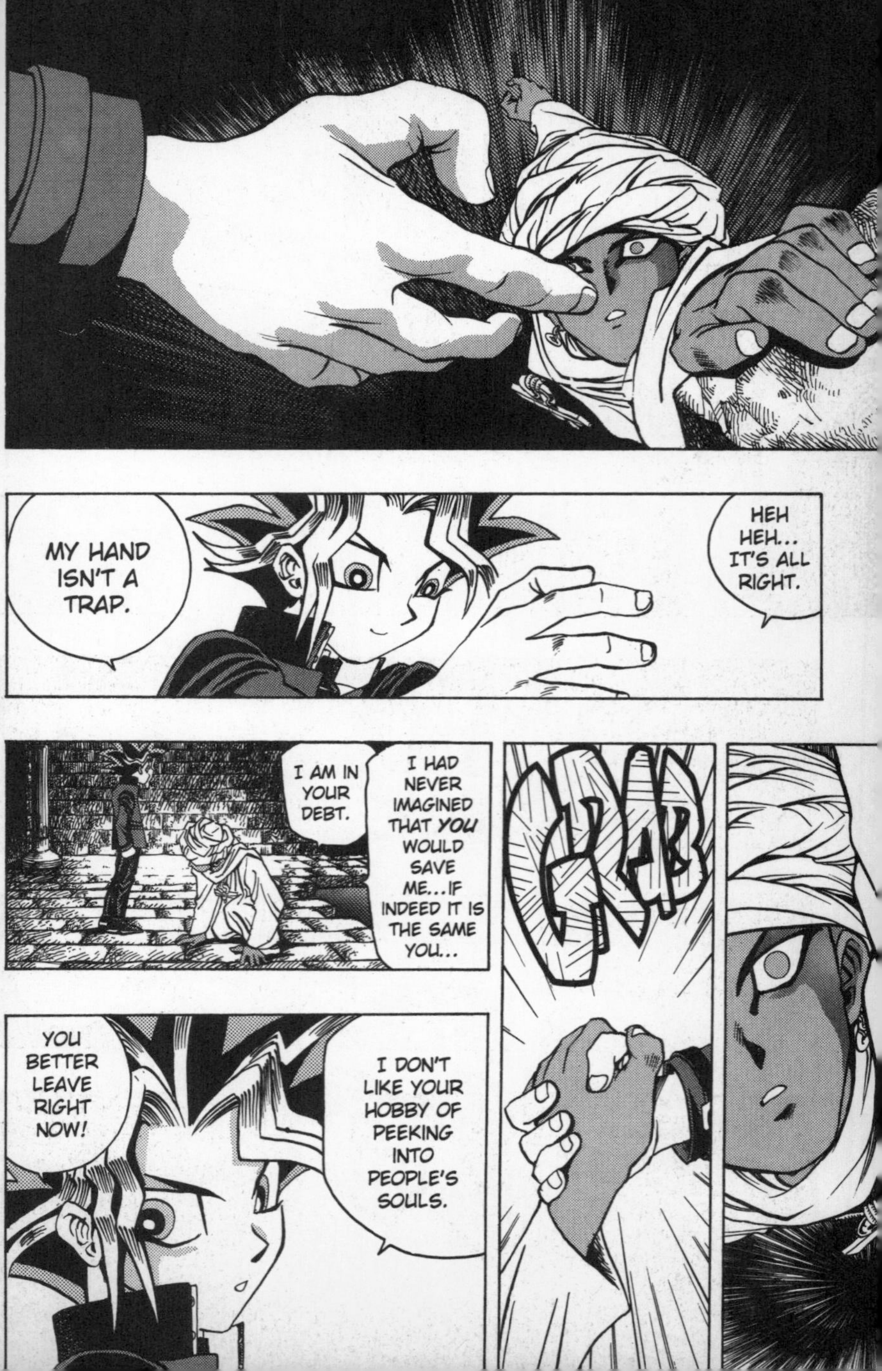
HEH HEH... IT'S ALL RIGHT.
MY HAND ISN'T A TRAP.
GRAB
I HAD NEVER IMAGINED THAT *YOU* WOULD SAVE ME... IF INDEED IT IS THE SAME YOU...
I AM IN YOUR DEBT.
I DON'T LIKE YOUR HOBBY OF PEEKING INTO PEOPLE'S SOULS.
YOU BETTER LEAVE RIGHT NOW!

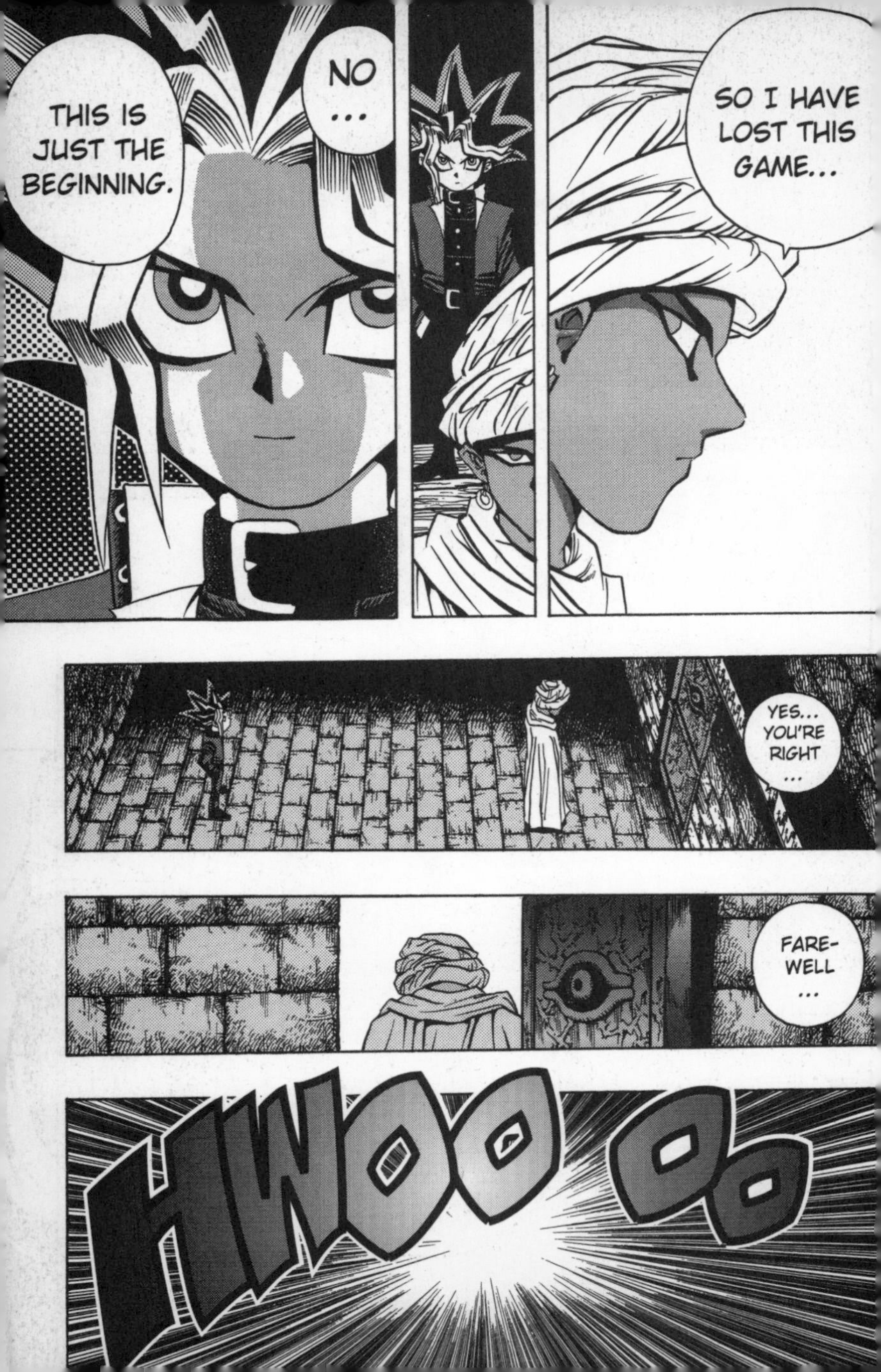
SO I HAVE LOST THIS GAME...
NO ...
THIS IS JUST THE BEGINNING.
YES... YOU'RE RIGHT ...
FARE-WELL ...
HWOOOO

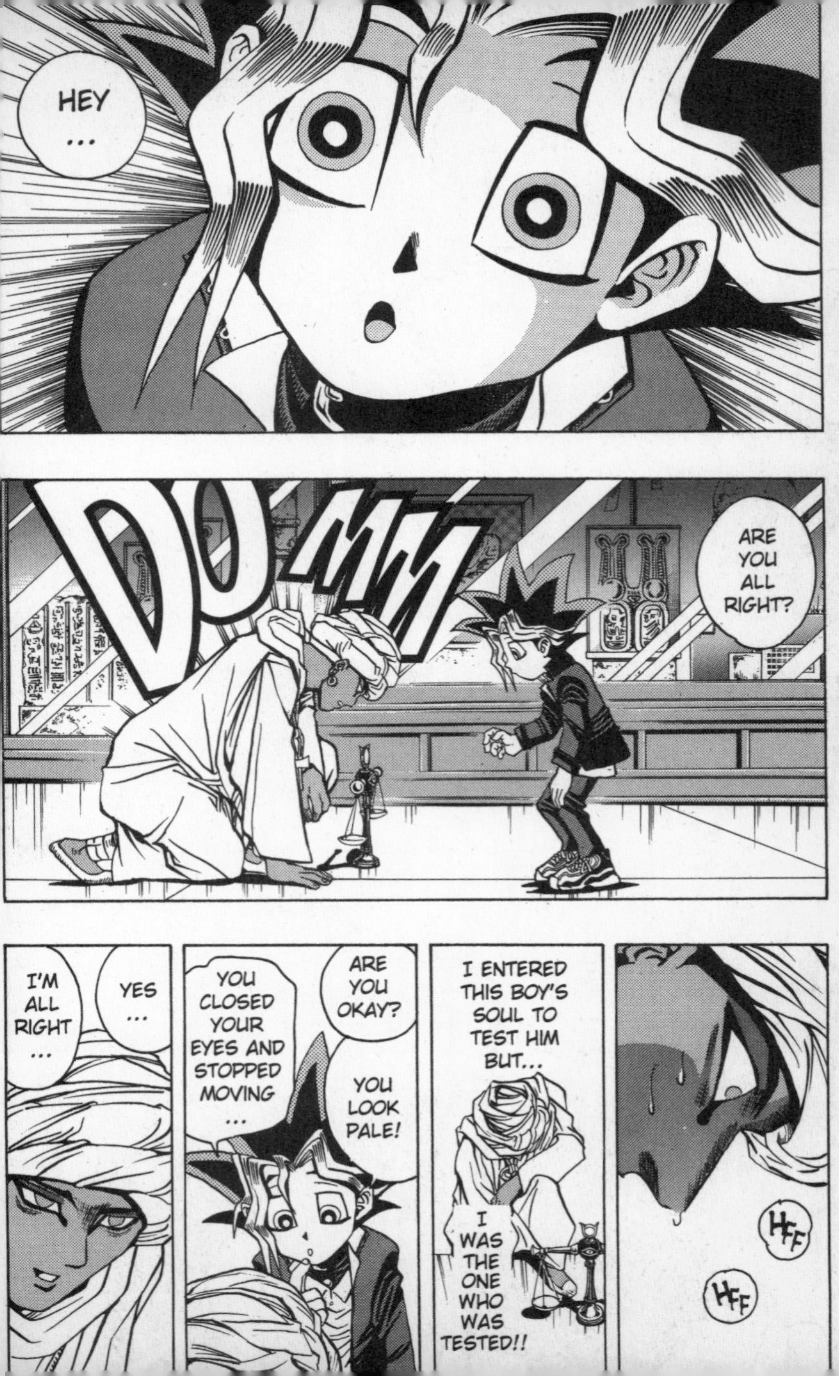
HEY ...
DOMM
ARE YOU ALL RIGHT?
HFF
HFF
I ENTERED THIS BOY'S SOUL TO TEST HIM BUT...
I WAS THE ONE WHO WAS TESTED!!
ARE YOU OKAY?
YOU LOOK PALE!
YOU CLOSED YOUR EYES AND STOPPED MOVING ...
YES ...
I'M ALL RIGHT ...

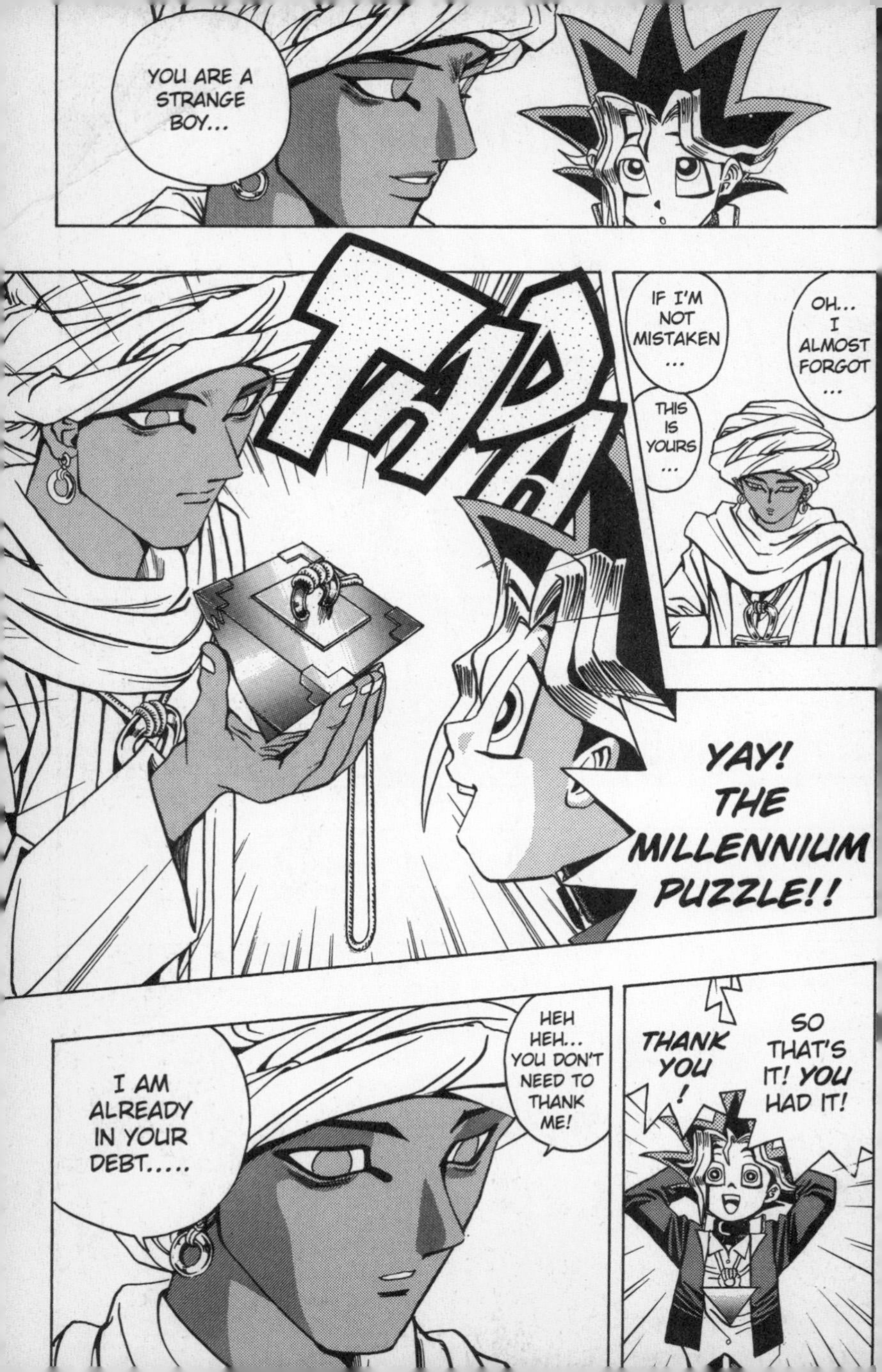
YOU ARE A STRANGE BOY...
OH... I ALMOST FORGOT...
IF I'M NOT MISTAKEN...
THIS IS YOURS...
YAY! THE MILLENNIUM PUZZLE!!
SO THAT'S IT! YOU HAD IT!
THANK YOU!
HEH HEH... YOU DON'T NEED TO THANK ME!
I AM ALREADY IN YOUR DEBT.....

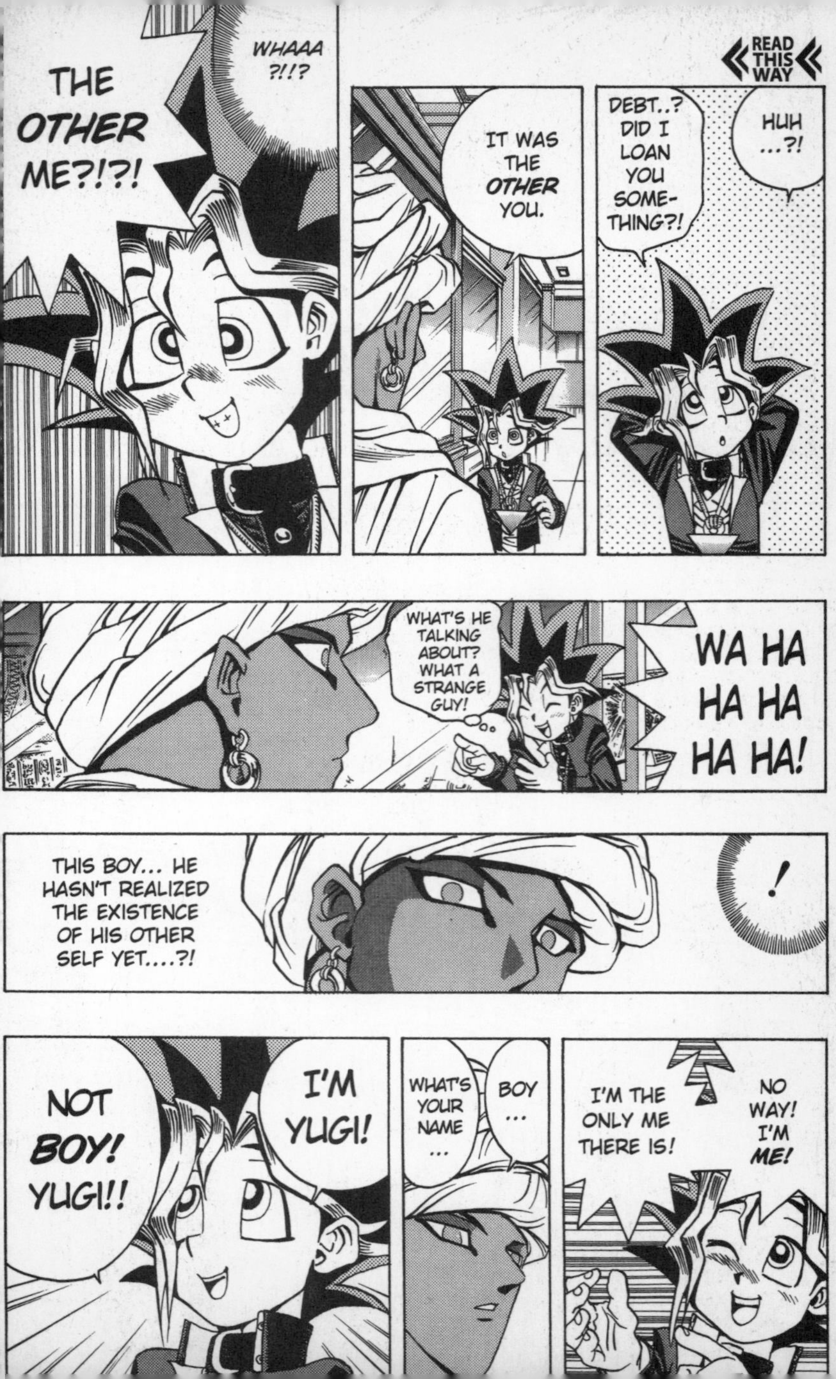
READ THIS WAY
HUH ...?!
DEBT..? DID I LOAN YOU SOME-THING?!
IT WAS THE OTHER YOU.
WHAAA ?!!?
THE OTHER ME?!?!
WA HA HA HA HA HA!
WHAT'S HE TALKING ABOUT? WHAT A STRANGE GUY!
!
THIS BOY... HE HASN'T REALIZED THE EXISTENCE OF HIS OTHER SELF YET....?!
NO WAY! I'M ME!
I'M THE ONLY ME THERE IS!
BOY ...
WHAT'S YOUR NAME ...
I'M YUGI!
NOT BOY! YUGI!!

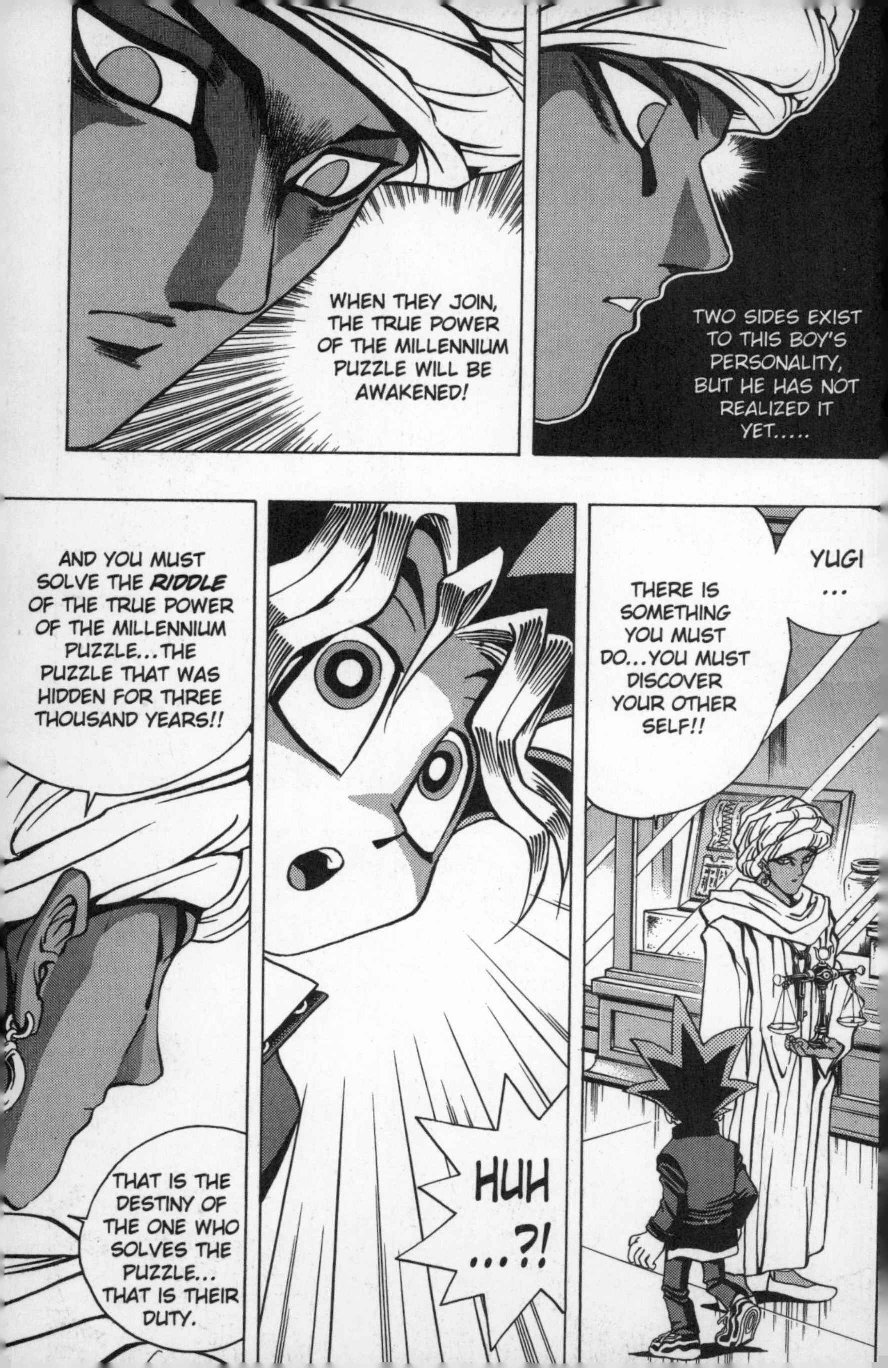
TWO SIDES EXIST TO THIS BOY'S PERSONALITY, BUT HE HAS NOT REALIZED IT YET.....
WHEN THEY JOIN, THE TRUE POWER OF THE MILLENNIUM PUZZLE WILL BE AWAKENED!
YUGI ...
THERE IS SOMETHING YOU MUST DO...YOU MUST DISCOVER YOUR OTHER SELF!!
HUH ...?!
AND YOU MUST SOLVE THE *RIDDLE* OF THE TRUE POWER OF THE MILLENNIUM PUZZLE...THE PUZZLE THAT WAS HIDDEN FOR THREE THOUSAND YEARS!!
THAT IS THE DESTINY OF THE ONE WHO SOLVES THE PUZZLE... THAT IS THEIR DUTY.

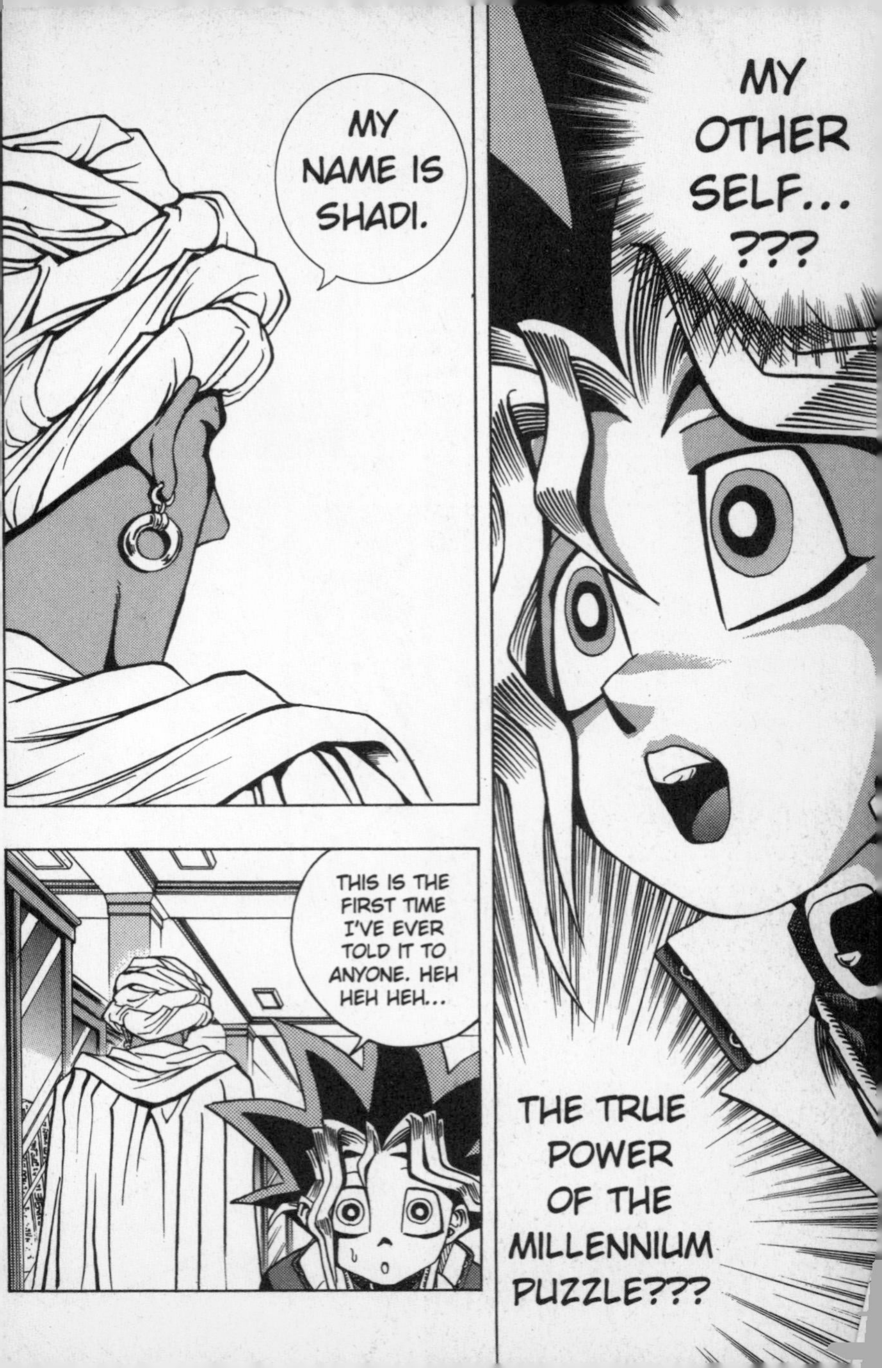
MY OTHER SELF... ???
THE TRUE POWER OF THE MILLENNIUM PUZZLE???
MY NAME IS SHADI.
THIS IS THE FIRST TIME I'VE EVER TOLD IT TO ANYONE. HEH HEH HEH...

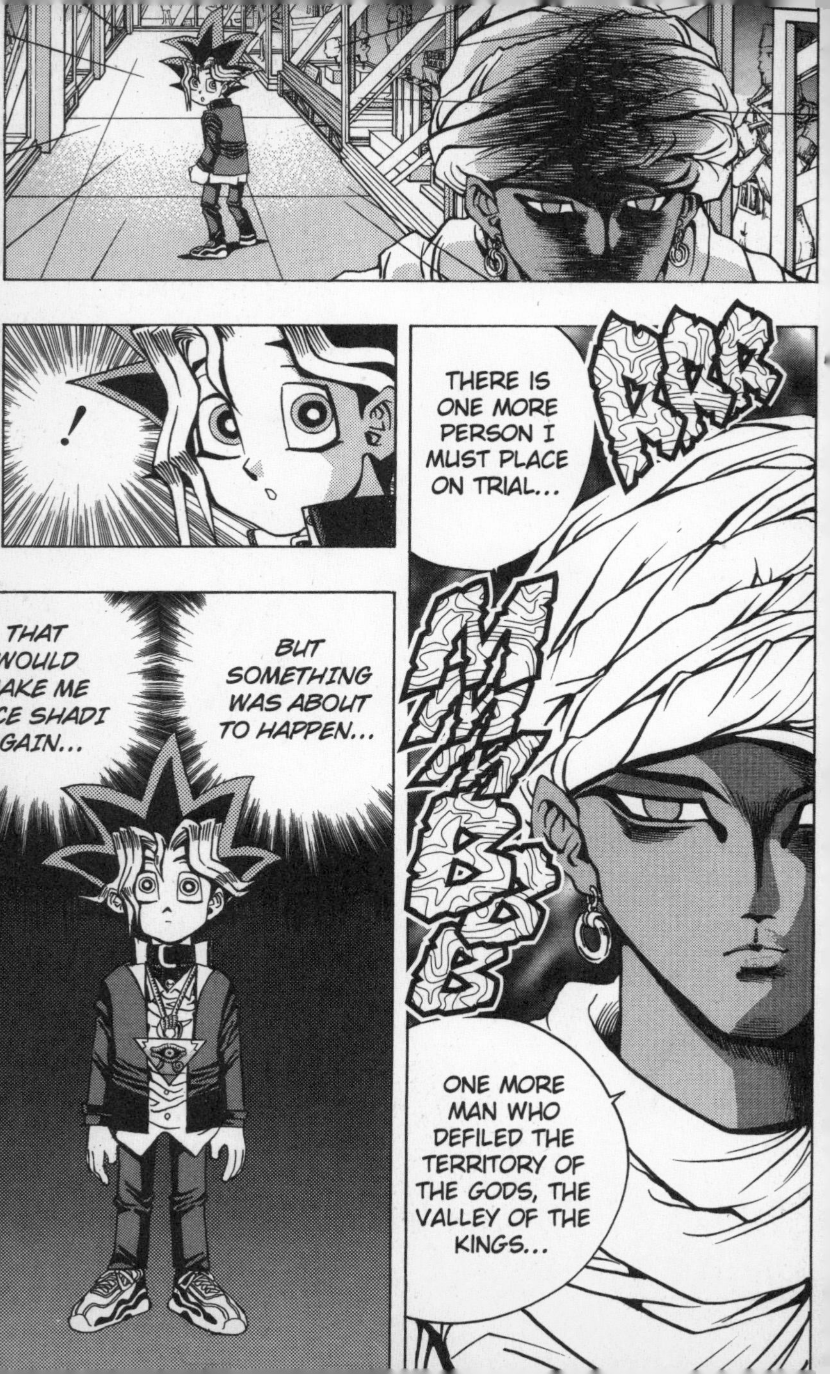
THERE IS ONE MORE PERSON I MUST PLACE ON TRIAL...
ONE MORE MAN WHO DEFILED THE TERRITORY OF THE GODS, THE VALLEY OF THE KINGS...
!
THAT WOULD MAKE ME FACE SHADI AGAIN...
BUT SOMETHING WAS ABOUT TO HAPPEN...

Duel 15: The Other Criminal

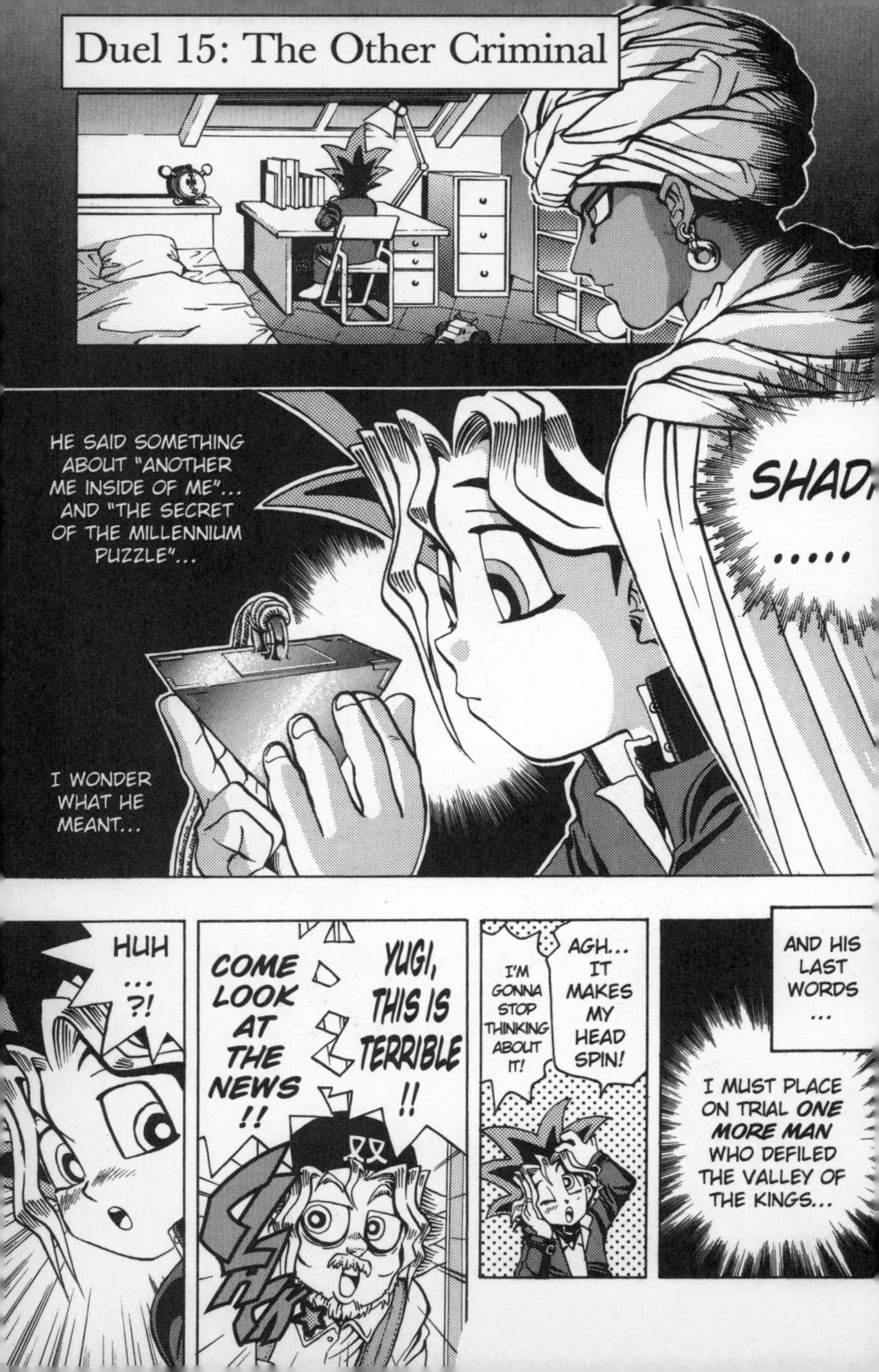
SHADI.....
HE SAID SOMETHING ABOUT "ANOTHER ME INSIDE OF ME"... AND "THE SECRET OF THE MILLENNIUM PUZZLE"...
I WONDER WHAT HE MEANT...
AND HIS LAST WORDS...
I MUST PLACE ON TRIAL ONE MORE MAN WHO DEFILED THE VALLEY OF THE KINGS...
AGH... IT MAKES MY HEAD SPIN!
I'M GONNA STOP THINKING ABOUT IT!
YUGI, THIS IS TERRIBLE!!
COME LOOK AT THE NEWS!!
HUH...?!

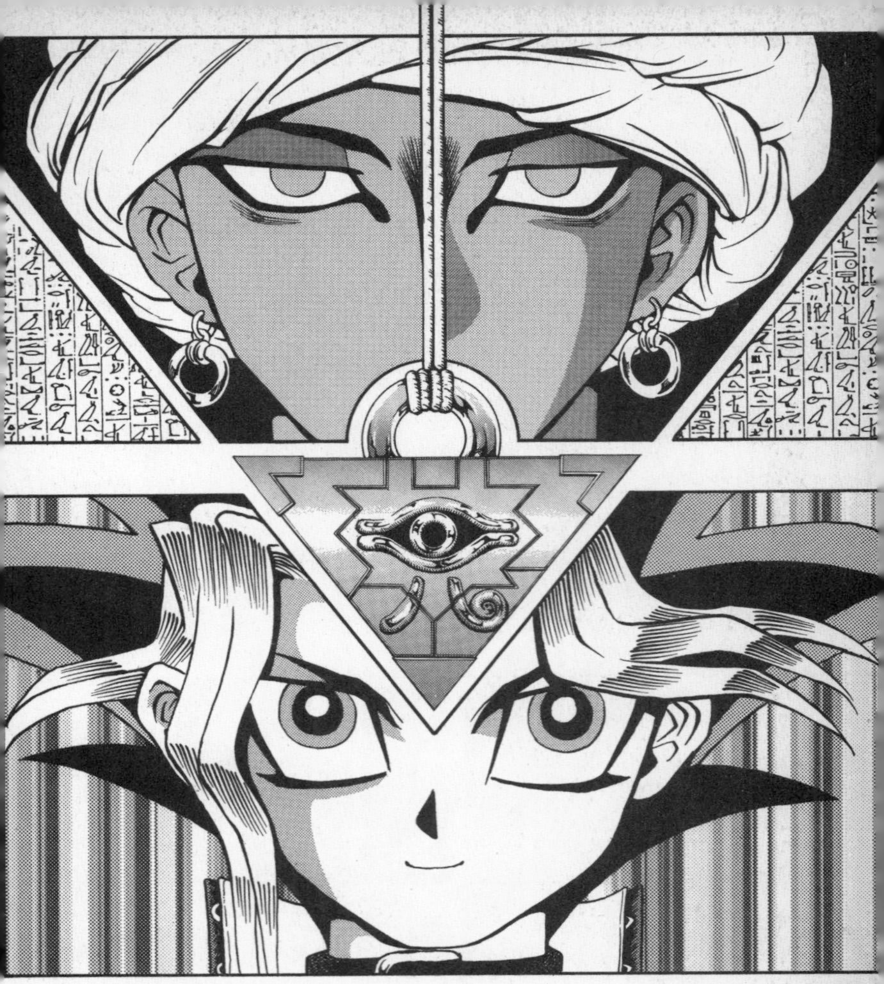

Duel 15:
The Other Criminal

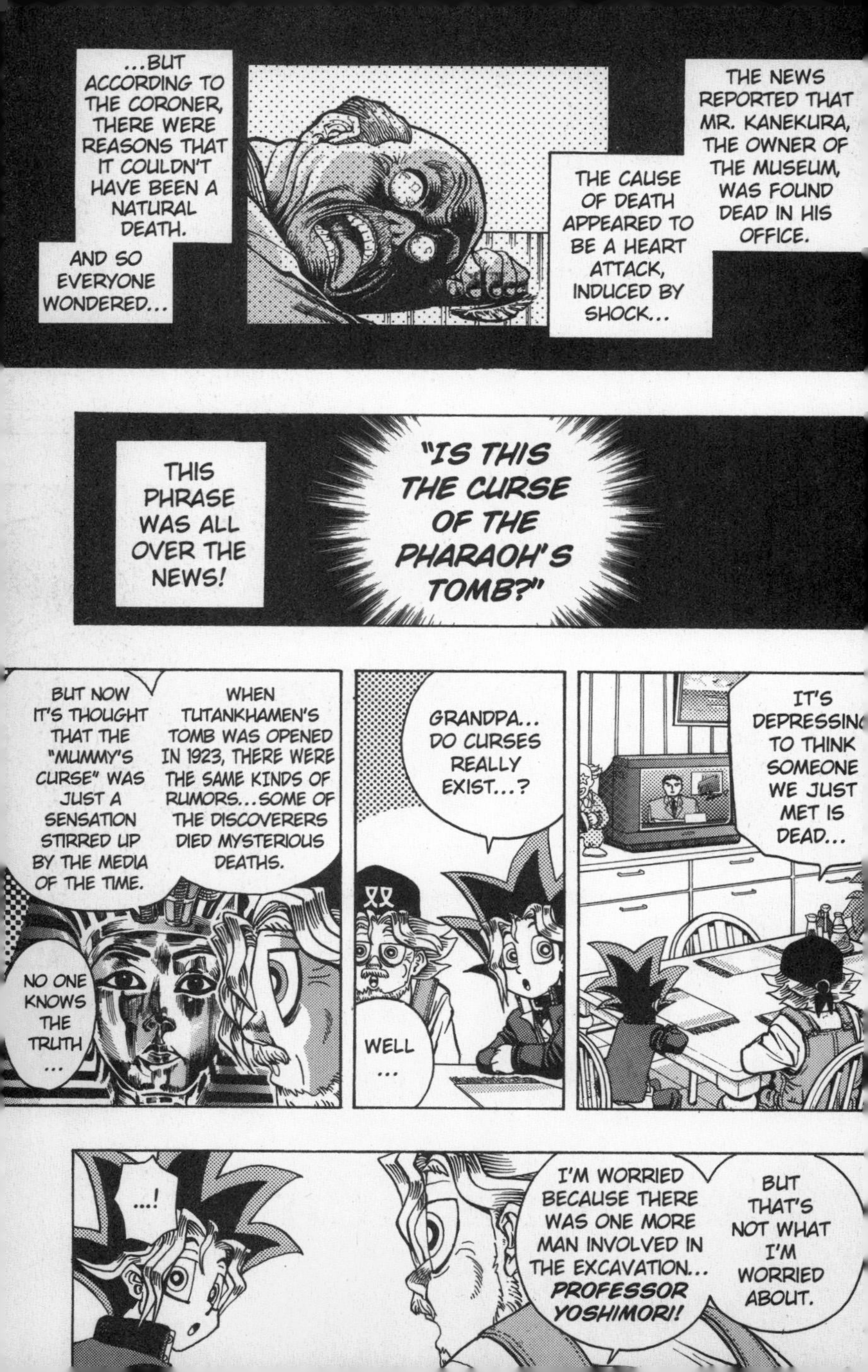
THE NEWS REPORTED THAT MR. KANEKURA, THE OWNER OF THE MUSEUM, WAS FOUND DEAD IN HIS OFFICE.
THE CAUSE OF DEATH APPEARED TO BE A HEART ATTACK, INDUCED BY SHOCK...
...BUT ACCORDING TO THE CORONER, THERE WERE REASONS THAT IT COULDN'T HAVE BEEN A NATURAL DEATH.
AND SO EVERYONE WONDERED...
"IS THIS THE CURSE OF THE PHARAOH'S TOMB?"
THIS PHRASE WAS ALL OVER THE NEWS!
IT'S DEPRESSIN TO THINK SOMEONE WE JUST MET IS DEAD...
GRANDPA... DO CURSES REALLY EXIST...?
WELL ...
WHEN TUTANKHAMEN'S TOMB WAS OPENED IN 1923, THERE WERE THE SAME KINDS OF RUMORS...SOME OF THE DISCOVERERS DIED MYSTERIOUS DEATHS.
BUT NOW IT'S THOUGHT THAT THE "MUMMY'S CURSE" WAS JUST A SENSATION STIRRED UP BY THE MEDIA OF THE TIME.
NO ONE KNOWS THE TRUTH ...
BUT THAT'S NOT WHAT I'M WORRIED ABOUT.
I'M WORRIED BECAUSE THERE WAS ONE MORE MAN INVOLVED IN THE EXCAVATION... PROFESSOR YOSHIMORI!
...!

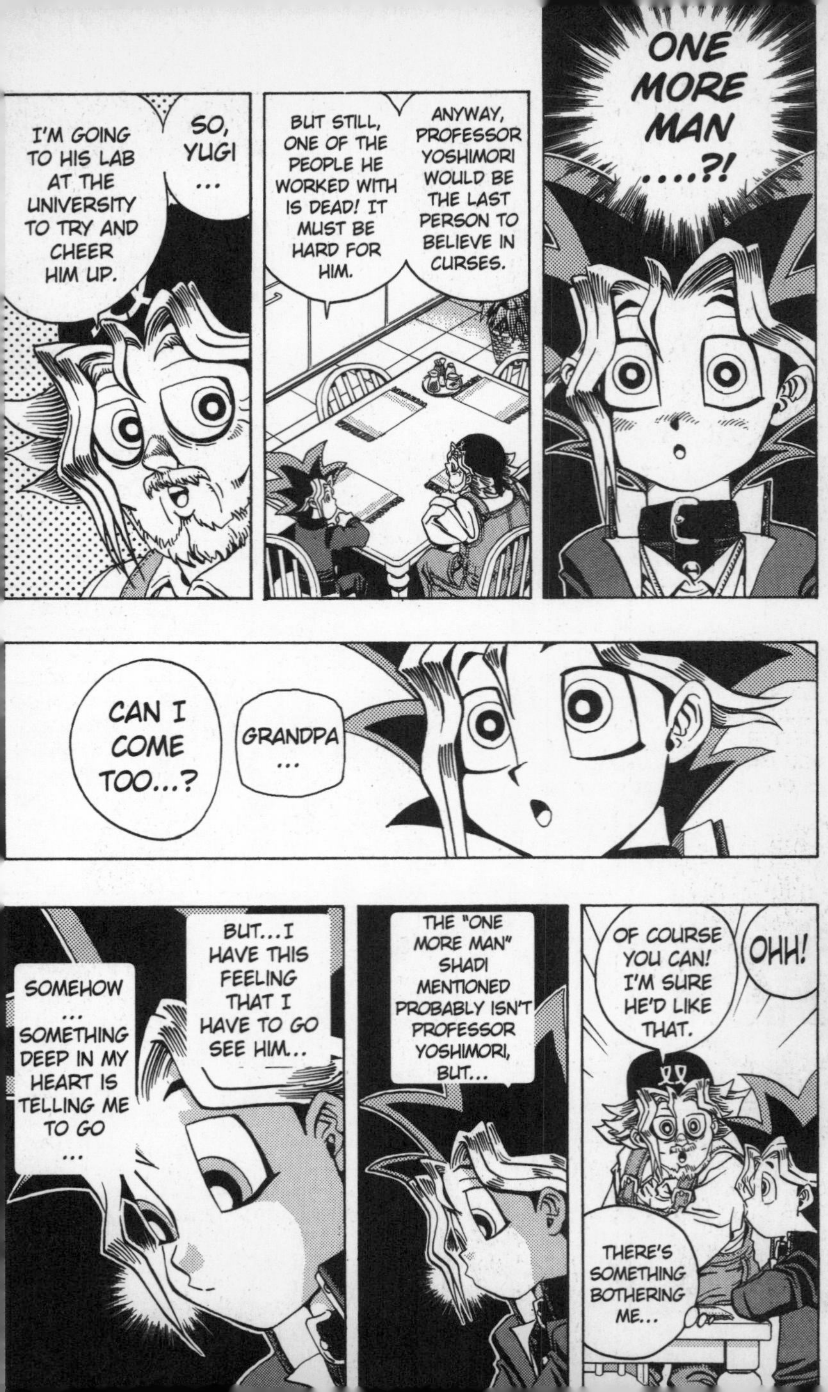
ONE MORE MAN ....?!
ANYWAY, PROFESSOR YOSHIMORI WOULD BE THE LAST PERSON TO BELIEVE IN CURSES.
BUT STILL, ONE OF THE PEOPLE HE WORKED WITH IS DEAD! IT MUST BE HARD FOR HIM.
SO, YUGI ...
I'M GOING TO HIS LAB AT THE UNIVERSITY TO TRY AND CHEER HIM UP.
GRANDPA ...
CAN I COME TOO...?
OHH!
OF COURSE YOU CAN! I'M SURE HE'D LIKE THAT.
THERE'S SOMETHING BOTHERING ME...
THE "ONE MORE MAN" SHADI MENTIONED PROBABLY ISN'T PROFESSOR YOSHIMORI, BUT...
BUT...I HAVE THIS FEELING THAT I HAVE TO GO SEE HIM...
SOMEHOW ... SOMETHING DEEP IN MY HEART IS TELLING ME TO GO ...

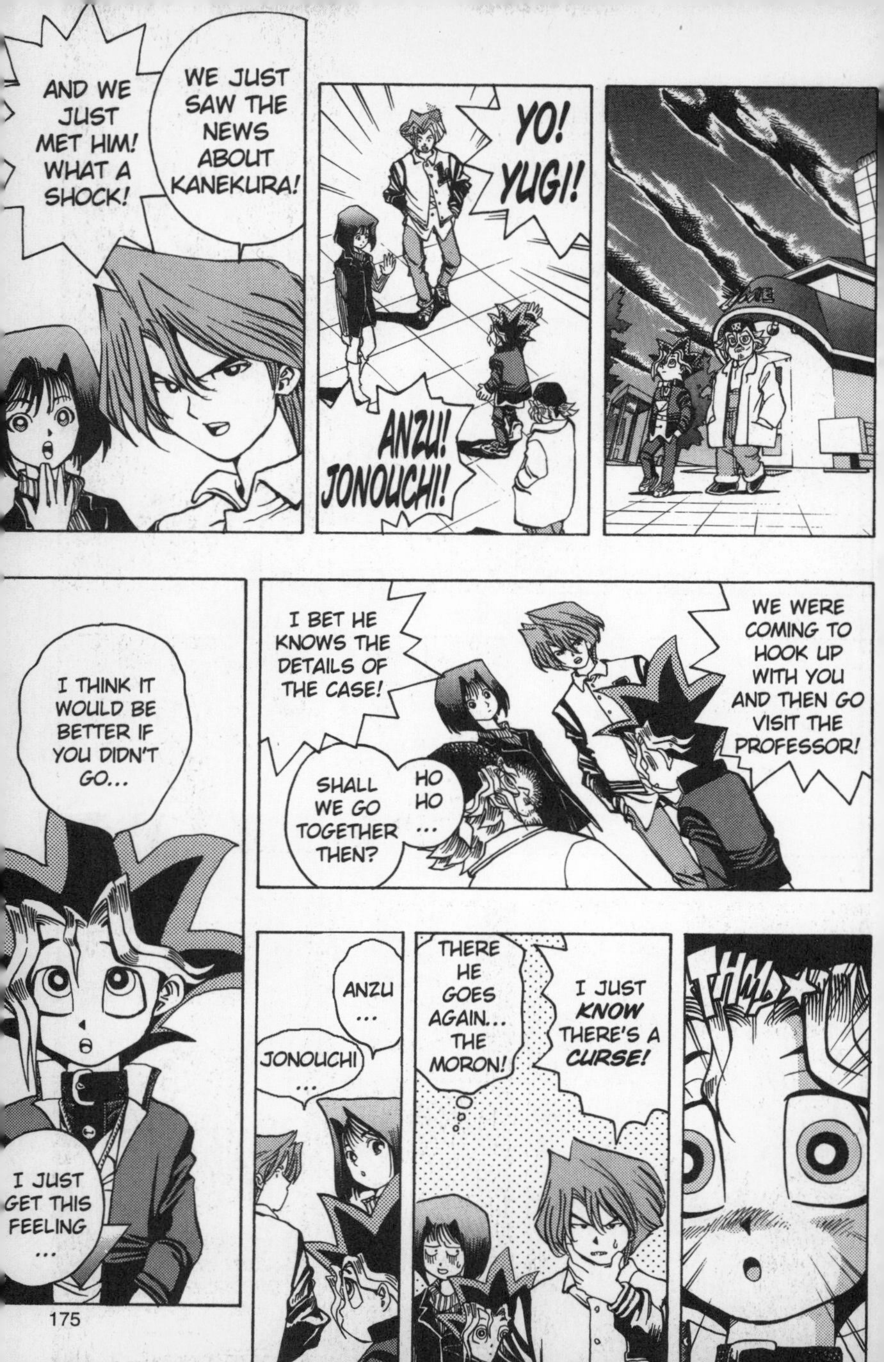
YO! YUGI!
ANZU! JONOUCHI!
WE JUST SAW THE NEWS ABOUT KANEKURA!
AND WE JUST MET HIM! WHAT A SHOCK!
WE WERE COMING TO HOOK UP WITH YOU AND THEN GO VISIT THE PROFESSOR!
I BET HE KNOWS THE DETAILS OF THE CASE!
HO HO ...
SHALL WE GO TOGETHER THEN?
THM
I JUST *KNOW* THERE'S A *CURSE!*
THERE HE GOES AGAIN... THE MORON!
ANZU ...
JONOUCHI ...
I THINK IT WOULD BE BETTER IF YOU DIDN'T GO...
I JUST GET THIS FEELING ...

WE'RE WORRIED ABOUT HIM JUST LIKE YOU ARE!

PROFESSOR YOSHIMORI SHOWED US AROUND THE MUSEUM!

HE SEEMS LIKE A GOOD GUY!

YOU'RE WORRIED THAT JONOUCHI'S AFRAID OF THE CURSE, AREN'T YOU?

WE'RE ALL RIGHT, YUGI!

YEAH! I'M NOT *REALLY* SCARED!!

HUH ...?

THEN LET'S BE OFF...!

HO HO ...

I'M SORRY FOR ACTING WEIRD...

YOU'RE RIGHT!

Y-YEAH ...

Archaeology Lab

Domino University

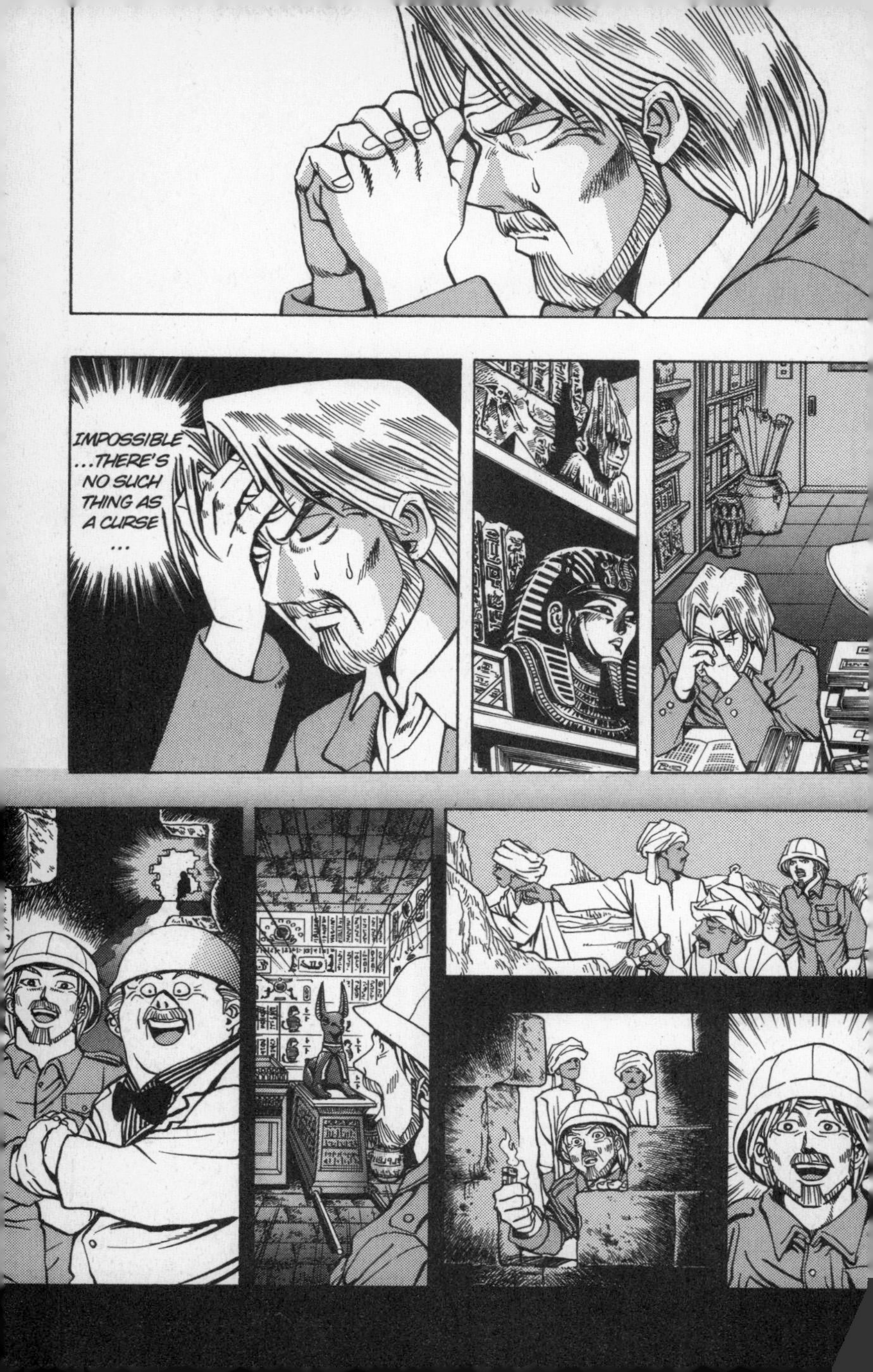
IMPOSSIBLE ...THERE'S NO SUCH THING AS A CURSE ...

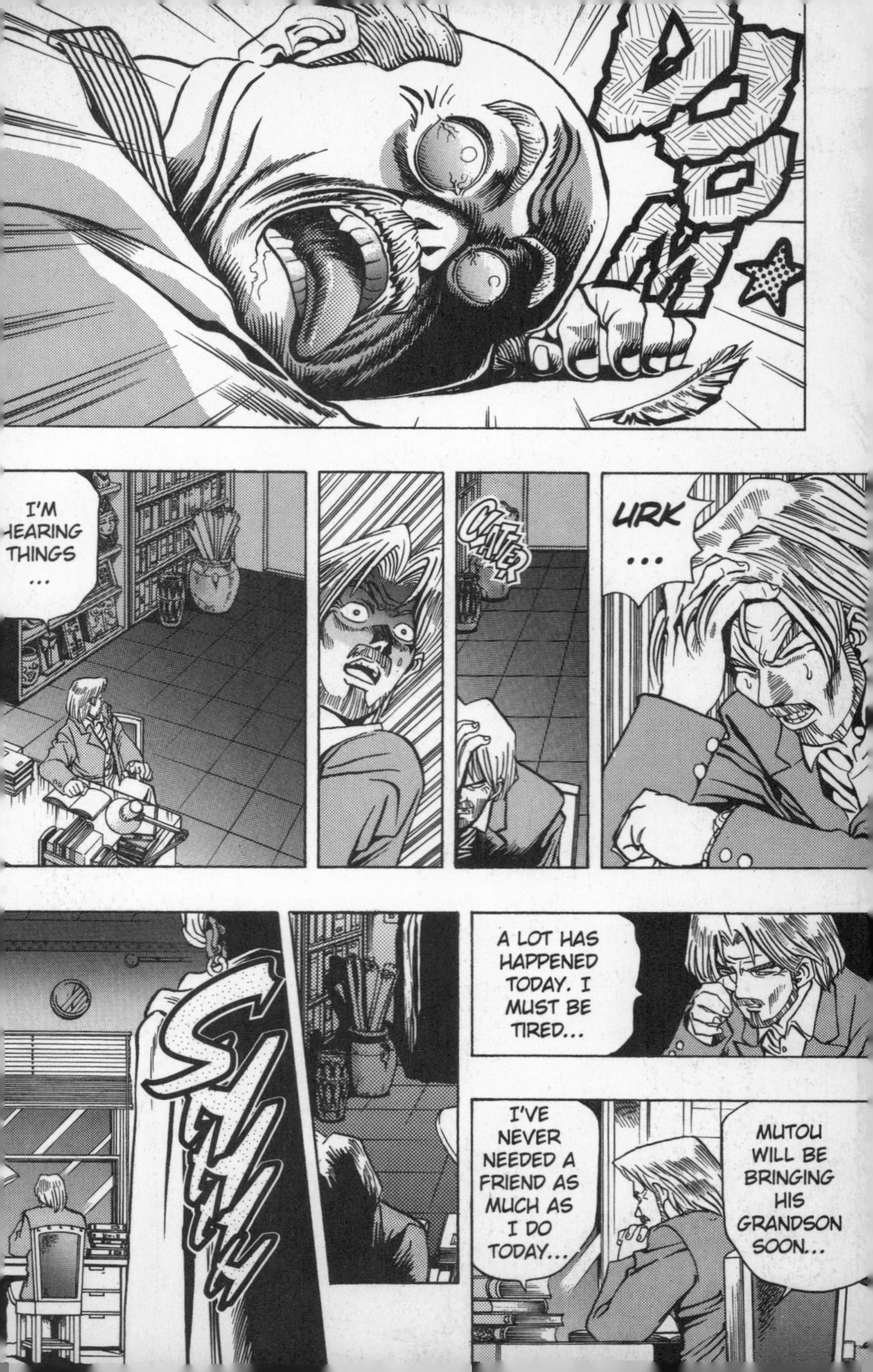

I'M HEARING THINGS ...
CLATTER
URK ...
A LOT HAS HAPPENED TODAY. I MUST BE TIRED...
I'VE NEVER NEEDED A FRIEND AS MUCH AS I DO TODAY...
MUTOU WILL BE BRINGING HIS GRANDSON SOON...

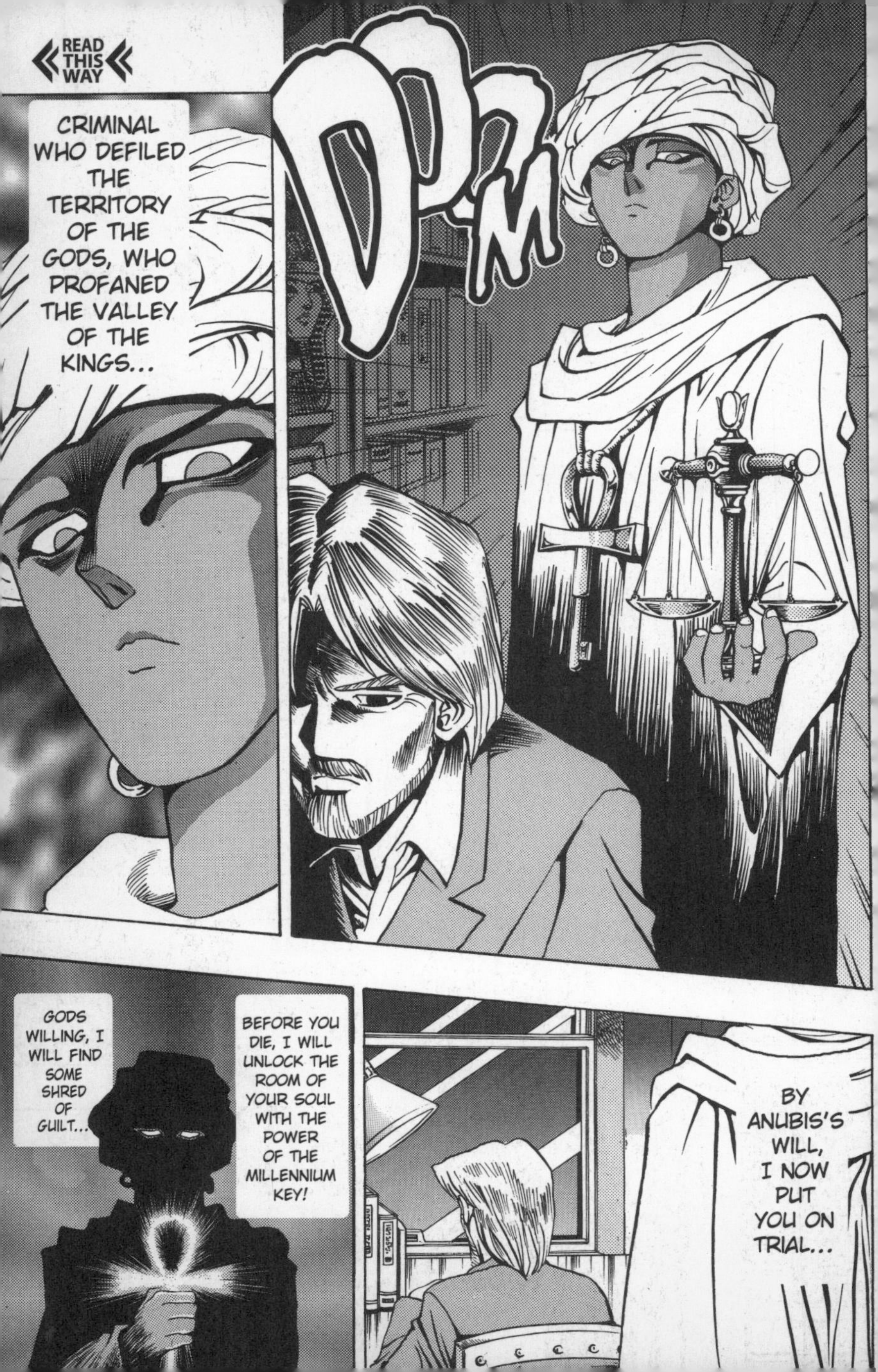
READ THIS WAY
DOOM
CRIMINAL WHO DEFILED THE TERRITORY OF THE GODS, WHO PROFANED THE VALLEY OF THE KINGS...
BY ANUBIS'S WILL, I NOW PUT YOU ON TRIAL...
BEFORE YOU DIE, I WILL UNLOCK THE ROOM OF YOUR SOUL WITH THE POWER OF THE MILLENNIUM KEY!
GODS WILLING, I WILL FIND SOME SHRED OF GUILT...

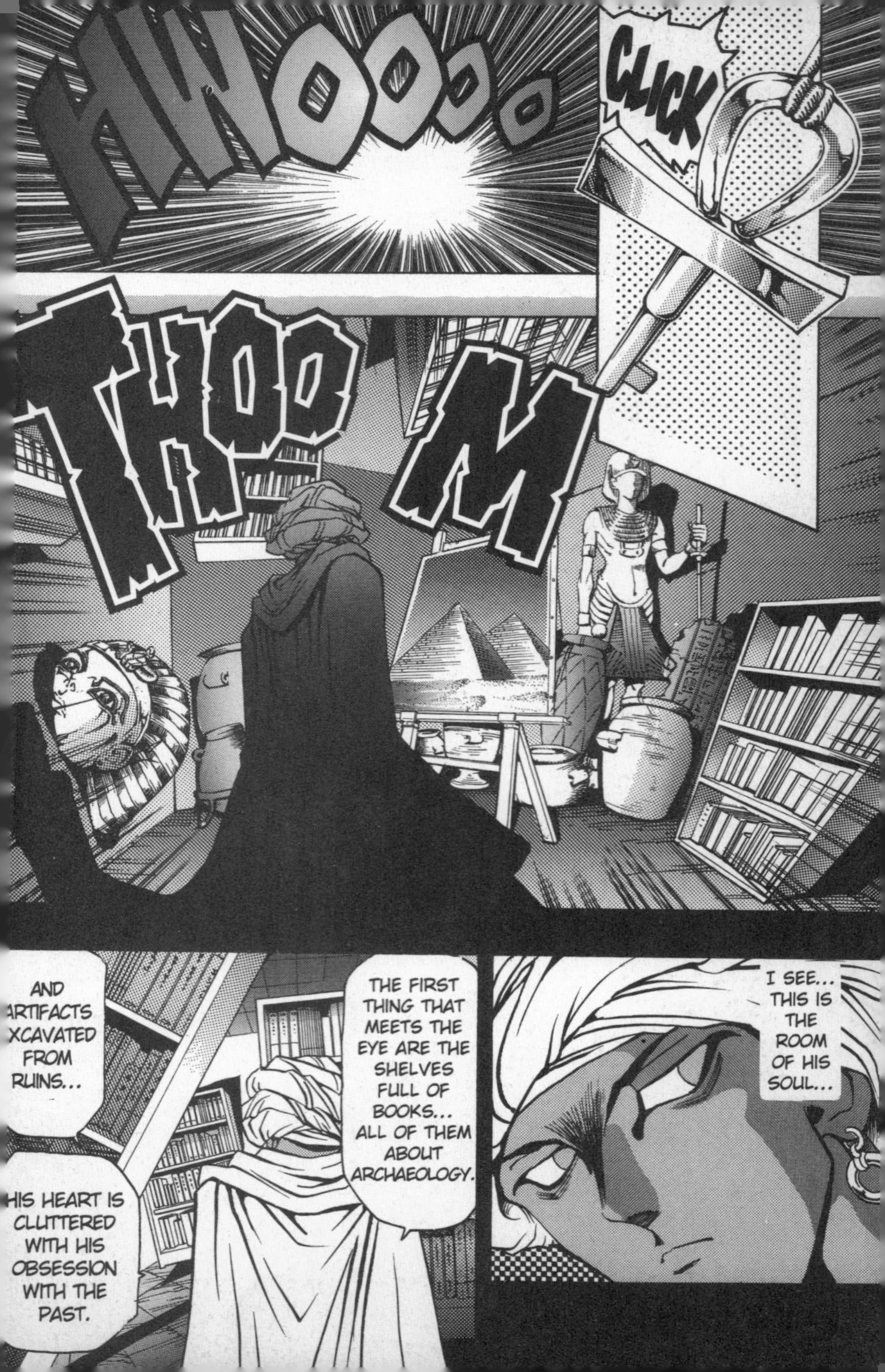
CLICK
WHOOOOO
THOOM
I SEE... THIS IS THE ROOM OF HIS SOUL...
THE FIRST THING THAT MEETS THE EYE ARE THE SHELVES FULL OF BOOKS... ALL OF THEM ABOUT ARCHAEOLOGY.
AND ARTIFACTS XCAVATED FROM RUINS...
HIS HEART IS CLUTTERED WITH HIS OBSESSION WITH THE PAST.

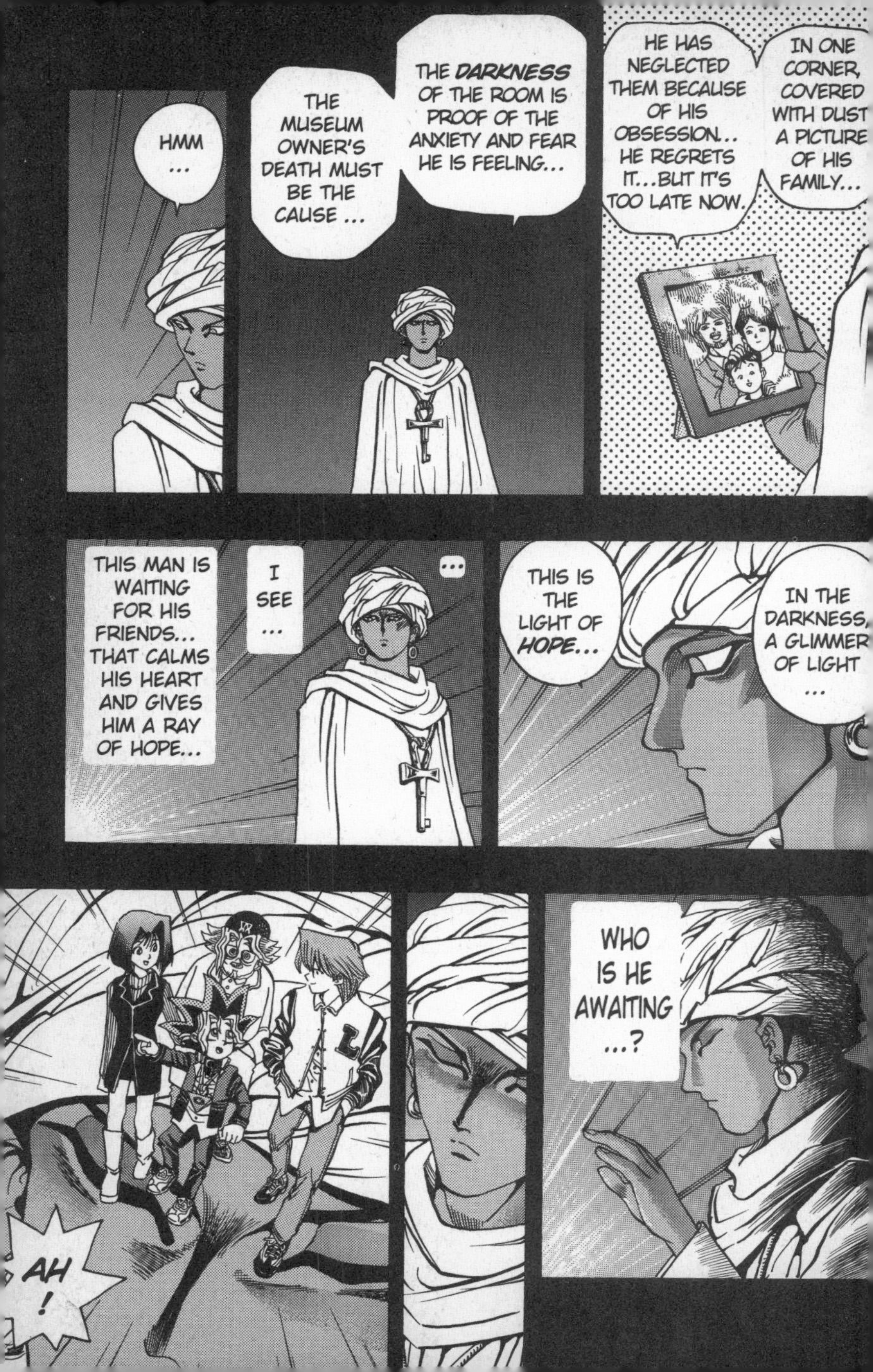
IN ONE CORNER, COVERED WITH DUST A PICTURE OF HIS FAMILY...
HE HAS NEGLECTED THEM BECAUSE OF HIS OBSESSION.. HE REGRETS IT...BUT IT'S TOO LATE NOW.
THE DARKNESS OF THE ROOM IS PROOF OF THE ANXIETY AND FEAR HE IS FEELING...
THE MUSEUM OWNER'S DEATH MUST BE THE CAUSE ...
HMM ...
IN THE DARKNESS, A GLIMMER OF LIGHT ...
THIS IS THE LIGHT OF HOPE...
...
I SEE ...
THIS MAN IS WAITING FOR HIS FRIENDS... THAT CALMS HIS HEART AND GIVES HIM A RAY OF HOPE...
WHO IS HE AWAITING ...?
AH !

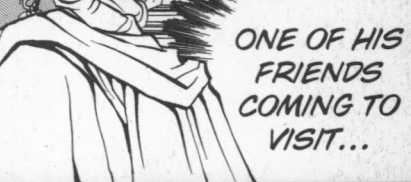

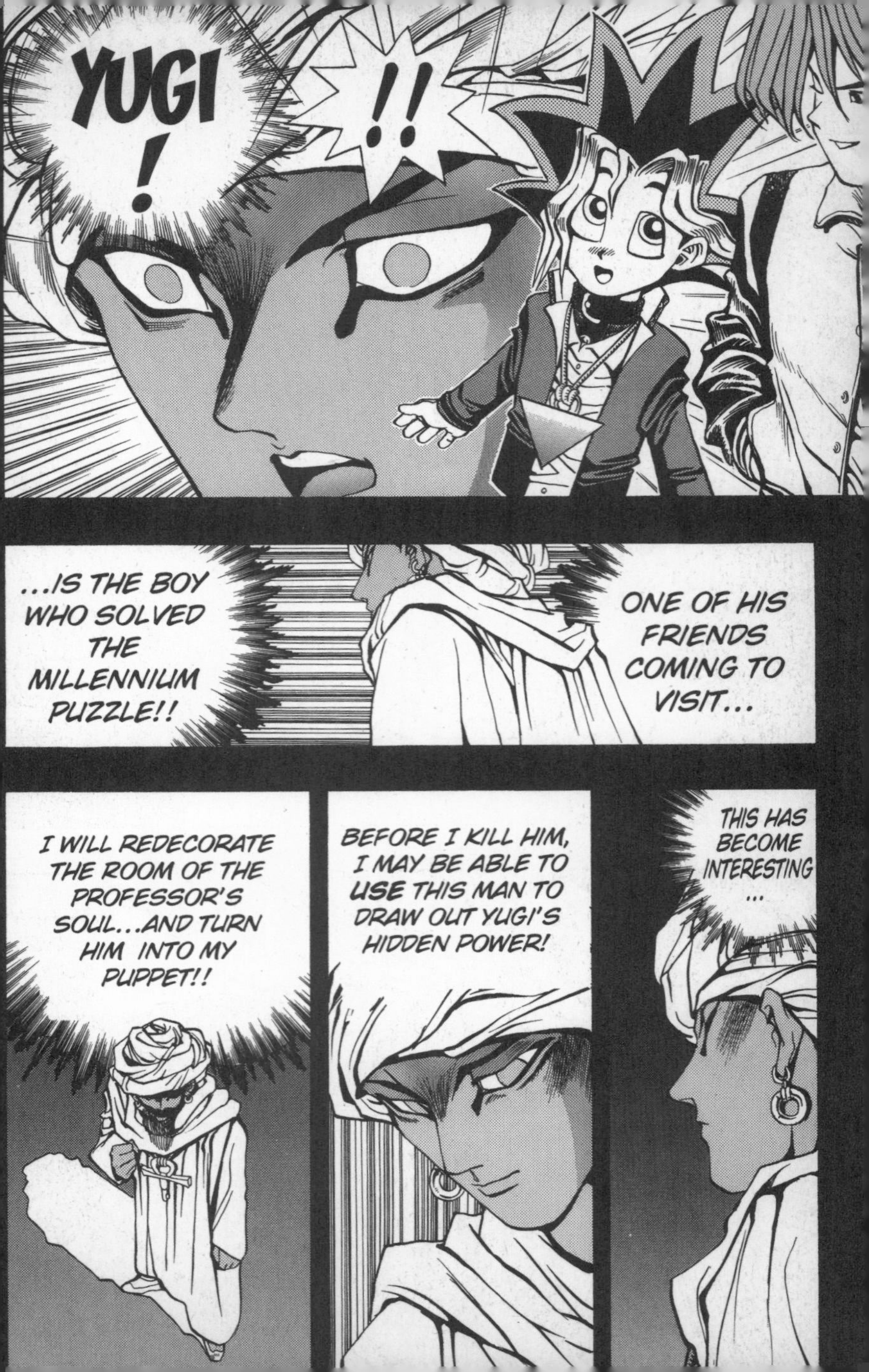

YUGI !
!!
ONE OF HIS FRIENDS COMING TO VISIT...
...IS THE BOY WHO SOLVED THE MILLENNIUM PUZZLE!!
THIS HAS BECOME INTERESTING ...
BEFORE I KILL HIM, I MAY BE ABLE TO USE THIS MAN TO DRAW OUT YUGI'S HIDDEN POWER!
I WILL REDECORATE THE ROOM OF THE PROFESSOR'S SOUL...AND TURN HIM INTO MY PUPPET!!

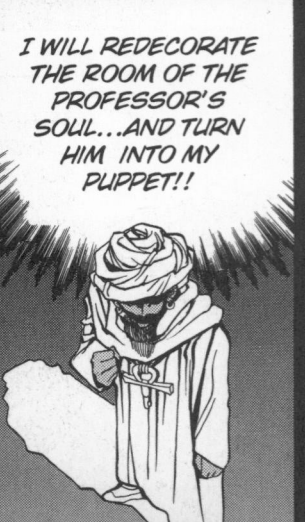

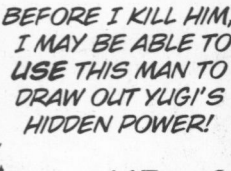

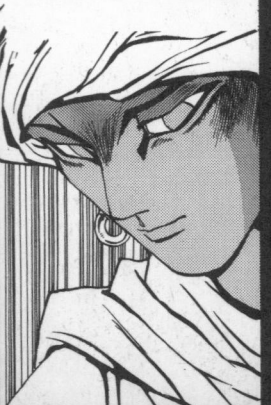

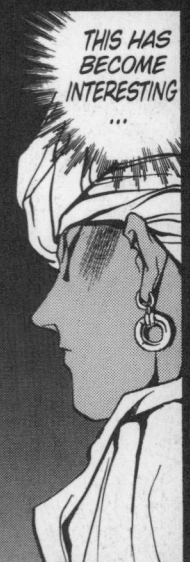

READ THIS WAY

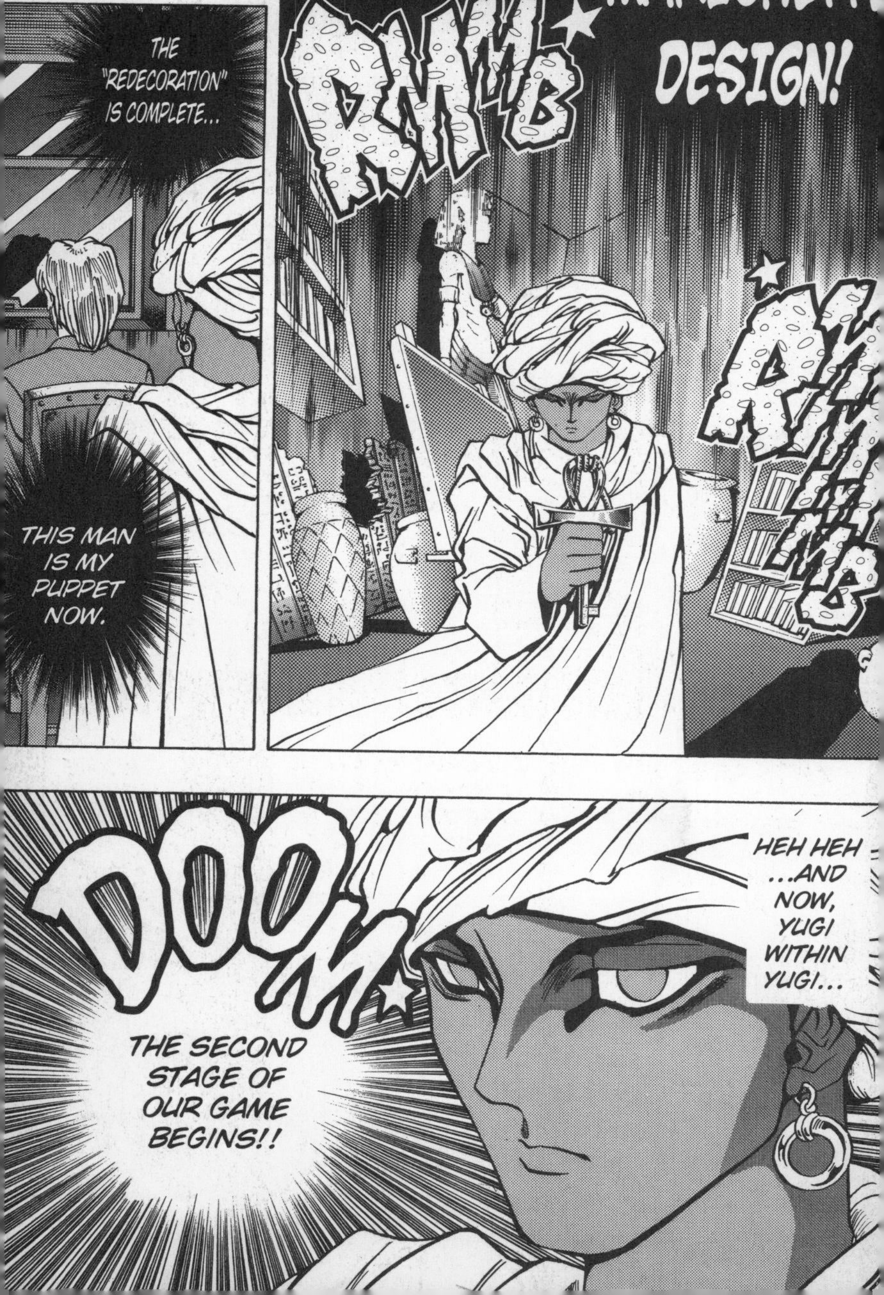
MARIONETT
DESIGN!
BAMB
THE "REDECORATION" IS COMPLETE...
THIS MAN IS MY PUPPET NOW.
HEH HEH ...AND NOW, YUGI WITHIN YUGI...
DOOM
THE SECOND STAGE OF OUR GAME BEGINS!!

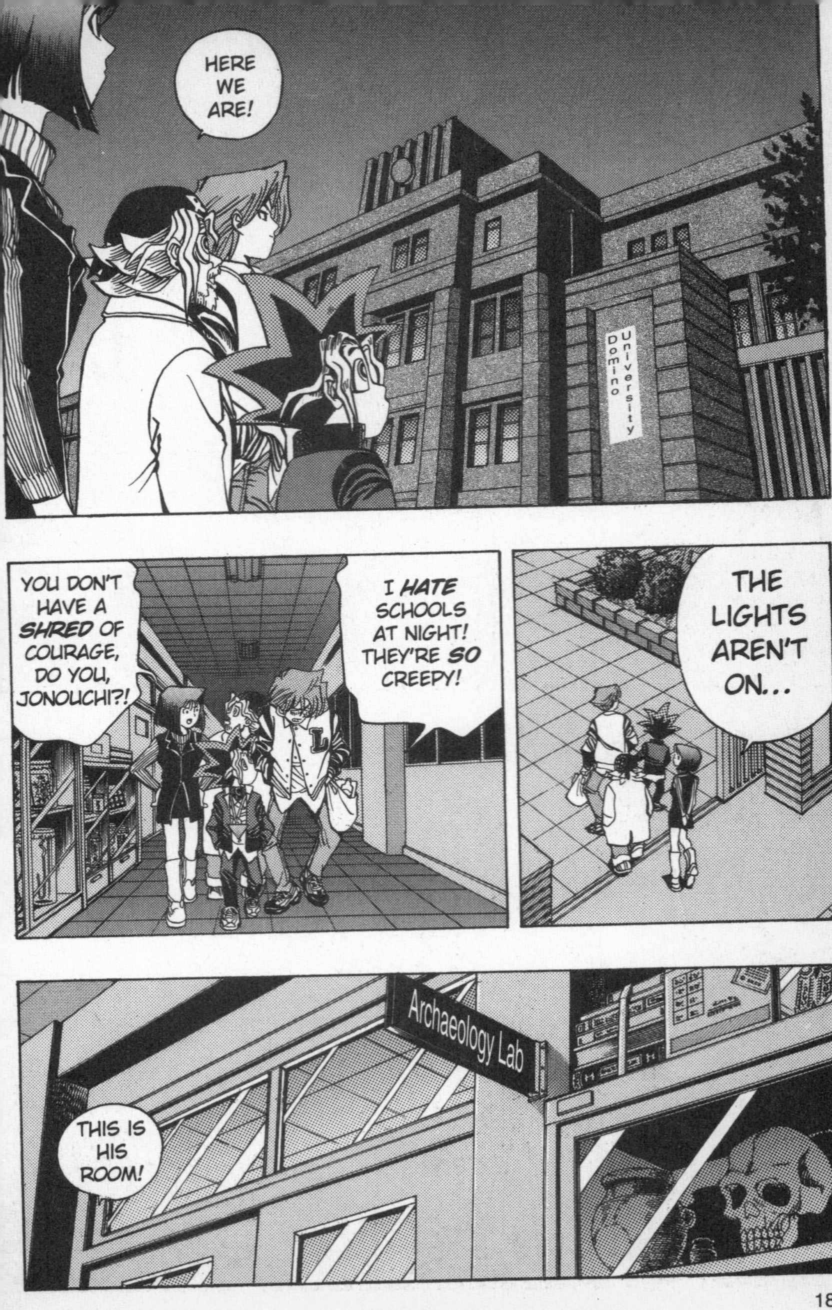
HERE WE ARE!
Domino University
THE LIGHTS AREN'T ON...
I *HATE* SCHOOLS AT NIGHT! THEY'RE *SO* CREEPY!
YOU DON'T HAVE A *SHRED* OF COURAGE, DO YOU, JONOUCHI?!
Archaeology Lab
THIS IS HIS ROOM!

READ THIS WAY

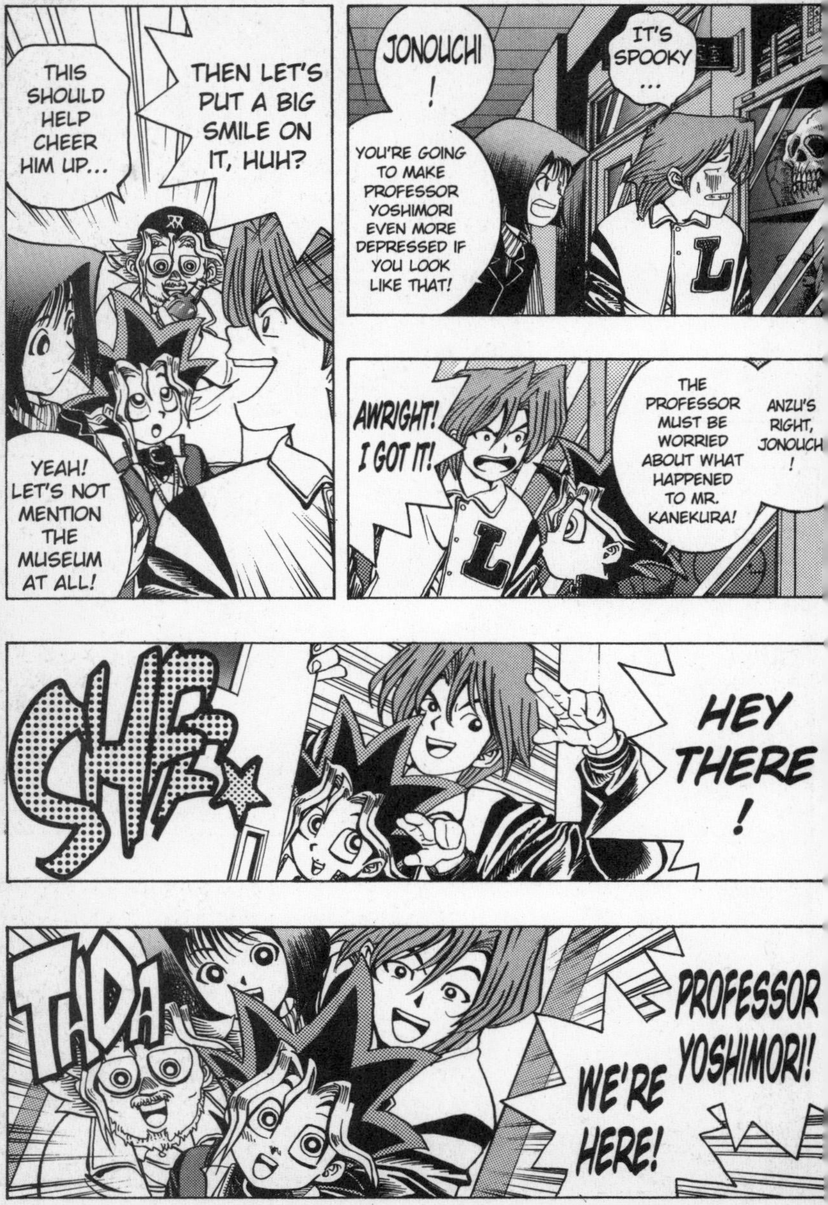
IT'S SPOOKY...
JONOUCHI!
YOU'RE GOING TO MAKE PROFESSOR YOSHIMORI EVEN MORE DEPRESSED IF YOU LOOK LIKE THAT!
ANZU'S RIGHT, JONOUCH!
THE PROFESSOR MUST BE WORRIED ABOUT WHAT HAPPENED TO MR. KANEKURA!
AWRIGHT! I GOT IT!
THEN LET'S PUT A BIG SMILE ON IT, HUH?
THIS SHOULD HELP CHEER HIM UP...
YEAH! LET'S NOT MENTION THE MUSEUM AT ALL!
HEY THERE!
SHF
PROFESSOR YOSHIMORI!
WE'RE HERE!
TADA

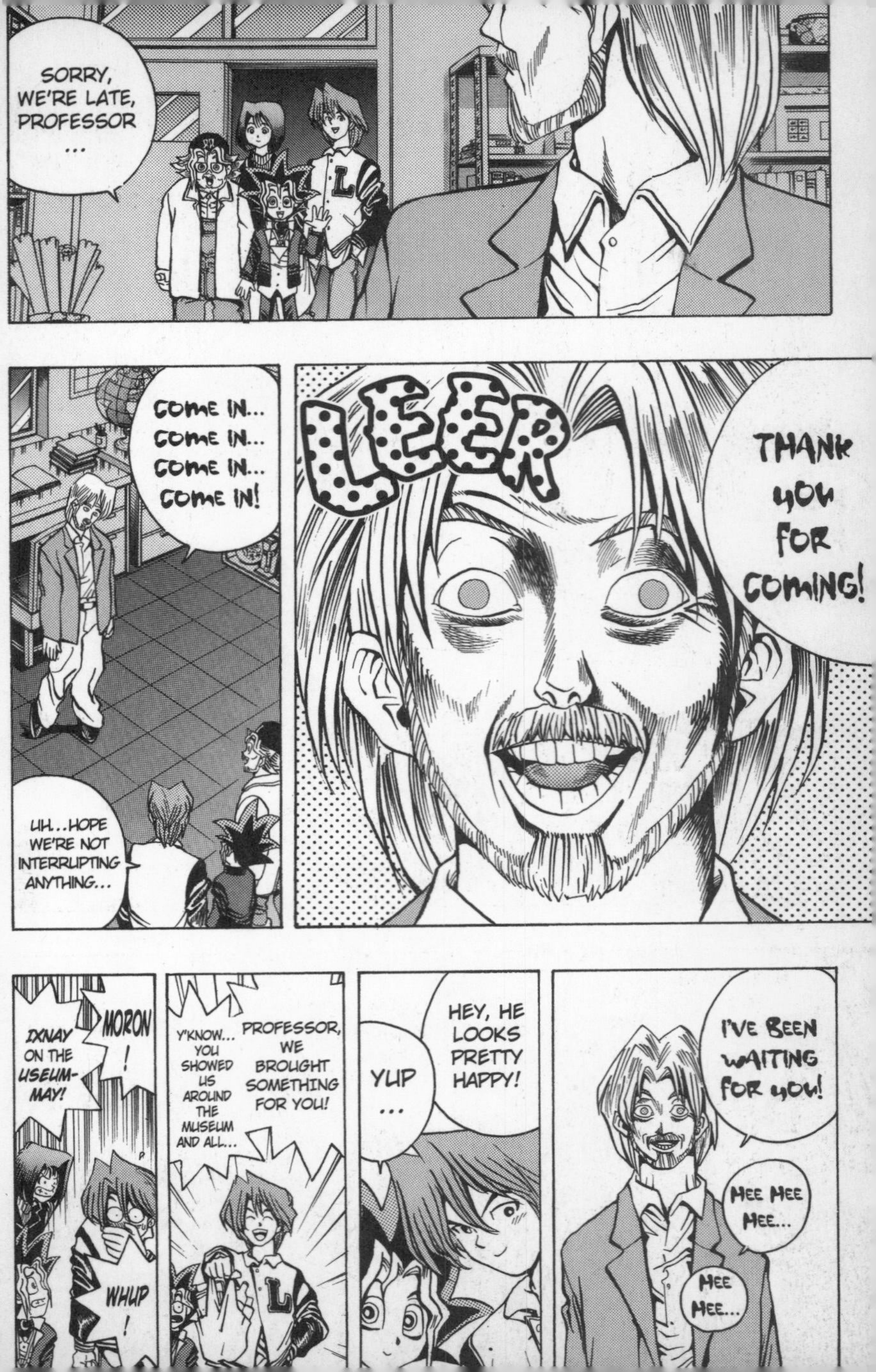
SORRY, WE'RE LATE, PROFESSOR ...
LEER
THANK YOU FOR COMING!
COME IN... COME IN... COME IN... COME IN!
UH...HOPE WE'RE NOT INTERRUPTING ANYTHING...
I'VE BEEN WAITING FOR YOU!
HEE HEE HEE...
HEE HEE...
HEY, HE LOOKS PRETTY HAPPY!
YUP ...
PROFESSOR, WE BROUGHT SOMETHING FOR YOU!
Y'KNOW... YOU SHOWED US AROUND THE MUSEUM AND ALL...
MORON!
IXNAY ON THE USEUM-MAY!
WHUP!

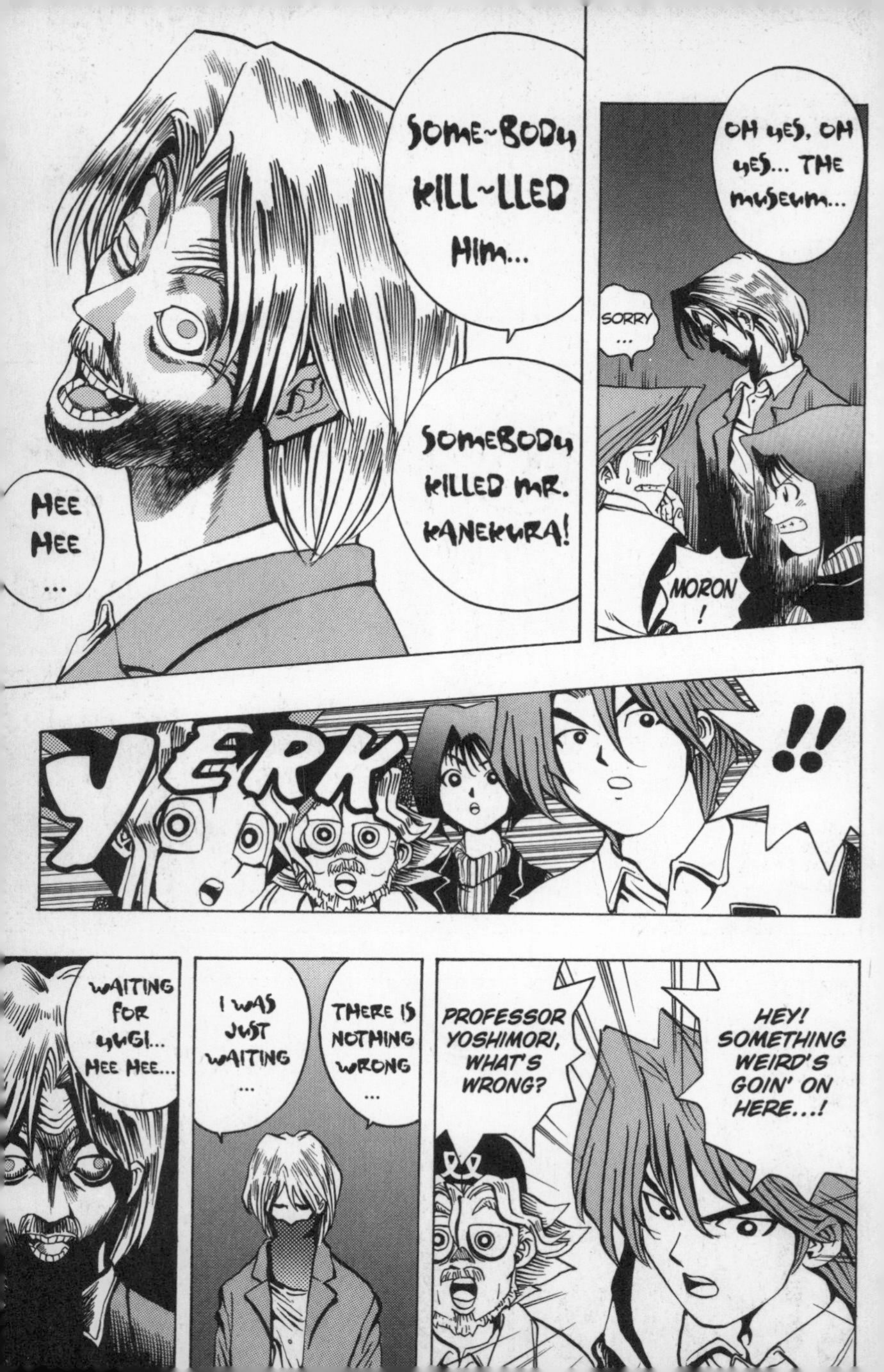
OH YES, OH YES... THE MUSEUM...
SORRY...
MORON!
SOME~BODY KILL~LLED HIM...
SOMEBODY KILLED MR. KANEKURA!
HEE HEE...
!!
YERK
HEY! SOMETHING WEIRD'S GOIN' ON HERE...!
PROFESSOR YOSHIMORI, WHAT'S WRONG?
THERE IS NOTHING WRONG...
I WAS JUST WAITING...
WAITING FOR YUGI... HEE HEE...

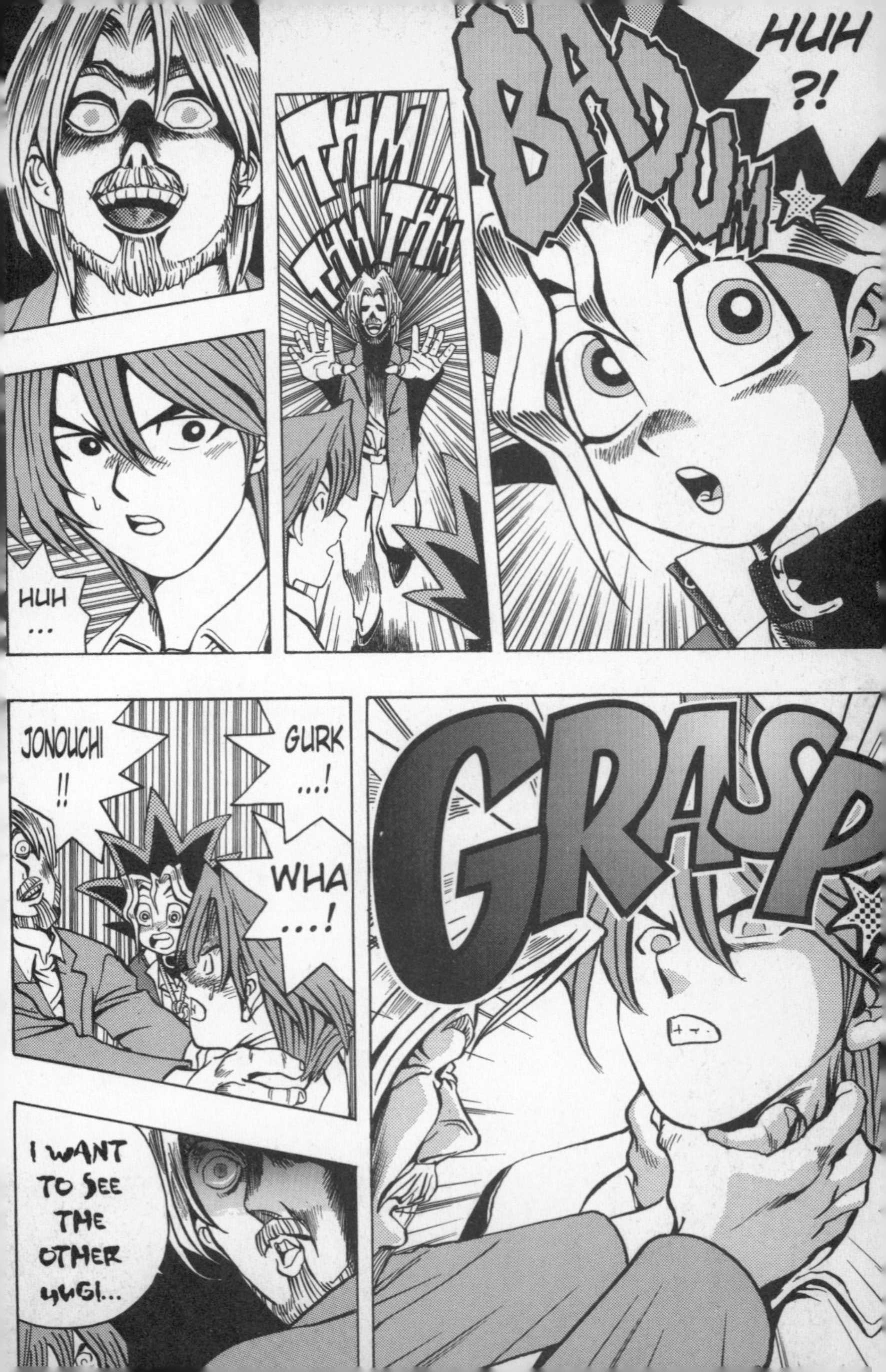
BADUM
HUH ?!
THM THM THM
HUH ...
GRASP
GURK ...!
JONOUCHI !!
WHA ...!
I WANT TO SEE THE OTHER YUGI...

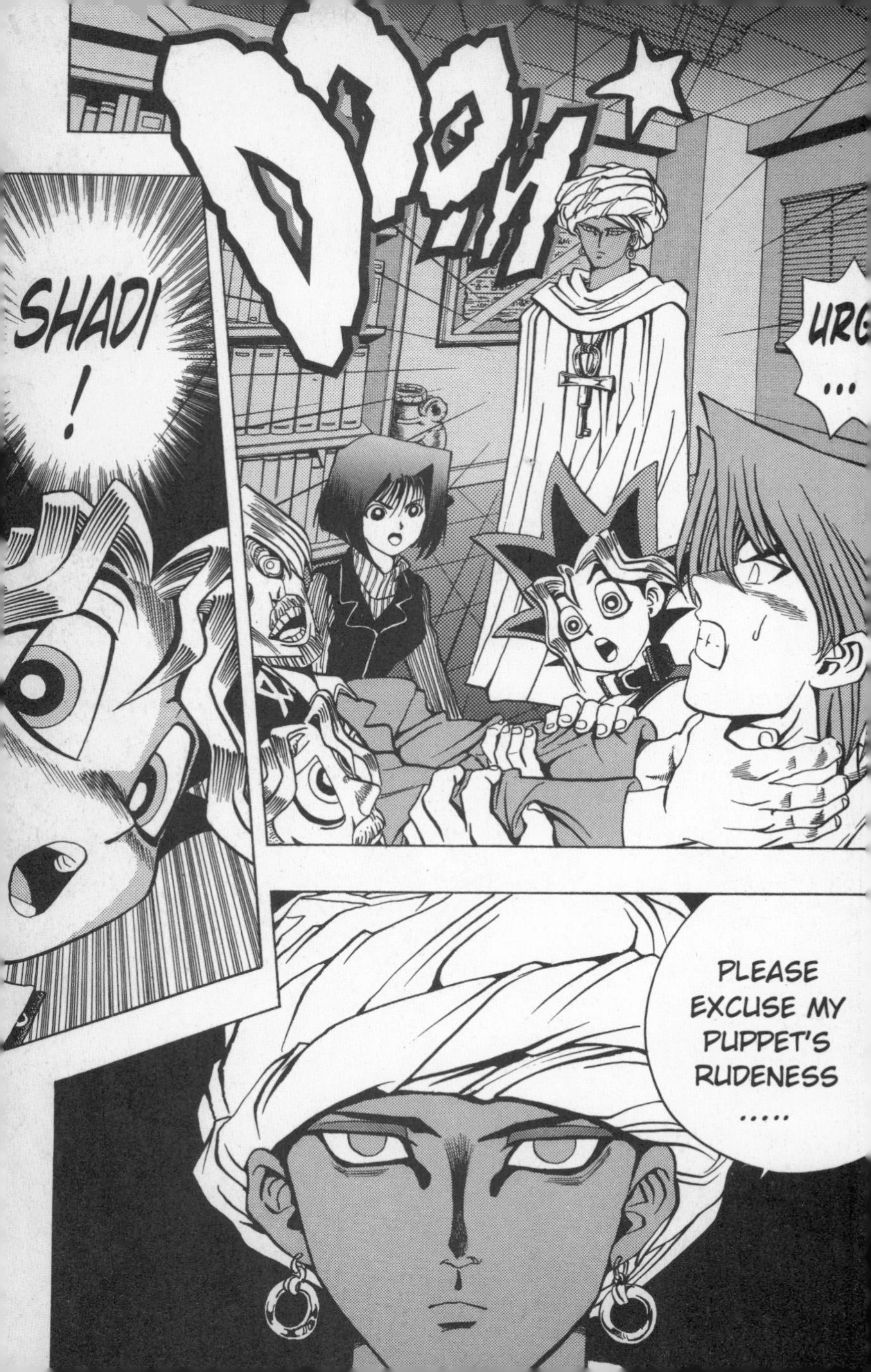
URG ...
SHADI !
PLEASE EXCUSE MY PUPPET'S RUDENESS .....

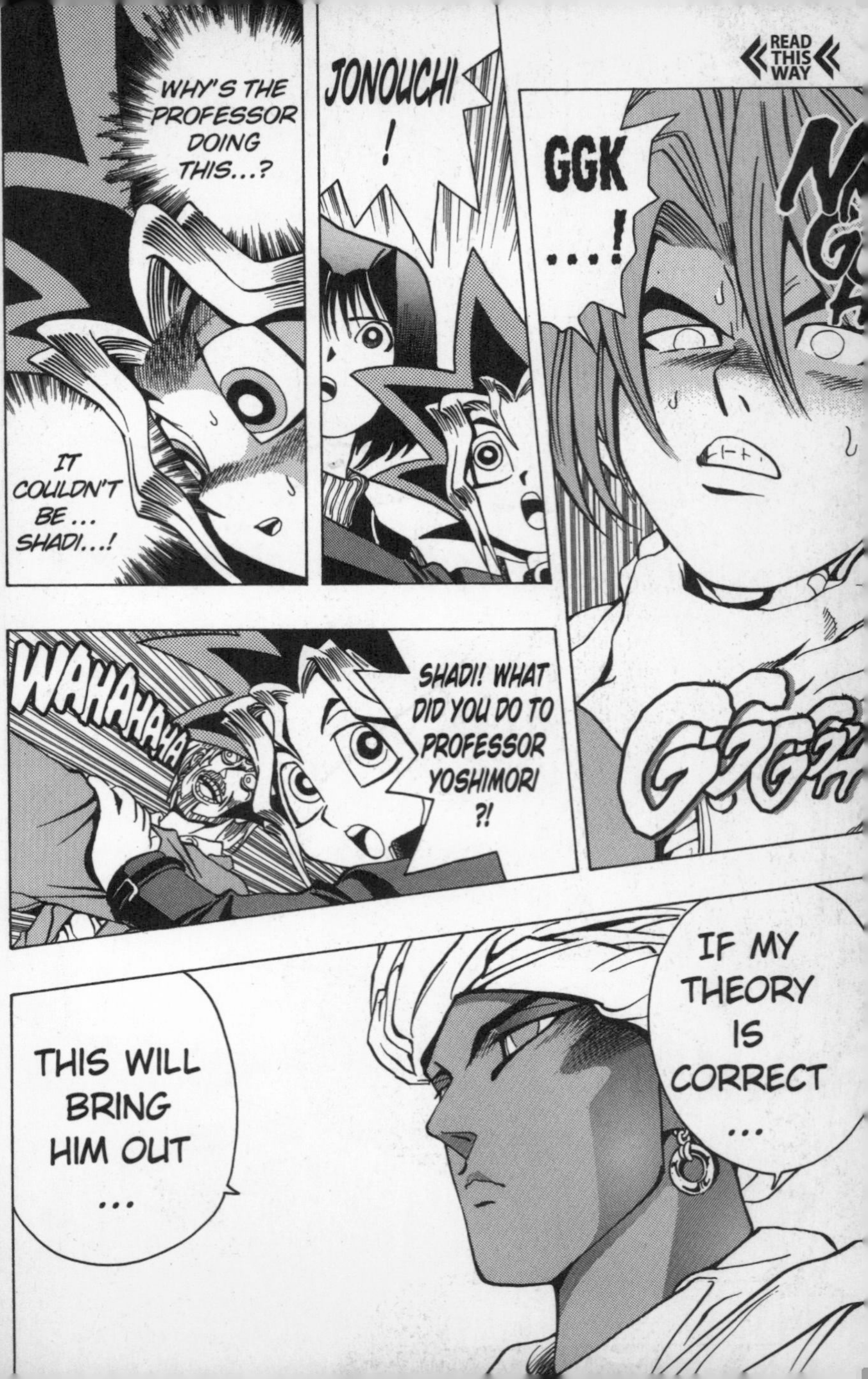
READ THIS WAY
GGK ...!
JONOUCHI !
WHY'S THE PROFESSOR DOING THIS...?
IT COULDN'T BE... SHADI...!
SHADI! WHAT DID YOU DO TO PROFESSOR YOSHIMORI ?!
WAHAHAHAHA
IF MY THEORY IS CORRECT ...
THIS WILL BRING HIM OUT ...

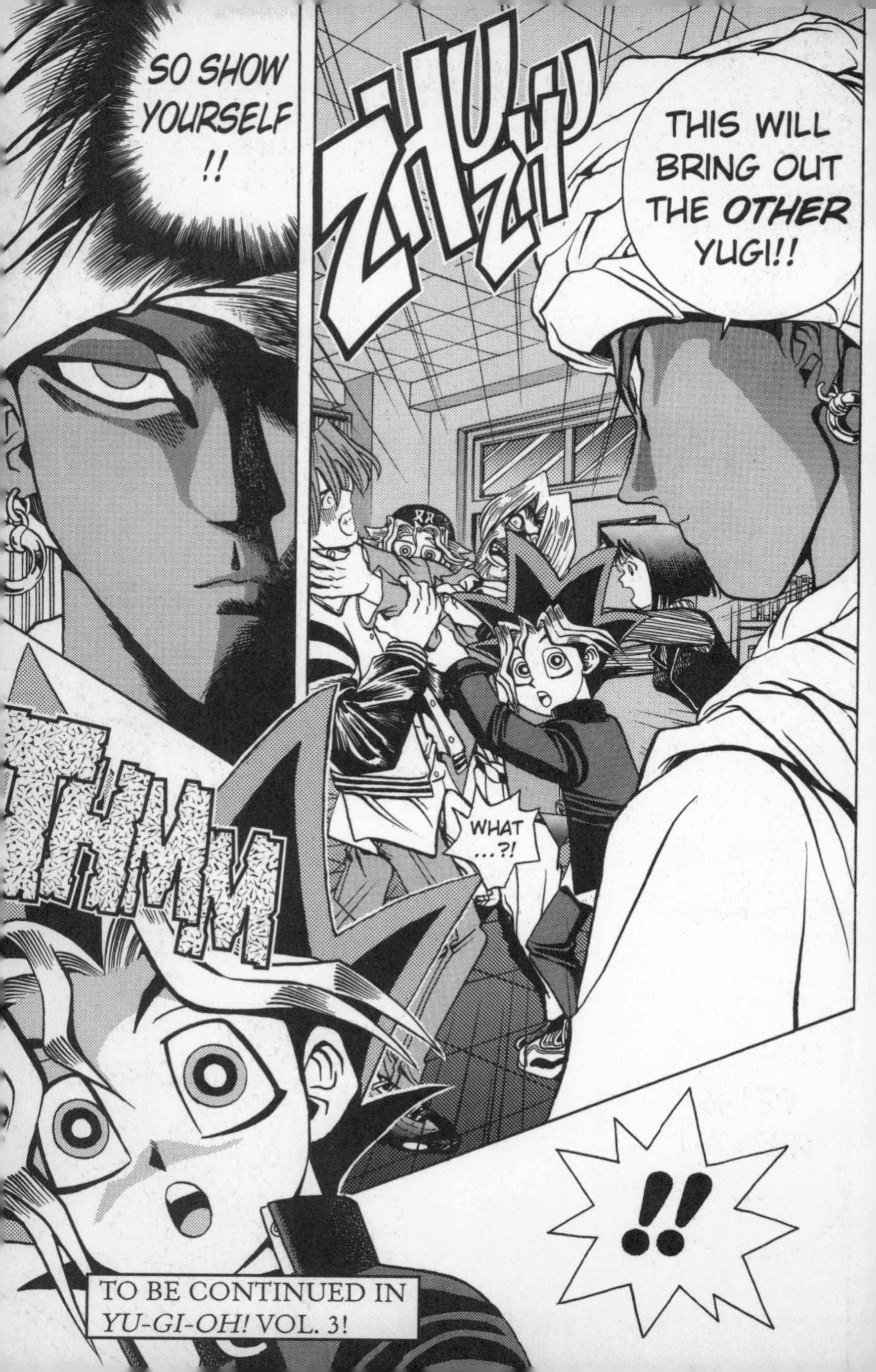
THIS WILL BRING OUT THE *OTHER* YUGI!!
WHAT ...?!
SO SHOW YOURSELF !!
THMM
!!
TO BE CONTINUED IN *YU-GI-OH!* VOL. 3!

MASTER OF THE CARDS

Duels 9 and 10 ("The Cards with Teeth") are the first appearance of collectible card games in **Yu-Gi-Oh!**. As **Yu-Gi-Oh!** fans know, the manga and anime version of the card game has simpler rules than the real-world version. Also, many of the card names are different between the English and Japanese versions. Here's a rundown of the cards in this graphic novel—the very first **Yu-Gi-Oh!** cards ever created by Kazuki Takahashi!

SUMMONED SKULL
[FIEND]
A fiend with dark powers for confining the enemy. Among the Fiend-Type monsters, this monster boasts considerable force.
ATK/2500 DEF/1200

1. Summoned Skull
Known as "Summoned Demon" in the original Japanese.

BLUE-EYES WHITE DRAGON
[DRAGON]
This legendary dragon is a powerful engine of destruction. Virtually invincible, very few have faced this awesome creature and lived to tell the tale.
ATK/3000 DEF/2500

2. Blue-Eyes White Dragon
In the manga, this card is extremely rare—only a few are supposed to exist.

RYU-KISHIN
[FIEND]
A very elusive creature that looks like a harmless statue until it attacks.
ATK/1000 DEF/ 500

3. Ryu-Kishin
Known as "Gargoyle" in the original Japanese.

BLACKLAND FIRE DRAGON
[DRAGON]
A dragon that dwells in the depths of darkness, its vulnerability lies in its poor eyesight.
ATK/1500 DEF/ 800

4. Blackland Fire Dragon
Known as "Dragon of Darkness" in the original Japanese.

MYSTIC LAMP
[SPELLCASTER/EFFECT]
This monster may attack your opponent's Life Points directly.
ATK/ 400 DEF/ 300

5. Mystic Lamp
Not actually played in the manga, this card doesn't have the same special powers that it does in the real-life game.

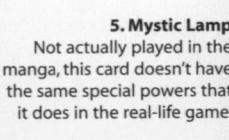

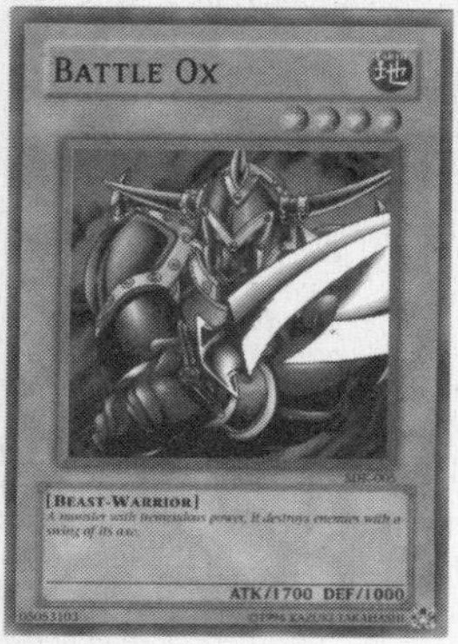
BATTLE OX
[BEAST-WARRIOR]
ATK/1700 DEF/1000

6. Battle Ox
Known as "Minotaurus" in the original Japanese. "Minotaurus" is the usual Japanese spelling of "Minotaur," the bull-headed monster from Greek myth.

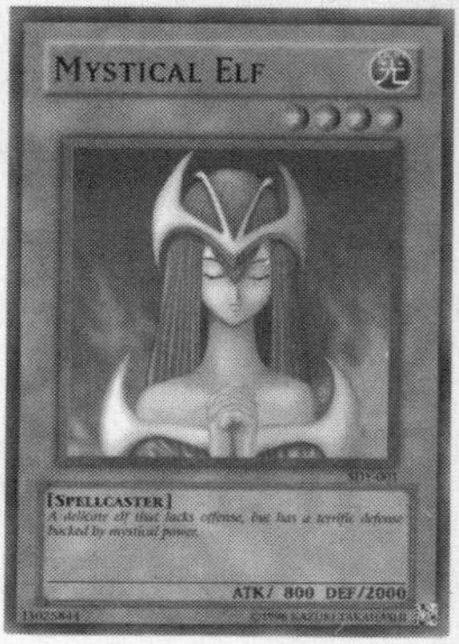
MYSTICAL ELF
[SPELLCASTER]
ATK/ 800 DEF/2000

7. Mystical Elf
Known as "Holy Elf" in the original Japanese.

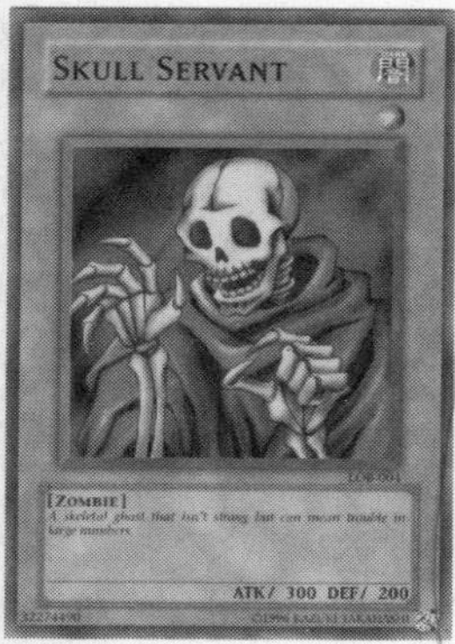
SKULL SERVANT
[ZOMBIE]
ATK/ 300 DEF/ 200

8. Skull Servant
Known as "Wight" in the original Japanese. A "wight" is an old English word for a ghost or a living corpse.

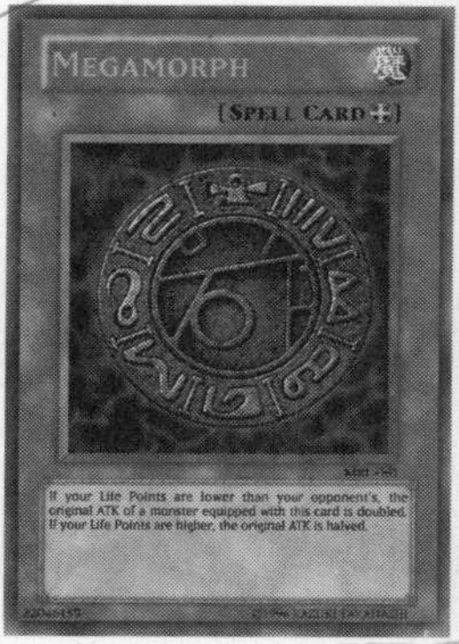
MEGAMORPH
[SPELL CARD]
If your Life Points are lower than your opponent's, the original ATK of a monster equipped with this card is doubled. If your Life Points are higher, the original ATK is halved.

9. Megamorph
In the real-life game, this card has different powers than it does in the manga, maybe so you don't have to do so much math to figure out 20% of your card's values. Because the manga and real-life cards have different powers, we translated the manga card's name as "Giant's Might" ("Become Giant" in the original Japanese).

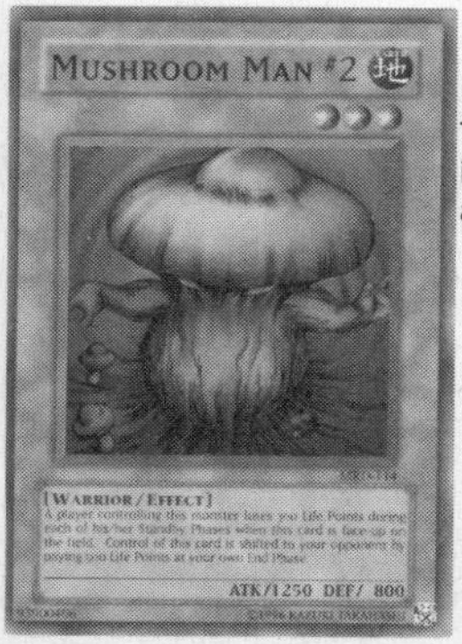
MUSHROOM MAN #2
[WARRIOR / EFFECT]
ATK/1250 DEF/ 800

10. Mushroom Man #2
This card only shows up briefly in the manga, and it has lower attack and defense values.

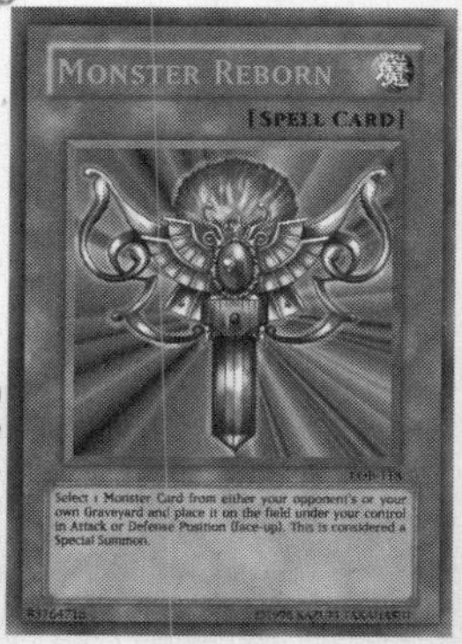
MONSTER REBORN
[SPELL CARD]

11. Monster Reborn
In the manga and the Japanese card game, the art for this card is an ankh—the Egyptian symbol of life and rebirth.

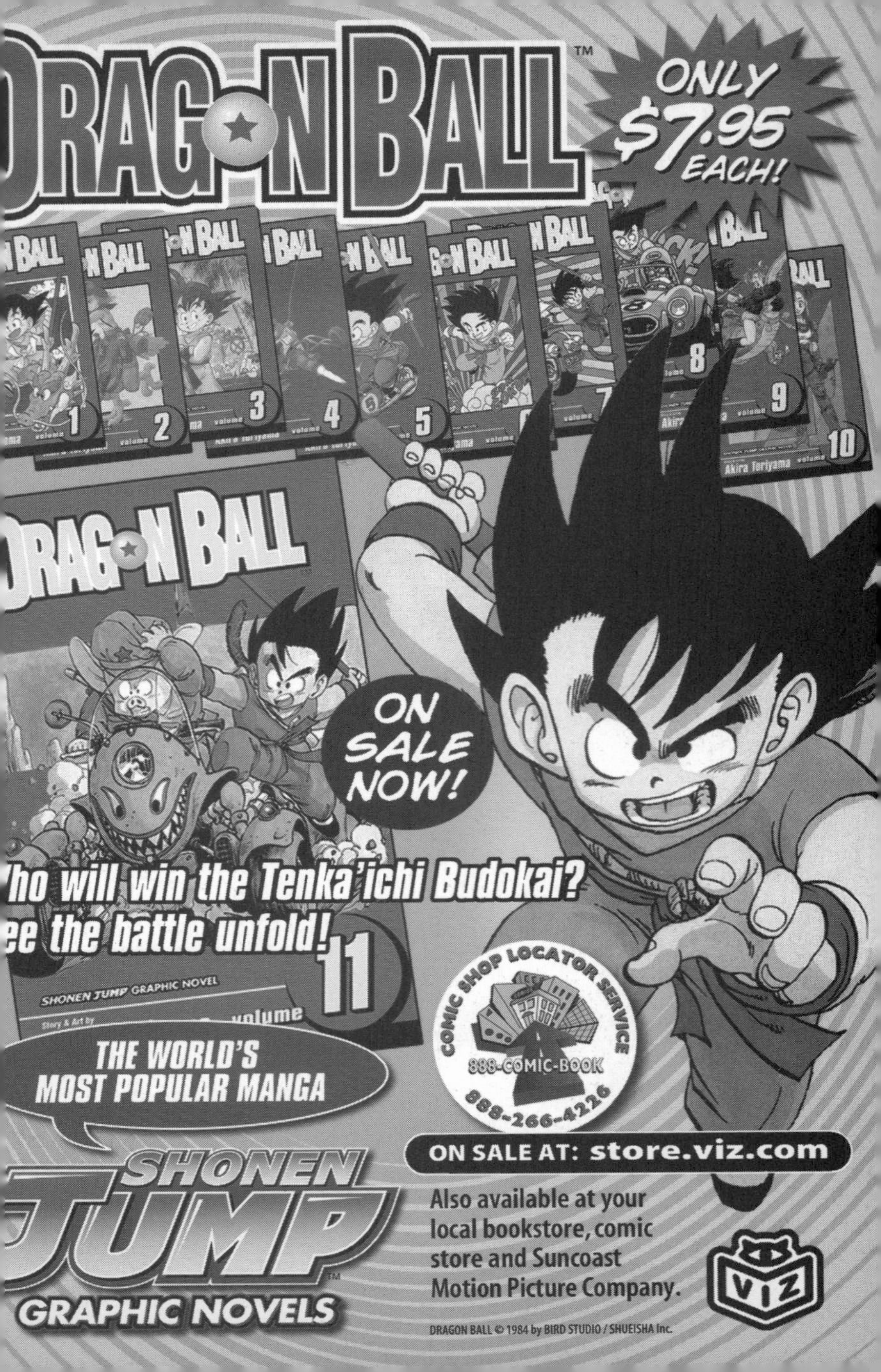
DRAGON BALL™
ONLY $7.95 EACH!
ON SALE NOW!
ho will win the Tenka'ichi Budokai?
ee the battle unfold!
SHONEN JUMP GRAPHIC NOVEL
volume 11
THE WORLD'S MOST POPULAR MANGA
SHONEN JUMP™ GRAPHIC NOVELS
COMIC SHOP LOCATOR SERVICE
888-COMIC-BOOK
888-266-4226
ON SALE AT: store.viz.com
Also available at your local bookstore, comic store and Suncoast Motion Picture Company.
VIZ
DRAGON BALL © 1984 by BIRD STUDIO / SHUEISHA Inc.

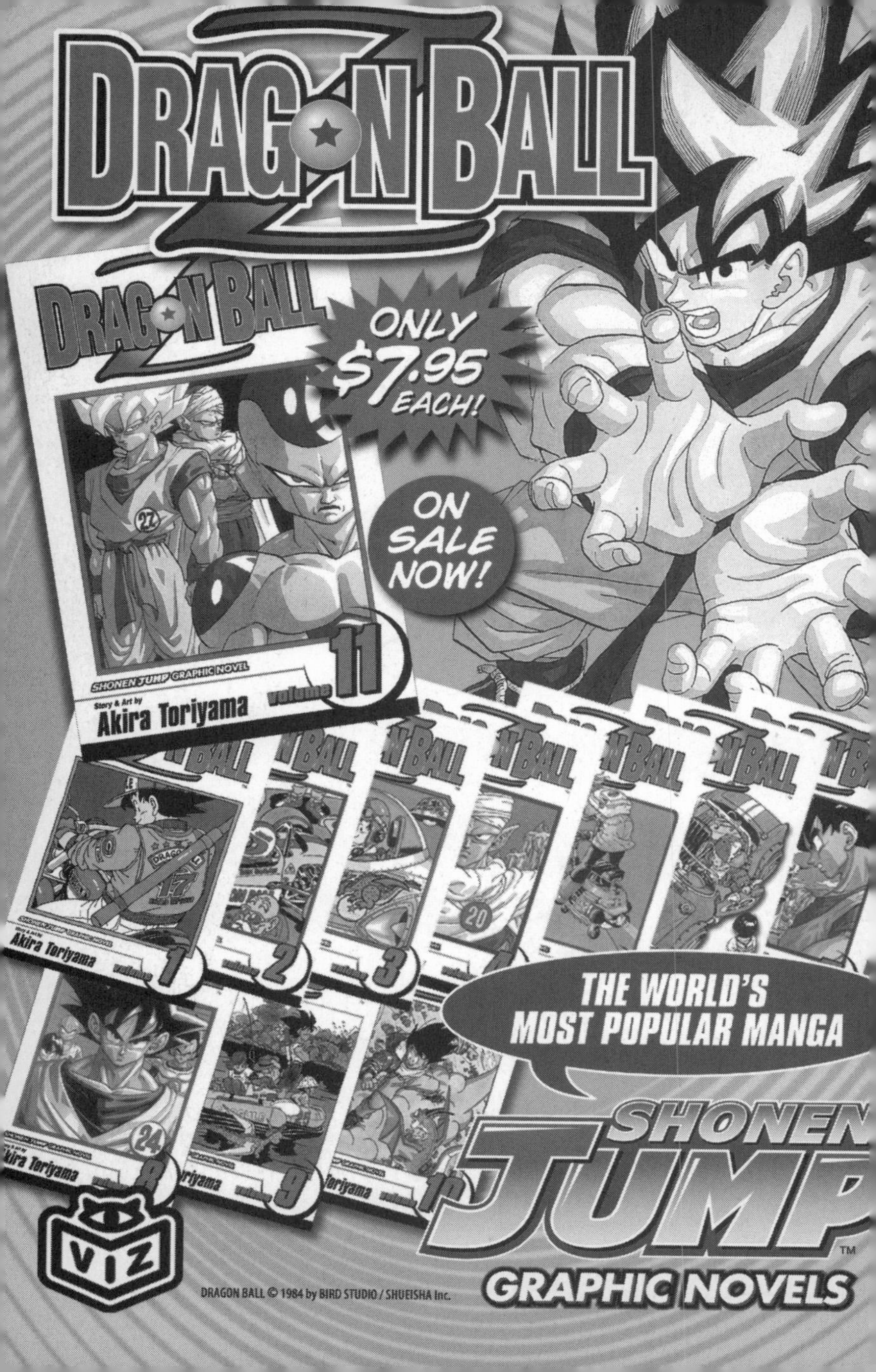
DRAGON BALL Z
ONLY $7.95 EACH!
ON SALE NOW!
SHONEN JUMP GRAPHIC NOVEL
Story & Art by
Akira Toriyama
volume 11
THE WORLD'S MOST POPULAR MANGA
VIZ
DRAGON BALL © 1984 by BIRD STUDIO / SHUEISHA Inc.
SHONEN JUMP™
GRAPHIC NOVELS

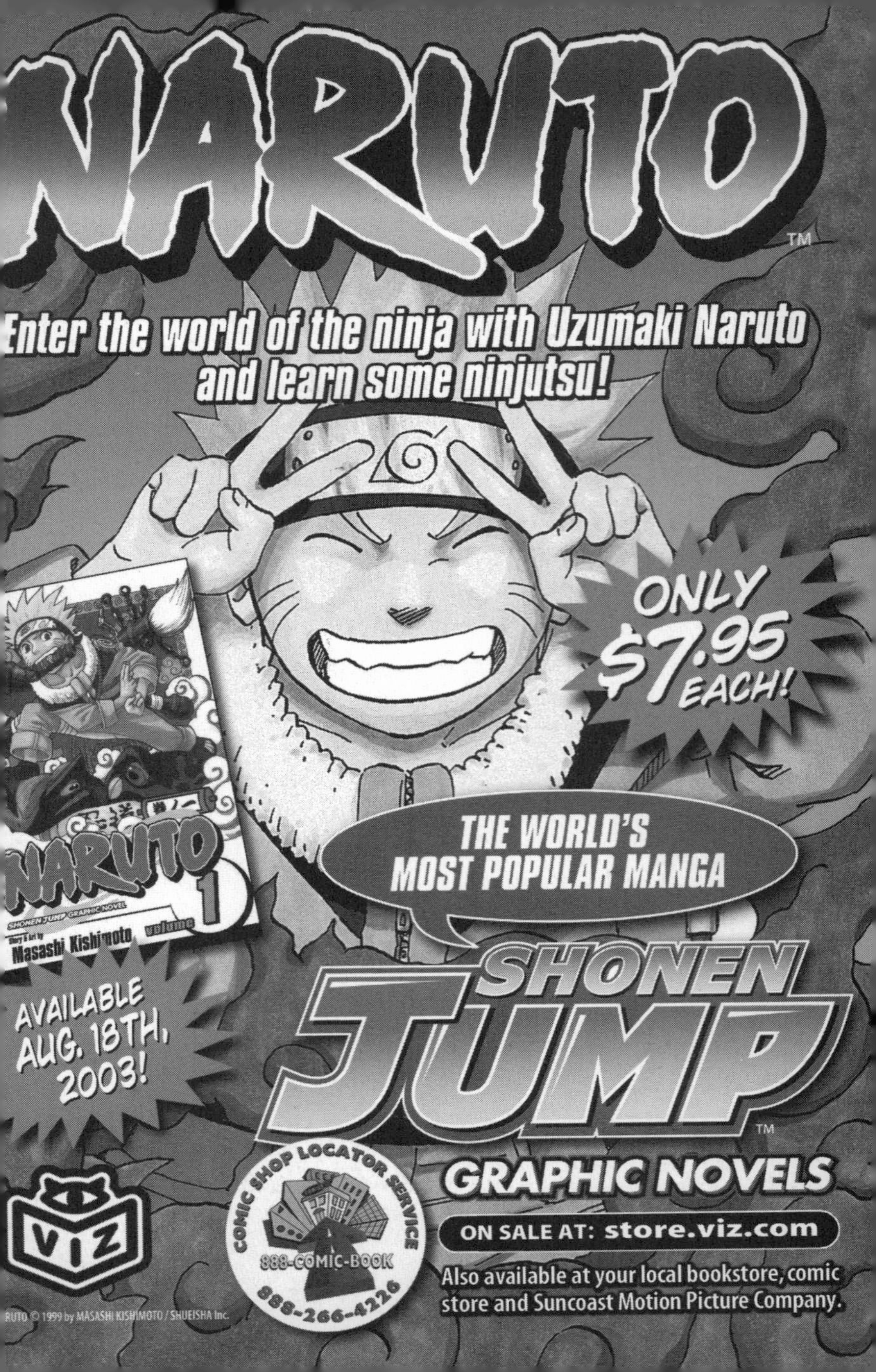

NARUTO™
Enter the world of the ninja with Uzumaki Naruto and learn some ninjutsu!
ONLY $7.95 EACH!
NARUTO 1
SHONEN JUMP GRAPHIC NOVEL volume
Story & Art by Masashi Kishimoto
THE WORLD'S MOST POPULAR MANGA
AVAILABLE AUG. 18TH, 2003!
SHONEN JUMP™
GRAPHIC NOVELS
ON SALE AT: store.viz.com
Also available at your local bookstore, comic store and Suncoast Motion Picture Company.
COMIC SHOP LOCATOR SERVICE
888-COMIC-BOOK
888-266-4226
VIZ
RUTO © 1999 by MASASHI KISHIMOTO / SHUEISHA Inc.

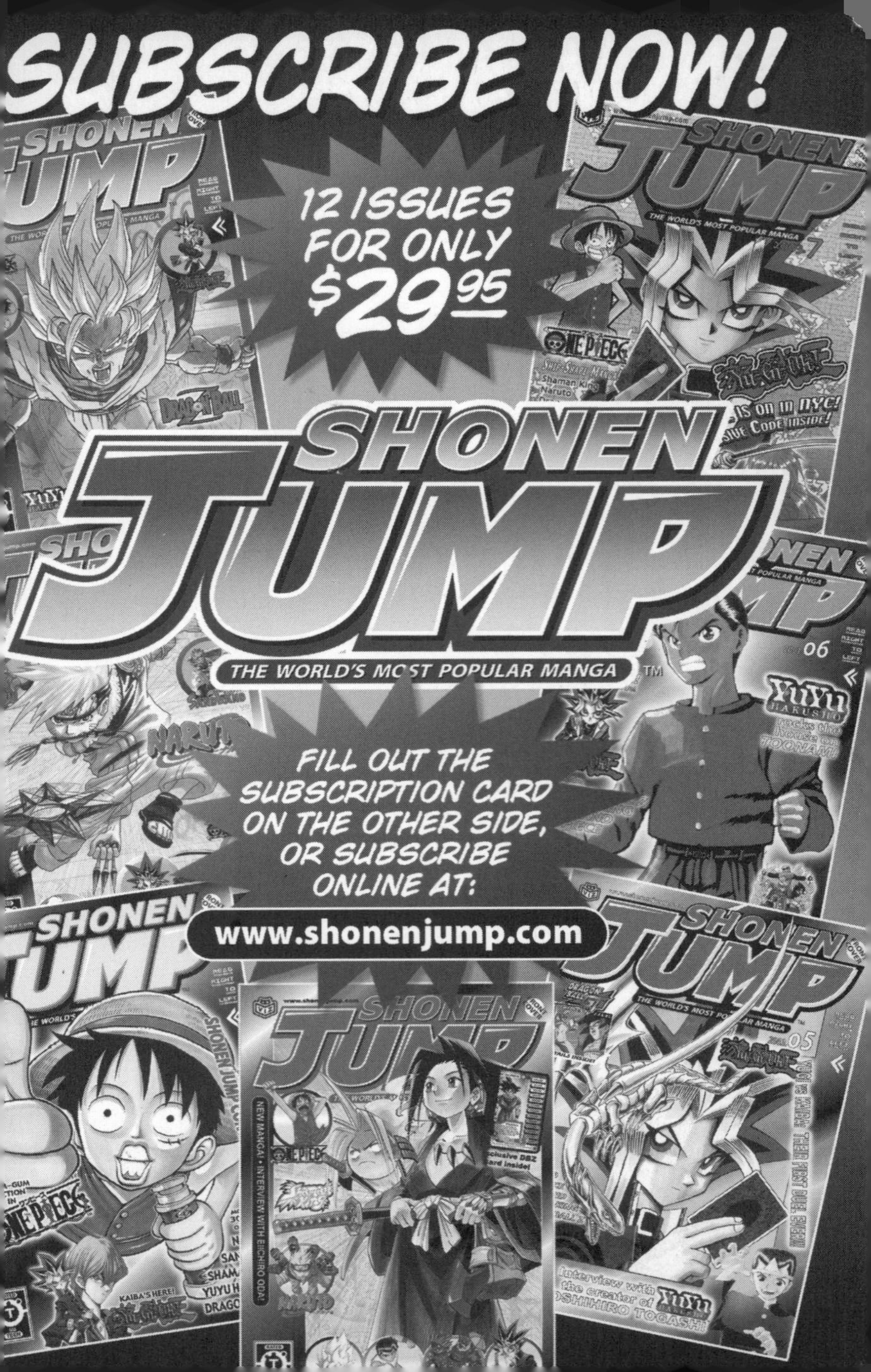
SUBSCRIBE NOW!
12 ISSUES FOR ONLY $29.95
SHONEN JUMP
THE WORLD'S MOST POPULAR MANGA ™
FILL OUT THE SUBSCRIPTION CARD ON THE OTHER SIDE, OR SUBSCRIBE ONLINE AT:
www.shonenjump.com

COMPLETE OUR SURVEY AND LET
US KNOW WHAT YOU THINK!

☐ Please check here if you DO NOT wish to receive information or future offers from VIZ

Name: CRiZey CHRiS CHriSMAn

Address: 181.zero wood drive

City: StuPiDSViLLE **State:** HiMe **Zip:** 1.00.00.

E-mail: WWW.Butt.BODER

☑ **Male** ☑ **Female** **Date of Birth (mm/dd/yyyy):** 1.00.00.91 (Under 13? Parental consent required)

What race/ethnicity do you consider yourself? (please check one)

☑ Asian/Pacific Islander ☑ Black/African American ☑ Hispanic/Latino

☑ Native American/Alaskan Native ☑ White/Caucasian ☑ Other: MNOO

What VIZ product did you purchase? (check all that apply and indicate title purchased)

☑ DVD/VHS DUMB AND DUMBeAcr

☑ Graphic Novel

☑ Magazines POOPE MR.POOP

☑ Merchandise

Reason for purchase: (check all that apply)

☑ Special offer ☐ Favorite title ☐ Gift

☐ Recommendation ☐ Other

Where did you make your purchase? (please check one)

☐ Comic store ☐ Bookstore ☐ Mass/Grocery Store

☐ Newsstand ☐ Video/Video Game Store ☐ Other:

☐ Online (site:)

What other VIZ properties have you purchased/own?

How many anime and/or manga titles have you purchased in the last year? How many were VIZ titles? **(please check one from each column)**

ANIME	MANGA	VIZ
☑ None	☑ None	☑ None
☐ 1-4	☐ 1-4	☐ 1-4
☐ 5-10	☐ 5-10	☐ 5-10
☐ 11+	☐ 11+	☐ 11+

I find the pricing of VIZ products to be: (please check one)

☑ Cheap ☑ Reasonable ☐ Expensive

What genre of manga and anime would you like to see from VIZ? (please check two)

☑ Adventure ☑ Comic Strip ☐ Detective ☑ Fighting

☑ Horror ☑ Romance ☑ Sci-Fi/Fantasy ☐ Sports

What do you think of VIZ's new look?

☑ Love It ☑ It's OK ☑ Hate It ☑ Didn't Notice ☑ No Opinion

THANK YOU! Please send the completed form to:

NJW Research
42 Catharine St.
Poughkeepsie, NY 12601

All information provided will be used for internal purposes only. We promise not to sell or otherwise divulge your information.